375

2,000 or more word term paper on one of
4 topics   Bibliography
    Plato
    Aristotle
    Epicureanism
    Stoicism   semester

Ch
96
2689/ 9
579

A STUDENT'S HISTORY OF PHILOSOPHY

THE MACMILLAN COMPANY
NEW YORK · BOSTON · CHICAGO · DALLAS
ATLANTA · SAN FRANCISCO

MACMILLAN AND CO., LIMITED
LONDON · BOMBAY · CALCUTTA · MADRAS
MELBOURNE

THE MACMILLAN COMPANY
OF CANADA, LIMITED
TORONTO

A STUDENT'S HISTORY OF PHILOSOPHY

BY

ARTHUR KENYON ROGERS, Ph.D.

FORMERLY PROFESSOR OF PHILOSOPHY IN YALE UNIVERSITY

THIRD EDITION

NEW YORK
THE MACMILLAN COMPANY

Published September, 1901. Reprinted October, 1902; July, 1904; July, 1905;
January, October, 1906.
Revised edition, July, 1907. Reprinted May, 1908; July, December, 1909, Janu-
ary, 1911; February, 1912; August, December, 1913; December, 1914; July, 1916.
March, October, 1917; January, 1918; April, 1919; July, 1920; June, November
1921; January, December, 1923; March, 1924; April, 1925; August, December
1926; April, December, 1928; August, 1929.
Third edition, February, 1932. Reprinted May, 1933 ; October, 1933 ; May, 1934 ;
January 1935; January, 1936 ; May 1937; January, 1938; February, 1940;
February, 1941; November, 1941; November, 1942; August, 1944;
June, 1945; August, 1946; August, 1947; February, 1948; April, 1948.
May, 1949.

PREFACE TO THE FIRST EDITION

I have tried in the present volume to give an account of philosophical development which shall contain the most of what a student can fairly be expected to get from a college course, and which shall be adapted to class-room work. What I have attempted to accomplish will be sufficiently covered in the following statements :—

1. The chief aim has been simplicity, in so far as this is possible without losing sight of the real meaning of philosophical problems. In summing up the thought of any single man, I have left out reference to the minor points of his teaching, and have endeavored to emphasize the spirit in which he philosophized, and the main problems in connection with which he has made an impression. Similarly, I have passed over many minor names without mention, unless some literary or historical interest creates the presumption that the student is already acquainted with them in a general way. Of course, the relative space that can most profitably be given to different topics is a matter of judgment, and I cannot hope that my choice will always be approved. But it is clear, I think, that the same principle can hardly be used in an introductory work that would suit more advanced students. I have tried continually to keep in mind the results that can reasonably be hoped for from a college class. So, for example, the medieval period is intrinsically of great importance. But, from the standpoint of an introductory course, it has also marked disadvantages, and I have, accordingly, only given it a brief space. Similarly, I have not attempted to trace the more technical lines of influence from one philosopher to another, as they are almost impossible for the student to grasp.

Whatever the success of the present attempt, I think there is a place for a book with this selective purpose alongside such a volume as, *e.g.*, Weber's.   The attempt to give a summary of all the important facts which a student with a more technical interest in philosophy would find useful, serves a valuable end, and an end with which the present volume does not pretend to compete; but it seems to me that the two aims are not altogether compatible in the same book.   The wealth of material is bound to confuse the beginner, no matter how clearly it is put.   I have attempted rather to create certain broad, general impressions, leaving further details to come from other sources.

2. Whenever I could, I have given the thought of the writers in their own words, particularly where the literary interest can be made to supplement the philosophical.   In this way it is possible to give the exposition an attractiveness which no mere summing up could have, and it will often supply, I think, by its suggestion of the personality back of the thought, a needed clew for the understanding of the thought itself.   I hope also it may be the means of arousing an interest in the masterpieces of philosophy at first hand, and may suggest that they have a really human and vital side.   The desirability of a considerable amount of such reading at first hand it is hardly necessary to insist upon.   The literary interest is also responsible for my giving one or two things an amount of space which is perhaps not entirely proportionate to their philosophical importance.

3. I have assumed that the study of the history of philosophy will centre about the systems of individual men; but I have tried also to bear in mind the need of relating these to the more general history of civilization.   This I have attempted through the medium of a somewhat mild reproduction of the Hegelian philosophy of history.   Doubtless this might have been made much more attractive and illuminating; but I do not think that, given the concrete knowledge that can be presupposed in the average student, it would be wise to attempt to make this aspect of the study otherwise than subordinate in a textbook.

In the lists of references which are added to nearly every section, the aim has been to give such as the student is likely to find helpful. The list might have been enlarged indefinitely, especially by the addition of French and German books; but these can so seldom be made use of by the college student to advantage that a reference to them did not seem necessary. I have to acknowledge my own obligation to very many of these volumes, perhaps to Windelband most of all.

Acknowledgments are due to the following publishers for their permission to utilize various translations of philosophical works: Macmillan & Co.; Geo. Bell & Sons; A. & C. Black; Paul, Trench, Trübner & Co.; Cambridge University Press; Henry Holt & Co.; Chas. Scribner's Sons; G. P. Putnam's Sons; Houghton, Mifflin & Co. In several cases acknowledgments are due also to the authors for a personal permission.

PREFACE TO THE THIRD EDITION

At the request of the publishers I have undertaken — a task I
should never have chosen for myself — the revision of an early philosophical venture which first appeared over thirty years ago. I
had strong misgivings in returning to a book into which I had not
looked for many years, and which represented no extreme amount
of labor in the first place. The misgivings were justified, though
perhaps not quite to the extent that I had feared. I have made
numerous minor changes on almost every page, and some considerable portions called urgently for a complete rewriting; but apart
from dropping out most of the Hegelian padding, the general plan
has been left pretty much as it was. More drastic alterations
would doubtless have produced a better book, but for this I had no
inclination; and I am not sure it would have been better for its
purpose. The only merit I have ever been disposed to claim is a
relative simplicity of treatment, which under American college
conditions still seems to me to be desirable; and further changes
might very well have detracted from this merit, such as it is. I
may add that the revision no more than the earlier edition pretends
to originality, or to much independent scholarship even.

I have had some trouble in deciding how far to go in bringing
the story of philosophy up to date. My own judgment would
have been to break off the narrrative a number of decades back; a
course in the history of philosophy seldom, I imagine, has much
time to spare for contemporary thought, and a cursory survey of all
deserving thinkers of the past and present generation would be of
doubtful educational value. However something seems to be demanded here; and I have compromised by picking out a few outstanding tendencies, for the most part such as have made some
popular appeal, and of which the average educated person therefore
already may be supposed to be aware. I have not even adhered

to this principle quite consistently; certain contemporary movements which might have qualified I have left out because I felt myself unable within a reasonable amount of space to give an account which appeared to me to possess the elements of intelligibility.

A. K. R.

ROCKPORT, MASS.
January, 1932.

CONTENTS

Contents

xiii

Contents

A STUDENT'S
HISTORY OF PHILOSOPHY

INTRODUCTION

§ 1. *Science and Philosophy*

Philosophy is one of those ambiguous terms which there is no great profit in trying to compress within the limits of a formal definition. The only way to arrive at any real sense of the meaning of philosophy is by philosophizing; and since this is something to which men are inclined in very different degrees, it is no wonder they should have held a variety of opinions about its nature and have disagreed about its human value. For the most part therefore it may be just as well to leave its actual meaning to take on shape as we proceed. Nevertheless there are a few general remarks which it will be desirable to make by way of preparation, particularly as they bear on one large distinction that will confront us at the start.

This is the distinction we are called upon to draw between philosophy and another great product of the human intellect — science. It is not always that the two have been on very friendly terms. The scientist more especially has shown a frequent disposition to look with disfavor on philosophy, and to contrast it as mere speculative guesswork with his own realistic methods and verifiable results; probably such an attitude never has been more prevalent or had a more respectable backing than at the present day. This hardly does justice however to what historically has been the close connection between the scientific and the philosophic problem. In the beginning it is almost impossible indeed to distinguish between the two with any great precision. Whether we are to call Thales and his immediate successors scientists or philosophers is largely a matter of choice; and from the age of Thales to the present time the developments of scientific and of philosophic thought have been so closely intertwined that neither can be really understood without the other.   Nearly all the greater and more creative periods of philosophy have had their roots in new discoveries about the nature of the world for which science primarily is responsible.   It would be possible — there always have been men to take this view — to interpret this entirely to the advantage of science, and to urge that philosophy is a mere parasite which adopts scientific conclusions only to pervert them by unwarranted speculative fancies.   But this leaves out of account important aspects of the actual situation.   While a good deal of valuable scientific work is no doubt of a purely factual sort, and makes no attempt to go beyond the description of phenomena and the determination of particular sequences, the greater scientists almost never stop with this.   Like the philosopher, they wish in some fashion to interpret their results; and to this end they not only enlist conceptual tools which have been given shape by the efforts of past philosophies, but frequently they go on to extend their conclusions to the world at large in a way that is indistinguishable from the methods which in the philosopher are made an occasion of reproach.

We may start with a characteristic which science and philosophy possess in common; they are both inspired by a large infusion of disinterested intellectual curiosity, a desire to know for the sake of knowing without much regard to immediate practical consequences and rewards.   It is the presence of this intangible spirit of disinterestedness, of critical detachment, which explains and justifies the leading rôle it has been customary to assign to Greece in the development of human thought.   There were elements of weakness in the Greek character which had unfortunate consequences later on as it came into contact with races of a tougher fiber.   It is on the whole rather deficient in those qualities of religious seriousness and of moral zeal which we find, for example, in the Hebrew. But the very absence of these qualities made it possible for the

Greek to undertake a task for which the Hebrew was unfitted. Religion and morality alike are naturally lacking in the power of self-criticism. They lay claim to an importance which makes it no easy matter to get outside them and view them in perspective; dogmatism and intolerance have been in consequence their usual fruit. A *philosophy* of religion and a *philosophy* of ethics presuppose on the other hand that we are freed to an extent from their immediate emotional compulsion and are trying impartially to appraise them; and this is a feat which no one prior to the Greeks had been able to accomplish. Such a disinterested outlook is closely connected with another gift which the Greeks possessed in a preëminent degree — the gift of artistic expression. Art is indeed the outstanding example of the disinterested outlook. Beauty, as Kant has said, gives us pleasure in the mere contemplation of itself, apart from the vulgar thought of possession and use. And we find in consequence Greek philosophy in its highest expressions connected with art hardly less intimately than with science. In fact philosophy, and to a lesser extent even science itself, has never lost its dependence on aesthetics. A sense for the same qualities at which the artist aims — simplicity, proportion, harmony — has constantly served to guide the scientist as well; a "beautiful" theory is a phrase that rises naturally to his lips. And all the major philosophies are in a real sense works of art, whose appeal lies often quite as much in the satisfaction with which the philosopher contemplates their intellectual neatness and logical precision as in their conformity with empirical fact.

It is worth pausing for a moment to take notice of one consequence of this relative separation from immediate needs; we ought not to expect either philosophy or science to show so intimate a connection with the economic sources of historical culture and development as that which we do undoubtedly discover in the case of religion or of morals. The popular vogue of a philosophy will no doubt be influenced by historical causes; and the philosopher himself cannot escape being moulded by his surroundings, and may have his mind turned in this or that direction by their dominant trend. But a major philosophy, at any rate, is far too individual a

matter, with its source in persisting human attributes and its outcome guided by an impersonal logic, to make it safe to carry too far
an objectively historical interpretation. As a matter of fact nearly
every type of philosophy since current has its representative in the
comparatively brief stretch of history which marks the fertile
period of Greek thought; and the responsibility for this rich output
lies pretty clearly not so much in the political and economic changes
in Greek life, though these often are enlightening, as in the more
general fact that the human mind for the first time had been set
free to indulge in a boundless curiosity about the world, and to
follow out new ideas to their conclusions.

Meanwhile it is not the similarity between science and philosophy,
but their differences, that we set out to consider. And since all the
fundamental motives that enter into what has commonly been
termed philosophy are present in Greek thought, it will assist in
what follows if we stop a moment to distinguish the most important.

The first difference is a relative one, to which it is not easy to set
hard and fast limitations; roughly however we may say that a man
is a scientist when he is trying to formulate the actual laws which
explain the facts and sequences in the world, while he enters the
field of philosophy as soon as he undertakes to lay down general
propositions about the ultimate nature of the world, in essence and
in the large. This last we may take to represent the fundamental
problem of philosophy, and it was clearly formulated by the Greeks;
what in the last analysis is *real?* what is the character of Being as
such? When one asks this question and attempts to answer it, he
becomes by that fact a philosopher, even if his main work lies elsewhere. It is because the question forces itself so inevitably upon
the mind of anyone who brings a disinterested curiosity to his contemplation of the world, that it is so difficult historically to separate
science and philosophy; nevertheless it is possible to draw a line
here with approximate exactness. If for example one is interested
in the precise relationships of space or number, he is a mathematician or a scientist; he becomes a philosopher when he raises the
question, What *is* space? Or again the scientist may for purposes
of causal explanation assume the existence of atomic structures, and

use them to account in detail for the behavior of physical objects; but if he asks himself whether atoms are ultimate constituents of reality, and if so in what relationship they stand to other apparent or possible realities — to meaning or purpose in the universe or to psychological feelings and sensations — he now is shifting to another problem and to other methods which men have agreed to call philosophical. Even the denial that anything at all exists deserving to be called real outside the facts and happenings which it is the business of science to explain is as such a philosophical rather than a scientific dogma. It is one thing to formulate the laws that phenomena reveal, and quite another to assert that beyond such empirical laws the human mind is incompetent to range; to say that only phenomena are real is to commit oneself to one theory of reality in particular, and so to pronounce on questions to which strictly scientific methods are unequal.

And in raising the point of method we come across a second distinction that can be drawn between philosophy and science. Without entering into a discussion of what is in itself one of the problems of philosophy, there is a difference here that lies upon the surface. Scientific method is primarily experimental; it involves putting theory to the test in terms of specific empirical consequences. When we turn to philosophy, however, experiment usually is found to be impracticable in view of the very general and comprehensive problems that are raised. The philosopher deals for the most part with ideas rather than events. A major portion of his task, in other words, has to do with a logical analysis of his terms, in the effort to rid them of self-contradiction, and to render them consistent not only with the facts of experience, but with the other general terms that thought employs. This is not a full account of philosophic method, nor is it indeed peculiar to philosophy; but whenever we find men concerning themselves on a large scale with the logical analysis and criticism of ideas we are usually justified in speaking of them as philosophers.

The third characteristic of the philosophic problem is a narrower and more specific one. The scientist, like the ordinary man, takes it for granted that we have a certain amount of valid knowledge;

and he sets about making this knowledge more exact and dependable. But when the problem of philosophy is raised, it very soon is seen that this assumption might be called in question. The real no doubt is what it is. But before reality can be talked or reasoned about, it must first have filtered through our thinking processes; and it becomes a distinct possibility therefore that this separation between knowledge and the thing it knows may affect our confidence in the results of knowing. It is even conceivable that we and our organs of appreciation may be so constituted as to make it impossible we should ever cross the gulf. For most purposes we do not need to entertain this possibility. But if we are to be thorough-going — and philosophy which fails to be thoroughgoing is hardly worth the effort — we are bound, before we commit ourselves finally to any judgments about the real, to examine the processes by which reality becomes known to us as human beings. The theory of knowledge therefore, or, as it technically is called, epistemology, has almost from the start been of very great significance for the philosopher's problem; and when we find it engaging men's attention we can be pretty sure that we are in the field of philosophy rather than of science.

There is one final problem belonging to philosophy which in its way is the most important one of all; at any rate it is here that the philosopher comes into closest contact with the needs and interests of men generally. Just as the work of the physical sciences may be supplemented by the more general and speculative effort to identify the ultimate nature of the realities with which physics deals, so the social and psychological interests of man may take on a more universal form comparable to the quest for reality in the outer world. Instead of asking about the nature of Being we may ask about the nature of the Good; and the Good itself is, or very well may be, one form of the real. Philosophy here has turned into what we are accustomed to call a "philosophy of life." This means we once more are adopting the critical and intellectually disinterested point of view; instead of stopping with particular forms of human good in their popular acceptance, and enlisting these in the cause of getting practical results, we are setting out to ask what goodness really *is*, and how it may throw light on the possibility of a genuinely unified and satisfactory plan of living. And now for such a question to be answered fully we might need to take one further step, by showing how the good as a goal for human life stands related to that larger reality which we call the world of nature. This is at any rate the ultimate quest on which most of the greater philosophies have embarked — a quest which, could it ever be successful, would give us a solution of the riddles which set philosophy on its way.

GENERAL LITERATURE

WHOLE PERIOD:

Lange, *History of Materialism*, 3 vols.
Lewes, *Biographical History of Philosophy.*
Weber, *History of Philosophy* (revised edition).
Windelband, *History of Philosophy.*
Turner, *History of Philosophy.*
Sidgwick, *History of Ethics.*
Hunter, *History of Philosophy.*
Cushman, *Beginners' History of Philosophy*, 2 vols.
Thilly, *History of Philosophy.*
Alexander, *A Short History of Philosophy.*
Webb, *History of Philosophy.*
Durant, *The Story of Philosophy.*
Marvin, *History of European Philosophy.*
Articles in *Encyclopædia Britannica* and in Hastings' *Encyclopedia of Religion and Ethics.*

ANCIENT PHILOSOPHY:

Benn, *The Greek Philosophers*, 2 vols.
Benn, *The Philosophy of Greece considered in Relation to the Character and History of its People.*
Grote, *History of Greece.*
Mayor, *Sketch of Ancient Philosophy from Thales to Cicero.*
Windelband, *History of Greek Philosophy.*
Zeller, *Outlines of the History of Greek Philosophy.*
Marshall, *Short History of Greek Philosophy.*
Gomperz, *The Greek Thinkers*, 4 vols.
Diogenes Laertius, *Lives of the Philosophers* (Bohn's Library).
Bussell, *The School of Plato.*

Caird, *The Evolution of Theology in the Greek Philosophers.*
Hyde, *Five Great Philosophies of Life.*
Adamson, *Development of Greek Philosophy.*
Appleton, *Elements of Greek Philosophy.*
Dickinson, *The Greek View of Life.*
Bakewell, *Source Book of Ancient Philosophy.*
Stace, *Critical History of Greek Philosophy.*
Fuller, *History of Greek Philosophy*, 3 vols.
Burnet, *History of Greek Philosophy*, Vol. I.
Taylor, *Greek Philosophy.*
Translations in Loeb's Classical Library and Bohn's Library.

MODERN PHILOSOPHY:

Höffding, *History of Modern Philosophy*, 2 vols.
Höffding, *Modern Philosophers.*
Royce, *Spirit of Modern Philosophy.*
Falckenberg, *History of Modern Philosophy.*
Lecky, *History of the Rise and Influence of the Spirit of Rationalism in Europe*, 2 vols.
Adamson, *The Development of Modern Philosophy*, 2 vols.
Levy-Bruhl, *History of Modern Philosophy in France.*
Calkins, *Persistent Problems of Philosophy.*
Merz, *History of European Thought in the Nineteenth Century.*
Rogers, *English and American Philosophy since 1800.*
Forsyth, *English Philosophy.*
J. Seth, *English Philosophers and Schools of Philosophy.*
Gunn, *Modern French Philosophy.*
Sorley, *History of English Philosophy.*
Ruggiero, *Modern Philosophy.*
Rand, *Modern Classical Philosophers.*

I. GREEK PHILOSOPHY

THE SCIENTIFIC PERIOD

§ 2. *The Milesian School. Thales, Anaximander, Anaximenes*

1. *Thales*. — Greek philosophy, in its distinctive sense, had its start at Miletus in the early part of the sixth century B.C. Miletus was the richest and most powerful of the Greek cities on the coast of Asia Minor. Situated on the great trade routes through which most of the commerce of the world then flowed, Asia Minor had reached a high degree of prosperity and cultivation; Croesus, the Lydian monarch, still remains the popular synonym for enormous wealth. Along with this there had followed, it is true, the consequences that usually attend conspicuous material prosperity. The social sanctions which a more primitive culture had found in custom and religion were beginning to break down; and no longer buttressed by these sanctions, the aristocracy of trade which had displaced the earlier Greek feudalism was in constant trouble with the populace and their demagogic leaders. The culture which grew up about the courts of powerful rulers shared in the defects of the society which fostered it; it was artificial, somewhat sentimental, and inclined to sceptical disillusionment and pessimism. Its chief intellectual product took the form of lyric poetry, which occupied itself with the personal feelings of the poet especially in the field of love, and which had little to do with larger social interests except as these found expression in partisan animosities generated by the clash of patrician and plebeian. At the same time it was a genuine culture of its sort; wealth had brought opportunity for leisure, and this leisure the active Greek mind had been quick to turn to account.

It was in such an atmosphere that science and philosophy took their rise; and the credit for taking the first step is universally ascribed to *Thales*. About Thales himself we have very little authentic information. Various anecdotes about him have come down to us which may or may not be true. One popular story is that he fell into a well while gazing at the stars; but this has the appearance of being one of those favorite jests on the impracticality of the philosophic temper rather than a fact of history. At any rate we are told other things that hardly fit in with the character of a dreamer; he is said for example to have shown his sagacity by foreseeing a bumper olive crop and cornering the market in oil. More historical perhaps is the statement that he predicted an eclipse of the sun that put an end to the fighting between Lydians and Medes. According to another account he attended Croesus on an expedition in the capacity of military engineer, and diverted for him the course of the river Halys; and he is credited with a realistic statesmanship in the attempt to induce the Ionian cities to unite in a confederacy to meet the threat against their liberties.

Our knowledge of Thales' philosophical opinions is practically limited to the statement that he found the cause of everything in *water*. This may seem a slight foundation for a philosophic reputation, and of course it does not go very far toward either a scientific or a philosophic explanation of the world. What gives it its importance is not its success as a theory, but the nature of the question which we have ground for thinking Thales was the first to ask. The thing at which he is aiming is a "cosmology" — a comprehensive attempt, in other words, to account for the universe in naturalistic terms; what is the elementary sort of reality, the primary substance, out of which things as we know them in experience arise as a consequence of its fundamental nature? We may contrast with such an attitude two products in particular of the intellectual past. Attempts on a grand scale to account for the universe existed long before Thales' day, and with some of these he was perfectly familiar. Practically every race has its cosmogonies, so-called; the one we are most familiar with is that which meets us in the book of Genesis. A cosmogony represents an effort by the primitive mind to make itself a little more at home in a mysterious and threatening world; it is a confused mixture of various motives

— religious, moral, fanciful — with roots stretching back so far into the dim past that we can only guess at what they originally may have meant. As a product of the imagination it may possess to a slight extent that quality of disinterestedness which belongs also to the scientific spirit. But cosmogonies, notwithstanding a dash of crude empirical observation that may enter into them, are negligible for the growth of human thought, because they are wholly lacking in the sort of method that alone can give reliability to knowledge. A scientific cosmology breaks completely with all such ungrounded fables; it looks for the cause of things, not in mythological fancies, but in actual physical agents which it sees at work, and which it can subject potentially to some sort of experimental testing.

Along with religious cosmogonies there was another and much more useful intellectual product of the past to which Thales had access. There is a sense in which the beginnings of science may be traced back to earlier civilizations, more particularly those of Babylonia and Egypt. Asia Minor was in easy touch with both — one reason doubtless why the intellectual development of the Ionian colonies was ahead of that of Greece. Thales consequently was in a position to learn whatever there was to be learned from such sources, and we are told indeed that he was the first to introduce geometry into Greece and to write a history of mathematics. But this does not deduct substantially from his originality; for the earlier sciences, if we may call them such, differ markedly from science as through the Greek influence we have come to think of it. At best they were purely observational in their nature. Thus the priests had for centuries been making laborious records of cyclical changes in the heavens, and these were of the greatest service to the later science of astronomy; but their own final interest in these facts lay in the realm of astrology and divination rather than in that of scientific explanation, to which they seem not to have made the first advances. In a similar way arithmetic and geometry among the Egyptians represented a utilitarian rather than a scientific interest, and took the form of practical rules of thumb, capable only of approximate exactness, for use in the market or for measuring fields and pyramids.   It was the Greeks who first turned these into an abstract science of exact mathematical relationships, and so made possible the immense part which mathematics since has played in enlarging our understanding of the world.

Why Thales picked out water as the ultimate substance is conjectural, but it is not difficult to see plausible reasons for his choice. Water has the mobility that might seem to go along with the power of universal transformation.   It does as a matter of fact appear to be intermediate between two other forms of matter; it solidifies into ice, and passes into steam or mist.   It is essential to growth and generation everywhere.   The process of transformation might appear to be taking place visibly in nature.   The sun draws water, which then is given back in the form of rain; and the rain in turn sinks into the ground where it is converted into the manifold products of the soil.

It is worth stopping here a moment to observe that, as will soon appear, when Greek science talks about such things as water, air and fire it is not so much the actual objects of experience that it has in mind, as it is certain general qualities of matter in the form more especially of pairs of opposites — the cold and the hot, the moist and the dry, the hard and the soft, light and darkness.   These still are thought of to be sure as "things," for the distinction between things and qualities had not yet been drawn; nevertheless it is what we nowadays should call the qualitative side of things that thought primarily is trying to explain and reduce to some kind of unity.

2. *Anaximander*. — The second Milesian philosopher is *Anaximander*.   Anaximander would seem to have made explicit that contrast of physical opposites of which mention has just been made, and to have been led by this to abandon the search for a single determinate substance from which everything else can be derived. It is probable he felt that Thales, in making water ultimate, was giving an undue importance to the "wet," whereas a true theory must take account of the principle of "justice" between opposites, and not exalt one at the expense of the other; if the wet had a

monopoly of reality, by this time it would be holding undisputed sway, and nature as we know it would have disappeared. Nor is it easy to see how any particular thing should be able to turn into something different; the notion of a change of quality is to say the least obscure. For reasons of this sort Anaximander was led to give up the search for any single ultimate element, and to find the original source of things in a boundless something (τὸ ἄπειρον) out of which empirical differences arise. From this source the opposites are "separated out"; they are not derived one from another. The processes of nature are due to the temporary encroachment of one opposite on the other — an encroachment which is then corrected by a movement in the contrary direction; thus winter encroaches on summer only in turn to be driven back as the "hot" gets the upper hand.

Anaximander's cosmology, growing out of this general conception, shows strikingly how far in a short time the Greek mind had been able to travel toward an essentially scientific way of looking at the world. Since the original mass is unlimited, ours is not the only world; at any point in it a world process may be set up, due to a sort of vortex or whirling motion in the Boundless. Our world does not rest accordingly on anything, but swings free in space; it has the shape of a cylinder, and we live on the upper surface. The sun, moon and stars are rings of fire surrounding the earth; since however they are obscured by air or mist we do not see them as rings, but only see the apertures through which the fire escapes "as through the nozzle of a pair of bellows." Eclipses are due to the stoppage of these apertures. Living creatures arose from the moist element as it was evaporated by the sun; man was like a fish in the beginning. Land animals are the result of adaptation to a new environment. To show that man must have sprung from a lower species Anaximander uses a very modern-sounding argument. Other animals quickly find food for themselves, while man alone requires a lengthy period of suckling; had he originally therefore had his present form he would never have survived.

3. *Anaximenes.* — *Anaximenes*, the last of the early Milesians, turns back from the Boundless to a renewed attempt to assign to

the primary source a determinate character. This was made possible by his more precise account of that process of transition from one form to another which his predecessors had left undefined ; he identifies change, that is, with the empirically verifiable process of condensation and rarefaction. But instead of following Thales and finding the ultimate element in water, Anaximenes turned to air or vapor or light mist. This might not unnaturally be suggested by his account of change. Mist condenses into water ; when it is dilated and becomes rarer it passes into the shimmer of heat or fire. And this probably was reinforced by another motive, which is significant as an illustration of what was to be the growing tendency of philosophy to turn from meteorology to physiology as a source of scientific explanation — a natural tendency in view of the strides that were being made in the art of medicine. We still speak of the "breath of life," as if air were the vital principle that animates the human frame. And just as the soul, being air, holds the body together, so Anaximenes thinks of the world as itself a living organism whose processes are maintained by inhaling the breath or air which encompasses it.

§ 3. *The Pythagoreans*

1. The Milesian School came to an end with the fall of Miletus in 494 B.C., though its doctrines reappear and continue to influence the course of scientific thinking. Before, however, following the main trend of the cosmological development that had thus been started, something will need to be said about another and relatively independent strain which was also to have an important influence on the course of thought. It was to do this in particular by turning attention to one of the most essential conditions of scientific progress. Mathematics is a halfway house between science and philosophy. In so far as it deals directly with ideas rather than with things its affinity is with philosophy, and on its speculative side it often in fact has played a leading rôle in systems of metaphysics. On the other hand it is so bound up with natural processes, and is so essential alike to exact description and to prediction, that the sciences almost without exception would be lost without it.

As physical theory took its rise in Asia Minor, so the new development belongs also not to Greece proper, but to the Greek colonies in southern Italy. *Pythagoras*, the founder of the movement, was an Ionian, a native of the island of Samos, and we are told that he had originally been a disciple of Anaximander; but sometime in the latter part of the sixth century he left his city, for political reasons it is likely, and settled at Croton. Here he established a community, or brotherhood, which was partly religious, partly scientific, and, in course of time at any rate, partly political. Its political activity was the source of constant trouble; Pythagoras was himself compelled to leave the city, and after his death the brotherhood was driven out with much loss of life and property. Following this expulsion the survivors settled in other Greek cities, where they continued to exert a powerful intellectual influence.

Pythagoras himself has come down to us as a semi-mythical figure, and about his real teachings there has been a wide difference of opinion. This comes in part from the difficulty in determining how much is due to Pythagoras and how much to the later Pythagoreans; and it is complicated by the fact that two distinct strains enter into Pythagoreanism whose connection is at first sight not too obvious. It was both a religious community, and a scientific and philosophical school. Later on the two motives were found incompatible and tended to part company; there seems no good ground for doubting however that originally they existed in conjunction, and that Pythagoras was responsible for both. Both at any rate were familiar to Socrates and Plato, and both contribute important elements to an understanding of subsequent Greek philosophy as it has come down to us through its historically most important representatives.

2. To appreciate the religious or mystical side of Pythagoras' teaching it will be necessary to have a few words first to say about Greek religion in general. We are most familiar with this in its mythological form. It is questionable however whether the array of deities that constitute the Greek pantheon really entered vitally into the religious life of the Greek people. Even in Homer the gods are treated too cavalierly to make it easy to think of most of

them as the objects of any very sincere religious feeling or worship; and with the increase of sophistication, in Ionia in particular, religious scepticism became pretty much the vogue. The scientist still continued to talk about the gods. But more and more these came to be identified with natural processes or with the natural universe as a whole, and religion, if it still can so be called, to pass into a pantheism which had little connection with its historic meaning; we shall meet presently this tendency in full swing in connection with the name of Xenophanes. One difficulty in particular lay in the way of taking the traditional Greek mythology too seriously. The ribald stories told about the gods, their all-too-human failings, seemed to the cultivated Greek, no less than to us today, entirely incredible; Plato for example takes much pains to show that such tales are inconsistent with anything like religious or moral reverence, and so will have to be rejected.

As always is the case however, scepticism was confined to the educated classes, and did not spread far among the masses of the people. The average Greek, like the average man everywhere, stuck to the religion of his fathers, and took it seriously enough to resent, with violence at times, any meddling with it. Even cultivated Athens has the invidious distinction of having banished one philosopher and put to death another on grounds nominally religious. It has however to be noticed here that popular Greek religion had little to do with theology, or with emotional fervor even. It was primarily a matter of ceremonial rites which safeguarded the routine of life and lent it dignity. The real objects of its worship were not the greater deities, but humbler and often local ones connected more directly with men's everyday affairs. What accordingly the populace resented was not the holding of heterodox beliefs, but the undermining of familiar habits. The Athenian democracy was suspicious with some reason of attacks on settled customs; and that the new opinions were chiefly current among their traditional aristocratic foes did not help to recommend them.

Meanwhile there was another form that Greek religion took which is not identical either with a rationalistic pantheism or with the rites and observances which it was the business of the priests to handle. Religion is more deepseated than theology, or than custom even. It appeals to the emotions also; and in all ages there are people who demand this emotional satisfaction. The worship of Dionysus in particular had furnished an outlet for such emotional cravings through the instrumentality of orgiastic practices — frenzied dancing, intoxication, the induction of a state of trance that seemed to release the worshiper from his human limitations; and these practices were safeguarded by esoteric rites which were called the mysteries, and which were jealously guarded against the curiosity of the uninitiated.

This worship of Dionysus was given a more distinctively moral significance in the Orphic religion — so called because it connected itself with the mythical poet Orpheus — which had gained a wide following all over Greece. Orphicism found its adherents for the most part in the humbler classes of society; it was looked down upon by most reputable people, and it had indeed features that offered an excuse for this disparagement. Nevertheless it was the expression of a real religious need, such as we may always expect will be in evidence when social life is undergoing profound disturbances and the old landmarks are threatened. The same conditions that among the cultivated classes in Ionia had given rise to a refined disillusionment with life, among the people resulted rather in a heightened sense of sin, the resort to ritualism and asceticism as a method of salvation, and the return to a religious fundamentalism represented by those obscure and superstitious roots of religion that go back to man's savage ancestry.

And along with this certain new ideas came likewise to the front that were foreign to the accepted notions of the Greeks — ideas that will meet us again in Socrates and Plato. These center about the notion of immortality, conceived now as a vital reality and not as the colorless existence of shades in a gloomy underworld. For Orphicism, immortality is both a personal hope and a way of life. True life is not to be found here on earth; what men call life is really death, and the body is the tomb of the soul. By reason of its bodily contamination the soul is forced to pass through an indefinite series of reincarnations, taking on this form or that according as it has been more or less true to its immortal nature.   And the aim of religion is redemption from the wheel of birth, and so from the body with its desires and sensations, through a system of purifications which finally will free the immortal and preëxisting soul from its earthly trammels, and bring it to the regions of the blest where it will dwell forever with the gods.

3. On its first or religious side it is this Orphic doctrine of salvation that meets us in Pythagoreanism, though it connects itself here with the worship of the Delian Apollo rather than with Dionysus.   The brotherhood was a community engaged in the quest for religious purification or purgation, through practices which at their lower level had slight connection with philosophy.   Some of the rules of the order have come down to us, and they throw an interesting light upon its character.   Do not sit on a quart measure; do not eat the heart; do not stir the fire with iron; do not look in a mirror beside a light; do not eat beans; when you rise from the bedclothes roll them together and smooth out the impress of the body : these are a few that are sufficiently characteristic.   Most of these rules seem so trivial that later there was a disposition to interpret them metaphorically, and to find in them some hidden wisdom.   But anthropology makes it plain that they are simply primitive survivals based on the notion of magic and taboo; the final injunction, for example, is one form of the superstition, to be met with everywhere, that similarity between objects, or close contiguity, implies a causal relationship as well, so that if an enemy can get access to an effigy that suggests me or to some object connected with my person he is in a position to do me harm.   These survivals seem to have appealed to Pythagoras as a suitable instrument for bringing about a reform of the luxury and license which marked the age, and which have made the neighboring city of Sybaris a byword for self-indulgence; a religious revival nearly always tends to turn back to the authority of ancient customs in which the religious feeling is deeply implicated, particularly on its more gloomy side.

But purification did not stop with ritual and magic; the community had other and more intellectual interests as well which were pressed into the same service. We know that it busied itself with the art of medicine and with musical studies. Now medicine has an obvious connection with the idea of "purgation." And as medicine is a purge for the ailing body, so is music for Pythagoras a purge for the soul. That such a notion is not arbitrary is shown by the use to which Aristotle later on puts it to explain the nature and effects of tragedy, and it was not an unfamiliar idea before Pythagoras' time; the Corybantic priests had used wild strains of music in the treatment of hysterical patients in order to bring on exhaustion followed by a healthy sleep.

But there is a higher method of catharsis still; and here at last we come into contact with philosophy and science. To Pythagoras is probably to be attributed the famous doctrine of the Three Lives. Just as there are three sorts of people who attend the Olympic games — those who come to buy and sell, those who come to compete, and those who come simply to look on — so mankind in general may be classified as lovers of wealth, lovers of honor, and lovers of wisdom (φιλόσοφοι); and this last type is higher than the other two. To the love of wisdom then, to the calm and disinterested pursuit of science, Pythagoras looked for the culmination of that same moral process of purification which started with ritual and taboo. Philosophy, so Socrates is made to say in one of his Pythagorean moods, is the highest music; in the contemplation of absolute truth one may find the serenity which frees him from the distractions of the body and prepares him for an ultimate release.

The special subject matter of this discipline was mathematics; and Pythagoras' philosophy is summed up in the doctrine that things are *numbers*. If we take number in its abstract modern sense, as distinguished from concrete things that can be numbered, it is not easy to make much of this statement. In a general way we may indeed compare it with the notion, underlying all modern science, that the aim of scientific inquiry is the discovery of mathematical or numerical relationships; and it is in this direction that in fact the Pythagorean philosophy is pointed. But Greek thought was still in far too crude a state for such a conception of scientific method to become fully explicit; and in any case it hardly explains how numbers could come to be *identified* with things. For this some interpretation is required.

The first thing to notice is that for the Pythagoreans the units of number are conceived as physical points — points, namely, which are not disembodied abstractions without length, breadth or thickness, but which possess actual magnitude. This is indeed a very primitive way of representing numbers — by dots arranged symmetrically so as easily to be recognized, as we still arrange them on dice for example. And in this way evidently we are brought back more closely to the world of extended objects than the term "number" might at first suggest. At least we can see how geometrical figures might be generated from such points or units, and possess certain definable properties in consequence; and it is not impossible, accordingly, to think of objects as figurate constructs which give definite shape to an original indeterminate stuff or matter. To be sure we cannot go very far with this without getting into trouble; spatial forms may be so conceived, but what of the more concrete things of experience such as dogs and men? We are told how one of the later Pythagoreans went about this; he drew a pattern of some natural object and proceeded to fill it in with pebbles or counters, the number of the object in question, its specific form or formula, being represented by the number of the pebbles. The difficulties are still more apparent when we turn to abstract conceptions; when we are told for example that justice is a square number, that opportunity is represented by the number seven, and marriage by the number five — the first harmony between the male (odd) and the female (even) — we clearly have entered the region of pure fancy.

Generalized, the Pythagorean philosophy gets expression in a conception of the cosmos as the union of two factors — the Unlimited, and the Limit; in other words, as the last paragraph has suggested, it is due to a process whereby empty space — though as a matter of fact the notion of space had not as yet been distinguished from that of an indeterminate and boundless stuff which Pythagoras, following Anaximenes, conceived as air — is measured off and given determinateness through the imposition of a pattern or enclosing figure. It has been suggested that we may get a picture of what Pythagoras has in mind if we think of the spectacle of the starry heavens — a field of darkness dotted and marked off by points of light; in fact darkness is for the Pythagoreans just a sort of mist or vapor. The whole character that actual reality takes on for us would thus be due to "forms" capable of receiving a mathematical expression — a doctrine that was to issue in Plato's famous "theory of Ideas," as it has usually been called, and through him to influence all subsequent thought.

4. Historically however it is very likely that the first suggestion of the "number theory" may have come from another source; at any rate it is here that its greatest scientific significance is found. The most important scientific discovery by Pythagoras lies in the field of music. He was the first to discover, by experimenting with a vibrating cord, that the intervals of the scale which strike the ear as concordant are associated with invariable and definite proportions in the length of one string to another; between the four perfectly concordant notes of the lyre the two middle notes stand in the relation of arithmetical means to the two extremes. It is in this conception of a "mean," a definite ratio or proportion, that Pythagoras brings to light for the first time a tool capable of a genuine scientific application in the modern sense; conceivably indeed it might turn out to be a universal tool, and the key for unlocking nature's secrets. If high and low can thus be brought together, so too might the other opposites of Greek scientific thought; at any rate a new way of conceiving nature has been disclosed to the philosopher. The opposites neither pass into one another, nor are "separated out"; things in the world are due to a "blend" or mixture of extremes, and have their specific character in terms of a balance between the "too much" and the "too little." Pythagoras was himself not in a position to make any further use of this conception for the purposes of physics; but in a less exacting field it was capable of an immediate extension. It could be applied for instance to the field of medicine; health is in a similar way the balance of the opposites in the body — the hot and the cold, the wet and the dry — while disease comes from the lack of such a proper

balance.   So again the possibilities for ethics are apparent, as Plato
and Aristotle in particular were to show.   In this way, then, the
forms which are imposed on the Unlimited take on the character of
quantitative formulas which express the specific nature of an object,
numbers meanwhile still retaining the quality of spatial magnitude
which gives them a standing in the physical world.

§ 4. *Heracleitus*

1. In the preceding speculations one notion in particular had
been implicit which had not as yet received the attention it
deserved.   The Milesians had assumed the fact of *change* as something self-evident, and they had assumed, too, that there must be
an underlying unity to this changing world.   But here are two ideas
certain to make trouble as soon as they are distinctly recognized.
The reality which changes must all the time be one and the same
reality at bottom, or else there is no meaning in the statement that
it changes.   Nothing changes except as it becomes different from
what it was before; and there is no "it," no "something which"
changes, unless there is an identity, or sameness, which persists
through the successive moments of change.   And yet if it changes
it must be different from itself, and so not one reality, but more
than one; it must at once persist, and pass away.   How are these
seemingly very opposite notions — the one and the many, sameness
and difference, permanence and change — to be reconciled and
combined?   Greek thinkers were presently to be very much engaged with problems such as these; and one of the chief contributing causes was the new turn given to philosophy by *Heracleitus*.

Heracleitus was an Ephesian, of aristocratic family and high
position.   It already has appeared that there was much in the
political condition of the cities of Asia Minor to force the reality of
change upon men's notice; this shows for example in the lyric
poetry of the period, with its fondness for dwelling on the endless
vicissitudes of fortune and the uncertainty of human life and happiness.   Apart from the perils that grew out of external relations to
the great Oriental powers, there was within each city an ever present
danger from civil strife; Heracleitus was himself among those who

had suffered from these conditions, and it was very likely his contempt for the democratic tendencies of his day which turned him from public life to philosophical pursuits. His reputation for gloomy misanthropy gave him in antiquity the title of the Weeping Philosopher; while the Delphic character of his writings — they require, says Socrates, a Delian diver to get at the meaning of them — caused him to be designated as Heracleitus the Obscure.

Heracleitus gets rid, implicitly at least, of the difficulty of reconciling permanence with change, by the denial that any such thing as permanence exists at all. There is no static Being, no unchanging element; change, movement, is Lord of the universe. Nothing ever is, but everything is becoming; all things are passing, and nothing abides. "You cannot step twice into the same river, for fresh waters are ever flowing in upon you." [1] Man is no exception; he is "kindled and put out like a light in the night-time." Heracleitus formulates this conception by saying that — not Water or Mist, but — Fire is the ultimate ground of the world. "All things are exchanged for Fire, and Fire for all things, as wares are exchanged for gold, and gold for wares." This is not intended to be figurative; Heracleitus means literal fire, just as Thales meant literal water. But it is fire as it embodies primarily the fact of change. Nor could his thought perhaps have found better expression than in terms of the all-transforming, shifting flame, ever passing away in smoke, ever renewing itself by taking up the substance of solid bodies which undergo destruction that it may live. We have the *appearance* of permanence, just as the flame *seems* to be an identical thing; in reality however its content is every moment altering.

This doctrine — that everything, as Plato maliciously puts it, is in a flux like leaky vessels, that there is no rest or permanence anywhere in the universe, no solid foothold which is not, the very moment we try to occupy it, silently shifting beneath us — may seem to us at first to be as paradoxical as it appeared to his contemporaries. The natural reaction finds expression in the jest

[1] This and succeeding quotations from the earlier philosophers are taken from Burnet's *Early Greek Philosophy*, A. & C. Black.

which puts Heracleitus' argument in the mouth of a debtor who does not wish to pay — how can he be liable, since he is not the same man who contracted the debt? We are not easily satisfied to give up identity and permanence in things; if an object has already come to be something different before we can give a name to it, how are we to make any articulate utterance at all? When we reflect, however, we see that, in spite of difficulties, this is very like the accepted views of modern science. For science also there is nothing that stands still. The stone that seems to lie unchanged and motionless is, on the one hand, whirling through space along with the planet which bears us with it on its surface, while on the other hand it is itself a little world of quivering forces where the most intense activity reigns. Our own bodies too are changing every moment of our lives, and our minds are changing with them; there is no such thing as stopping the flow of consciousness without blotting it out altogether. Heracleitus has laid hold accordingly of a highly important feature of reality, which will need to be taken account of in every future attempt at philosophizing.

2. Is there, then, no unity at all to the world? If so, how can we account for even the appearance of permanence? Heracleitus does not deny unity of a sort. But the unity is not one of unchanging substance; it is what we call nowadays the unity of law. The process of change does not take place in an unregulated and lawless way; it is *rhythmical* change, kept within the bounds of definite proportions. As the heavenly fires are transmuted successively into vapor, water, earth, so a corresponding series of transformations ascends upward to fire again, only to start once more on the same ceaseless round. The universe is thus a closed circuit in which an ascending and a descending current counterbalance each other — an "ever-living Fire with measures of it kindling and measures going out." It is this opposition of motions, and the measured balance between them, which produces the delusive appearance of rest and fixity; a "thing" is constituted, not by the presence of identical elements, but by a relatively constant content due to the fact that what is lost in one direction is compensated by the returning process.

To repeat then, nothing in the world is self-contained and self-complete; everything is forever passing into something else, and has an existence only in relation to this process. "Fire lives the death of earth, and air lives the death of fire; water lives the death of air, earth that of water." This is the first philosophic statement of the famous *doctrine of relativity*, which in one form or another has played an important part in subsequent thought down to the present day. And not only is everything passing into something else, but it is forever passing into its opposite. All reality is born of the clash of opposing principles, the tension of conflicting forces. "Homer was wrong in saying: Would that strife might perish from among gods and men! He did not see that he was praying for the destruction of the universe; for, if his prayer were heard, all things would pass away." Strife is "father of all, and king of all." This union of contrasts Heracleitus is never weary of tracing out. Organic life is produced by the male and the female, musical harmony by sharp and flat notes. The painter creates his harmonious effects by the contrast of colors. The sea is the purest and the impurest water; fish can drink it and it is good for them, while to men it is undrinkable and destructive. It is the same thing in us that is quick and dead, awake and asleep, young and old; we cannot lay our finger on the moment when youth becomes old age, since neither term has any meaning except in contrast to the other. "God is night and day, winter and summer, war and peace, hunger and satiety; but he takes various shapes, just as fire when it is mingled with different incenses is named according to the savor of each."

The same thought Heracleitus applies to the treatment of the ethical life. Just as the light and the heavy, the warm and the cold, plenty and want, are relative terms, so likewise are good and evil. "Physicians who cut, burn, stab and rack the sick, then complain that they do not get any adequate recompense for it." "Men would not have known the name of justice if there were no injustice." "It is not good for men to get all they wish. It is disease that makes health pleasant and good; hunger, plenty; and weariness, rest." What we call good or bad has no existence except in relation to a possible worse or better; were either of the related terms wanting the moral life would cease to exist. At least this is true of human morality, though Heracleitus still speaks of God himself as one to whom all things are "fair and good and right."

3. One other problem begins faintly to emerge in Heracleitus — what has been referred to as the problem of knowledge. Since the vulgar notion is that the things which the senses reveal to us are more or less solid and permanent, a distinction has to be drawn between sense knowledge, which is fallacious and the source of all kinds of illusion, and that true wisdom which consists in a perception of the underlying unity of the various opposites. And this last becomes possible because man is no mere separate individual, but a part of the all-comprehending Fire that constitutes the universe; he can know objective truth because in essence he is identical with that truth. This connects itself in Heracleitus with his doctrine of the upward and the downward paths; it is from the ascending current, toward the everlasting Fire, that knowledge derives — the dry soul is the wisest and best — while pleasure, folly, sleep and death are due to the downward path and the encroachment of the moist. Heracleitus finds a proof in the phenomena of drunkenness; the drunken man is "led by a beardless lad, tripping, not knowing where he steps, having his soul moist."

The answer given by Heracleitus to the problem of philosophy is one which is likely to grow in force the more one thinks of it. But can we be really satisfied to stop here? Can the fact of law furnish all the unity and permanence our thought requires? What *is* measure or law, indeed, over and above the multitude of particular facts and changes, each distinct and unrelated? If it is only an ideal fact in our minds, it has no constitutive force in the material world without; and if it is a material fact, does it not furnish simply another element to be brought into unity, and not a unifying bond at all? At any rate it hardly satisfies our first feeling of what the situation calls for; instinctively we seek to find a solid and permanent background for this universal flow of events, an unchanging subject of change, which shall bind the multiplicity into a real whole, and give us something definite to grasp and rest upon. This factor of permanence, of static Being, which Heracleitus denied, is brought into a one-sided prominence by an opposing group of thinkers, whose connection with the city of Elea, in southern Italy, has given them the name of the Eleatic School.

§ 5. *The Eleatic School. Xenophanes, Parmenides, Zeno, Melissus*

1. *Xenophanes.* — The reputed founder of the Eleatic school was *Xenophanes*, an older contemporary of Heracleitus and a native of Colophon, whence he fled in consequence of the Persian conquest of Ionia. Xenophanes was however not in reality a philosopher in the proper sense; he was a poet turned satirist and religious reformer. As a satirist, he sets himself against the florid and artificial culture of Magna Graecia — its luxuries, its purple garments, its fops "proud of their comely locks, anointed with unguents of rich perfume" — in favor of an ideal of plain living and high thinking, of simplicity, moderation, and good taste. In like manner he ridicules the exaggerated athleticism of the day — the preference of muscle to brains, "strength to wisdom" — and the immaturity and affectation of its intellectual interests; "there is nothing praiseworthy in discussing battles of Titans, or of giants and centaurs, fictions of former ages, nor in plotting violent revolutions." As against this he exalts the true life of intellect. And Xenophanes' conception of the intellectual life has a distinctly modern flavor. It is modern in its sceptical caution. "There never was nor will be a man who has clear certainty as to what I say about the gods and about all things; for even if he does chance to say what is right, yet he himself does not know that it is so. But all are free to guess." And more especially is it modern in its naturalism. It is this naturalistic strain that was the main source of Xenophanes' influence, and that gives him such philosophical importance as he may possess.

It has appeared already that the movement of Ionian science, and the tendency of a sophisticated culture as well, had been away from popular religion. Xenophanes is the most outspoken representative of this enlightenment. His impatience with the intellectual futility and low moral grade of many of the old beliefs and stories about the gods leads him to a sharp polemic against the popular theology. "Homer and Hesiod have ascribed to the gods all things that are a shame and a disgrace among men, thefts and adulteries and deceptions of one another." "But mortals think that the gods are born as they are, and have perception like theirs, and voice and form." "Yes, and if oxen and lions had hands, and could paint with their hands and produce works of art as men do, horses would paint the forms of the gods like horses, and oxen like oxen. Each would represent them with bodies according to the form of each." "So the Ethiopians make their gods black and snub-nosed; the Thracians give theirs red hair and blue eyes." In truth there is One God, the greatest among gods and men, comparable to mortals neither in form nor thought; without toil he swayeth all things by the thought of his mind; and he abidest ever in the selfsame place moving not at all, nor does it befit him to go about now hither, now thither.

We are not however to suppose that this is meant to be a profession of monotheism in the ordinary sense; the One God of Xenophanes is expressly said to exclude all anthropomorphic elements. What Xenophanes is really trying to assert is, not that the reality of the universe is God as the religionist uses the term, but that what we name God is the one eternal and unchanging world of nature. It is true attributes are assigned to nature which later came to be regarded as spiritual or immaterial. But this means only that the Greeks had not yet succeeded in making distinctions which to the modern mind may seem fairly evident; down to the time of Plato we shall find philosophers attributing such qualities to reality without a suspicion that they may be casting doubt thereby on its strictly physical existence.

2. *Parmenides*. — It is not impossible that, as tradition tells us, the real founder of the Eleatic school, *Parmenides* of Elea, may originally have been a disciple of Xenophanes, and have been influenced by his pantheistic doctrine of the One. But if so he was at least to give it a direction vastly more significant for philosophy. Parmenides is one of the great philosophical thinkers of pre-Socratic times, in some ways possibly the greatest. It was he

who turned philosophy explicitly from cosmological speculations to an examination of ideas or concepts. This does not mean that he converted reality into a merely logical existence; he continued to think of it as physical, and indeed he has been called by one recent critic the father of Materialism. But his method is that of logic rather than of physical explanation; it is the method of removing inner inconsistencies from our thought, and requiring reality to submit to the demands which consistent thinking makes upon it.

Parmenides' chief work, which has come down to us only in fragments, takes the form of a poem, or at least of verse, since Parmenides was not a poet by natural endowment. In the exordium he represents himself as borne on a chariot, attended by the Sun maidens, through the gate of Day and Night into the realm of Day. He arrives at the palace of a Goddess, who welcomes him and proceeds to instruct him in the two ways of Truth and of deceptive Belief. The second part of the poem deals with the way of Belief, and contains cosmological speculations which modern scholarship has shown to be identifiable in considerable part with the cosmology of Pythagoras. It has been plausibly conjectured, therefore, that Parmenides is telling us of his own philosophical conversion from Pythagoreanism to a new and more adequate philosophy; and the reason he takes the trouble to expound the way of error is, presumably, in part that he wishes to contrast his former with his latter state, and in part that he is setting forth the erroneous doctrines which his followers will be called on to meet and to refute.

Of all philosophical systems, that of Parmenides is perhaps the most paradoxical. It is based on the absolute denial of change and multiplicity in the world, and their reduction to pure illusion. Only the One exists, and that One is eternal, immutable, immovable, indivisible. The practical refutation of this, by facts, is perfectly easy; it does not describe the world as we actually know it, and if the world really were such a world, then all philosophies with their reasonings about Being would themselves be wiped out along with everything else that is partial. The illusions which philosophy attempts to correct would be impossible even as illusions. Parmenides' philosophy, however, does not pretend to be based on empirical facts; it declares that facts themselves must be subjected to the laws of thought or logic, and if they prove to be self-contradictory must be rejected. If we cannot think them we have no right to call them facts. "What can be spoken and thought *is;* for it is possible for it to be, and it is not possible for what is nothing to be." So long as thought is true to itself no effort can make the being of Not-being intelligible; and if it is not intelligible, if it is incapable of being thought, it does not exist. Only Being exists, eternal, immovable, unchanged. It cannot have come into being, for to do this it must have arisen either from something or from nothing. It cannot have arisen from nothing, for nothing is the absence of the real; it cannot have arisen from something, for there is nothing other than what *is*. Being cannot be divisible, since it is all alike, and there is no more of it in one place than in another to hinder it from holding together, nor less of it, but everything is full of what is. There can be no break between its parts; to say that such a break is real is to say that it itself is Being or body, and so body is continuous after all. It is without motion; for it could only move in space, and space either is or is not. If space is, it is Being, and Being moves in Being, which is equivalent to saying that it is at rest. If space is nothing, it does not exist, is Not-being, and so nothing can move in it. Being must be finite, for it is in need of nothing, while if it were infinite it would stand in need of everything. As it cannot *be* in one direction any more than in another, it must be spherical in shape, since the sphere is the only figure of which this can be said. Being is thus an eternal, self-complete, spherical, motionless, solid body, beyond or apart from which there is pure nothingness.

3. *Zeno and Melissus.* — The paradoxical arguments of Parmenides, appearing as they did at a time when the human mind was first beginning to taste the delights of metaphysical inquiry, had an immense influence. Among his more immediate adherents the best known are *Zeno* of Elea, and *Melissus* of Samos, the latter a general who won a victory over Athens in 442 B.C. Melissus came

to be the recognized spokesman of the Eleatic philosophy in his day, though he did little more than restate Parmenides' position. His only important innovation is his rejection of Parmenides' finite ball of Being; he argued that since the real can only be limited by empty space, and since there is no empty space, Being must be infinitely extended.

Zeno, an older contemporary, is much better known to us through his exceedingly acute attempts to strengthen the Eleatic doctrine by a counter-attack intended to show that the difficulties it involves for common sense are matched by difficulties equally as great for those who believe in multiplicity and change. He does this by the logical device of taking his opponent's position as a premise, and showing that this leads either to two opposite conclusions that contradict one another, or else to a reductio ad absurdum. For example, if things are many and made up of parts, as his pluralistic contemporaries maintained, the parts must be just as many as they are, and neither more nor less. On the other hand if things are many, each part is capable of division, and these parts in turn can be divided in an endless process. Consequently things are both finite and infinite in number. Again, if there is space it will be *in* something; for all that is is in something, and what is in something is in space. So space will be in space, and this space in another space, and so on ad infinitum; and this is an absurdity. Another argument, a favorite in later times, deals with the relation of part to whole. The effect of a sum of units ought to be no more than the sum of the effects produced by each separately. Drop a grain of millet seed, and it will make no noise. Drop a whole measure of seed and it will. If consequently a whole is made up of parts then — unless a noise can be compounded out of silences — a single seed ought to make a noise, which as a matter of fact it does not do.

Zeno's most famous arguments are those by which he attacks the possibility of motion. If a thing moves from one point to another, it must first pass through half the distance; before it can do this it must traverse a half of the half, and so on forever; it has therefore to pass through an infinite number of points, and this is impossible in a finite time. The same difficulty appears in the paradox of Achilles and the tortoise. Achilles never can overtake the tortoise, because, while he is reaching what at any moment is the tortoise's starting point the latter will have gained a certain amount of ground; and as Achilles always must reach first the position previously occupied by his competitor, the tortoise will forever keep just a little ahead. Similarly of the flying arrow. In order that an arrow flying through space should reach its destination, it must successively occupy a series of positions. But at any moment we may choose it is in a particular place, and therefore is at rest, since an object is at rest when it occupies a space equal to itself. And as no summing up of states of rest can result in motion, it can never move. These puzzles have exercised the human mind ever since Zeno's day, and even now there is no universal agreement as to how they should be solved. To realize their historical significance however, one needs to note the particular opponents against whom they were directed. What Zeno would appear to have had in mind is the Pythagorean assumption that lines are made up of discrete points; and on this showing his arguments are sound.

§ 6. *The Pluralists. Empedocles, Anaxagoras, Leucippus and Democritus*

1. *Empedocles.* — The conclusions which the Eleatics had reached were naturally a challenge to all contemporary thinkers who took an interest in scientific explanation, since, if accepted, they wiped out at a stroke the whole world with which science deals. Philosophy now takes accordingly a new start, as various thinkers attempted to rescue the Ionian speculations from this logical impasse. They did this by giving up the search for any single element out of which things can be derived, and by substituting a plurality of independent units; and by this path they arrived ultimately at a goal which represents the high-water mark of Greek physical science — that so-called atomic view of the structure of reality, which was destined later on under more propitious circumstances to become the working theory of modern science.

Empedocles, with whom this new tendency takes its start, was a native of Sicily, and a man of note and political influence. His extensive knowledge, and his skill in medicine, caused him to be regarded as the possessor of almost supernatural powers — a reputation which he seems not to have taken any trouble to disclaim. A mixture of charlatanism with what is essentially a true scientific spirit has not been uncommon at periods when new possibilities of knowledge are beginning to dawn upon men's minds; Paracelsus is a more modern illustration. At such times there seem no limits to what science can hope to accomplish. "And thou shalt learn," Empedocles says at the beginning of his great philosophical poem, "all the drugs that are a defence against ills and old age, since for thee alone shall I accomplish all this. Thou shalt arrest the violence of the weariless winds that arise and sweep the earth, laying waste the cornfields with their breath; and again, when thou so desirest, thou shalt bring their blasts back again with a rush. Thou shalt cause for men a seasonable drought after the dark rains, and again after the summer drought thou shalt produce the streams that feed the trees as they pour down from the sky. Thou shalt bring back from Hades the life of a dead man." If science has not done precisely these things, it has enabled men to perform wonders almost as great in the way of controlling natural forces; it is only the desire to reach these results by short cuts, and the failure to perceive that they require a long process of patient investigation, that turns men's thoughts in the direction of occult powers, in the manipulation of which they are partly self-deceived, in part conscious deceivers.

Whatever deductions we may need to make, however, we do find in Empedocles a real perception of the value and necessity of true scientific knowledge. Man is by nature weak, ignorant and self-deluded. "For straitened are the powers with which their bodily parts are endowed, and many are the woes that burst in on them, and blunt the edge of their careful thoughts. They behold but a brief span of a life that is no life, and, doomed to swift death, are borne away and fly off like smoke. Each is convinced of that alone which he has chanced upon as he is hurried to and fro, and idly fancies he has found the whole. So hardly can these things be seen by the eyes or heard by the ears of men, so hardly grasped by their mind !"   Our only salvation is through knowledge, or science ; and in his own philosophy, Empedocles thinks that he has found the key to man's enfranchisement.

Empedocles had felt the force of Parmenides' reasonings ; but he could not rest content with their one-sidedness.   Change and generation undoubtedly exist, and have somehow to be explained. Now even if Parmenides' proof of the non-existence of empty space be allowed — and Empedocles follows him in this — one possibility of motion still remains.   The parts of the solid mass might conceivably change their position with reference to one another without the need of empty space between them, one part slipping continuously into the place left vacant by its neighbor just as the parts of water seem to do.   There would be no gain in this if each part were exactly the same as every other.   But if we conceive a primitive difference in the nature of the parts, then their shiftings of position might be utilized to account for the changing phenomena of the sensible world.   This is Empedocles' new thought : generation is merely change of composition.   "There is no coming into being of aught that perishes, nor any end for it in baneful death, but only mingling, and separation of what has been mingled."   "When the elements have been mingled in the fashion of a man, and come to the light of day, or in the fashion of the race of wild beasts or plants or birds, then men say that these come into being ; and when they are separated, they call that, as is the custom, woful death." "Just as when painters are elaborating temple offerings, men whom Metis has well taught their art — they, when they have taken pigments of many colors with their hands, mix them in a harmony, more of some and less of others, and from them produce shapes like unto all things, making trees and men and women, beasts and birds and fishes that dwell in the waters, yea, and gods that live long lives, and are exalted in honor — so let not the error prevail over thy mind that there is any other source of all the perishable creatures that appear in countless numbers."

This marks the path accordingly by which the reconciliation of change and permanence was to be attempted. If reality is One the arguments of Parmenides are irrefragable, and the world of generation has no existence. But if reality is Many, and not One, then we can account for both factors; permanence belongs to the elements themselves, change to their shifting relations. So by setting up four separate elements — Earth, Water, Air and Fire — Empedocles thought that he could explain, through their varying combinations, those apparent differences in the world of individual objects which Parmenides had left himself no way of accounting for even as illusion.

In another direction, also, Parmenides' influence would seem to have been felt. By the earlier philosophers motion had been taken for granted; matter possesses in its own right the power of change. By his doctrine of the absolute immobility of Being, Parmenides had detached this quality of motion from the conception of matter; and Empedocles finds it necessary therefore to have recourse to a separate principle in order to start bodies moving again. So he is led to postulate, in addition to his four elements, two other agencies to which he gives the names of Love and Hate — names which should not however lead us to suppose that he looks on them as any less material than the other elements. Love acts in a way to bring about a complete intermixture of the unlike elements, "as a baker cementing barley meal with water." Hate breaks up this intermixture, and allows the natural affinity of elements of the same kind to have its way. The history of the universe is thus an oscillation of two alternate movements. At the start Hate is at the outside of the sphere, with all the elements in complete union. Then Hate is drawn inside and gradually drives Love to the center, only to be forced out again as the reverse process begins. To the rivalry between the two agencies the actual phenomena of change are due. The stage of the world in which we ourselves are living is that in which Hate is encroaching on Love.

One point in Empedocles' cosmology is worth referring to, since it anticipates in a rather bizarre form a very modern scientific doctrine. This is his conception of an organic evolution — an evolution that takes place, however, in the other stage of the world process where Love is getting the upper hand. The limbs and organs arose in separation to begin with — "heads without necks, arms bereft of shoulders, eyes in want of foreheads" — and combined at first to produce all sorts of monsters, "oxen with heads of men and men with heads of oxen"; organic forms as we know them are the result of the struggle for existence between these accidental variations, and the survival of the fittest.

One other problem which already has appeared in Heracleitus receives a somewhat fuller treatment at the hands of Empedocles — the problem of knowing. We can know everything because we are ourselves compounded of everything. All the elements enter into our make-up — earth to form the solid parts, water the liquid, air the vital breath, fire the soul. We are able to perceive any particular thing, therefore, because we *are* that thing; like is known by like. "For it is with earth that we see earth, and water with water; by air we see bright air, by fire destroying fire. By love do we see love, and hate by grievous hate." Empedocles explains sensation by a theory — afterwards to be made more precise by Democritus — of effluences thrown off by objects, and entering the body through pores adapted to their several natures.

2. *Anaxagoras*. — With the name of *Anaxagoras* we come for the first time into connection with the city of Athens. Anaxagoras was not himself an Athenian citizen, being a native of Clazomenae in Ionia; but he resided in Athens for some years, and was a prominent figure in the brilliant circle which surrounded Pericles. Anaxagoras was the first victim of the distrust toward the new philosophy which the Athenian people later on were to display in the more famous case of Socrates. His naturalistic explanation of the sun as a red-hot stone "larger than the Peloponnesus" led to an accusation of impiety, though it is very likely that a political animus lay behind the charge; at any rate he was thrown into prison, and escaped only at the price of leaving the city.

Empedocles had thought that by the admission of four distinct elements the infinite variety of the world could be explained; this appeared to Anaxagoras an impossibility. The qualities revealed in the world are too multitudinous for so limited a machinery; we cannot stop short with four elements, but must postulate an indefinite variety of qualitative characters. These qualitatively simple facts — hot and cold, moist and dry, and the like — are everywhere diffused in nature; indeed in each individual bit of matter regardless of how finely it may be divided — and it may be divided to infinity — all of them without exception are present. There is no such thing as an ultimate particle that is simple in its nature; everything is in everything else, and things are not "cut off from one another with a hatchet." On the other hand, the constituents are combined in varying proportions in the "seeds" of things, and in this way we may account for the vast variety among the objects which the empirical world presents. We name a thing after the quality that strikes the senses most forcibly; snow, for example, is black as well as white, but we call it white because the white predominates.

Along with this hypothesis, Anaxagoras is celebrated in antiquity as the originator of one other doctrine in particular. Parmenides' argument had left him, as it had left Empedocles, in a position where he needed an outside source of movement. Now the starting point in science is the recognition that the world is not the purely haphazard affair that many of its phenomena might at first sight lead us to suppose, but that, most conspicuously in its larger processes such as the changes of the seasons and the movements of the heavenly bodies, it shows evidence of harmony and order. But law or order, because it is intelligible, it is natural, for unsophisticated thought at any rate, to regard as a product of intelligence. And when it is considered, further, that creatures possessing life and thought have the apparent power of self-movement and self-direction, it is easy to see why Anaxagoras should have been led to identify the moving principle of the universe with Mind. On the one hand then are the elements, entirely inert, while over against them, and not itself a mixture like the rest, stands Mind or Nous, which alone is self-moved, and which is the cause of motion in everything else.

This is the first explicit separation of the rational life of mind, under its own proper name, from its entanglement with the rest of the universe; and it marks an important step in philosophical analysis. With Anaxagoras indeed the conception still remains confused and obscure. Notwithstanding its distinction from the elements, Nous still remains a material agency; it is the thinnest of all things, which because it is unmixed and contains no parts of other things is able to master them — to know and move them. Nor does Anaxagoras put his new principle to use in explaining natural phenomena in detail; it serves only to start the whirling movement that sets up the cosmos. In one of the Platonic dialogues we have an account of the disappointment Socrates had felt when he came to the study of Anaxagoras' system. He had been told that here everything was accounted for by Mind, and he had in consequence expected to find the purpose of things pointed out to him — the earth's shape for example, or the motions of the heavenly bodies, explained by reference to the end they serve. And instead of this he found Anaxagoras having recourse to just the same agencies — air and ether and water — that were to be met with in the other philosophers.

One other novelty appears in a correction which Anaxagoras makes to Empedocles' theory of sense perception; we perceive by unlikes rather than by likes. Sensation is produced through the stimulation of one opposite by another; witness the indifference of the body to temperatures similar to its own. The cold is known by the warm in us, the sweet by the sour, the fresh by the salt, in virtue of our deficiency in each. This is why normally we cannot see in the dark; we see by means of the dark pupil of the eye, and no image is cast on a surface where the color is the same.

3. *Leucippus.* — The doctrine of atomic elements took its final step in *Leucippus*, and in his greater pupil *Democritus* of Abdera. The issue of this new atomism lay in a denial of all differences in quality among the elements, and a return to the Eleatic conception of being as mere body stripped of qualitative characteristics. Since however Leucippus was not prepared to abandon the reality of change, and since he accepted, equally with his predecessors, change in spatial position as the only agency competent to explain phenomena, he was forced to admit what the Eleatics had denied,

and to assume that empty space has in some sense a real existence. In this way the solid lump of being which for Parmenides had constituted reality now gets split up into an infinite multitude of reproductions of itself in miniature, or atoms. These atoms, too infinitesimal to be visible to the eye, and differing from one another only in shape, size, position and arrangement, are eternal and unalterable, and individually possess indeed all the characteristics of Parmenides' Being except its immobility. They and their changing relationships alone are real; all else is appearance, to be explained ultimately in terms of these real movements in space. The random movements of the atoms as they oscillate in all directions and impinge on one another may anywhere set up a vortex or whirling motion. This brings atoms similar in shape and size together, as the shaking of a sieve sorts out millet, wheat and barley, or as waves sort the pebbles on a beach; and in this way Empedocles' elements — earth, water, air and fire — come into being. As in a whirlpool, the larger bodies move to the center, while the smaller are forced toward the outside; and so a world process is under way.

In Leucippus we have the first clear statement of a philosophical materialism in its ordinary modern meaning — the reduction of true reality, that is, to what later came to be known as the primary qualities of body. This has proved to be a point of view of the greatest significance for scientific thought; by its reduction of qualitative to quantitative differences it made possible, in particular, that application of mathematics to the treatment of phenomena which is essential to the modern notion of a scientific law. Leucippus gets rid of the last temptation to a teleological explanation of events by restoring motion to the elements as an original possession; with all the data required for an understanding of the world thus immanent in the atoms themselves, there was no longer any need to appeal to Love or Nous, or to anything except the necessary laws of mechanical impact. Mind or soul is only a particular form of atomic matter; it is composed of the fire atoms, which are the smallest, smoothest and most active of all, and which dart about in all directions like motes in a sunbeam. These soul atoms exist everywhere, though they are only endowed with sensation when they come together in certain quantities, as they do in the human body; consciousness accordingly will disappear again when the body is dissolved.

4. *Democritus.* — The scientific elaboration of this standpoint at the hands of Democritus (about 460–360 B.C.) was one of the great philosophical achievements of antiquity. Democritus is to be classed indeed, not with the earlier philosophers, but rather with Plato and Aristotle, whom he rivals in the comprehensiveness of his system. For one thing, he goes beyond his predecessors in the more elaborate treatment which he gives to the knowledge problem. This is a problem which had grown more insistent with the progress of science, and the growing rift between ordinary sense perception and scientific thought. Democritus finds a solution in his theory of "images" — a theory which remained influential even down to the time of Locke, and which is given a certain verisimilitude if we remember that in vision an image is actually present in the pupil of the eye. External objects, according to this theory, shed copies or images of themselves; these enter the sense organs which are fitted to receive them, and by setting in motion the soul atoms give rise to perception. Differences in color are due to the smoothness or roughness of the impinging images; taste and smell to differences in the shape of the atoms; and so on for all the sense properties. By this doctrine Democritus is able also to offer an explanation of the important and perplexing fact of error or mistaken knowledge. The images do not reach our senses quite so spick and span as when they started on their journey, but are more or less battered and distorted by their progress through the intervening air; this explains why things seem indistinct at a distance, and why if the distance is great enough they cannot be seen at all. Were no obstacle thus present "we could see an ant crawling on the sky." Also as they enter the sense organs there is a similar distortion; they do not fit exactly into the pores or cavities, and so are still further abraded and wrenched from their original form.

So far we have a theory that would seem to point to a thoroughgoing relativity of knowledge such as we shall meet presently in connection with certain of the Sophists. And as regards the senses Democritus not only admits but insists that this is so. "By the senses we in truth know nothing sure, but only something that changes according to the disposition of the body and of the things that enter into it or resist it." Here lies the explanation of the fact that there are so many variations in the way different men perceive the same objects, and the fact that the same man may feel a thing as sweet or bitter, pleasant or painful, according to his physical state. Sight, hearing, smell, touch, taste are consequently bastard forms of knowledge; in reality there are only atoms and the void. But in saying this we already are presupposing that not all knowledge shares the liabilities of the senses; we "know" the atoms, and such knowledge by hypothesis is true and adequate. How is this possibility of true knowledge to be accounted for?

In looking for an answer Democritus has to keep of course to his universe of atoms; but he does not need to go far for a solution. True thought is caused by the finer images which copy the atomic structure of things, and which are able to reach the soul atoms, not through the disturbing senses, but more directly; for the soul is not localized in the senses merely, but is diffused throughout the body, so that the finer images may get into immediate touch with it. Furthermore the motion of these images is less violent. Sensation, being due to larger and coarser images, throws the soul into violent commotion and thus results in perceptions more or less confused; whereas the atomic images give rise to a gentler motion of the soul which eliminates confusing disturbances.

And in this last consideration we have a point of contact with certain ethical conclusions by which Democritus' philosophy is rounded off. As might be expected, his ethical theory takes a hedonistic form. Pleasure and pain alone are what determine happiness; "the best thing for a man is to pass his life so as to have as much joy and as little trouble as possible." But between pleasures we are able to discriminate; and the ordinary pleasures of the senses no more constitute true happiness than sense perception constitutes true knowledge. The pleasures of the senses differ with different people, as sensations do; they are too transitory to form the content of real happiness, and they pass too easily into pain. The mind must judge between pleasures and weigh their relative values. For the reflective mind, accordingly, the true end of life is to be found not in tumultuous pleasures or in external goods, but in the calm of body which is health, and the calm of soul which is cheerfulness. "He who chooses the goods of the soul chooses the more divine; he who chooses the goods of the body chooses the human."

LITERATURE

Burnet, *Early Greek Philosophy*, 3rd ed.
Fairbanks, *The First Philosophers of Greece*.
Zeller, *Pre-Socratic Philosophy*, 2 vols.
Scoon, *Greek Philosophy before Plato*.
Patrick, *Heracleitus on Nature*.
Symonds, *Greek Poets*, Vol. 1.
Benn, *Early Greek Philosophy*.
Bailey, *The Greek Atomists and Epicurus*.
Cornford, *From Religion to Philosophy*.
Robin, *Greek Thought and the Origins of the Scientific Spirit*.

THE EARLY MORALISTS

§ 7. *The Sophists*

1. *The Growth of Critical Inquiry.* — So far the powers of the Greek mind had been directed chiefly to the theoretical solution of the cosmological problems that are connected with processes in nature; and along this line the results had been somewhat remarkable. In a comparatively short space of time a conception had been elaborated which is strikingly similar to that on which modern science has most commonly proceeded. The reduction of qualitative to quantitative differences, the connection of mathematics with scientific method, the resolution of all phenomenal bodies into a multitude of minute moving particles or atoms, of all change into change of position on the part of these atoms and all efficiency into mechanical impact, is expressed with a definiteness that leaves little to be desired.

But now this development comes abruptly to an end, and for nearly two thousand years the course of human thought takes, in its dominant aspects, a different direction. One reason for this lay in the very merits of the atomic hypothesis; it was the natural culmination of the problems which the Ionians had inaugurated, and having arrived at this point the Greeks could go no further until a new instrument had been created. It is here the great difference lies between ancient science and that of the present day. Modern science is no mere guess at the ultimate nature of things in general, but an experimental investigation of the way in which things in particular really act. It is this which gives it its immense influence on modern life. To know the actual *laws* of things is to be able to control them; and this practical service is what renders science one of the most powerful instruments of growth in civilization that has ever been devised. The Greeks, on the contrary, had not reached the point where they could master the concrete behavior of objects. Their atomism is less a science than a philosophy, intent chiefly on the theoretical interest of reducing complexity to a single formula. As such it has no great contribution to make to the concrete human ends out of which the larger movements of human thought always flow; it is not far enough advanced to touch human life on the practical side, like modern science, while it is plainly inadequate to satisfy the spiritual interests of man. It was only natural therefore that physical speculations should for a time be subordinated to the more pressing problems which have to do with individual and social conduct, that is, to Ethics; it was not till these had in their turn been to some extent worked out that the human mind was able to come back with profit to the physical aspects of the universe.

Meanwhile, in a negative way, the theories of the physical philosophers had helped prepare for this subsequent movement — a movement which represents most characteristically the genius of Greek thought. At first philosophy had directed its criticism only against such ideas as were primarily theoretical in their nature, and had left comparatively untouched the realm of conduct. Any real tampering with the foundations of social life would indeed at the start have been strongly resented; a society based on the morality of custom and tradition cannot afford to allow too free an examination of its sanctions. Indirectly, however, philosophy had helped to undermine these sanctions. Morality and the social life always stand for the mass of men in close connection with religious ideas and practices, and this especially is true of early society, where religion is still intimately bound up with every detail of life. The physical philosophies had weakened materially the hold of popular religion for a multitude of educated men. The stories about the gods, offensive alike to the scientific and to the moral sense, began to be rationalized and explained away; and while philosophers might not go to the length of denying outright the gods' existence, still the clearly defined conceptions of the past were all the time being attenuated into a vague naturalistic pantheism whose connection with concrete conduct was very slight indeed. This growth of naturalism, and the decay of an active belief in the old mythology, shows itself plainly, for example, in the Greek historians. There is already in Herodotus a fair development of the historical spirit which stops to weigh the evidence even in the case of stories that are sacred. In spite of a good deal of native piety, Herodotus is glad to rationalize when he sees his way to it; thus he explains the legend of the rape of Europa as perhaps growing out of what was historically a capture by pirates. And in Thucydides we have a thoroughly modern historian whose narrative has become purely secular, and who has nothing to do with anything except human and natural motives. When therefore the ideas of conduct came themselves in turn to be criticized, they already had lost some of their vitality.

There had always been a certain amount of ethical reflection among the Greeks. The early moralists had indeed been content with the enunciation of disconnected ethical and prudential maxims with moderation as their keynote — maxims whose social and political applications were partisan rather than fundamental. Still this moralizing was already symptomatic of a growing spirit of unrest and a sense of insecurity. Meanwhile the tacit acquiescence in the status quo, the unquestioning acceptance of law as obligatory and divine, the merging of the individual life as a matter of course in the community life, could hardly remain unchallenged under the conditions that marked Greek politics during the sixth and fifth centuries. Constant revolutions and changes of government, and the increasing spread of democratic principles, made it impossible that the old attitude should be persevered in. So too the appearance everywhere in the Greek cities of the Tyrant, a vigorous personality who, often from the rôle of popular hero, ended by setting up his private will as absolute, had impressed on the age a stamp of egoism and individualism which was not conducive to a reverence for tradition. In this social turmoil, with the old ideals based on the life of custom yielding to new circumstances, it was natural that thoughtful minds should turn to the task of finding some more substantial basis for law and justice and morality, and of vindicating at the bar of reason the institutions which hitherto had been accepted on authority. This sense of the conflict between the new and the old we may see in the development of the Greek drama. In the earlier dramatists, Aeschylus and Sophocles, it is still more or less implicit, and takes the form of a deepening of the ethical consciousness and a moralization of the older Greek mythology. But in Euripides it has come to full self-expression, and its issue is a pervasive scepticism and individualism and modernity which makes it very clear how far thought had advanced from its primitive caution.

2. *The Sophists.* — Among the influences responsible for bringing this change of attitude to consciousness the appearance of the Sophist was not the least important. The Sophistic movement was in the main an outgrowth of the political conditions of the time. For a young man of good birth the natural career to look forward to was in connection with the political life of his city; and for this, as well as for the still more fundamental purpose of self-defence against the jealous suspicion of his democratic neighbors, the almost indispensable qualification was the ability to speak persuasively in public. A demand arose accordingly for teachers who should train men for public life; and this demand the Sophists undertook to meet. The representatives of the higher education of the day, they made the teaching of wisdom a profession. As there were no settled seats of learning they wandered from city to city, picking up their pupils wherever they could find them. The basis of their work was apt to be rhetorical; but with the abler Sophists this was broadened out to cover the field of an all-round and liberal culture. Any knowledge that was available of the working of the human mind, of history, literature or grammar, of logic or the forms of argument, of political constitutions, of the nature of justice or of virtue, was regarded as appropriate to the end in view. And so in the case of the greater Sophists we meet with men possessed of a varied learning, made acceptable through the cultivation of a high degree of skill in presentation.

All this seems innocent enough, and hardly sufficient to justify the hostility and suspicion with which the Sophists were generally regarded by the populace, and by such reactionary upholders of tradition as Aristophanes. Grounds for this suspicion were not however lacking. Practically there was always a chance that the Sophistic skill might be prostituted to undesirable purposes. In Aristophanes' *Clouds* the worthy Strepsiades, driven to his wits' end by the debts in which his son has involved him, is represented as turning to the Sophist Socrates for the means to extricate himself by cheating his creditors; and when, after he proves too stupid himself to master the new learning, his son takes his place, and ends by winning his suits in the courts, the latter shows himself a proficient disciple by ill-treating his own father, and then justifying his actions in true sophistic style. And apart from such chances for abuse there were other reasons for the popular distrust. Naturally the Sophists found their clients mainly in the aristocratic classes, where alone the adequate leisure could be looked for, as well as the ability to pay the rather stiff fees they were inclined to ask. And to acquire the reputation of being hangers-on to the aristocracy was of course not a way to popular favor.

Nor was a more fundamental ground for suspicion wholly lacking. Men do not like to have the foundations of their lives disturbed; and when these foundations have no better warrant than unthinking custom, any habit of unrestricted inquiry and discussion is an apparent menace to security. Just the admission that each man has the right to test the truth of anything whatsoever by referring it to his private judgment seems at first to do away with the possibility of public standards. Such a risk was heightened, as has been remarked, by the practical aim of the Sophistic teaching. The goal of the politician is not so much truth as victory. This made it necessary that, like the modern lawyer, he should be nimble-witted enough to take any side, to seize any loophole of argument, to be able, if need be, to make the worse appear the better reason — a procedure likely to obscure rather than clarify the ultimate principles of truth if any such there be. On this basis it easily was possible for a way of thinking to arise that should reduce society to a crowd of private individuals, each looking out for his own interests — a conception which had its counterpart in that atomism in the outer world with which the theories of the physical philosophers were familiarizing men's minds.

In the case of the earlier and greater Sophists we are not justified in assuming any intention thus to undermine the foundations of society or to promote an extreme scepticism and individualism. For the most part these were men of excellent moral ideals, who honestly meant to train their pupils to a life of virtue and usefulness in the state; the famous *Choice of Hercules* by Prodicus, and the discourse of Protagoras in Plato's dialogue, keep safely to the path of a familiar and rather commonplace morality. At the same time forces had been put in motion to which it was no easy thing to set a limit. The conditions tending to break down the sacredness traditionally attaching to social law and custom had had one result of particular importance. This was the growing recognition of a distinction between existing laws and prescriptions of morality, and those ultimate principles of justice and legality which reason can disclose — as it came to be expressed, between what is right only by custom or convention and what is right by *nature*. At the start this might be meant to justify genuine morality as against mere convention; but once started on such a line there was no telling what might be the outcome. The almost universal assumption which lies back of moralizing reflection and ethical exhortation in early times — that virtue and justice are the only safe way of getting on in the world, and should be sought as a matter of far-sighted prudence — becomes less obvious as it is pondered over. To the intelligence enlightened by the casting off of unthinking habits of moral judgment it does not seem evident that the righteous always prosper and the wicked come to grief. Injustice has its full share, if not more than its share, of the good things of life, and apparently enjoys them none the less for the crimes that have been committed to procure them. If then the motive of conduct is one's own advantage and happiness — and what other end can maintain itself? — and if the fear of the gods, whose very existence is in question, is no longer before the eyes of the emancipated man, have virtue and justice themselves any other title to our respect than mere convention? It may be advisable often to yield to the prejudice in favor of these things; but if we can disregard them safely, and it is clearly to our interest to do so, it is folly to allow words like "injustice" and "evil" to stand in our way.

There were not lacking men to draw this final conclusion. In the last resort, might is right. The law of nature is to satisfy, if we can, those appetites which nature has implanted in us in common with the rest of her creatures. "For nature herself intimates that it is just for the better to have more than the worse, the more powerful than the weaker, and in many ways she shows among men as well as among animals that justice consists in the superior ruling over and having more than the inferior. . . . If there were a man who had sufficient force, he would trample under foot all our formulas and spells and charms, and all our laws, sinning against nature; the slave would rise in rebellion and be lord over us, and natural justice would shine forth." [1] These conclusions were not often so nakedly expressed but they were in the air, not so much as the opinions of any group of individual thinkers as a state of mind in "that great Sophist, the Public"; it is no Sophist, but a practical politician and man of the world, a despiser of philosophy, who stands in Plato as the most extreme and outspoken representative of the gospel of force. "The Sophists do but fan and add fuel to the fire in which Greece, as they wander like ardent missionaries about it, is flaming itself away." [2]

3. *Protagoras and Gorgias.* — In Plato's dialogue, the *Protagoras*, we have an interesting picture of what the Sophists and their activities were like — a picture which we have no reason to suppose is not drawn to life, and which probably is no less true in that it is given a slightly satirical twist as viewed through the humorous eye of Socrates. Three of the four most famous names among the Sophists are in Athens, and a meeting has taken place at the house of Callias. Two of them play a minor role in the dialogue, as they do in the history of philosophy. *Prodicus* of Ceos is known as an early grammarian of a sort, whose specialty is the discrimination of synonyms — an art which he proceeds at once to show off when the

[1] Plato, *Gorgias*, 483. This, and the subsequent quotations from Plato, are from Jowett's translation, Oxford University Press, American ed. by Chas. Scribner's Sons.
[2] Pater, *Plato and Platonism*.

chance arrives in the dialogue. *Hippias* of Elis was a universal genius and foe to specialism, prepared to lecture on any subject, and claiming a proficiency in every art; he is said to have appeared at the Olympic games gorgeously attired in a costume entirely of his own making down to the ring on his finger. Both are entirely over-shadowed by *Protagoras*, the greatest figure of his day among the Sophists. The dialogue starts with an account of the excitement among the intelligentsia of Athens as the news goes about that Protagoras is in the city, the hurried gathering of his admirers be-fore daybreak, the visit of Socrates and a younger friend to Callias' house where they find Hippias already answering questions about astronomy, Prodicus still abed but talking continuously in a boom-ing voice, and Protagoras walking up and down and discoursing to eager listeners. "As for me, when I saw their evolutions I was delighted with the admirable care they took not to hinder Protag-oras at any moment by getting in front, but whenever the master turned about and those with him, it was fine to see the orderly manner in which his train of listeners split up into two parties on this side and on that, and wheeling round formed up again each time in his rear most admirably." Of Protagoras himself the picture drawn is respectful if not enthusiastic; at least there is no trace of hostility on Plato's part. Protagoras is slightly pompous and dogmatic and does not take to criticism very kindly; he is dis-posed to monopolize the conversation and to discourse at great length in spite of Socrates' efforts to keep him to the point, to be more inclined to rhetoric than to accurate definition, and much more ready to instruct others than to learn himself. But on the whole he appears in a not unfavorable light as a man of learning, intelligence and eloquence, fully persuaded that he is promoting the good of his hearers and of society in general.

Protagoras' chief contribution to philosophy does not appear in the dialogue that goes by his name, but elsewhere Plato examines it in considerable detail.[1] It is summed up in the still famous phrase, Man is the measure of all things. It is not wholly clear how far Protagoras meant to go in this; perhaps it was intended pri-

[1] In the *Theaetetus*.

marily to repudiate the metaphysical pretensions of the early philosophers, and to call philosophy back to man and man's affairs as the only thing which it is really important for us to know. But it certainly was understood by later thinkers, Plato included, as the expression of a thoroughgoing scepticism. Things are to me as they appear to me, and to you as they appear to you, and no ground exists for saying that one opinion is any truer than the other. There are many facts of experience that lend verisimilitude to such a claim, more particularly when it is applied to the facts of sense perception; and since these facts had already been exploited by philosophers, as Protagoras must have been aware, it seems unlikely he would have put the matter as he did if he had not intended in some sense to subscribe to the sceptical consequences. Against this is the difficulty to be noted that he apparently did not draw the practical conclusions that might seem to be implied. In the dialogue there is no evidence of real moral scepticism, for example; on the contrary, Protagoras accepts almost ostentatiously the same conceptions of virtue and the social good that are held by the ordinary man.

Plato in the *Theaetetus* suggests a possible way out of the apparent contradiction. About any matter of opinion it is possible to make two opposite statements; but while both may equally be "true" — — since we have no test of truth other than that it seems true to this or that individual — nevertheless one may be "better" than another; it is more serviceable, that is, to human life. And as the sense perception of the man in normal health is better than the equally "true" or real sensations that result from diseased or imperfect organs, so the common sense of mankind which has been embodied in laws and accepted social institutions has a similar pragmatic claim on our acceptance. It is the business of the educator to bring about by words the same change which the physician works by the aid of drugs. You cannot say that the sick man because he has one sort of sense impression is foolish, while the healthy man is wise; and in the same way education does not aim to make men wiser, but to produce mental health by changing the worse state into the better. Plato does not give the impression that this was an explanation that Protagoras actually advanced; but it would explain what seems to have been his attitude in practice. Thus he argues in the dialogue, as against the point made by Socrates that virtue has no teachers, that all men are teachers of virtue; we pick up knowledge from the common life about us, though this has to be extended by the familiar processes of education, by occasional correction from the laws, and by the wisdom of superior men, of whom Protagoras does not deny that he is one. A more explicit scepticism might appear to be implied in another passage that has been preserved. "With regard to the gods," Protagoras writes, " I cannot feel sure either that they are or that they are not, nor what they are like in figure; for there are many things that hinder sure knowledge, the obscurity of the subject, and the shortness of human life." It was not however with speculative theology that Greek religion was concerned, but with the observances of public worship; and we have no reason to suppose that here too Protagoras was not ready to conform to custom.

The next most important Sophist was *Gorgias*, who also has given his name to one of Plato's dialogues. Gorgias was a native of Sicily, and was already advanced in years when, in 427 B.C., he came to Athens as an ambassador from his city. His interest lay more in the direction of rhetoric than did that of Protagoras, and his influence on the development of prose style was considerable. As a philosopher his reputation rests on his sceptical extension of the Eleatic argument against Not-being to the knowledge of Being likewise; he sought to prove, first, that nothing *is*, secondly, that if there is any thing we cannot know it, and, finally, that even if we could know it we could not communicate our knowledge to anyone else. Here at any rate the probability would appear to be that Gorgias' real purpose is not to expound a serious philosophy of scepticism and nihilism, but rather to demolish the pretensions of metaphysics in the interest of more practical concerns.

§ 8. *Socrates*

1. *Socrates* (469–399 B.C.) was the son of an Athenian sculptor, but abandoned his father's profession for the more congenial pursuit

of philosophy. There is no more picturesque figure in the history of Greece. In personal appearance the very opposite of the Greek ideal, with protruding eyes, thick lips, snub nose and a peculiar gait, this was forgotten when one came under the charm of his personality and his conversation. And conversation was the business of his life. Living in the most frugal manner, his meat and drink of the cheapest sort, without shoes to his feet the whole year round, and clinging to a single threadbare cloak that served for summer and winter alike, he spent his time in the market-place or wherever men came together, satisfied if only he could find some one with whom to talk about the questions in which he took a perennial interest. "I have a benevolent habit," he says jokingly in one of Plato's dialogues, "of pouring out myself to everybody, and I would even pay for a listener if I couldn't get one in any other way." In consequence of his moderate and abstemious life his powers of endurance were remarkable. On military campaigns, besides showing great bravery in battle, he had an extraordinary power of sustaining fatigue and going without food; "and when during a severe winter the rest either remained indoors, or, if they went out, had on no end of clothing, and were well shod, and had their feet swathed in felts and fleeces, in the midst of this Socrates, with his bare feet on the ice, and in his ordinary dress, marched better than any of the other soldiers who had their shoes on." His courage was shown in peace as well as in war. When acting as president of the prytanes he had declined, in face of the popular clamor, to put to vote illegally the resolution condemning the generals at Arginusae; and once again, in the perilous times under the Thirty Tyrants, he had, at the risk of his life, refused to act contrary to the laws at their bidding. This combination of rectitude of character with striking intellectual gifts — a combination which his personal peculiarities served rather to heighten than obscure — gave to Socrates an influence unequalled by any thinker of his day.

Socrates' youth and early manhood were contemporaneous with the most brilliant period of Athenian history. About the enlightened democratic leader Pericles there was gathered a galaxy of famous men drawn from the fields of literature, philosophy and art.

Philosophy was represented in particular by Anaxagoras, but other eminent thinkers visited the city from time to time. Socrates seems not to have met Anaxagoras, but there is reason to believe that he was fully alive to the new scientific ideas that had made such a stir throughout the Hellenic world. When Aristophanes set out to satirize the intellectual modernism of the day in his comedy the *Clouds*, he chose Socrates to represent it. Socrates appears as the head of a school or Thinking Shop. One scientific tendency regarded Air as the instrument of thought; Socrates accordingly is found by his visitors suspended in a basket that he may get plenty of pure air for his thinking. With his disciples he is engaged in various scientific investigations, such as measuring the distance fleas can jump in terms of their own footprints. Aristophanes has often been regarded as intending here not to draw a picture of the historic Socrates, but only to give Socrates' name to a composite picture of the scientists and Sophists generally. But this, highly unlikely in itself, is made still more improbable by the fact that Plato also definitely tells us that Socrates had passed through a period when he was much concerned with the physical speculations that were exercising the minds of scientists at the time — whether we think with air or blood or fire, whether organisms are brought about through a sort of fermentation by heat and cold, what is the cause of destruction and decay, and the like.[1]

That he later abandoned such interests was due mainly, it would seem, to the vein of practicality which is one of his leading characteristics. He found the theories of the scientists altogether too speculative and pretentious to suit him; there was too much guesswork in them, and they really didn't explain things after all. In his later life, in the period when we know most about him, his intellectual interests had taken accordingly a different direction. Here we enter very controversial ground. There is no agreement among scholars about the actual character of Socrates' contributions to philosophy, and the account that follows must therefore be taken as open to dispute. The trouble comes partly from the fact that we have two pictures of him that are very far apart. Xenophon

[1] *Phaedo,* 96

depicts him merely as an edifying moral teacher, and one whose range of ideas, moreover, does not extend beyond the customary moral and religious commonplaces. In Plato, on the other hand, he is a genuine and original philosopher, with an explicit theory of the universe which anticipates, if indeed it is not identical with, the one that has commonly been attributed to Plato himself. There is a growing tendency to believe that Plato's account is on the whole nearer to the truth; but even if we grant this, difficulties still remain in the way of distinguishing between Socrates' own ideas and the additions which Plato made to them. It will be necessary therefore to proceed with caution if we are not to get in trouble.

Plato's account, which on the surface seems to be intended, up to a point at least, to be genuinely biographical, is in brief as follows: [1] Dissatisfied with the explanations of the physicists, Socrates had turned eagerly to what he had been told was Anaxagoras' attempt to account for things in terms of Mind. But this too disappointed him; after all he found the new philosophy falling back on purely mechanical causes just like those that had preceded it. Accordingly he was led to strike out a new path. Instead of looking to the physical world, he turned his gaze within to the intellectual essences which the mind itself reveals. What is the cause of beautiful objects, for example? It is not their lovely color, or their shape, or any other of the particular qualities that in a given case may or may not be present. Can it be anything else than Beauty itself, absolute and intrinsic Beauty, in which the things we call beautiful somehow share? This means that physical explanations are on the wrong track. We are not to say, for instance, that one man is greater or smaller than another by a head; that is saying, first, that the greater is greater and the smaller is smaller by the same thing, and, secondly, that since a head is small the greater man is greater by something which is small. No, it is greatness alone that makes great things great, smallness that makes small things small, beauty that makes things beautiful, goodness that makes things good. That there exists such a thing as absolute beauty, absolute goodness, absolute equality, Socrates takes as self-evident; it is an

[1] *Phaedo*, 96–102.

assumption which, however he arrives at it, he never for a moment doubts.

If then we take this as a starting point, where does it lead us? Some things to begin with we can say with considerable assurance. In the first place, Socrates is now concerned with the life of the spirit rather than with physical science. This by itself was a revolutionary innovation, and marks a fresh stage in the history of thought. Socrates' philosophy is primarily a moral philosophy; it is occupied with questions about virtue, the good, the ends that lend value to human living. Furthermore — on this point all the accounts agree — we know that Socrates identified virtue with *knowledge;* and he believed that in some real sense virtue is no mere collection of separate virtues but is one and indivisible. We have to ask therefore what more concretely he may be supposed to mean by this.

2. We may start from an incident in Socrates' life to which he apparently attached some importance. As he tells the story in Plato's *Apology*, the report had come to him that Chaerophon, a friend of his, had put to the oracle at Delphi the question: Is any man living wiser than Socrates? and the reply had been that Socrates was indeed the wisest of mankind. Unable, in the consciousness of his own ignorance, to understand this, and yet not wanting to doubt the word of the god, Socrates had gone from one man to another who was reputed wise that he might test this wisdom; and in every case he had found a conceit of knowledge with nothing in reality to back it. A little questioning had quickly brought to light that each man was as ignorant as he of all the higher concerns of human life; the only difference lay in the fact that all the rest supposed themselves to be very wise indeed, whereas Socrates, though he was as ignorant as they, at least knew that he knew nothing. He concluded, therefore, that it was this consciousness of his own ignorance to which the oracle had been referring, and that, by thus commending him, the god had chosen him out as an instrument for pricking the bubble of universal self-deception. Convinced profoundly that knowledge alone is salvation, he saw that the first and essential step toward getting rid of the

confused mass of opinion going by the name of knowledge was to make its inadequacy apparent. He was the divinely appointed gadfly given to the state, "which is like a great and noble steed who is tardy in his motions owing to his very size, and requires to be stirred into life."

On the negative side, accordingly, Socrates believed he had a mission to show up the false claims of that which ordinarily goes by the name of human wisdom, but which really is ignorance parading in the guise of knowledge. Throughout his life this occupied a good share of his endeavor. The process was kindly and sympathetic in dealing with his friends or with anyone who showed an open mind; it was more caustic and ironic where an arrogant dogmatism was in evidence. But it is the first essential if a man is ever to arrive at that true knowledge in which virtue consists. "Know thyself" is the first duty of man; and self-knowledge Socrates looked in vain to find. The carpenter, the smith, the flute player, the pilot, each knows his own business; he trains himself for one definite thing, and he can tell you what that thing is and what purpose it serves. But for his vocation as a man there is no special training and no teachers. There were the Sophists to be sure, who professed to educate men in the virtues of citizenship. But when one came down to cases this amounted only to a training in the superficial arts of the politician; as to what really constitutes the good of man and of the state — what in itself virtue is — they are as ignorant as any one. But if we need knowledge for the simplest and humblest pursuits, most of all do we need it for that pursuit which is ultimate and supreme. Socrates' task is thus fundamentally a moral and religious one. "Men of Athens, I honor and love you; but I shall obey God rather than you, and while I have life and strength I shall never cease from the practice and teaching of philosophy, exhorting every one whom I meet after my manner, and convincing him, saying: O my friend, why do you, who are a citizen of the great and mighty and wise city of Athens, care so much about laying up the greatest amount of money and honor and reputation, and so little about wisdom, and truth, and the greatest improvement of the soul, which you never regard or heed at all?"

Socrates begins, then, by shaking the foundations of a false assurance of knowledge. Starting in with an appearance of agreement, and a depreciation of his own wisdom as compared with that which his interlocutor undoubtedly possesses, he induces the latter to offer a definition of the matter in hand. Then by a series of skilful questions he develops the most contradictory conclusions from this, until, as Euthyphro says, "somehow or other our arguments, on whatever grounds we rest them, seem to turn round and walk away"; and the one with whom he is arguing is compelled to confess that he has never carefully considered the subject, and that his notions about it are based on mere confused opinion. This is the famous Socratic *irony*.

But implied in this is a more positive assumption. If the elements of knowledge did not exist below the surface of opinion, we should have no standard by which to correct our first thoughts. Socrates' questioning is intended, therefore, not to leave men confused and doubting, but to disentangle and bring to light what implicitly is there already; he is an intellectual midwife to bring truth to its birth. If knowledge is possible at all, then down beneath the unessential differences due to individual prejudices and opinions there is something on which men agree, or can be led to agree. The method of philosophy will consist in stripping off these outer husks and laying bare the universal element which they conceal; only when we thus have got down to fundamentals, when instead of taking our terms for granted in a dogmatic way we have tested their credentials and found out what really and essentially they stand for, do we have anything that deserves to be called real knowledge.

Now in the first place such a statement means at least as much as this, that Socrates has gone beyond the sceptical and individualistic tendencies implicit in the Sophistic movement. Instead of looking for man's nature in those private desires, feelings and sensations which separate him from other men, he looked rather to the rational elements that bind all men together in the bonds of a valid knowledge and a universal moral insight. It was this tendency which Plato and Aristotle carried on, and which in their hands was to shape Greek thought in the form which left its most significant and lasting impress on the future. What we have now to examine is the sense which it bore to Socrates himself.

3. In Xenophon's picture Socrates appears, as has been said, as a rather plodding exponent of the customary virtues, for which he has neat and commonplace definitions to which he leads his hearers up by a process of questioning that only in appearance represents a genuine search for truth still undiscovered. It is a radically different Socrates that we meet in Plato. Even in the shorter and simpler dialogues which were undoubtedly the first to be written, there is almost no trace of the didacticism which makes out of Socrates an earlier Dr. Johnson; while he is engaged with the same general subjects as in Xenophon — justice and temperance, piety and courage — it is in the spirit of the truthseeker rather than of the exhorter. If there is one thing about Socrates that is well attested, it is the profession he makes of his own ignorance; and the almost entire lack of definite conclusions in these dialogues, while perplexing to the reader, must be regarded therefore as far truer to historical fact than Xenophon's cut-and-dried definitions.

There is also a much more important and fundamental difference. This meets us most conspicuously in a second group of dialogues, including among others the *Phaedo*, the *Symposium* and the *Phaedrus*, where Plato's literary art comes near to attaining its highest perfection; and since one cannot go much farther in the interpretation either of Socrates or of Plato until he has formed some opinion about this, it will be necessary to consider it more carefully. Briefly it has to do with a very decided touch of mysticism attributed to Socrates — a mysticism which in a thin and sentimentalized form has reached us in the so-called doctrine of "Platonic love," and which historically connects itself with the Orphic mysteries and with Pythagoreanism on its religious side. Are we justified in ascribing this to Socrates — who in that case must have been a very different sort of man indeed from the sort that Xenophon presents — or does it come originally from Plato, who creates a new and unhistorical Socrates to serve as his mouthpiece?

As against this last alternative it is not very easy to suppose, for one thing, that Plato's literary conscience would have permitted him to take such liberties with the character of a well-known Athenian, only recently martyred, whom he himself held in affectionate remembrance. In the *Symposium*, for example, where a particularly lifelike portrait is drawn for us, we find Socrates present at a banquet with his cronies, each of whom contributes to the entertainment an after-dinner eulogy on Love; if now Plato when he comes to Socrates goes out of his way to represent him as temperamentally at very near the opposite extreme of character from what he really was, he at least is sinning against every canon of art. Nor are other difficulties lacking. Plato as we know him from his dialogues was an intellectually fastidious man whom we scarcely should expect to find much attracted by the homely and somewhat uncouth Orphic theology and life unless it came recommended to him from some trusted source, and no such likely source can be pointed to other than Socrates himself; it was only later that Plato seems to have come into direct contact with the Pythagoreans, and then chiefly on the mathematical and scientific side. In Socrates' case, on the contrary, the evidence goes to show that an Orphic tendency did actually exist. The inner voice which spoke to him every now and then to hold him back from some course of conduct, the disposition to take dreams and oracles seriously as divine messages, his notorious trances — at one time when in camp, to the amazement of his fellow soldiers who timed him, he stood in a trance out of doors from early morning on one day till sunrise on the next — all indicate the presence of a mystical vein.

We seem fairly safe in following Plato, then, and assuming that among Socrates' beliefs the traditional doctrines of the Orphics and Pythagoreans held an important place — the doctrine of the body as the tomb of the soul, of transmigration as a moral economy through which the deeds of the body are punished or rewarded by reincarnation in a lower or a higher form, of a realm of true reality above the world of sense to which the soul aspires, and of philosophy as a method of salvation whereby the soul, through feeding on the truth congenial to its divine nature, is enabled to escape the wheel of birth and attain to the final consummation of a unity with God.

To the body are due our aberrations and failures to see the truth; "it draws the soul down into the region of the changeable, where it wanders and is confused; the world spins around her, and she is like a drunkard when under their influence." "For the body is a source of endless trouble to us by reason of the mere requirement of food, and also is liable to diseases which overtake and impede us in the search after truth, and, by filling us so full of loves, and fears, and fancies, and idols, and every sort of folly, prevents our ever having, as people say, so much as a thought. For whence come wars and fightings and factions? whence but from the body and the lust of the body?" "Each pleasure and pain is a sort of nail, and rivets the soul to the body, and engrosses her, and makes her believe that to be true which the body affirms to be true; and from agreeing with the body, and having the same delights, she is obliged to have the same habits and ways, and is not likely ever to be pure at her departure to the world below, but is always saturated with the body." Philosophy alone is the means through which enfranchisement is to be secured. "When returning into herself the soul reflects, then she passes into the realm of purity and eternity and immortality and unchangeableness which are her kindred; and with them she ever lives, and is not let or hindered. There she ceases from her erring ways, and being in communion with the unchanging, is unchanging; and this state of the soul is called wisdom." [1] It is but partially indeed that we can attain this in our present life, for we are still clogged by the weight of the body; before the common variety of soul can attain its true destiny it must pass through many reincarnations and undergo many adventures. Only the soul of the philosopher may pass at once to the celestial realm and be purged completely from the taint of earth.

4. It is this general background which we find implied in Socrates' discourse in the *Symposium*. Love — the subject of the *Symposium* — is not, as the previous speaker had declared, possession, but the desire for a good in which the soul as yet is lacking; for no man desires what he already has. What is its true object

[1] *Phaedo*, 79, 66, 83

then? Socrates' answer he professes to have learned from a wise woman of Mantineia. Eros is neither a God nor a mere mortal, but a spirit intermediate between the two. He is the child of Plenty by the beggarmaid Need, inheriting from both his parents; and it is thus his nature to aspire after something of which he feels his present lack. Moreover Love desires the possession of its good eternally; this is why parents wish to perpetuate themselves in their offspring, and why men aim at an enduring fame. But the longing for an eternal good does not stop here; it manifests itself in higher and more adequate forms. It will pass from beautiful bodies to beautiful souls, from these to the beauty that informs social laws and institutions, then to the intellectual beauties of the sciences. And still one higher stage remains — the search of the philosopher for the supreme beauty which finally shall satisfy the soul's cravings. "He who has learned to see the beautiful in due order and succession, when he comes toward the end will suddenly perceive a nature of wondrous beauty, not growing and decaying, or waxing and waning, not fair in one point of view and foul in another, or in the likeness of a face, or hands, or any other part of the bodily frame, or in any form of speech or knowledge, nor existing in any other being; but Beauty only, absolute, separate, simple, everlasting, which without diminution and without increase, or any change, is imparted to the ever growing and perishing beauties of all other things. He only uses the beauties of earth as steps along which he mounts upward for the sake of that other Beauty, going from one to two, and from two to all fair forms, and from fair forms to fair actions, and from fair actions to fair notions, until from fair notions he arrives at the notion of absolute Beauty, and at last knows what the essence of Beauty is." [1]

Here once more we have arrived then at the point to which we were brought in Plato's account of Socrates' intellectual development — the conviction that behind the flux of sensible appearance, and somehow capable of explaining it, there lies a most real world which is subject neither to generation nor decay, and which, whatever else we may say about it, we can at least be assured is the abode

---

[1] *Symposium*, 211.

alike of perfect Beauty and of perfect Goodness. And if we are justified in actually ascribing this to Socrates, it is here we shall plainly have to look to find that virture which is knowledge, and which constitutes the end of the Socratic search. From such a standpoint all the virtues will be one at bottom; for it is only the oneness of the universal good that makes particular good things possible at all. And knowledge in the strictest sense *is* virtue, not a mere means to its attainment in the sense that a knowledge of economics is a way of getting money; the beatific vision is itself the goal of life and the end of striving. So too a man cannot *really* know the good and still follow evil; he cannot look upon its perfect beauty without loving it, and love will constrain his action.

Now this result, if we accept it, will make it necessary to revise one traditional way of understanding the Socratic quest. It has often been supposed, largely through the influence of Xenophon once more, that Socrates' main interest lay in drawing up logical definitions of the several virtues, framing adequate intellectual "concepts" of them. If this had been the case, there seems no reason why he should have continued to insist so strongly on his ignorance; such concepts are not beyond the reach of an acute intelligence, and Xenophon in fact represents Socrates as having no great trouble in arriving at them. It is true that absolute Good and absolute Beauty also might be conceived as the outcome of such a logical process of stripping away particular differences and leaving behind only what is common. But this also is an easily attainable goal; and in neither case have we any satisfactory explanation for what in Socrates is most distinctive — the love and fervor which the good is able to inspire in him.

It is just this emotional appeal that the mystical strain in Socrates accounts for. After all, when we get down to fundamentals, it is on moral assurance and not on ignorance and scepticism that Socrates' chief emphasis is placed. We may not have what science or common sense calls knowledge. But in his soul man does know the good, and it is just the need of clarifying this knowledge he already implicitly possesses that guides the philosopher in his task. "This is the point in which, as I think, I am superior to men in general,

and in which I might, perhaps, fancy myself wiser than other men
— that whereas I know but little of the world below I do not suppose that I know.   But I *do* know" — and here the positive side
comes in — " that injustice and disobedience to a better, whether
God or man, is evil and dishonorable, and I will never fear or avoid
a possible good rather than a certain evil."

Knowledge is thus in the last resort the knowledge of those spiritual "values" which are innate in man's constitution, and which
reveal to him the true nature of the ends that lend significance to
his existence.   This is why they cannot be taught in the ordinary
sense.   You cannot *make* a man admit that anything is good unless
he himself has the power of feeling this is so; the true business of
the teacher is not to convey new information or to put into the mind
ideas that were not there before, but to lead his pupils to see and
appreciate on their own account the truths by which men live.
Such knowledge cannot therefore be a product of conceptual definition.   It is an insight native to man's moral being, which has to be
presupposed before any attempt at definition can get under way;
the task of philosophy is not to create it by what we now call logical
induction, but to clear away the confusing unessentials by which
it has been overlaid.   The very fact that we can judge particular
things to be imperfect shows that we already have a standard by
reference to which they fall short.   Take an instance from geometry : We never have seen the perfect circle, and yet we know that
any given circle comes short of perfection; how can we know this
except as we are able to compare the visible circle with the ideal
circle for which it gives the cue, and which we never can see with
the bodily eye?   And if thus it is impossible to suppose such
patterns to have sprung from sense experience, they can only be
explained as traces left upon the soul in a previous existence.
Knowledge is *recollection;* before that union with the body which
has immersed it in the world of sense, the soul lived in the realm of
true reality where it came face to face with God and the changeless
Ideas.

So far perhaps we are entitled to go.   But there is one further
step that is more debatable.   It has appeared that Socrates had

probably been influenced by the Pythagorean philosophy. Now Pythagoreanism had two sides. On one side it is a method of salvation first of all, a way of escape from the imperfections of the bodily existence into a purer realm where man becomes one with the divine; and it is with this that the doctrine of the *Symposium* most obviously connects. But Pythagoras had been a scientist as well, who wished to account for the empirical world with which science is primarily concerned. This likewise he did through his theory of Forms — the universal mathematical patterns which, imposed on the Unlimited, bring the structure of the world as we know it into being.

Beauty and Justice and the Good are then Pythagorean Forms. But they no longer are conceived by Socrates as "numbers." Socrates has shifted the whole problem from the outer to the inner world, from science to morals; the things of which, since they are not physical, the Pythagoreans had been unable to give any coherent account, now represent the proper and essential meaning of the forms, though other forms more closely connected with the world of nature may still be thought of as existing. And with the immaterializing of the forms a new set of problems arises for the philosopher. How are forms, no longer physical in character, to be connected up with the world with which physics deals, and how do they account for — how even can they be reconciled with — the processes of nature where things have no continuing existence but are all the time coming into being and decaying? And if there are many forms, how are they to be thought of as related alike to one another and to the comprehensive Good? Socrates may or may not have busied himself with questions such as these, and so have been the originator of that specific "theory of Ideas" of which Plato has traditionally been regarded as the author. But the evidence is less conclusive here than for his acceptance of forms in their religious or mystical significance; and since we know that these were in any case problems that much exercised Plato, we may follow the usual practice and reserve their treatment to a later point, leaving the question open as to just how the credit is to be divided.

5. It is not strange that Socrates should have raised up enemies as well as friends. Few people can bear with equanimity the public exposure of their own ignorance; and Socrates' conception of his moral mission made him careless of the hard feelings he might excite. He fell, too, under the public suspicion which the sceptical and irreligious tendencies in the Sophistic movement had aroused in the minds of lovers of the old ways, although he was himself of a deeply religious nature and an observer of the customary forms of worship. More important still, his political sympathies were in question; and the Athenian people were in a suspicious mood. Socrates probably had not hesitated to expose the faults of democracy, and he had had close relations with some of the young aristocrats, notably Alcibiades the stormy petrel of Athenian politics, and Critias, who had been a leading spirit in the aristocratic revolution that had just had a brief day of power. Not long after the overthrow of the Thirty, therefore, he was publicly accused of denying the gods of the city and of corrupting its youths, and was brought to trial. If he had been willing to adopt a conciliatory tone he probably would have escaped; but he refused to lower himself by flattering the people when he was conscious of no guilt, and he was condemned to drink the hemlock.

"And Crito made a sign to the servant; and the servant went in and remained for some time, and then returned with the jailer carrying the cup of poison. Socrates said: You, my good friend, who are experienced in these matters, shall give me directions how I am to proceed. The man answered: You have only to walk about until your legs are heavy, and then to lie down, and the poison will act. At the same time he handed the cup to Socrates, who in the easiest and gentlest manner, without the least fear or change of color or feature, looking at the man with all his eyes, as his manner was, took the cup and said: What do you say about making a libation out of this cup to any god? May I, or not? The man answered: We only prepare, Socrates, just so much as we deem enough. I understand, he said; yet I may and must pray to the gods to prosper my journey from this to that other world — may this, then, which is my prayer, be granted to me. Then holding the cup to his lips, quite readily and cheerfully he drank off the poison. And hitherto most of us had been able to control our sorrow; but now when we saw him drinking, and saw too that he had finished the draught, we could no longer forbear, and in spite of myself my own tears were flowing fast; so that I covered my face and wept over myself, for certainly I was not weeping over him, but at the thought of my own calamity in having lost such a companion. Nor was I the first, for Crito, when he found himself unable to restrain his tears, had got up and moved away, and I followed; and at that moment Apollodorus, who had been weeping all the time, broke out into a loud cry which made cowards of us all. Socrates alone retained his calmness: What is this strange outcry? he said. I sent away the women mainly in order that they might not offend in this way, for I have heard that a man should die in peace. Be quiet, then, and have patience. When we heard that we were ashamed, and refrained our tears; and he walked about until, as he said, his legs began to fail, and then he lay on his back, according to the directions, and the man who gave him the poison now and then looked at his feet and legs; and after a while he pressed his foot hard, and asked him if he could feel; and he said, No; and then his leg, and so upwards and upwards, and showed us that he was cold and stiff. And he felt them himself and said: When the poison reaches the heart, that will be the end. He was beginning to grow cold about the groin, when he uncovered his face, for he had covered himself up, and said (they were his last words) — he said: Crito, I owe a cock to Asclepius; will you remember to pay the debt? The debt shall be paid, said Crito; is there anything else? There was no answer to this question; but in a minute or two a movement was heard, and the attendant uncovered him; his eyes were set, and Crito closed his eyes and mouth.

"Such was the end, Echecrates, of our friend, whom I may truly call the wisest, and justest, and best of all the men whom I have ever known." [1]

[1] *Phaedo*, 117.

§ 9. *The School of Megara.   Aristippus and the Cyrenaics.*
Antisthenes and the Cynics

1. *The School of Megara.* — Along with the more important development of Socrates' teaching which we shall meet with when we
come to Plato, there were several distinct schools which traced their
origin to him, some of them as far apart as they very well could be.
One of these, whose interest lay primarily in metaphysics, was the
school of Megara founded by *Euclides*.   Euclides besides being a
disciple of Socrates was also an Eleatic; and he used Socrates'
conception of the Good to give a more significant content to the
Parmenidean One, with which indeed it might well appear to have
an affinity by reason of its character of universality and indivisi-
bility and unchanging being.   As an Eleatic, Euclides denied
of course the reality of the world of sense; and the way he went
about to prove this was by the form of argument which Zeno had
popularized, and which came to be called Eristic.   This method
later developed into a rather cheap form of logical quibbling
such as we come across in several of Plato's dialogues; this
gave it a bad name, though a real problem underlay it to which
Plato was the first to supply an answer — the problem of what
we really mean when we say that a thing "is" or "is not" so
and so.

More permanently important for the later history of thought
were two other tendencies — the Cynicism of Antisthenes, and the
Cyrenaicism of Aristippus.   Both of these turn their backs on
metaphysics, and connect themselves rather with Socrates' ethical
interest; and in them we meet with the first clear and definite
formulation of two great types of ethical theory which ever since
have been engaged in bitter strife with one another.   It is natural
to suppose that both alike could profess to go back to Socrates only
because Socrates had left so many loose ends in his own ethical
doctrines.   That virtue is man's highest good, and that virtue is
intimately bound up with knowledge or insight — of this he was assured.   But virtue is good for what? for its own sake?   This does
not seem altogether satisfactory to men's ordinary way of thinking;

to say that the supreme good is virtue, and that virtue is insight into the good, might appear to be going in a circle. And if we try to go farther there is only one answer that seems obvious and unambiguous to common sense; the end is happiness or pleasure. All men will agree that pleasure is a good in its own right, needing no justification by reference to a remoter end; and it is the only good about which they would so agree.

2. *The Cyrenaics.* — Such a way of thinking, into which Socrates must no doubt have seemed to fall at times, especially when meeting men on their own ground, is erected by *Aristippus* of Cyrene to the position of a central doctrine. Such a doctrine probably never has received a more clear-cut formulation than in this its first fully articulate expression. Aristippus turns away completely from the outer world, about which, as the Protagorean scepticism had shown, we can have no valid common knowledge, to the one thing that we can really know and that really holds an interest for us — our own feelings and sensations. Here, in the feeling of pleasure that comes immediately home to me, I have something that I do not need to test by any further standard. It neither demands nor is capable of proof; if it is felt as good it really *is* good, because goodness has no other meaning than felt goodness. It makes no difference if another man declines to call it good, or indeed if I change my own belief about it; the only good with which I am concerned is what is good for *me*, and good for me *now*. Between pleasures there is no intrinsic difference of quality, of higher and lower; all pleasures alike in the end are pleasures of the body, and the only thing we need to ask is, which is the most pleasurable? Furthermore, since we live only in the present, it is the pleasure of the moment that concerns us. We have nothing to do with a past no longer in existence, or with a future that has not yet come to be; not only does present feeling have a vividness and poignancy which is lacking in memory and anticipation, but we cannot tell anyhow what the future consequences are going to be, and so we are likely if we give them too much thought to lose the substance for a shadow. The wise man therefore will take pleasure as it comes, and make the most of it; the ideal of life is to live from

moment to moment filling each with the fullest delight that sense and mind alike are capable of receiving.

Unfortunately for Aristippus, however, this is a plan of life which simply cannot be lived up to in any literal way. Our acts have consequences which we do not intend, and so in our well-meant pursuit of pleasure we continually are blundering upon pain and loss. In practice therefore he was forced to modify to an extent the thoroughgoing nature of his doctrine, and allow a place for the Socratic insight. Only the wise man can be truly and permanently happy — he who does not let himself be carried off his feet by the rush of his passion, who can enjoy while at the same time he stands above enjoyment as its master. He must have the ability to weigh and compound his pleasures rightly and, while he seizes on the fleeting moment, at the same time to look beyond the moment and choose in view of the probable consequences he foresees. Since it is the part of wisdom therefore to avoid pain as well as to win pleasure, the life of sensuous enjoyment will have to be checked and moderated somewhat in favor of the less intense but safer joys of the mind. It is not that any shame attaches to the senses, or that any higher law exists to which they are subordinate. There is no particular reason why I should not commit a so-called "immoral" act if the temptation is great enough and I can get away with it; a wise man, says *Theodorus*, "may steal and commit adultery and sacrilege at proper seasons, for none of these actions is disgraceful by nature if one can put out of sight the common opinion about them which owes its existence to the consent of fools." However, prudential reasons do exist for going slowly — not only the popular discredit that attaches to certain acts, but the more active penalties that society may inflict, as well as the natural consequences that follow from immoderate indulgence.

Of course it follows that society will have no constitutive part to play in a rational scheme of life. The good at which I aim is my own good and not the general happiness, as modern hedonists commonly have been disposed to hold. Cyrenaicism is not indeed, like its Cynic rival, positively anti-social. The wise man will take the world as he finds it, and pick up such pleasures as he can from

the social amenities. But society, while it may be the source of
certain secondary values, has no intrinsic worth; friendship for
instance is not disinterested, but has its justification in what I can
get out of it for myself. And certainly the philosopher will not
spend himself for the benefit of the state. "I do not dream for a
moment," Xenophon makes Aristippus say to Socrates, "of ranking
myself in the class of those who wish to rule. In fact, considering
how serious a business it is to cater for one's private needs, I look
upon it as the mark of a fool not to be content with that, but to
further saddle oneself with the duty of providing the rest of the
community with whatever they may be pleased to want. If any
one desires to have a heap of pother himself, and be a nuisance to
the rest of the world, I will educate him in the manner suggested;
but for myself I beg to be enrolled amongst those who wish to spend
their days as easily and pleasantly as possible." After the same
fashion Theodorus: "It is not reasonable that a wise man should
hazard himself for his country, and endanger wisdom for a set of
fools."

There are various contributions that Cyrenaicism might be
thought to make to an ethical ideal, but since they stand out much
more clearly in the later form given to hedonism at the hands of
Epicurus there will be no need to dwell upon them here. It is true
hedonism leaves no room for refined sentiments about the good
and the just, for the beauty of righteousness or the nobility of duty.
But in compensation it offers a clearcut view of life with no non-
sense about it, lending itself to what is intellectually the simplest
and most straightforward of all ethical theories, and appealing
powerfully to the natural man. The drawback is that the universe
does not always seem to be arranged for the purpose of enabling
gentlemen to avoid all disagreeable duties and to live "as easily
and pleasantly as possible." Accordingly this logic of experience
led among the later Cyrenaics to a growing tendency to shift the
emphasis from the positive feeling of pleasure to the negative good
of a freedom from pain — a tendency that reached its culmination
in the open pessimism of *Hegesias*. Hegesias feels so strongly how
ill-calculated life is to yield even a balance of pleasure that he

denies it any value. "Life only appears a good thing to a fool; to the wise man it is indifferent." Instead he turns his eyes to the painlessness of death; and this thought he presented so persuasively that he was known as the "advocate of death" or suicide.

3. *The Cynics.* — As against Aristippus, *Antisthenes* and the Cynics took their start from another and more characteristic side of Socrates' teaching. "Virtue for virtue's sake" is a moral slogan which has certain obvious advantages over pleasure in the way of edification. But before adopting it we have the preliminary and not quite easy task of deciding what it means. When we hear such a phrase today the meaning usually is not far to seek; it stands for the supremacy of the conventionally accepted moral duties about whose authority men are never to ask questions. But this has nothing in common with the Cynic meaning; in fact they outraged public sentiment by their attack on such conventional virtues. It was in a very different direction that the Cynic looked for the content to virtue that was necessary to give it rational standing.

The hint toward their own doctrine came from Socrates, if not expressly from his words at any rate from his life. Xenophon calls attention to this side of Socrates in the reply which he represents him as making to Antiphon when he is taunted with his frugal way of living and with the absence of all pleasures from his life. "Again, if it be a question of helping our friends or country, which of the two will have the larger leisure to devote to these objects? he who leads the life which I lead to-day? or he who lives in the style which you deem so fortunate? Which of the two will adopt a soldier's life more easily? the man who cannot get on without expensive living, or he to whom whatever comes to hand suffices? Which will be the readier to capitulate and cry mercy in a siege? a man of elaborate wants, or he who can get along happily with the readiest things to hand? You, Antiphon, would seem to suggest that happiness consists in luxury and extravagance; I hold a different creed. To have no wants at all is, to my mind, an attribute of godhead; to have as few wants as possible the nearest approach to godhead." Whether the particular instance is historical or not, there can be no doubt that one of the things in Socrates that most impressed his contemporaries was the simplicity of his life, and its freedom from the pressure of those wants and ambitions that complicate living for the ordinary man.

Here accordingly Antisthenes found the answer he was looking for. If virtue, as the rational conduct of life, is to be an end in itself, and bring satisfaction quite apart from anything outside it, it follows that the course of our life must be freed as much as possible from the chances of the outer world, whi h are constantly liable to interfere with our happiness if this is made dependent on them. It must be freed from everything that does not lie wholly within the power of the mind itself; and this can only come about as we suppress the desires which make things attractive or fearful. That is the only rational and virtuous life which has the fewest possible wants, and which is thus, in so far as may be, self-centered and self-sufficient.

Such an ideal might well be interpreted in a way to make it decidedly inviting to a mind with any tinge of moral enthusiasm. The Cynic however ran the risk of losing much of its appeal by pressing it rather far. In his opposition of "nature" to convention, he set out to rid himself not only of those artificial wants that complicate and enervate life, but of all ties whatsoever that bind a man to the rest of the world. Antisthenes found a logical basis for this attitude in his strong opposition to that other side of Socrates' teaching, developed by Plato in particular, which finds true reality in the universal "forms" rather than in the particular things in which they are embodied. For Antisthenes, particulars alone are real; a man is just himself and not an instance of a more inclusive class, and to find himself he has accordingly to strip off the qualities that make him a social being in favor of a few residual wants that cannot be escaped — sex and food and shelter. Thus marriage and the family go by the board, since the fundamental needs of sex and reproduction can be satisfied without them. All forms of government are rejected as equally bad. Nationality and patriotism have no place among the virtues for one whose country is the entire world. The economic arrangements of society are useless if a man has no economic wants that cannot easily be met. Religion as a system of rites and institutions interjected between man and the gods is entirely unnecessary. The Cynic thus places himself deliberately outside the current of the world's life, but it is not because, like the early Christian, he finds here no abiding city and so looks for another and a heavenly. He breaks all national and civic bonds, not to enter into some higher life, but to be free from bonds altogether. Like the Cyrenaic he is a cosmopolitan, a citizen of the world; but in neither case does the term stand for any enthusiasm for humanity, but only for a negation of social duties. In the midst of civilized society he tries to live in a state of nature and lead the existence of a savage. *Diogenes* wanders about Greece with his beggar's staff and wallet, having no other shelter than a tub, and throws away his cup as a last useless luxury on seeing a child drink from his hands.

Such an attitude might call for sympathy as a somewhat ostentatious acceptance of an enforced exclusion from the goods of civilization. Cynicism was, indeed, essentially the philosophy of the poor man, who already knew what it was to feel wants unsatisfied before he made a virtue of his necessity. But the Cynic did not stop here. Common decency itself he places among the conventions of which he prides himself on being rid; and doctrines such as the community of women, and even the harmlessness of eating human flesh, are propounded in a rather offensive form. Under these conditions ethical and intellectual ideals could hardly in the end survive. When the human relationships that constitute the central fact of the ethical life were torn away the result was naturally a moral temper that sometimes approached the grossness of the animal; and with no content for the intellect to feed upon it too could have no healthy growth. The dominant characteristic of most of the Cynics came to be a Pharisaic pride in their own spiritual poverty, which showed itself in a flaunting of their peculiarities in the face of every one, and in an arrogant criticism of others; I see your pride, says Socrates to Antisthenes, through the holes in your cloak. The independence which they prized almost more than anything else was the freedom of a sharp tongue which held no man in reverence — an independence typified by Diogenes ordering Alexander to stand out of his sunlight. The truth in Cynicism passed over to the later Stoics, as the Cyrenaic philosophy was revived in Epicureanism; but in Stoicism this is so much more impressively formulated that we may postpone any further consideration of it for the present.

LITERATURE

Zeller, *Socrates and the Socratic Schools.*
Grote, *History of Greece*, Vol. 8.
Taylor, *Varia Socratica.*
Taylor, *Plato's Biography of Socrates.*
Plato, *Earlier Dialogues.*
Xenophon, *Memorabilia.*
Forbes, *Socrates.*
Watson, *Hedonistic Theories.*
Grote, *Plato and the Other Companions of Socrates.*
Seth, *Study of Ethical Principles.*
Pater, *Marius the Epicurean.*

held important positions ... in the ... democracy. ... by the family ... ... Athens ... ... The ... to ... ... Sparta ... ... produced by ... ... It is much ... more ... ... my outline ...

PLATO AND ARISTOTLE

§ 10. *Plato*

Plato was born in 427 B.C., and so was still under thirty when Socrates was put to death. He came from a distinguished family on both his father's and his mother's side, the latter tracing her descent to a kinsman and friend of Solon, the great Athenian lawgiver. The political sympathies of the family were traditionally with the democracy, and Plato had looked forward to a political career in Athens. But the course of political democracy at the close of the fifth century was not of a sort to encourage this ambition in him, and Socrates' execution seems even to have left him not quite certain of his personal safety; at any rate he left the city soon after, and for some ten years we have little reliable information about him. He stopped for a time at Megara with Euclides, Socrates' Eleatic follower; and at the end of the period we find him in southern Italy, where he must have come into first-hand contact with the leaders of Pythagorean thought. Here he also made an acquaintance which was to have consequences later on. Dion, a brother-in-law of Dionysius the famous tyrant of Syracuse in Sicily, was an able man with intellectual interests, and through his friendship Plato was led to make his first visit to Syracuse; but he was too outspoken to hit it off very well with Dionysius, and according to tradition the tyrant handed him over to the Spartans who sold him into slavery.

At about the age of forty Plato was back in Athens. By this time he had written the minor dialogues, and in all likelihood a major part at least of a second group — including among others the *Protagoras*, *Phaedrus*, *Phaedo* and *Symposium* — in which his literary art reaches its highest perfection. Soon after his return he founded the school which was to make him the most prominent intellectual figure in Greece throughout the rest of his life. This was established on his private estate situated near the Academy, a gymnasium just outside the city; and it almost immediately became the educational center of Greece, attracting students from every part of the Hellenic world. To this school Plato devoted the remainder of his life, his teaching being interrupted however by two episodes.

These had to do with Plato's only incursion into active political affairs, though indirectly his influence was considerable; the Academic curriculum was in fact largely directed toward a training in political science and statesmanship. After the death of Dionysius he was persuaded by Dion to come to Sicily and undertake the education of Dionysius the Younger. Dionysius, at that time a man of about thirty, while possessed of some natural ability was almost totally uneducated; his father had been suspicious of his heir and probable successor and had kept him from taking any part in public matters. Here was an opportunity such as Plato had looked forward to; the union of supreme authority in a state with the possibility of a true philosophical training might conceivably result in the philosopher-king of his imagination, and a sense of duty led him somewhat reluctantly to try his hand. At first he was measurably successful, and made an impression on the young king's nature. For a time philosophy was the fashion in the Sicilian court; the floors were strewn with sand, and the courtiers suspended their revels and busied themselves tracing geometrical figures. But Dionysius' nature was too feeble and court influences too much opposed to a reign of virtue and reason for this to keep up very long; and at the outbreak of a war Plato was permitted to follow his inclinations and return to Athens. He still remained however on good terms with Dionysius, and some correspondence passed between them; and when later Dionysius insisted that he fulfil a promise to return to Syracuse he allowed himself again to be persuaded. The second venture was even less successful than the first, and Plato, thoroughly disillusioned, had some difficulty in getting away. Finally Dionysius was induced to let him depart and he came back to Athens, this time for good. Plato died in 347 B.C.

I. ETHICAL AND SOCIAL PHILOSOPHY.   THE REPUBLIC

1. *The Republic.* — It is in the *Republic* that we find the most comprehensive expression of what the world has come to think of as the Platonic philosophy, and it will offer therefore the best starting-point for a summary.   In writing the *Republic* Plato may have drawn, and probably did draw, to an indefinite extent upon reminiscences of Socrates; but the large impression which it leaves is that we are dealing here with a thinker who has a more carefully reasoned system of philosophy than we can easily attribute to Socrates himself.   The whole volume is a cumulative argument, into which there are subtly interwoven opinions on almost every subject of philosophical importance; of the Socratic casualness and "ignorance" there are few signs.   And as a matter of fact the book seems most readily explained in terms of a Platonic rather than a Socratic purpose.   Like the *Phaedrus*, which was written at about the same period in Plato's life, and which has the appearance of being meant to justify the need of a more thorough training for public life than rhetoric in its common acceptation gave, the *Republic* has many of the earmarks of a manifesto or prospectus of the new school which Plato had just started or was about to start.   A considerable portion of the book is engaged directly in laying down the essentials of a sound education, starting from the earliest years of childhood, and culminating in a university curriculum.   Still more fundamentally, it has to do with the possibility of an education that shall fit a man for public life; the central plot of the book is concerned with virtue in the form of "justice," alike as the end of individuals and of the state, and we are led up to the first systematic attempt at a political science.   We may accordingly assume that here the Socratic thought has passed through the mind of Plato and represents, roughly at any rate, his own views at the moment.

2. *The Nature of Justice.* — As in Socrates, the underlying question one has first to answer before education can proceed is the question, What is the nature of the end in which man finds his well-being, the "virtue" which is the expression of his proper function as a man?   The discussion starts from a consideration

of the particular and very typical virtue — justice. Men say that justice is honorable and good; what is their ground for such a statement? In point of fact, unless they simply take it for granted on the evidence of a general moral agreement among mankind, they usually go to work to substantiate and to recommend it by an appeal to consequences. "Parents and tutors are always telling their sons and their wards that they are to be just; but why? Not for the sake of justice, but for the sake of character and reputation, in the hope of obtaining some of those offices and marriages and other advantages that Glaucon was enumerating as accruing to the just from a fair reputation; and they throw in the good opinion of the gods, and will tell you of a shower of blessings which the heavens, as they say, rain upon the pious. And this accords with the testimony of the noble Hesiod and Homer, the first of whom says that for the just the gods make

> ' The oaks to bear acorns at their summit, and bees in the middle,
> And the sheep are bowed down with the weight of their own fleeces.'

And Homer has a very similar strain; for he speaks of one whose fame is

> ' As the fame of some blameless king, who like a God
> Maintains justice, for whom the black earth brings forth
> Wheat and barley, whose trees are bowed with fruit,
> And his sheep never fail to bear, and the sea gives him fish.'

Still grander are the gifts of heaven which Musaeus and his son offer the just; they take them down into the world below, where they have the saints feasting on couches with crowns on their heads, and passing their whole time in drinking; their idea seems to be that an immortality of drunkenness is the highest meed of virtue. But about the wicked there is another strain; they bury them in a slough, and make them carry water in a sieve; that is their portion in the world below, and even while living they bring them to infamy."[1]

But what if one sees fit to doubt the cogency of this appeal? What if, as he looks about the world, he sees the wicked triumph

[1] *Republic*, 363.

and the righteous man despised, injustice seated in high places tyrannizing over the just and making their lot miserable? What if his reason tells him that the gods of whom the poets sing are only myths, or, if they exist, have no concern with human affairs; and so men can look beyond the grave, with no fear of meeting there with any punishment for their misdeeds? Is there still any reason why a man should follow justice rather than its opposite? Doubtless the *reputation* for justice passes current in the world for a certain value; but if one could keep the appearance without being hampered with the reality, would he not be so much the better off? Suppose we take the most extreme case imaginable — an unjust man who possesses all the things that men call blessings, and who, in spite of his inner corruption, contrives that every one should deem him righteous, and passes to his grave full of years and honors; and, over against him, the just man who has no reward whatever beyond his own consciousness of rectitude, who goes through life a prey to every kind of wretchedness and misfortune brought on him by his very righteousness, and who, moreover, has the reputation everywhere of being actually unjust. Can we still say in such a case that the life of the just man alone is truly blessed, or that justice is anything but an evil?

Yes, says Plato; in spite of all it is only the just life that has any real worth. The consequences in the way of pain or pleasure make not the slightest odds. The good man who suffers unjustly is still more to be envied than the tyrant who persecutes him. The wrongdoer who enjoys his ill-gotten gains unmolested is not the happier for his immunity; rather he is the more miserable if he be not made to meet with retribution. This then is the paradox which Plato's theory of the good must justify.

Clearly it will be necessary to know, first, just what it is we mean by justice and the just life; and the need for answering this leads Plato to attempt a psychology of the human soul. For if virtue is an attribute of man's nature, we must be able to define in what this nature consists.

In its primitive form the soul, or ghost, had commonly been conceived as a sort of fine matter, which in Homer may be seen separating itself from the body like a smoke at death, and about which there centered such vague notions as the Greeks possessed of immortality and of future retribution or rewards. But in this sense the soul plainly is of small account as an explanation of the concrete processes that make up our actual experience. Toward a more empirical psychology the Greeks also had made some progress in an unsystematic way; it had been a necessity, indeed, of their political life. When political affairs are carried on by free discussion, and influence won not by arbitrary force but by persuasion, a certain rough knowledge of the workings of the human mind is indispensable. The successful orator must to a certain extent have classified men in types, and made himself familiar with the sort of motive that is likely to appeal to each; and thus there had grown up a considerable body of practical wisdom that dealt with psychological processes. The beginnings of a more scientific treatment had likewise been made by the philosophers; in particular, thought had oeen separated from sensation, and of sensation various theories were current. And among the Pythagoreans, under the influence of their religious motive, the soul itself had reappeared as a philosophically significant conception, and crude beginnings made towards its analysis.

The method of psychology was still, however, too little developed to permit Plato to go at his task directly by an examination of the individual consciousness; and so he approaches it in a roundabout way. What we are after is to get an understanding of what justice is as applied to the human soul. But the word "justice" is also used in an objective sense, in connection with the life of the state. If we turn first then to the study of justice as it is writ large in the state, we shall make our task an easier one; afterwards, unless the two are quite distinct, we can transfer our results to the more obscure problem, or at any rate can get a clew for its solution. What then is justice in the state?

Without going into detail, it is enough to say that Plato finds the essence of justice in *order*. The end of the state is the common good, and injustice makes this unattainable; it sets men at variance with their neighbors, and renders harmonious action impossible.

Justice is accordingly a state of things where each man has his own work to do, and does it without trying to go outside his proper sphere and take on himself the function which some one else is better fitted to perform; it is "minding one's own business." Now in any self-sufficing state there will be three classes of citizens needed. There is the working class, the farmers and artisans, on whose shoulders rests the burden of providing the material goods without which life and civilization are impossible; the special virtue that belongs to this class is obedience, self-control or temperance. Above them is the warrior class on whom devolves the defence of the state against attack; and their chief virtue, naturally, is courage. Finally there are the rulers, who must be possessed first of all of wisdom. Justice will consist in the right coördination of these separate classes, each with its characteristic virtue. When each attends to its own business we have an ordered and harmonious whole, in which all the parts work smoothly together, not in the interests of one individual or of one class only, but for the common good of all. And such a state is what we call a just state.

When we take this clew and apply it to the individual soul we find that an analogy exists. To the lower class there corresponds, we may say, that more ignoble part of man's nature — the sensations, desires and appetites. These have in themselves no principle of order, and are only tolerable as they are brought under the sway of some higher faculty which subjects them to the rule of temperance. This higher power is the mind, or reason, wherein wisdom resides; and as it is the function of the appetites to obey, so it belongs to the mind by divine right to rule. Between these, and corresponding to the warrior class in the state, there is a third faculty which it is less easy to define. This is the forceful, energetic side of man's nature, which Plato calls spirit (as we use the adjective "spirited"). This is not in itself ignoble, as are the sensations and appetites; it is the basis of certain very admirable virtues — the heroic virtues, as opposed to those that are due to wisdom. Since however it is in itself unintelligent, and liable to turn into blind passion, it stands on a lower level than reason; it also is the servant of mind, though a servant which by helping tame the unbridled desires of the lower nature is a potential ally rather than a hindrance. These three faculties are in some real sense distinct; if man's nature were one and indivisable it would be impossible to explain how it comes to pass that the reason often has to fight with all its strength against the sensuous desires. On the other hand they are not separate and unrelated. Our lower faculties are intended to be subject to and used in the service of the higher; the body is for the sake of the soul.

3. *The Ethical Ideal.* — This relation Plato expresses elsewhere in the famous figure of the charioteer and the winged horses. One of these is of noble origin, and the other of ignoble; and so naturally there is a great deal of trouble in managing them. The noble steed is striving continually to mount to the region of the heavens, where it may look upon the images of divine beauty and wisdom that are proper to its nature; the ignoble is ever dragging it down to the earth and earthly delights. Now just as, in the state, justice consists in the proper subordination of the different classes, so the just soul is one in which a similar subordination of parts exists; where the charioteer has got control of his steeds and can guide them to the heights of heaven; where the body submits itself to the sway of the soul, the beast in man to that part of him which is truly human. "For the just man does not permit the several elements within him to meddle with one another, but he sets in order his own inner life, and is his own master, and at peace with himself; and when he has bound together the three principles within him, and is no longer many, but has become one entirely temperate and perfectly adjusted nature, then he will begin to act if he has to act, whether in a matter of property, or in the treatment of the body, or in some affair of politics or of private business; in all which cases he will think and call just and good action that which preserves and coöperates with this condition, and the knowledge which presides over this, wisdom; and unjust action that which at any time destroys this, and the opinion which presides over unjust action, ignorance."[1]

Why then is virtue honorable and to be desired? Just because

[1] *Republic,* 443.

man is man and not a brute; because he cannot win any true and
lasting satisfaction except as he realizes his essential manhood.
What advantage is it to him if he gain the whole world and lose
his own soul? "How would a man profit if he received gold and
silver on the condition that he was to enslave the noblest part of
him to the worst? Who can imagine that a man who sold his
son or daughter into slavery for money, especially if he sold them
into the hands of fierce and evil men, would be the gainer, however
large might be the sum which he received? and will any one say
that he is not a miserable caitiff who sells his own divine being to
that which is most godless and detestable, and has no pity. Eri-
phyle took the necklace as the price of her husband's life, but he is
taking a bribe to compass a worse ruin." Virtue is the health of
the soul; without it there is nothing but disease and deformity.
"If when the bodily constitution is gone life is no longer endurable
though pampered with every sort of meats and drinks, shall we be
told that life is worth having when the very essence of the vital
principle is undermined and corrupted, even though a man be
allowed to do whatever he pleases, if at the same time he is forbidden
to escape from vice and injustice, or attain justice and virtue?"[1]
The wicked man vainly imagines that his is the life of liberty; it
has neither order nor law, and this he deems joy, and freedom, and
happiness. He does not know that he is in reality a slave — a
slave to his passions and no longer master of himself. In spite
then of appearances and all that men may say, it is only the virtuous life that brings true and lasting happiness.

4. *Social Philosophy.* — It is clear that in such an ideal a sceptical
individualism in the moral and social life has been transcended. Indeed it is transcended so completely that we run some risk of losing
whatever element of value it may contain. The private nature of
a man, in the interpretation which Plato goes on to give, has all the
time a tendency to be thrust into the background by that universal,
rational element which he has in common with other men, and
which makes him first of all a member of the state and a part of the
universe. To be sure it is no longer the purely traditional order of

[1] *Republic*, 445, 580.

society which Plato exalts to the position of arbiter in man's life. His Republic is an ideal fashioned by reason, and differing in many respects from anything that history has to show. But when the ideal has once been set up it is to rule with a rod of iron. Since men cannot be trusted always to know their true interests and prefer them to those that are more specious and evanescent, the state must have the authority to force them into the ways of righteousness. For the democratic state with its ideal of liberty and equality Plato has slight respect; of all the forms of government that are not entire perversions a democracy is the worst. "No one who does not know would believe how much greater is the liberty which animals who are under the dominion of men have in a democracy than in any other state. For truly the dogs, as the proverb says, are as good as their she-mistresses, and the horses and asses come to have a way of marching along with all the rights and dignities of free men, and they will run at anybody whom they meet in the street if he does not get out of their way, and everything is just ready to burst with liberty." [1] Men however are not equal, and it is only a perversion that the worst should rule the best. People will be vastly better off if they cease bothering their heads about affairs of state, and turn over the conduct of their lives to those whose wisdom gives them the right to rule. Then only, with a philosopher-king who knows what is best, and a state that will submit itself to wise direction, shall we have a remedy for the ills of the world, and a chance for man to realize his highest good.

Based as it is, then, on the conviction that the claims of the state come first, and that the mass of men are not of themselves capable of living the true life of reason, Plato's Republic represents the carrying out in the strictest way of paternalism in government. Everything must bow to the supposed interests of the whole. It has appeared already that the citizens are to form three classes, or castes, though the separation is not hard and fast; according to the promise which children show they are to be advanced or degraded into a higher or a lower class than that in which they happen to be born. The lower class does not receive much attention from Plato;

[1] *Republic*, 563.

its duty is simply to obey its rulers blindly and perform faithfully the tasks imposed upon it.   It does not possess the rights of citizenship; no free citizen is allowed to earn his living by an illiberal trade.   The industrial life is for Plato a degradation, and renders attention to the true art of living impossible; society has consequently to be built up on the basis of a large class of men who fail to share in its spiritual benefits, though in some ways they are freer to enjoy themselves than are their rulers.

To produce the right kind of citizen there is devised an elaborate social machinery.   In the first place children are to be examined at birth, and those who do not appear physically strong and perfect are to be put out of the way, with due regard to decency and order. The survivors are then to be subjected to a rigid system of state education, whose provisions, once established, are not to be altered by a hair.   Even the playthings for children are carefully selected and no innovations are to be allowed under severe penalties; for if change once begins even in small things, no one can set limits to it. As soon as possible a child's capacity is to be determined by experts and his place in the social system settled for him; and thereafter educational methods are all directed to the inculcation of a spirit of unquestioning obedience.   In the case of the guardians this supervision follows the citizen throughout his life; for it is of no avail, Plato thinks, to make laws concerning the public relations of men unless we regulate their private life also.   "In the first place, none of them should have any property beyond what is absolutely necessary; neither should they have a private house with bars and bolts, closed against any one who has a mind to enter; their provisions should be only such as are required by trained warriors who are men of temperance and courage; their agreement is to receive from the citizens a fixed rate of pay, enough to meet the expenses of the year and no more, and they will have common meals and live together, like soldiers in a camp.   Gold and silver we will tell them that they have from God; the diviner metal is within them, and they have therefore no need of that earthly dross which passes under the name of gold, and ought not to pollute the divine by earthly intermixture, for that commoner metal has been the source of many unholy deeds; but their own is undefiled. And they alone of all the citizens may not touch or handle silver or gold, or be under the same roof with them, or wear them, or drink from them. And this will be · their salvation, and the salvation of the State." [1] Even wives should be held in common, and children should be brought up by the state and kept in ignorance of their real parents. By doing away with private interests in this wholesale fashion, and by compelling men to have their pleasures and pains in common, Plato hoped to eliminate those occasions of discord which grow out of separate and clashing aims among the citizens. The history of the Roman Catholic priesthood shows how powerful an instrument it is actually possible to create in this way.

So in every possible direction the state is to be guarded carefully from all influences that might seem in any way harmful. It is to be isolated as much as possible from foreign trade and foreign intercourse. Amusements and the arts are to be under strict supervision. All music that is emotional and exciting in its nature is to be prohibited, and the theater to be put under a ban. Poetry is to be subjected to a strict censorship, and everything whose moral tendency is not immediate and apparent is to be rejected regardless of its artistic excellence. The poet is to be confined to singing the praises of virtue and hymns to the gods; no suggestion is to be tolerated that the way of vice might have its attractions or that virtue sometimes proves a thorny road. And finally religion, which of course likewise is to be under the control of the state, will add the fear of divine vengeance to the political checks on conduct.

2. THE "THEORY OF IDEAS"

1. We are ready now to turn to the general presupposition which underlies this treatment by Plato of the problems of ethics and of politics. This we shall find in a certain attitude which he adopts toward "knowledge" and its possibilities — an attitude which gets expression in the theory of "ideas," or "forms," which we have already met in Socrates, and with which Plato's name has ever since been in a special way connected.

[1] *Republic,* 416.

The starting-point of the theory, in Plato as in Socrates, is the certainty that truth exists, and that truth is stedfast and abiding. Various current theories had cast doubt on this. There was the "flowing philosophy" of Heracleitus which emphasized the relativity of knowledge; Plato had himself been influenced by this, and he continued to regard it as essentially a true account of the world of phenomena and change which sense reveals. We have met the same tendency in Protagoras and his famous utterance that "man is the measure of all things." To any such philosophy regarded as a final word, Plato was unalterably opposed. Why, so he asks in the *Theaetetus*, should the "truth" that all truth is relative be more true than its opposite? it is true to the man who thinks it so, and that is all. "The best of the joke is, that Protagoras acknowledges the truth of their opinion who believe his opinion to be false; for in admitting that the opinions of all men are true, in effect he grants that the opinion of his opponents is true." We cannot then give up our belief in knowledge; a consistent scepticism would have to be completely speechless. And knowledge implies fixity, an abiding nature somewhere; for it would no longer be knowledge if a transition were going on in it continually.

Socrates had pointed out where this fixity is to be looked for. It is present, not in the flux of sense experience, but in thought. Philosophy has to do with the common nature which makes a thing what it is; with those essential characteristics which by their presence in the individual object constitute it more than a mere individual. If we want to know what a man is, or what is virtue, it is not enough to name this or that man, or to enumerate a string of virtues; different men are not different in kind, but each is a man by reason of a nature that belongs to man as such.

Such fixed and universal ideas, consequently, constitute the truth of which the scientist and the philosopher are in search. But where are we to look for the abiding place of the object to which these true ideas refer, of which they are valid? In the sense world we can find no such object; there everything is ephemeral, in constant process of change. Is it a mere fiction then? That would be intolerable. Are there to be real objects corresponding to our sensations, and nothing real to correspond to thought, whose dignity is so much greater, and to which we bring our sense perception to be tested? No, along with the world of perception with its change and unrest there must be another realm. This is the realm of true and abiding existence. On the one hand are the individual things which we see when we open our eyes; and these are given over without reserve to multiplicity, relativity, the Heracleitean flux. To this sense world belongs all the uncertainty that the individualist and the sensationalist had found in knowledge; it is in truth a perpetual process of change which will not stand still long enough to give rise to the possibility of an authoritative standard. But for just this reason it can be only a phenomenal world, and not the world of true being. This latter is the world of the Idea or Form — absolute, abiding, without variableness or shadow of turning, which sensation never can attain to, but thought alone. "Over against that world of flux,

> ' Where nothing is, but all things seem,'

it is the vocation of Plato to set up a standard of unchangeable reality, which in its highest theoretic development becomes the world of eternal and immutable ideas, indefectible outlines of thought, yet also the veritable things of experience; the perfect Justice, for example, which if even the gods mistake it for perfect injustice is not moved out of its place; the beauty which is the same yesterday, to-day, and forever. In such ideas, or ideals, eternal as participating in the essential character of the facts they represent to us, we come in contact, as he supposes, with the insoluble, immovable granite, beneath and amid the wasting torrent of mere phenomena." [1]

Such a tendency to find the highest truth in "universals" has of course always had to meet with strong opposition alike from popular and from scientific thinking. "Nominalism" — the view that only particulars are real — may easily seem to be the only natural way of looking at the facts, as well as the only way likely to be scientifically fruitful. How can that exist which is nothing in

[1] Pater, *Plato and Platonism.*

particular, but only something in general? Is "man" anything more than the abstraction of a certain number of characteristics which we have seen in individual men, and which now are held together in the mind? The thought of man is real, indeed, as *my* thought; but has it any other reality, except as we go back again to the particular men from whom the qualities were abstracted? How are we possibly to conceive of that as having any actual existence which is neither an inch, nor a foot, nor a yard long, nor possessed of *any* definite length, but which is only length in general?

However we have only to go a little deeper to see that Plato's problem was very far from being an artificial one. Do we not constantly assume that, through the thought which transcends particular objects, we are getting nearer to the truth? For whom is the tree or the flower more real, the child who sees it barely in its separateness in space, or the naturalist for whom it epitomizes the history of ages dead and gone and sends forth lines of relationship to all living things? And yet it is in terms of "ideas" that this wider knowledge is embodied. We are stating more and more adequately what "kind" of a thing it is, interpreting it in terms of general notions. That our ideas are *valid* of reality we cannot possibly refuse to say without destroying the worth of thinking altogether. And if valid of the real world, must they not somehow be present in that world?

We come closer to the real force of Plato's thought if, instead of such a concept as "man," we substitute the notion of a scientific *law*. Put in such terms, we find ourselves almost compelled to think of the "idea" as something real and ultimate. The law of gravitation is a "universal," an unchanging truth, which we distinguish from the particular events in which it finds expression; and yet we hardly feel satisfied to suppose that it has no reality apart from our faculty of generalization, and that it stands for nothing in the outer world over and above the separate events themselves. So too for our "ideals"; ideals tend naturally to claim objective validity, and not a subjective existence simply. Particularly compelling is the impression we get when we turn our eyes to that great system of relationships which constitutes the subject-matter of mathematics. Here are truths which are not physical at all, though they apply to physical things; moreover they are true universally and eternally. The truth about the angles of a triangle does not come into existence when the human mind for the first time perceives it; and the fact that there are many mathematical relationships which man never has made and never will make the object of his thought does not in the least prevent their being true and valid. We may hesitate to say that they eternally "exist." But that they have *some* sort of being independent both of things and thoughts we find it very difficult to avoid supposing.

2. This natural "realism" is, then, the starting-point of Plato's theory; and it remains to ask how he himself meant it to be interpreted. Here we come up against the difficulty that already has been mentioned; just how is Plato's own belief related to what he had learned from Socrates? To this only a tentative answer can be given here; but a few things can perhaps be said without trespassing too much on controversial issues.

We need to call attention in the first place to a divergence between the theory of forms as it meets us in the group of dialogues belonging to the middle period of Plato's literary activity, and what we have reason to suppose represents his teaching in the Academy. We know from Aristotle that this last took on a more definitely Pythagorean guise; the forms are expressly identified with "numbers." There is almost no ground for thinking that this last doctrine was a Socratic doctrine. Plato may very well have been led to it through his later contact with the Pythagoreans in southern Italy. However it is reasonable to suppose that before this happened he had already been introduced to the forms, or universal natures, or essences, by Socrates, and had passed through a period when he thought of them more nearly in their Socratic meaning.

Nor does it seem likely he would have been oblivious to the ultimate questions which they raised, or would have failed in his own thinking to make some effort to straighten matters out. What sort of metaphysical being attaches to these forms, or first principles of explanation? how do they get connected with particular objects? how can they in their eternal and immutable existence be supposed to give rise to change and generation? While both the religious and the scientific interest, not always distinguished sharply, find a place in Plato's pages, we can feel fairly confident that it was the second that to his natural turn of mind appealed most strongly, since it is with such an interest that we later on find him occupied almost exclusively; at any rate to Plato as an educator it is the scientific use and not the mere contemplation of the forms that was bound to be of most concern.   We may illustrate the difference by two competing pictures of the philosophic life which find a place in the dialogues.   In the one case — and this seems the sense it had primarily for Socrates — it means a life freed from the fetters of the body and from the sensual pleasures which contaminate the soul — a freedom attainable in the occasional moments of mystical experience which Plato seems to imply that Socrates had enjoyed, though only completely attained in another form of existence when the body has been left behind.   The other and, it would seem, more distinctively Platonic ideal of the philosophic life has a quite different complexion; it is the theoretic life, the life of pure scientific thinking released from practical demands upon our time and effort. Here the thing that makes all the trouble is not primarily the sensual but the "sensible" — that character attaching to sense perception which sets the problems the scientist has to answer. To such a philosophic temper the ordinary business of mankind yields but slight entertainment.   "Political ambition and office getting, clubs and banquets, revels and singing maidens, do not enter into the philosopher's dreams.   Whether any event has turned out well or ill in the city, what disgrace may have descended to anyone from his ancestors, male or female, are matters of which he no more knows than he can tell, as they say, how many pints are contained in the ocean."   "The truth is that only the outer form of him is in the city; his mind, disdaining the littleness and nothingness of human things, is flying all abroad, as Pindar says, measuring with line and rule the things which are under and on the earth and above the heaven, interrogating the whole nature of each and all, but not condescending to anything which 's within reach."[1]

[1] *Theaetetus*, 173.

The acceptance of the Socratic forms made it imperative, then, if scientific knowledge is to be attained, that certain fundamental questions of theory should be met; what is the nature of these forms, and how in particular do they stand related to the world of sense? On Socrates' showing, the best answer might appear to be the answer which in the earlier dialogues finds expression in the doctrine of "participation." A particular object, that is to say, is the meeting point of independent and self-contained and immutable forms; it is an individual of which various universal terms can be predicated, and in which somehow they are present to lend that universal character which alone takes things out of the flux of sensation and makes them an object of knowledge. But Plato does not seem to have found this answer quite sufficient. As we see from the *Parmenides* in particular, he was quite conscious that such a mode of statement lays itself open to serious logical objections. In the *Parmenides* the reality of the forms is still assumed as something beyond question, but the effort to bring them into relation to the world of things is shown to be beset with many troubles. However we elect to put it — that things "participate" in the forms, or that they "imitate" the forms — we find ourselves in difficulties. The difficulties get no solution in the dialogue, and whether Plato ever arrived at an answer that fully satisfied him it is a little hard to say; certainly he was not able to convince his pupil Aristotle. Meanwhile we do know that he tried at any rate to give a more precise account of the nature of the forms themselves, and that in this attempt he was influenced by the Pythagorean doctrine.

3. A hint of this new development may perhaps be found in the *Republic*. Here mathematics appears in his curriculum as the study which in a preëminent degree brings us into contact with the real. But even the intellectual rigor of mathematics still falls a little short of what knowledge ought to be; mathematics leads to necessary conclusions when you admit its premises, but these premises are not themselves seen to be necessary. The mind will not rest satisfied until they in their turn can be shown to follow from a further premise which is intelligible in its own right; and so the crown alike of education and of science is to be found in an ultimate discipline

which Plato calls Dialectic, and which we probably should speak of as metaphysics.

What Plato seems to be trying to say is that the source of all reality is to be looked for in an ultimate kind of truth from which mathematical truths themselves can be derived, and which by way of mathematics can then be used for explaining the actual patterns that make up the structure of the world. It is not easy at the present day to make sure just what this doctrine was; Plato himself tells us in a letter that it was not to be found in his written works. It was apparently too subtle and difficult to have much chance of being understood except through the direct contact of teacher with pupil; it could not be set forth by reasoning or logic, since by hypothesis the final truth from which all derivative truths arise is something not to be demonstrated, but only to be seen directly. What Plato appears to be aiming at is, in brief, the derivation of arithmetical number from more elementary concepts — the reduction of mathematics ultimately to logic. And he does this by finding the essence of number in the product of a Limit, or the One, and of the Unlimited or Continuous. This last is in a certain sense Not-being; but only in the sense, not that it is "nothing," but that it is not *anything in particular* until it gets some particular or quantitative expression by combining with the One. Plato adds to this the further doctrine that the number series does not, as the Pythagoreans held, start from the unit, but from zero; it includes the infinitely small as well as the infinitely great. To the continuum which makes number possible, therefore, Plato gives the name of the Indeterminate Dyad, or the Great and Small; and he apparently looks to this conception for a solution of the puzzles about incommensurables which had been forcing themselves on the attention of mathematicians.

Reality is thus an ideal system which has its logical and principled basis in the imposition of definite limit or measure on an indefinite continuity, and which is represented in the concrete sciences by the mathematical relations constituting the forms or patterns which reason seeks to discover as the truth underlying the world of sense. And it is in this light therefore that we shall have to interpret the notion of the Good, which remains Plato's name for reality in its highest reach. The Good, according to Aristotle, is to be identified with the One which combines with the Indeterminate Dyad; it is, in other words, the principle and source of *measure*, which, as Plato tells us in the *Philebus*, ranks highest in the list of goods, higher even than beauty, mind and wisdom. Plato is thus continuing in a sense the Socratic tradition of the Good as an eternally real object residing in a supersensible world. But the meaning he intends this to convey is a different one. The ethical and religious fervor of Socrates has given place to a fervor that is primarily speculative; and we are told accordingly that listeners who came to Plato's famous lecture on the Good went away much perplexed because they heard of nothing but numbers, and geometry, and astronomy, and the One.

Why then did Plato continue to call by a name that stands for "value" a reality conceived by him in terms of human understanding first of all? Not, we may suppose, because he was thinking of those human values which the term good naturally suggests; to suppose indeed that the eternal and unchanging realm of logical and mathematical truth should suffer the intrusion of a merely human teleology would be in Plato's view a desecration. This last appears even in the *Republic* as belonging to the lower world of appearance, and it is related to an absolute good, not as identical with its essence, but, like all finite things, as dependent on it for such measure of reality as it may possess. Teleology has to be interpreted in the last analysis in the light, not of human functions, but of that aesthetic value which for the man of intellect attaches to rational order as such — an order that finds its most striking expression in the "beautiful" relationships of mathematics. "Everything that is good is fair, and the fair is not without measure." It is in this absolute sphere where the power of the good has retired into the region of the beautiful that we apparently are to look for the good as such — in the eternal logical perfection of "system," and not in the temporal connection of means with ends. Only here does human teleology find its real significance. The ears and the eyes are for a purpose. but it is not the crude purpose of satisfying natural needs; it is in order that, through perceiving the movements of the heavenly bodies and the harmonies of musical sounds, they thus may introduce the mind to the true objects of its desire.

3. THE LATER DIALOGUES

1. It remains to give more briefly some account of the dialogues which Plato wrote well after the Academy was founded, and which, though they are much less familiar to us through their relative neglect of the literary and dramatic graces, really represent his maturest thought. Two of these, the *Parmenides* and the *Theaetetus*, are probably the earliest of the group, and were composed not very far apart. About the *Parmenides* a word already has been said. The *Theaetetus* is a critical examination of the nature of knowledge. Here Plato takes up the two current types of theory — that knowledge is sensation, and that knowledge is thought or judgment — and finds neither satisfactory. The doctrine of Protagoras and of Heracleitus leads to a thoroughgoing relativism which makes knowledge impossible; we find nothing on which to rest our feet till we pass beyond sensations to those common attributes — unity and difference, sameness and otherness, and the like — which we reach not through the senses but by thought. But the Eleatic or Megarian attempt to explain knowledge in terms of judgment is equally unsuccessful. The fatal difficulty is its failure to explain the possibility of error. Either you know what you are judging about, or you do not. If you do know, you cannot judge falsely; if you do not, your mind is a mere blank and you cannot make any judgment at all. Various ways of evading the difficulty are canvassed, but none of them are found to be successful. On the one hand, then, we have a theory for which nothing is true, and on the other a theory for which everything is true; and neither is good enough to account for actual knowledge. Here Plato drops the investigation, and leaves the matter in the air.

2. The *Sophist* belongs to a later period in Plato's life, and here some of the questions raised in the *Theaetetus* come up again. One difficulty in particular, which had proved a puzzle to preceding

thinkers, and to which the paradoxes of the Eleatics had been chiefly due, now gets a solution. This is the difficulty attending "predication"; how can we say that a thing is *not* so and so? To this Plato gives the answer: "is not" does not mean "does not exist." It means "is other than"; it has a logical and not an existential significance. If we say then that an object is not beautiful, not-beautiful is not a name for nothing, but for all the things other than the things that are beautiful; and these not-beautiful things *are* just as truly as the things that are beautiful. In this sense not-being is as real as being, and the difficulties raised by Parmenides' philosophy have been removed. We can now see how error is possible; a false belief that Theaetetus is flying is not a belief about nothing, but a belief which asserts that he is doing something different from the thing he actually is doing. Meanwhile, and in particular, the way now is open for bringing the various general concepts or categories of thought into some sort of intelligible connection or system — a necessity if knowledge or science is to be rendered possible. Not all such general attributes can combine, or be predicated one of the other; we can say for instance that motion and rest both *are*, or partake of being, but not that rest is motion, or that motion is rest. It is the business of philosophy to work out these connections, and so combine the Many and the One.

3. The *Philebus*, a dialogue of Plato's old age, is noteworthy partly from the fact that it shows his attitude toward an important problem which had been, and was to continue to be, much discussed by ethical philosophy, and also because the method which he uses brings us closer than does anything else in his writings to his fundamental metaphysics. The place that pleasure ought to hold in the rational life raises questions which had received frequent but unsystematic treatment in the earlier dialogues. Just how Socrates himself had stood on such a question is a little difficult to say; it may be doubted whether he ever committed himself to any very explicit doctrine. Probably, as was said before, we are safer in looking to his life than to his teaching; here indeed a pretty well-defined attitude appears. Pleasure is not something necessarily

and essentially base; Socrates did not refuse to enjoy simple and natural pleasures when they came his way. The case against pleasure is not that it is bad, but that it is unimportant. So long as we can take it or leave it alone, so long as it does not "possess" us, we do not need to bother very much about it. But pleasure is dangerous because it has so strong a tendency not to stop here, but to usurp a place that does not by right belong to it; and then it becomes a positive evil by blocking the way to man's true end and good.

To this last judgment Plato undoubtedly subscribed. When he condemns pleasure, as he often does, what he has in mind in the first instance is this disrupting influence pleasure is likely to have on a rationally ordered life; he is expressing primarily his instinctive repugnance to excess, disorder, disproportion and the haphazard life of license and riot that results from an undisciplined gratification of man's lower nature. There is a natural tendency in such an emphasis to pass to the opposite extreme, and Plato is not free from this temptation. The higher pleasures, he quite definitely believes, are the pleasures of the mind, and at times he seems on the point of regarding these not only as higher but as self-sufficient. But this is a personal preference, and not "science." A scientific theory of ethics must start by accepting the facts of man's experience; and just as the theory of knowledge has to find a place both for sensation and for judgment, so a theory of ethics must take account alike of pleasure and of wisdom as constituents of human good.

That pleasure alone is not sufficient to constitute a worthy end hardly needs much proof. There is no good which men call desirable — money, position, beauty — which may not, if it fall into the hands of a fool, bring about his ruin; of what avail is it to possess a gold mine if we do not know how to use our wealth except to bring harm on ourselves? Pleasure then "ranks not first, no, not even if all the oxen and horses and animals in the world in their pursuit of enjoyment thus assert, and the many, trusting in them as diviners trust in birds, determine that pleasure makes up the good of life, and deem the lust of animals to be better witness than the inspirations of divine philosophy." Above pleasure there is a higher principle by which pleasures must be judged. " Do we not say that the intemperate has pleasure, and that the temperate has pleasure in his very temperance? that the fool is pleased when he is filled with foolish fancies and hopes, and that the wise man has pleasure in his wisdom? and may not he be justly deemed a fool who says that these pairs of pleasures are respectively alike?" It is as in the case of aesthetic taste. The excellence of music may be measured by pleasure, but the pleasure must not be that of the chance hearer; " the fairest music is that which delights the best and best educated, and especially that which delights the one man who is preëminent in virtue and education." [1]

But neither is wisdom to be identified with the good to the exclusion of pleasure. Certainly this is not the case if wisdom is accompanied by positive pain. About a state of wisdom that is neither pleasurable nor painful there might be more chance for dispute; such we may deem the felicity of the gods to be. But Plato is ready to admit that to the natural man the thought has no attractions. The supreme end consequently will combine the two. "Here are two fountains that are flowing at our side; one, which is pleasure, may be likened to a fountain of honey; the other, which is a sober draught in which no wine mingles, is of water pure and healthful. Out of these we may seek to make the fairest of all possible mixtures."

It is with the principles governing this mixture that the philosophical scientist is concerned. Plato starts with the principle to which attention earlier was called; the highest rank among possible goods is to be assigned to "measure." The ultimate reason why we cannot take pleasure as our standard is that pleasure, as a form of feeling, is a continuum, an indefinite more or less of quality without the quantitative determinations that lend themselves to exact knowledge; pleasure can be brought within the confines of the good only in so far as feeling receives the impress of limit or measure. Assuming then that the first place will belong to measure, and to the symmetry, beauty and perfection of the ideal type in which measure gets expression, it will be the particular business of the scientist to

[1] *Laws*, 658

estimate the various grades of knowledge and of pleasure that have a right to enter into the loveliest mixture.

Here we may say at once that, as between thought and pleasure, thought indubitably will at least have the higher place; if a thing is good in proportion to the presence of measure in it, it is obvious that mind, whose essence it is to deal with exact relationships, must be much more closely akin than pleasure is to the divine mind which is the cause of order in the cosmos. Moreover in the realm of knowledge there is a gradation. Knowledge will differ in reality or truth in proportion to the reality of the objects with which it deals — which means that it will be valuable in proportion to the presence of number in it. The highest rank therefore will belong to the dialectical knowledge of the philosopher. But less exact forms of mind will also find a place in so far as they too in their degree aim at precision — science, art and even true opinion.

In the lower half of the scale stand pleasures; and these too can be arranged in a relative order of value. Pleasures differ in their purity — their relative freedom from attendant pain. The intellectual pleasures are the purest, and will stand therefore at the top. But there are other pleasures also that Plato does not reject. Certain of the senses — notably sight and hearing — have pleasures which are attended by no consciousness of want or pain, and are therefore relatively pure; here belong in particular the aesthetic pleasures of line, color and harmony. And in addition there are "necessary" pleasures — the natural pleasures of biological desire when these are kept within the bounds of health and temperance. All these may be called "true" pleasures, and as such they have a place in the good life.

Meanwhile it has to be noted that while pleasures are allowed to enter into the fairest mixture, it is not their quality of pleasureableness that gives to them this right. Pleasures are "good" not because they are pleasant, but by reason of the presence in them of the measure that alone gives value. "Purity" is thus to be regarded as an intrinsic rather than a utilitarian ground of preference. It is not because of our dislike for pain that pure pleasures appeal to the philosopher, but because purity is itself an aesthetic quality and so a good; pleasure that runs true to type is better than pleasure obscured by a combination with its opposite, in the same way that a little pure white is fairer and truer than a great deal that is mixed. And equally of necessary pleasures; it is only for the sake of the rational life that we need to consider them. We should indulge natural desires, Plato had said in the *Republic*, just enough to lay them to sleep and prevent them from interfering with the higher life of thought; by calling them necessary, the philosopher means that if it were not for their necessity he would have no interest in them.

Meanwhile there remain false pleasures also, from which the element of measure is lacking; and these will be excluded from the mixture. Some of them are false in the sense that they are contaminated by their connection with false opinion; we look forward with anticipation to consequences that never actually materialize. Or we may overestimate the worth of pleasures by reason of their being mixed up with a preceding painful state that colors them by contrast; here belong the pleasures of excess, which seem to be the most intense of all, but whose intensity is really dependent on an exaggeration of desire and so on attendant pain. Such pleasures have no true being, and they are not therefore to be reckoned in the class of the good.

4. The *Timaeus* is a book which had a large influence on the religious philosophy of the Middle Ages, but which is apt to prove a puzzle to the modern reader. It is the only one of Plato's dialogues to deal with the problems of physical science; and it takes the form of a cosmology along Pythagorean lines. Its present interest lies however largely in the appearance of a new side of Plato's philosophy for which his earlier works will hardly have prepared us. One of the great difficulties that any doctrine of forms presents is that of accounting for the fact of generation, change or motion. There is no obvious cause for this in the forms themselves, since these are changeless and eternally perfect; among them there is, to be sure, the form or idea of motion, but the idea of motion does not move. Plato finds a true cause in the notion of the "soul." The soul alone among the objects of experience does not only move, but

is self-moved; this power of self-motion constitutes indeed the definition of a soul, and Plato uses it as the basis of one of the several arguments by which he undertakes to prove the soul's immortality.

In the *Timaeus*, then, this notion is used to solve the problem of a world of generation, which is due to a Soul eternally self-moved and having the power of imparting motion. God is not the only being to whom the term applies; he has created subordinate souls as well — a cosmic soul and other lesser ones, including gods and men. But God is the ultimate and supremely good soul, and it is he who is responsible for those motions which are "good" — which reveal the presence of order and system in the world such as is most conspicuous in the motions of the heavenly bodies. Incidentally Plato in the *Laws* uses the notion of subordinate souls to explain the fact of evil; since God is wholly good, he cannot be responsible for bad or disorderly motions in the lower world. Meanwhile although God is good, he is not *the* Good, which has its own being as the source of the pattern which God follows in his creation of the world. The details of this creation it is not necessary to stop upon, especially as for Plato himself they do not represent knowledge or science in the strict sense, but only more or less mythological approximations to the truth. It is enough to note its more general metaphysical outcome; corporeal things are the result of a mixture of form with the "bastard" concept of space, the physical "elements" being conceived as geometrical solids which embody the principles of number.

5. In the *Statesman* and, in particular, the *Laws*, Plato returns to the problems of political science — including that of public education — which he had dealt with in the *Republic*. Here the treatment is much more realistic, and aims in detail to meet actual Greek problems. The thoroughgoing communism of the earlier dialogue is abandoned — though plenty of occasion still is found for Plato's paternalistic bent — as well as any real hope for the appearance of a philosopher-king. Plato now places his reliance on sound constitutional principles — a reign of law administered by the best minds — with a constitutional monarchy standing as the

best available type of government. The *Laws*, probably the last book of Plato's to be published, possesses a good deal of human interest and represents some of Plato's ripest thinking, but it is far too detailed to lend itself to a summary.

6. *The Academy.* — The school which Plato founded, and which was called the Academy, continued in existence several centuries after his death, although it passed through a number of vicissitudes. At different periods of its existence it represents different tendencies, and is known successively as the Older Academy, the Middle Academy, and the New Academy. Plato's real successor however is not found among the more orthodox followers who formed the Academy, but rather in Aristotle, the originator of a new and rival school.

LITERATURE

Plato, *Dialogues.*
Van Oordt, *Plato and his Times.*
J. Seth, *Study of Ethical Principles.*
Nettleship, *Lectures on the Republic of Plato.*
Nettleship, *Theory of Education in Plato's Republic* (in *Hellenica*)
Bosanquet, *A Companion to Plato's Republic.*
Zeller, *Plato.*
Pater, *Plato and Platonism.*
Ritchie, *Plato.*
Martineau, *Types of Ethical Theory.*
Grote, *Plato and the Other Companions of Socrates,* 3 vols.
Collins, *Plato.*
Shorey, *The Unity of Plato's Thought.*
Shorey, *Idea of the Good in Plato's Republic.*
More, *Platonism.*
More, *Religion of Plato.*
Stewart, *Myths of Plato.*
Stewart, *Plato's Doctrine of Ideas.*
Barker, *Political Thought of Plato and Aristotle.*
Barker, *Greek Political Theory. Plato and his Predecessors.*
Taylor, *Plato.*
Taylor, *Plato. The Man and his Work.*
Field, *Plato and his Contemporaries.*
Lodge, *Plato's Theory of Ethics.*
Burnet, *Platonism.*
Adam, *Plato: Moral and Political Ideals.*

§ 11. *Aristotle*

Aristotle was born in 384 B.C. at Stagira, a town of Thrace. He came from a family of physicians, and his father was court physician to the king of Macedon. At the age of eighteen he turned definitely from his ancestral calling to enter Plato's Academy at Athens; Plato was at that time around sixty years of age. Aristotle remained a member of the Academy for eighteen years, leaving Athens only when Plato died. Four years later he was called by Philip of Macedon to conduct the education of his son Alexander, afterwards to be called the Great, and then a boy of thirteen. About 335 B.C. he returned to Athens and founded his own school, the Lyceum, in a grove outside the city sacred to Lyceius; the school got the name of the Peripetetic school from Aristotle's practice of walking up and down as he discussed matters with his pupils. Twelve years later, being threatened with prosecution for impiety and for his Macedonian connections, he went into voluntary exile, dying almost immediately thereafter in 322 B.C.

In passing from Plato to Aristotle we are conscious of a marked change of atmosphere, though this is probably more noticeable than it would have been were we in possession still of Aristotle's own published works, whose literary merits were highly thought of by antiquity. Instead the writings that have come down to us bear the earmarks of lectures or lecture notes intended for instruction in the Lyceum; and they have the defects attaching to such a purpose, being highly technical, often repetitious or else unduly sketchy, and not infrequently obscure. At any rate they show the long step thought has taken away from the imaginative unity of the earlier Platonic dialogues in the direction of scientific specialization. Here we are in contact with the type of mind which we now are accustomed to think of as the scientific type. This does not mean that Aristotle is no metaphysician. He combines in himself as few philosophers have done the scientific with the metaphysical interest, and throughout his multitudinous investigations in detail there runs a single principle by which he undertakes to gather up and unify the whole preceding course of philosophical and scientific thought.

I. METAPHYSICS, LOGIC, PHYSICS, BIOLOGY, PSYCHOLOGY

1. *Form and Matter.* — We may take a start from a doctrine on which Aristotle lays some stress, and by reference to which he proposes to correct the deficiencies latent in all previous systems. This is his doctrine that any complete way of explaining things involves a fourfold distinction in the term "cause"; there is the material cause, the efficient cause, the formal cause and the final cause. To take an example — say a manufactured article like a chair — the material cause is the wood out of which the chair is made, the efficient cause is found in the muscular movements by which the material is fashioned, the formal cause is the ideal pattern in the workman's mind which guides these movements, the final cause is the purpose to which the finished object is to be put. It is a defect in all previous philosophies that none of them has realized the need of taking all of these considerations into account for a full explanation, though each individually has been recognized in one connection or another. Thus the elements of the Ionians are material causes; they are the stuff out of which everything is constituted. Again, Love and Hate in Empedocles, or Nous in Anaxagoras, are a recognition of the second principle, since their only function is to impart motion to the elements. And the Pythagoreans, and Plato in particular, had contributed the notion of a formal cause. The business of a systematic philosophy is now to give, not one of these, but all of them their due.

It is one type of cause in particular however — formal cause — that plays the outstanding rôle in Aristotle's reconstruction of philosophy; and his meaning can best be approached by first considering what he has to say about this. It is one of the leading motives of his Metaphysics — a collection of writings so called from the fact that in a later collection of his works they came after the treatises on physics ($\mu\epsilon\tau\grave{\alpha}$ $\tau\grave{\alpha}$ $\phi\upsilon\sigma\iota\kappa\acute{\alpha}$) — to show that the Platonic doctrine of forms cannot be accepted as it stands, and to put in its place a more adequate conception. Generally speaking, his objection lies against what he regards as Plato's disposition to separate the forms from the actual things of experience. Plato already had himself, in the *Parmenides*, noticed the objections that can be raised to a belief in such transcendent forms, and these objections Aristotle repeats and amplifies. It would be impossible to prove the existence of such forms if they were separate from the world to which we and our knowing processes belong; nor, if they existed, should we be able to explain by reference to them anything whatever in this lower world from which we have so carefully removed them. The statement that things "imitate" the forms or "participate" in them is only a metaphor which conveys no genuine meaning. But it does not follow that the form has no existence, and that the only reality is the world of individual objects. The form does exist, and it is a very essential part of reality; only it exists *in* the world, and *in* things, not outside of and apart from them.

The best way to gain a notion of what Aristotle means by this is to take a concrete illustration. We shall find the most enlightening illustration in what we call an organism. What is it we mean by an oak tree, for example? Is it merely a collection of the particular parts that go to make it up as an object in space? But where shall we start to make such an analysis? If we take the acorn — and there surely is a sense in which the oak already exists in the acorn — we shall get one result; if we wait till the tree is full grown we shall get another and a very different one. The idea of the tree, that is, evidently includes more than is present at any one moment of the tree's existence; all the processes by which it changes from the acorn to maturity also belong to the complete notion of what a tree is. Nor is this all. Any mere description of the parts misses the *unity* of the organism, that which makes it a single object; we must also introduce into the idea of the tree as a whole the relation of each part to the other parts and to the entire organism. If there were no "form" or type, if the particular facts were everything, there would be no tree, but only a series of molecular changes. Looked at from one standpoint the tree can no doubt be reduced to a succession of such changes, entirely continuous with all the other changes in the universe. But a tree is, for our knowledge, more than this; it is a single process, possessing as an organism its own peculiar *unity of end*. Only again it is not an end that comes literally at the finish — such an end is but the end of death ; nor does it exist in any sense outside the life of the tree. The life process is itself the end ; the tree fulfils the purpose which it embodies in the very act of growing.

This is essentially what Aristotle means. As the tree is nothing outside the whole process of growth, regarded as bound into a unity by its relation to the organic type, so the concept in general does not exist separate from the material world of generation, but only *in* that world. Matter and form are relative terms, neither of which has any real existence apart from the other. Matter is the organic process looked at from the side of potentiality, of what as yet is unrealized, as the acorn is the material from which the oak will spring. This does not mean that matter is some "thing," an actual bit of stuff out of which the world is made. The material which goes into things may indeed in a secondary sense be called their matter ; but it is already a particular "kind" of matter which, in however rudimentary a form, possesses definite characteristics. Pure matter does not "exist" ; it is in the strict sense just potentiality or possibility — the possibility of the realization of form. Form on the other hand is the same process on the side of actuality or fulfilment. It is the inner meaning expressing itself concretely in material shape, the end which governs the series of particular changes ; it also in itself is an abstraction, and becomes an object of knowledge only as it is embodied in a "thing." The transition from the potential to the actual is motion, or evolution, or development. True existence thus is something not apart from the phenomenal world, but realized in it ; it is possibility made real, the potential actualized, Aristotle's *entelechy*.

Such a conception would apparently involve, if taken seriously, an important change in philosophical standpoint ; it would substitute a reality which is changing or dynamic for an all-complete perfection, as indeed Heracleitus had already done when he made reality a process of Becoming. There is another side however to Aristotle's theory which prevents our taking this too strictly. A different type of illustration will suggest the point. Aristotle does not confine his examples to organic life, where matter and form are

in truth only distinguishable and not separate, but also turns frequently to illustrations from human workmanship, especially in
artistic creation. Take a statue for example; the reality of the
statue is the marble shaped to body forth the sculptor's ideal.
Here we have two sides again — the material which furnishes the
conditions for the artist's work, and the idea in his mind that represents the pattern which his activity follows and the end toward
which it is directed. But there is a degree of separation here that
did not exist in the case of the tree. The two things have a relation,
it is true. Even in the rough the marble may be said to be not
something altogether separate and independent, since the sculptor
sees in it the possibility of realizing his ideal; and his ideal is not
the mere dream it would have been apart from the possibility of
being realized in the marble. Still, in the illustration, the form
and the matter both have a real existence before they meet in the
statue.

If we apply this illustration to the world at large, it leads to the
conception of a graded series of realities, each step in the series
revealing more and more those universal relationships which go to
render it intelligible, an object of true knowledge. In the actual
world of generation the formal element exists nowhere in more than
a relative degree of purity. Everything is alike matter and form —
matter to what lies above it in the scale, form to what is lower down.
The marble is matter to the statue, but it is not pure matter; it
also has definite characteristics, and so in relation to a lower grade
of matter it stands itself as form. The tree is form in relation to the
elements that are taken from the soil to further its growth, matter
in relation to the house which is made from its timber. But when
we reach the upper limit the situation changes. The rational types
which reveal themselves in the world process are not, for Aristotle,
actually generated by the process as such, as in modern philosophies
of evolution. Rather, they are eternally implied as the necessary
condition for the world's intelligibility. At the end of the series,
therefore, lies that which no longer is relative merely, but absolute;
it is pure Form, beyond which there is nothing to which it can
stand in the relation of matter.

Here we seem to be getting pretty close after all to that separation of form from the empirical world which Aristotle criticizes in Plato. Aristotle saves himself however, technically at least, by resorting to theology. Even in the supra-sensible realm pure form does not exist as such. It is Aristotle's doctrine that nothing can *exist* which is not an individual substance; and form is by definition not individual, but universal and abstract. But while it cannot exist in its own right it may exist, even without matter, if we can find an immaterial substance to embody it. Such an individual substance is God. God is absolute mind with no touch of the corporeal. His is the life of pure thought that has no foreign content — thought that thinks itself. Unmoved himself, he is the mover of the universe, not as an active agent, but as the final end of all, the ideal toward which the whole creation moves by an inner necessity, as the beautiful and the good stir our endeavor to realize them not by anything they themselves do, but by the appeal they make to our desires as worthy of being realized. God is spirit without body, mind without sense, pure activity without action or desire.

Aristotle's philosophy thus has two aspects. As science it issues in a teleological hierarchy of existents; it is an impressive attempt to bring together all the facts of man's experience into a graduated scale of forms or species, each gathering up into itself the meaning of what had gone before, while at the same time it faces ahead toward something higher, more rational, and more self-complete. On the other hand this whole process is topped by a half metaphysical, half religious doctrine where dualism reappears in a different guise. It is the first aspect that is mainly responsible for Aristotle's influence on subsequent thought, though as the propounder of what has perhaps a right to be called the first clear formulation of a philosophic theism the other side as well is by no means negligible. We may however overlook this for the most part in what remains to be said about his philosophy.

2. *Logic.* — And first a word about scientific method in general as Aristotle conceives it. Aristotle's most perfect achievement is his Logic, found chiefly in the collection of writings called the *Organon*. Of course there had been before his time some isolated

treatment of logical details, and Zeno and other philosophers had made significant contributions to the technique of argument; but there was no connected body of logical doctrine. Aristotle not only succeeded in creating such a science, but he did his work so thoroughly that, in its special field, it has remained practically unchanged ever since. Formal Logic as it is called — the analysis of the processes of deductive argument as this is taught to-day — does not differ essentially from the formulation which Aristotle gave it over two thousand years ago.

Aristotle's logic centers about two things in particular — definition, and the syllogism. Definition aims to set forth the character of those natural types which represent the cleavage into which the world of nature falls, and which are presupposed as the forms that render explanation possible; technically it consists in subsuming a species under the next higher or more general concept or genus, from which it is distinguished by means of its distinctive character or "difference." The syllogism, or process of proof, establishes the necessary logical connection between concepts through the medium of two premises and a middle term, which last, by standing in a relation to each concept separately, uncovers the relation of one to the other.

At the present day it is universally recognized that formal logic has a very secondary value for scientific thinking; the syllogism represents in an abstract and somewhat artificial form processes involved in human argument, and it is more or less useful in pointing out possible defects or fallacies, but no one supposes that it tells the scientist how to go to work to discover the actual constitution of the world. But for Aristotle, with his theory of forms, this is just what logic was supposed to do. It is the business of science to demonstrate by means of the syllogism those properties of objects which follow from the definition of the species, on the basis of certain necessary principles of thought, some of them, like the laws of contradiction and of excluded middle, being common to all the sciences alike, while others, like the axioms of mathematics, are peculiar to a limited group. We cannot in this way arrive at all the facts which the actual world presents; there are other accidental or contingent characters which depend on conditions external to the form or essence of the species. But this is not science in the strict sense. Science, true knowledge, is *necessary* knowledge, and only through the syllogism is such knowledge to be attained. The various characteristics in which members of a class differ from one another are therefore not capable of being brought within knowledge in the scientific sense; we can "know" that Socrates is mortal, but not that he is snub-nosed and talkative.

3. *Physics.* — It would be impossible here to give more than a hint of the way in which Aristotle goes on to apply his general conception to the wealth of detail he has gathered together. We have seen that each successive stage in the complexity of the world process stands to its predecessor in the relation of form to matter. At the bottom stands pure matter, which is not what we should call a form of matter at all, but a principle, an abstract condition of the real, a mere limit to the process of explanation. The first stage in the actual development of nature is to be found in the primitive elements of Earth, Water, Air and Fire. These are no longer pure matter, but in them matter has taken on a definite though still a very elementary form; they constitute the formed matter which all the more complex objects of experience presuppose. From the elements we pass upward through mechanical changes and changes of quality to organic life; in organisms we advance from the vegetative life of the plant to the animal soul which is capable of sensation and motion, and from the animal soul to man in his true essence as a rational being, each step being governed by an upward impulse toward the next succeeding step which constitutes the goal toward which it is striving. And every successive stage, once more, gathers up within itself the preceding stage. Mechanical and chemical changes still take place in the organism; the vegetative soul — the life principle — persists in the animal; and all alike are presupposed in the exercise of the practical reason.

The physical theories of Aristotle are his least important contribution; they are not particularly original, and they do not always represent the best insight even of his own day. One point however is worth noting here, since it calls attention to the dangers involved in subordinating science to a metaphysical principle. To the four elements already mentioned Aristotle adds a fifth. This is almost infinitely finer than the other four, and is free from generation and decay; and it is the stuff out of which the heavens are made. For the super-terrestrial regions represent to Aristotle by far the most perfect product of nature — so perfect that they all but attain to the apotheosis of pure Form. In the undeviating regularity of the movements of the heavenly bodies, and in the circular motion which, without end or beginning, comes closest to what is eternal and unchanging, we find the most adequate embodiment of form in the physical universe. Indeed it has only one imperfection, that it does move. The circular motion of the celestial element is far superior to the rectilinear motion of terrestrial things; but it still falls short of the motionless serenity, the activity without change, of God, and shows therefore the presence still of matter, however refined.

4. *Biology and Psychology.* — Aristotle is more at home when he reaches the biological stage, as we might perhaps have expected in view of his family traditions; here he has collected a mass of original observations, and his treatment has an importance for the later growth of the biological sciences. The general outcome is an evolution from the simple to the increasingly more complex and more perfect — an evolution, however, where the successive forms are not in the Darwinian sense the result of the evolving process, but where the entire process is brought into being and directed by the formal essences that define each fresh species, all pointing to the highest organic form — man. The development passes from simple and homogeneous parts like flesh and bone, through the heterogeneous part or organ, to the unitary organism, which in turn rises to still higher forms as organs and functions are multiplied. The "form" that serves as the principle for explaining living creatures is called the soul, which is distinguished as vegetative, animal and rational in the order of relative perfection. In becoming aware of its real essence the soul makes explicit the unconscious teleology of nature, and sets this up as a conscious end, or final cause. The goal toward which it moves in its desire for completion is the highest or

rational soul. It is their adaptability to the ends of reason that explains the bodily organs peculiar to man: thus through his erect carriage his parts assume the "natural" position of up and down, and the fore legs are replaced by more efficient organs; sensitivity is increased by the development of heart and brain — the blood is for Aristotle the seat of sensation, and the brain is a means of cooling and tempering the heat of the blood; there is a shedding of excrescences like horns and feathers, which are due to surplus matter not fully utilized; and the greater smoothness in the texture of the skin refines the sense of touch — the primary sense.

The same method also is applicable to psychology; here Aristotle's treatment is often suggestive, and many of the things he has to say about memory, desire, the processes of sensation, the unity of consciousness, the association of ideas, are anticipations of modern psychological doctrines. By regarding the human soul as the entelechy of the body, in whose service the whole body is enlisted, Aristotle has in particular a way of avoiding the dualism which was until quite recent times a characteristic of modern psychological thinking; the subject-matter of psychology is the whole psycho-physical man, and not mind by itself. Dualism in another form however still persists; the "reason" responsible for the whole process of generation is itself an eternal essence which enters from without, and through which man is made part of a world that is not in time at all. At the start knowledge is utilitarian and instrumental. But in proportion as the bodily needs are satisfied, and opportunity for leisure is provided, knowledge is freed from its service to the practical life and becomes an end for itself in which, as will appear, man's highest felicity consists.

2. ETHICS, POLITICS, AESTHETICS

1. *The Summum Bonum.* — It is Aristotle's treatment of ethics and political science that chiefly recommends him to the modern reader. Here he takes his start from Plato's query: What is the end of life, the highest good? If we were to ask the opinion of men in general, we should find most of them agreeing both that happiness, and virtue, enter into the composition of the good; and we

have accordingly to settle on the meaning of these terms. Here again Aristotle's metaphysics helps him out. The end of a thing is the fulfilment of its " form," the realization of the potentialities of its own intrinsic nature. If then we are able to define that which constitutes a man as such, we can determine what is for him the *summum bonum*.

"Perhaps it seems a truth which is generally admitted, that happiness is the supreme good; what is wanted is to define its nature a little more clearly. The best way of arriving at such a definition will probably be to ascertain the function of Man. For as with a flute player, a statuary, or any artisan, or in fact anybody who has a definite function and action, his goodness or excellence seems to lie in his function, so it would seem to be with Man, if indeed he has a definite function. Can it be said, then, that while a carpenter and a cobbler have definite functions and actions, Man, unlike them, is naturally functionless? The reasonable view is, that as the eye, the hand, the foot, and similarly each several part of the body, has a definite function, so Man may be regarded as having a definite function apart from all these. What then can this function be? It is not life, for life is apparently something which man shares with the plants, and it is something peculiar to him that we are looking for. We must exclude, therefore, the life of nutrition and increase. There is, next, what may be called the life of sensation. But this too is apparently shared by Man with horses, cattle and all other animals. There remains what I may call the practical life of the rational part of Man's being. But the rational part is twofold; it is rational partly in the sense of being obedient to reason, and partly in the sense of possessing reason and intelligence. The practical life, too, may be conceived of in two ways, but we must understand by it the life of activity, as this seems to be the truer form of the conception. The function of Man, then, is an activity of soul in accordance with reason, or not independently of reason. Again, the functions of a person of a certain kind, and of such a person who is good of his kind, for example, of a harpist and a good harpist, are in our view generically the same, and this view is true of people of all kinds without exception, the superior excellence being only an addition to the function; for it is the function of a harpist to play the harp, and of the good harpist to play the harp well. This being so, if we define the function of Man as a kind of life, and this life as an activity of soul, or a course of action, in conformity with reason, if the function of a good man is such activity or action of a good and noble kind, and if everything is successfully performed when it is performed in accordance with its proper excellence, it follows that the good of Man is an activity of soul in accordance with virtue, or, if there are more virtues than one, in accordance with the best and most complete virtue. But it is necessary to add the words 'in a complete life.' For as one swallow or one day does not make a spring, so one day or a short time does not make a fortunate or happy man." [1] And, finally, we have to add to this certain external conditions that are favorable to virtuous living — health, beauty, money, luck — not because they are good in themselves, but because without them man's nature normally does not get a fair chance to express itself.

Happiness or well-being, then, consists in the unobstructed realization of man's rational nature; it is the active and continuous exercise, under sufficiently favorable conditions, of this nature functioning at its best. In this there clearly is a place for pleasure; indeed in Aristotle's psychology pleasure is to be explained precisely as a necessary concomitant, a superadded perfection, attending upon activity in so far as it is successful. Accordingly he is not afraid to use the word pleasure freely. "Happiness is the best and noblest and pleasantest thing in the world, nor is there any such distinction between goodness and nobleness, and pleasure, as the epigram at Delos suggests:

> "'Justice is noblest, health is best,
> To gain one's end is pleasantest.'"

This of course does not justify any and every pleasure. "Pleasures are desirable, but not if they are immoral in their origin; just as wealth is pleasant, but not if it be obtained at the cost of turning traitor to one's country; or health, but not at the cost of eating any

[1] *Ethics*, I, 6, Welldon's translation, The Macmillan Company.

food however disagreeable." Nor are we speaking of purely trivial pleasures. "Happiness does not consist in amusement. It would be paradoxical to hold that the end of human life is amusement, and that we should toil and suffer all our life for the sake of amusing ourselves." The pleasure ranks according to the excellence of the faculty exercised; and so while the highest virtue is by that very fact the highest pleasure also, happiness, or well-being, as the activity of that part of our nature which is most truly human, is a better term to use than pleasure. "It is reasonable not to speak of an ox, or a horse, or any other animal, as happy — even of a child. For happiness demands a complete virtue and a complete life."

In calling pleasures better or worse in proportion as they are attendant on a higher or a lower function, we are already precluded from expecting very much from them in the way of actual guidance in the moral life. Before pleasures can themselves be judged we have to rank men in terms of virtue or of character; in fact the only practicable way of defining a good pleasure is by saying that it is the pleasure which the good man would choose. When people are in a good state of health, it is the things which are truly wholesome that will seem wholesome to them; and, similarly, moral health is the condition which determines whether a man's desires will correspond to what actually, and not in appearance only, constitutes his happiness. The great word in moral theory is not pleasure, but virtue. It remains to ask therefore what this virtue is that constitutes the proper excellence of man.

2. *The Nature of Virtue.* — We may note to begin with that, as a consequence of the division of man's soul between intellect, and the lower desires and impulses which are only capable of acting in subjection to reason without being rational in their own right, virtue may take two forms — *intellectual* and *moral* virtue. Since reason is the essential element in man, it follows that the highest excellence is to be found in the life of philosophy — of pure rational insight or contemplation. The pleasure of speculation is of all pleasures the highest, the most continuous, the purest, the most self-sufficient, in the degree that the reason is divine in comparison

with the rest of the constituents of man's nature. Moral virtues are human; this one is godlike. "Our conception of the gods is that they are preëminently happy and fortunate. But what kind of actions do we properly attribute to them? Are they just actions? But it would make the gods ridiculous to suppose that they form contracts, restore deposits, and so on. Are they, then, courageous actions? Do the gods endure dangers and alarms for the sake of honor? Or liberal actions? But to whom should they give money? It would be absurd to suppose that they have a currency, or anything of the kind. Surely, to praise the gods for temperance is to degrade them; they are exempt from low desires. We may go through the whole category of virtues, and it will appear that whatever relates to moral action is petty and unworthy of the gods. Yet the gods are universally conceived as living, and therefore as displaying activity; they are certainly not conceived as sleeping like Endymion. If, then, action, and still more production, is denied to one who is alive, what is left but speculation? It follows that the activity of God, being preëminently blissful, will be speculative, and, if so, then the human activity which is most nearly related to it will be most capable of happiness." [1]

However it is not with the super-life of the theoretic reason that the bulk of Aristotle's treatise deals. Primarily he is concerned as a scientist with the natural history of man's ethical experience; and the great majority of men of course never reach the highest stage at all. Reason can only mean for them moral reason, or reason in the secondary sense in which it enters into and directs their practical activities rather than as it constitutes a final end in itself. We have to determine therefore in what a life according to reason in this less ultimate sense consists.

To begin with, nothing deserves to be called a virtue unless it is the outcome of rational choice. A purely natural and spontaneous impulse is not as yet a virtue, though it may be the starting-point for one. Thus an instinctive disregard of risks is not the same thing as courage in the moral sense; true courage exists only when dangers are faced deliberately and for the sake of some worthy end.

[1] X, 8.

We may admire such a temperamental gift of nature, but we do not praise it; and it is one of the empirical differentia of a virtue that it is an object of praise.

Again, this act of deliberate choice must not stop with a desultory exercise, but must attain a quality of permanence and dependability. A virtue is a *habit* of rational choice; to produce a virtue we must not only use our reason, but we must act repeatedly in the way reason directs until this sort of action has become a second nature. "It is neither by nature, nor in defiance of nature, that virtues are implanted in us. Nature gives us the capacity of receiving them, and that capacity is perfected by habit." As builders learn by building, and harpists by playing the harp, so it is by doing just acts that we become just. "As in the Olympian games it is not the most beautiful and strongest persons who receive the crown but they who actually enter the list as combatants, so it is they who act rightly that attain to what is noble and good in life." Even philosophy will not make a man virtuous till it is put into practice; those who imagine otherwise are like people who listen attentively to their doctors, but never do anything that their doctors tell them. Virtue stands accordingly for a definite habit of mind, brought about by a repetition of acts in which the impulse is directed by voluntary and intelligent effort in such a way as to express man's essential nature.

But here a further question will arise. In order that we may have a virtue, desire must be subjected to the rule of reason. But on what principle does reason act? The resultant pleasure is no test, for we have already seen that pleasure itself presupposes a prior standard in the shape of the good man with his character already formed. The "rational" will therefore need some further definition if it is to serve as a practical guide.

Such a principle Aristotle finds in his famous doctrine that virtue is a *mean*. An impulse has in it the possibility of giving rise to a virtue by taking the middle course between the two extremes of excess and deficiency. "The first point to be observed is, that in such matters as we are considering deficiency and excess are equally fatal. It is so as we observe in regard to health and strength; for we must judge of what we cannot see by the evidence of what we do see. Excess or deficiency of gymnastic exercise is fatal to strength. Similarly an excess or deficiency of meat and drink is fatal to health, whereas a suitable amount produces, augments and sustains it. It is the same, then, with temperance, courage and the other virtues. A person who avoids and is afraid of everything and faces nothing becomes a coward; a person who is not afraid of anything but is ready to face everything becomes foolhardy. Similarly, he who enjoys every pleasure and never abstains from any pleasure is licentious; he who eschews all pleasures, like a boor, is an insensible sort of person." [1] In like manner liberality lies between avarice and prodigality, modesty between impudence and bashfulness, sincerity between self-disparagement and boastfulness, good temper between dulness and irascibility, friendly civility between surliness and obsequiousness, just resentment between callousness and spitefulness, high-mindedness between littleness of mind and pompousness. Put in a somewhat less mechanical way, moral virtue is the sort of action that meets *adequately* any situation that confronts us; the mean of right giving, for example, is to give to the right person the right amount, at the right time, for the right cause and in the right way.

It is fairly obvious, however, that this definition of virtue as a mean, even allowing that it is more widely applicable to the several virtues than it appears to be, still falls a good deal short of a definite rule of guidance. If human impulses lent themselves to anything like an exact mathematical treatment, we should indeed have a serviceable instrument. But this is not the case, as Aristotle is of course quite aware; the point which avoids alike the too much and the too little is a highly indefinite point that will differ with circumstances and with different agents, just as an amount of food suited to a vigorous constitution will for another man be excessive. What in fact the principle amounts to is simply a restatement of the familiar Greek ideal of moderation; it is only in appearance that it lends itself to scientific precision. Aristotle adds to be sure a few practical suggestions that help out

[1] II, 2.

a little. Thus in aiming at a mean we should avoid obvious extremes, and when we cannot hit the mean exactly should take the lesser of two evils; we should observe the things to which we are particularly prone and force ourselves in the opposite direction, as we pull a crooked stick straight by bending it backward; we should always be on our guard against the enticements of pleasure, since pleasure is not conducive to impartiality of judgment. But something more than these desultory bits of moral counsel is required before we shall be in a position in practice to determine the actual content of the rational life.

The way in which Aristotle goes to work to satisfy this need calls attention to the fundamental conservatism of his ethical outlook; in general it consists in pointing us to the standards already implicit in the wisdom of the past. The good is not something each one has to discover for himself by the aid of his private reason. He can presuppose the true "form" of man already in the best achievements of the race; the touchstone of moral truth is the settled character of those persons in whom the highest insight of Greek society is embodied. Just as in the case of a refined gentleman in whom good breeding has become instinctive, the wise man in a moral sense does not need for the most part to fall back on explicit reasoning. He sees instinctively, by means of a certain moral tact that grows up gradually in anyone of naturally good disposition through his contact with the world, that this under the circumstances is for him the proper course; and the more he grows in wisdom and experience the easier the perception comes. For the most part we are pretty safe accordingly in following the undemonstrated assertions and opinions of old, experienced and prudent men; and if the judgment of the wise and the judgment of the many coincide, we have as sound a reason for accepting it as we can very well expect. All this is the easier for Aristotle in that he does not feel under obligation to take account of a vast variety of personal aims such as complicate for the modern man the problem of self-realization. While ethics is not for him a science — human conduct is too much immersed in the contingent to permit of this — it approaches a science in so far as its subject-matter will permit; and here as elsewhere the business of science is with the universal — with the species rather than the individual. The good we are looking for is thus the good for man, not the good of this or that man in particular; and as such it is capable of a formulation which does away with many of the complications that arise when the end is defined in terms of my personal constitution, and which we shall have more reason therefore to expect to find realized in the historical process to which the "form" of man has given shape.

The ideal, then, for man in his everyday conduct, is set for him by the accepted moral opinion of the day. This means the "best" opinion; but the best is only that which is most respected and respectable — the opinion generally current among those who are recognized as pillars of the state. Accordingly we find Aristotle saying that a man's goodness is relative to the character of the state in which he lives, even though this means that he must in consequence fall short of the ideally good man in stature. There thus is no provision in his philosophy for growth in moral wisdom that shall render a man wiser than his age or nation.

There remains one further principle that can be employed to an extent in guiding conduct. The speculative wisdom which for Aristotle remains man's highest good is not itself engaged with the problems of moral action; it is speculation that has no other end beyond itself. But by this very fact it furnishes a goal toward which life may be directed. Practical wisdom is the steward of the household which procures leisure for the master — philosophy — by subduing the passions and keeping them in order. "Whatever choice or possession of the natural goods will most produce the contemplation of God, that choice or possession is best; this is the noblest standard, and any that through deficiency or excess hinders one from the contemplation of God and reverence of God is bad."

3. *Political Theory.* — Meanwhile man is more than an individual. By nature he is a political animal, who can attain his highest good only in society; and Ethics accordingly is subordinate to Politics. Society arises out of the physical needs of man, who because he is not self-sufficing has to coöperate with his fellow-man in order to be sure of subsistence; but this is not its sole or highest

ground. Originating in the bare needs of life, it continues for the sake of the *good* life. The state therefore, and the science which deals with the state, have an ethical rather than a merely utilitarian aim. "Political science is concerned with nothing so much as with producing a certain character in the citizens, or, in other words, with making them good, and capable of performing noble actions."

Aristotle goes on to discuss a variety of problems relating to the theory of government. Plato's ideal state is criticized with more or less effectiveness, particularly in its communistic features. As against Plato he argues, for example, that the happiness of citizens and classes ought not to be submerged in the requirements of the social organism, that an abstract devotion to the state cannot take the place of personal interests such as get expression in the family and in property, that the unity of society needs to be interpreted not as sameness but as coöperation between a variety of individual aims. Specifically, the aim of the state can perhaps be best expressed as a preparation for that life of leisure in which man's highest good will be found; like many others since his day, Aristotle conceives of civilization as sufficiently vindicated by the existence of a leisure class of high-minded and cultivated gentlemen, supported by the labor of a menial class of peasants and workers who alike from deficiencies of nature, and from the demands of their occupation, are excluded from the higher life and so from the real rights of citizenship. About the content of this life of leisure Aristotle is not entirely explicit. For the standards of a leisure class of wealthy *parvenus* he has nothing but contempt. Nor does art have anything like the part to play that it does in similar ideals in more recent days; the contemplation of works of art is only a form of amusement, while artistic craftsmanship belongs to the field of manual labor, so that too professional a skill in any of the arts is a disgrace to a free citizen. There remain, to occupy the time, the direction of the necessary affairs of household and of state, the pleasures of friendly intercourse among equals, and, in particular, the strictly intellectual work of the scientist and philosopher. To this may be added the vocation of a university professor who combines instruction with research — a profession that would seem to represent for Aristotle the highest reach of purely human felicity.

In his discussion of the forms of government Aristotle refuses to be content with setting up a single ideal. He has his own notion of what abstractly is the best form of government — the rule, namely, of a single man, provided we could find one preëminently wise and good. But a political treatise should recognize actual conditions; and in practice the "best" government is a relative term, and will differ with the character of the people who are to be governed. In general there are three sound types of government — monarchy, aristocracy, and polity or constitutional government. When one man stands out preëminently among his fellow-citizens a monarchy is, as has been said, the natural form; when a few men are obviously superior in virtue, an aristocracy. It is not to be forgotten, however, that mere numbers give a certain stability and massive wisdom in affairs of government; while the individual members of the multitude therefore may be inferior to a chosen few, yet, taken collectively, their wisdom may conceivably be superior, since they supplement one another. In particular, they may be the best judges of what affects themselves, as a guest is a better judge of a feast than the cook who prepares it. So also a mass of men is apt to be more incorruptible than a single man; while any permanent exclusion of the multitude from political office is likely to be dangerous. Each of the three types of government may be perverted, and we have as a result tyranny, oligarchy and democracy. This comes about when the ruling class ceases to aim at the common interest and has instead its own advantage in view. For the average state a mixture of the types is advisable; roughly this means a democracy modified by oligarchical principles such as property qualifications and a relative independence of the magistrates. The advantages are best secured in a state in which the middle class is strong; this is likely to be more permanent than where either of the extremes of wealth or poverty predominates, and is more conducive to the spirit of friendship and comradeship which flourishes only among equals.

To a large extent of course the reasonings of Aristotle apply to conditions dissimilar to those which any modern country has to meet. Greek society was founded on the institution of slavery — an institution which Aristotle justifies theoretically on the ground that some men find their whole life in bodily action and so are slaves by nature. Another important difference is suggested in his attitude toward the worker in general. No man can practise virtue, he declares, who is living the life of a mechanic or laborer; and the assertion that greatness is impossible to a state which produces numerous artisans but few soldiers, reveals a social condition far removed from modern industrial society. So again the fact that the principle of representative government lies beyond his vision renders it inevitable that the state of which he speaks should be very limited in size; a democracy in the modern sense, as distinct from the city-state of the Greeks, he is unable to imagine. Nevertheless, the *Politics* is interesting even at the present day, and at times its modernness of tone is striking.

4. *Aesthetics.* — The *Poetics* is rather slight in nature, but as the first attempt to treat in a separate way that side of philosophy which in its larger aspect is now known as Aesthetics it deserves some mention : —

"In the *Poetic*, Aristotle takes Plato's view of poetry as a branch of Imitation, and divides it into three parts, Epic, Tragic and Comic. All imitation is a source of pleasure, but the imitation of the poet or artist is not simple representation of ordinary fact, but of the universal or ideal which underlies ordinary fact; whence poetry is more philosophical than history. This is most conspicuous in Tragedy, where the characters are all on a grander scale than those of common life; but even Comedy selects and heightens in its imitation of the grotesque. Tragedy is not, as Plato thought, a mere enfeebling luxury; rather it makes use of the feelings of pity and terror to purify similar affections in ourselves, that is, it gives a safe vent to our feelings by taking us out of ourselves and opening our hearts to sympathize with the heavier woes of humanity at large, typified in the persons of the drama; while it chastens and controls the vehemence of passion by never allowing its expression to transgress the limits of beauty, and by recognizing the righteous meaning and use of suffering." [1]

The school which Aristotle founded was known as the Peripatetic school. It maintained an existence alongside the Academy till well into the Christian era, but produced no new doctrines of any great importance.

LITERATURE

Aristotle, *Organon, Metaphysics, De Anima, Nichomachean Ethics, Politics, Poetics, Rhetoric*. Translations: Welldon (*Ethics, Politics, Rhetoric*); Jowett (*Politics*); Wallace (*Psychology*); Hammond (*Psychology*); Wharton (*Poetics*); Smith and Ross (*Works*).

Zeller, *Aristotle and the Earlier Peripatetics*, 2 vols.

Grote, *Aristotle*, 2 vols.

Wallace, *Outlines of Aristotle's Philosophy*.

A. Grant, *Aristotle*.

Davidson, *Aristotle and Ancient Educational Ideals*.

Bradley, *Aristotle's Theory of the State* (in *Hellenica*).

Barker, *Political Thought of Plato and Aristotle*.

Ross, *Aristotle*.

Taylor, *Aristotle*.

Stocks, *Aristotelianism*.

Ross, *Metaphysics*.

Burnet, *Ethics*.

Newman, *Politics*.

[1] Quoted from Mayor, *A Sketch of Ancient Philosophy*, Cambridge University Press.

THE LATER ETHICAL PERIOD

§ 12. *Introduction*

With Aristotle, the period of great speculative systems comes for the time being to a close. In his successors the course of philosophy took a new turn, which it was to follow for several centuries.

The reason for this new departure there has already been occasion to notice; it is due to the breakdown of Greek political and social life. From Socrates to Aristotle philosophy had made an attempt to stem the current and to give a rational basis to that ideal of a corporate life which, resting originally on the foundation of a customary morality, had begun to totter when this morality was undermined alike by political ineffectiveness and by philosophical scepticism. But the attempt was not successful; we see a recognition of its hopelessness in the growing prominence assigned to the theoretic life as a substitute for an active participation in social interests. After the conclusion of the Peloponnesian War, and the fall of Athens, things went from bad to worse in Greece. Feuds and jealousies increased among the numerous petty states into which the country was divided. Personal ambitions led to the solicitation of foreign interference, especially from Persia; and the employment of mercenaries still further threatened the existence of freedom. With the loss of Greek independence, and the supremacy of Macedon, the failure of Greek civilization became a settled fact, however much the attempt might be made to nurse the forms of freedom. The appearance of isolated patriots only brought into clearer relief the incapacity for united action on the part of Greece as a whole; so that the final loss of all chance of independence by the intervention of the Roman power was in some ways a blessing to the country. After the capture of Corinth by Mummius, in 146 B.C., Greece became a Roman province under the name of Achaia.

It is not surprising therefore that philosophy turned away from the ideal of man as an organic member of a social order, and occupied itself instead with the private individual, and the way in which he might obtain such satisfaction as he could in the troublous times in which his lot was cast. A new social ideal with any vitality in it could only come into being after history had prepared the way. Meanwhile men must have something as a guiding principle; and to get this they looked in two directions. On the one hand there begins now to some extent that running after Oriental cults which forms a striking feature in the life of the Empire later on; more sober minds, on the other hand, turned to philosophy for guidance and comfort.

For the next few centuries, accordingly, philosophy assumes an intensely practical aspect; it aims to be nothing more nor less than a complete art of living. You pretend that you are not calculated for philosophy? says Diogenes; why then do you live, if you have no desire to live properly? "Philosophy," writes Seneca, "is not a theory for popular acceptance and designed for show; it is not in words, but in deeds. It is not employed to help us pass the day agreeably or to remove ennui from our leisure; it forms and fashions the mind, sets in order our life, directs our action, shows what ought to be done and to be left undone; it sits at the helm and guides the course through perplexities and dangers. Without it none can live fearlessly, none securely; countless things happen every hour which call for counsel, and this can only be sought for in philosophy. Whether fate constrains by an inexorable law, or God is judge of the universe and arranges all things, or chance without reference to any order impels and confounds the affairs of men, philosophy ought to be our safeguard. It will encourage us to obey God willingly, to obey fortune without yielding; it will teach us to follow God, to put up with chance." [1]

Furthermore in all its more important tendencies the philosophy of the next few centuries is practically agreed in this: that if there is any good attainable at all it must be found by each man within himself. Circumstances have passed beyond man's power

[1] *Letters*, II, 4.

of control; but if he cannot remedy the ills of the outer world he can at least make himself independent of it, can cultivate that philosophic calm and poise which finds all the elements of happiness within the mind itself, and thus can be put beyond the power of chance to harm. Both of the two more original philosophical currents of the period have primarily in view this practical end. Although they are reached by very different roads, the ἀπάθεια (freedom from emotion) of the Stoics, and the ἀταραξία (imperturbability) of Epicureanism, bear a close resemblance.

The same thing is true of another characteristic tendency of the time — Scepticism. A distrust of the powers of reason usually succeeds a period of great speculative activity. As the ideals which give rise to systems of thought in such a period lose their freshness, the theoretical gaps in the arguments on which they have been based begin to monopolize attention. And since ultimate beliefs always are at bottom a matter of faith rather than of demonstration, and no new enthusiasm had as yet appeared to back knowledge with conviction, a sceptical distrust of the possibility of knowledge was a natural outcome. But here too the interest was not primarily theoretical. Scepticism, like its rivals, is a discipline to prepare the mind for assuming such an attitude toward life as will enable it to secure what satisfaction it may. Such disinterested intellectual curiosity as remained directed itself largely to the investigation of literary, grammatical and historical details, where no great theoretical principles were involved.

The same lack of intellectual grasp which showed itself on the one hand in the sceptical abandonment of the possibility of knowledge and, on the other, in a painstaking collection of facts, gave rise also to the tendency to Eclecticism. Unable to deal with fundamental principles, there was a growing disposition to settle the disputes of philosophy by an uncritical combination of the various systems. The practical nature of the Roman mind, and its disinclination for metaphysical thinking, gave a special impulse to this tendency. And, finally, as the inability of philosophy by itself to satisfy men became more and more evident, a union of philosophy with religion was attempted, culminating in the religious meta-physics of the Neo-Platonists.

§ 13. *Epicurus and Epicureanism*

1. *Epicurus* (341–270 B.C.) was of Athenian descent, though he was born in the island of Samos. About 306 he founded his school, which was held in his own gardens at Athens. Here he gathered about him a group of enthusiastic disciples, including among their number even women and slaves, who were bound together by the closest ties of intimacy and friendship. In this group Epicurus reigned supreme. His followers regarded him with the utmost veneration — a veneration which is expressed in the words of Lucretius in later days: "For if we must speak as the acknowledged grandeur of the thing itself demands, a God he was, a God, most noble Mummius, who first found out that plan of life which is now termed wisdom, and who by trained skill rescued life from such great billows and such thick darkness, and moored it in so perfect a calm and in so brilliant a light." [1] His teachings were memorized by his pupils and accepted without change, down to unimportant details. So rigidly did he impress his views upon them that, in spite of the long life which the school enjoyed, its speculative opinions scarcely altered to the end. Partly for this reason, the names which represent the later history of the school are only of secondary importance; *Lucretius*, among its Roman adherents, is indeed famous, but rather as a poet than an independent philosopher.

Epicurus' philosophy is a combination of the hedonism of the Cyrenaics with the atomism of Democritus. First of all it is a hedonism — a theory of the end of life, the highest good. Like Aristippus before him, Epicurus found in pleasure the one obvious and undeniable good; even when we speak of virtue as a good, as no doubt we do and may, it is really the pleasure which accompanies the exercise of virtue that we have in mind. But here begin certain complications. When Aristippus had said these same things he

[1] *Lucretius*, V, l. 7, Munro's translation, Geo. Bell & Sons.

had been pretty clear what he meant; pleasure stood to him for just what it does to the ordinary man. Nor could Epicurus very well deny that such pleasure is a good; he declares indeed that no conception of the good is possible apart from bodily enjoyments, while Metrodorus, one of his followers, asserts baldly that everything good has reference to the belly.

But ethical philosophy is more sophisticated now than it had been in Aristippus' time; the stumbling-blocks in the way of pleasure-getting are more clearly recognized. And in endeavoring to take account of this Epicurus goes farther than he might seem to be justified in doing. In part he lays stress on the need for selecting our pleasures wisely, for avoiding those unregulated impulses which bring evils in their train, for preferring simple and natural joys to the questionable delights of luxury and extravagance; and in so far there is no inconsistency with his starting-point. But when he goes on also to disparage all positive pleasures in favor of a philosophic poise of mind (ataraxy), a quiet and undisturbed possession of one's faculties free from pain of body and trouble of spirit, it is not easy always to distinguish his position from that of his opponents, the Stoics; and he is sometimes led to adopt an attitude toward sensuous satisfaction hardly to be expected of a hedonist. He even takes up with the theory that positive pleasures represent no more than the relief that results from the removal of a pain. They are only the preliminaries therefore of a true satisfaction, which in itself is nothing but the freedom from pain which leaves the mind without craving and without agitation; pleasures may be varied, but they cannot be increased. "The end of our living is to be free from pain and fear. And when once we have reached this, all the tempest of the soul is laid. When we need pleasure is when we are grieved because of the absence of pleasure; but when we feel no pain, then we no longer stand in need of pleasure." [1] This calm of mind may even render a man contented in spite of physical tortures, if he will only assert his independence of adventitious aids to happiness and refuse to let himself be disturbed; torn on the rack the philosopher may exclaim, How sweet! So far

[1] Diog. Laertius, *Life of Epicurus*, § 27.

have we travelled from the conception of happiness as a mere agreeable titillation of the senses.

But whether or not Epicurus is logically consistent in his position, at any rate he created an ideal which appealed powerfully to a certain type of mind, and which even today, as a working theory of life, exerts a wide influence. It is not a strenuous ideal; it calls for no heroism or sacrifice. But this very fact constitutes its charm for certain moods which to few men are wholly unknown. And the attitude of opposition which, in the interests of an aesthetic simplicity, it assumes toward the more flagrant vices and follies, gives it a sufficient moral flavor to hide its more dubious aspects. What — so its burden is — does man's fret and ambition and busy toil after all avail him? Does all the boasted advance of civilization add one real pleasure to his life? Does it do anything, indeed, but plague him with added cares, and weary him with war and strife? He longs to be rich, and famous, and powerful, and is dragged hither and thither by his ambition, only to expose himself to envy and the daily risk of ruin, and win nothing in the end. A frugal subsistence joined to a contented mind alone is true riches. "If any one thinks his own not to be most ample, he may become lord of the whole world, and will yet be wretched." The wise man will not despise pleasure when it comes to him; but he will not be dependent on it. He will be able to get along contentedly with little, finding his satisfaction in the common things and incidents of life, and getting an added zest from the very consciousness of his ability to go without. "He enjoys wealth most who needs it least. If thou wilt make a man happy, add not unto his riches, but take away from his desires."

Epicureanism is then in one aspect, like the message of Rousseau in modern times, a summons to return from the complexities of civilization to nature and natural pleasures; to take life easily and simply, and cease to worry over trifles; to depend for happiness less on highly spiced foods and elaborate banquets than on a good digestion and the company of friends. This ideal was exemplified in the life of the early Epicureans. "When," says Seneca, "you come to the gardens where the words are inscribed: Friend, here it will be well for you to abide; here pleasure is the highest good: there will meet you the keeper of the place, a hospitable, kindly man, who will set before you a dish of barley porridge, and plenty of water, and say: Have you not been well entertained? These gardens do not provoke hunger, but quench it; they do not cause a greater thirst by the very drinks they afford, but assuage it by a remedy which is natural and costs nothing. In this pleasure I have grown old." [1] "For myself," writes Epicurus to a friend, "I can be pleased with bread and water; yet send me a little cheese, that when I want to be extravagant I may be"; and he boasts that while Metrodorus had only reduced his expenses to sixpence, he himself had been able to live comfortably on a less sum.

The parallel with Rousseau extends also to Epicurus' estimate of science and human learning. Although he finds his chief good in mental pleasures, he is very far from commending the strenuous intellectual life which Plato, for example, regarded as a man's highest source of happiness. He is quite as easy-going here as in the rest of his theory. Intellectual enjoyment means refined conversation, pleasant intercourse between friends, and not any anxious and soul-disturbing search for the hidden truth of things. For what commonly goes by the name of learning and culture Epicurus has little respect; he was himself not a trained thinker, and he did not require more than the rudiments of education for his disciples. If they were able to read and write they had all that was essential; mathematics, logic and rhetoric, the theory of music and art, the researches of the grammarian and historian, were disparaged by him as contributing nothing to human happiness, and so as a mere waste of time. "One need not bother himself," says Metrodorus, "if he has never read a line of Homer, and does not know whether Hector was a Trojan or a Greek." How does it happen, then, that the scientific explanation of the universe as represented in the theories of Democritus plays so large a part in the Epicurean teaching? Why does Epicurus insist upon this as an essential part of his philosophy and impose it dogmatically upon his followers?

[1] *Letters*, h, 9.

2. The primary reason is not that Epicurus had, like the modern scientist, a feeling for positive and concrete fact in opposition to the verbal subtilties of logic, grammar and metaphysics; it is an entirely practical reason. Physical science is, for Epicurus, an instrument for making possible that calm of mind in which the end of life consists. And it does this because it rids us once for all of that which is the greatest foe to inward peace and a contented acquiescence — namely, religion. "Will wealth and power," writes Lucretius, "avail anything to cause religious scruples scared to fly panic-stricken from the mind, and that the fears of death leave the breast unembarrassed and free from care? But if we see that such things are food for laughter and mere mockeries, and in good truth the fears of men and dogging cares dread not the clash of arms and cruel weapons, if unabashed they mix among kings and kesars, and stand not in awe of the glitter of gold nor the brilliant sheen of the purple robe, how can you doubt that this is wholly the prerogative of reason, when the whole life is withal a struggle in the dark? For even as children are flurried and dread all things in the thick darkness, thus we in the daylight fear at times things not a whit more to be dreaded than those which children shudder at in the dark and fancy sure to be. This terror therefore and darkness of mind must be dispelled, not by the sun and glittering shafts of day, but by the aspect and law of nature." [1]

It is the great work of science, then, to sweep aside the chimeras and religious scruples which make men slaves to their own diseased fancies, which upset the calculations of life, trouble all the future with superstitious fear, and put repose and happiness beyond their reach; and it does this by substituting a purely natural and mechanical explanation for events, and so making religion superfluous. Men have imagined that the world is made and ruled by gods whose favor they must secure and whose wrath they must propitiate. These gods are continually interfering in the affairs of men, punishing and rewarding, hurling the thunderbolt and sending plagues and earthquakes. The soul moreover is immortal, and so we must still look forward to possible vengeance in a future

[1] II, l. 43.

life and to the woes of Tartarus. Doubtless such stories had, with the rise of science and philosophy, long since come to be more or less discredited in the eyes of educated men. But now that everything in the world was in a state of change and the landmarks which had guided men were disappearing, the need for something to which to cling had begun to manifest itself in a return to the superstitions which it was supposed had been outgrown.

It is against this tendency that Epicurus sets himself. Only by ridding oneself of the vague hopes and fears which tear and distract the mind, and prevent it from finding its satisfaction in the present, can the true end of life be attained; and this is what science has accomplished. Only our ignorance lets us imagine that events are brought about by supernatural interference; true reason tells a different story. The lightning for example, the dreaded thunderbolt of Jove, is a purely natural fact — fire, it may be, struck out by the chance collision of the clouds; given atoms and the void in which they move, and we have the data for explaining everything. And if we do not have to fear the vengeance of the gods in this life, no more is there any reason why we should look forward to punishment in another world. This fear of hell seems to the Epicurean one of the greatest evils that religion brings in its train. But there is no place for hell in the world which science knows. "No Tantalus in a lower world fears the huge stone that hangs over him; the true Tantalus is he who vexes himself by a baseless dread of the gods, and fears such fall of luck as chance brings to him." The idea of immortality is a vain imagination; the soul of man is even more unenduring than the world about him. And if death for us ends all, why should we fear it? there are no evils it can bring, for there is no life or consciousness in the grave to which we go. "Where we are, death is not yet; and where death comes, there we are not."

In spite however of thus rejecting alike the threats and the consolations of religion, Epicurus does not deny altogether the existence of the gods. His theory of knowledge, adopted from Democritus, which requires for perception and thought alike an objective cause in the shape of filmy images which objects continually are shedding, leads him to accept the real existence of divine and glorious forms in order to account for man's belief in them. But such gods are neither to be feared nor loved. Living an un-ruffled life in the interspaces of the heavenly regions, "where neither winds do shake nor clouds drench with rains, nor snow congealed by sharp frost harms with hoary fall, an ever cloudless ether over-canopies them, and they laugh with light shed largely round. Nature supplies all their wants, and nothing ever impairs their peace of mind." Enjoying perfect felicity, they feel no concern for human things; the good and ill of the world alike fail to move them; wrapped in eternal repose, in want of nothing from us, they are neither to be gained by our prayers nor stirred by us to anger.

In spite of the fact therefore that Epicureanism allied itself with the scientific view of the world, it was itself singularly lacking in the scientific temper. Its interest was not in getting at truth, but in bolstering up the particular view of life which it wished to adopt. It lays in consequence but little stress on the details of scientific explanation. Certainty is not attainable, or even much to be desired; a phenomenon might very well be explained in more ways than one, and it makes little difference which explanation we choose to adopt so long as it enables us to exclude the supernatural. One point in particular would suggest that Epicurus had not the purely scientific interest very much at heart. For Democritus the atoms are subjected rigidly to law. This belief in law as universal Epicurus rejects. "It would be better to believe the fables about the gods than be a slave to the Fate taught by the physical philosophers; for the theological myth gives a faint hope of averting the wrath of God by giving him honor, while the Fate of the philosophers is deaf to all supplications." [1] So when he comes to account for the beginning of the world he departs from Democritus; as all the atoms naturally fall downward in a parallel direction, and fall equally fast so long as there is nothing to oppose them, they never would come into contact were it not for a primordial deviation from a straight line which must have been uncaused.

[1] Diog. Laertius, *Life of Epicurus*, § 27.

3. Some of the reasons for the success which Epicurus' teaching met have already been suggested. It offers a conception of life which is intelligible to the average man in his average moods. It is easily formulated, is free from mystical and transcendental elements, and calls for no flights of moral or intellectual enthusiasm. But this also might be thought to constitute a limitation. The charges of loose living frequently brought against Epicurus himself were certainly far from being true; and while in later times many who called themselves Epicureans made his doctrine an excuse for an unregulated pursuit of pleasure, this is by no means characteristic of the stricter members of the school, nor is it countenanced by the words of the founder. Pleasure and virtue are synonymous with Epicurus; it is impossible to live pleasantly without living wisely and well and justly, and it is impossible to live wisely and well and justly without living pleasantly. It might be argued that there is really nothing in Epicurus' premises which can fairly be opposed to the indulgence in any pleasure, provided it be pursued judiciously and with due regard to consequences. Acts of moral wrong-doing, to be sure, are opposed to certain prejudices on the part of mankind at large, and so if they are detected they will meet with punishment. But these moral prejudices are, for the philosopher, theoretically a matter of convention; if one can commit a crime and reap the benefits without discovery, there appears no good reason why he should refrain from gratifying his desires in the unconventional way. All that Epicurus can answer is, that even if the criminal is not found out the possibility of detection always will be present and, by rendering him continually uneasy, will destroy that peace of mind in which happiness consists. But whatever may be true in theory, in practice there is nothing necessarily immoral in the Epicurean way of life.

It is not the more flagrant abuses to which it may or may not lead that constitutes the special weakness of Epicureanism, but rather a certain flabbiness of moral fibre which it reveals even when it is at its best. It is, as Cicero calls it, a bourgeois philosophy; its very virtues have only to be turned at another angle to seem commonplace. Cheerfulness of mind, pleasant conversation, a life ordered by good taste and aesthetic moderation, are good in themselves; but they may be won at the expense of other qualities. Heroism, self-sacrifice, an honest enthusiasm for what is best in conduct or even in art — for these things Epicureanism would appear to have no place. It sets its face against ambition, and money-getting, and vulgar pleasure-seeking, not because there is a worthier life for man to lead, but because nothing after all is much worth while. I am no doubt a fool if I weary myself with striving after wealth and luxury, fame and position; but I should be equally a fool if I were to delude myself with fine phrases about virtue and humanity, patriotism and duty. "It is not our business to work for crowns by saving the Greeks, but to enjoy ourselves in good eating and drinking." Such a conception of life is crystallized in the Epicurean notion of the gods as they sit beside their nectar careless of the downtrodden race of men below. That this should have seemed the only true ideal of life, and that the Epicurean should find it unthinkable that one who had the power of attaining it should voluntarily take upon himself cares and responsibilities for the sake of others, is perhaps his severest condemnation.

LITERATURE

Zeller, *Epicureans, Stoics and Sceptics.*
Lucretius, *De Natura Rerum.*
Wallace, *Epicureanism.*
Courtney, *Epicureanism* (in *Hellenica*).
Pater, *Marius the Epicurean.*
Masson, *The Atomic Theory of Lucretius.*
Watson, *Hedonistic Theories.*
Hicks, *Stoic and Epicurean.*
Taylor, *Epicurus.*
Bailey, *The Greek Atomists and Epicurus.*

§ 14. *Zeno. The Stoics*

If Epicureanism was of a nature to appeal strongly to the world weariness of a society in which indolence and corruption had dulled the edge, in less strenuous minds, of any pronounced belief in virtue.

it was a very different sort of philosophy that would recommend itself to the typical Roman of the Republic, and to those men who carried on the traditions of the Republic. The same intellectual temper which in public life produced a Cato, received expression in the world of philosophy as Stoicism. It is true Stoicism is not Roman in its origin. But neither is it typically Greek, although Athens, as the intellectual center of the world, was naturally chosen by *Zeno* (340–265 B.C.), the founder of the school, as the most fitting place in which to establish himself as a teacher. Zeno was himself however a merchant of Cyprus, probably of Phoenician stock, and nearly all the succeeding heads of the school were born outside of Greece; so that the more ascetic temper which Stoicism displays may perhaps be traced in part to an Oriental strain. At all events Stoicism offered to the nobler minds of the day a welcome refuge from the trivialities of the life which surrounded them; and it succeeded in evolving a type of character and belief superior to anything that its contemporary rivals had to show.

1. *Metaphysics.* — Objectively, the Stoic philosophy is aiming at a result which has points of contact with Epicureanism. For both the true end of life might be described as freedom from disturbing desires and from the pressure of external things, and a discipline of the mind that shall enable it to find satisfaction within itself. For both the attaining of this end is the great aim of philosophy. But the real meaning of the end, and the attitude of mind for which it called, were in the two cases widely different. As the Epicurean went back to Aristippus and his doctrine of pleasure as the end of life, so the Stoics are connected with that development of Socrates' thought which, in the Cynics, made virtue the highest good. But whereas the Cynics had for the most part stopped with negative results, in the case of the Stoics the possession of a different theoretical background enabled them to correct in a degree the onesidedness alike of their predecessors and of their rivals the Epicureans.

Instead, that is, of accepting the individualism and atomism of Epicurus, they start from the other end. Reality is an organic whole, an intimate combination of form and matter, soul and body, through which one universal life pulsates. This connected whole is called indifferently God, or nature. Now man, like everything else, is a part of the universal nature; and in this way *conformity to nature* becomes a formula which has in it the possibility of giving some real content to the life of virtue. The Cynic protest against convention is translated into a positive law of duty; the knowledge in which virtue consists becomes a knowledge of the true nature of things, and virtuous conduct such conduct as will further the life of nature — of that whole to which we belong as parts, and which is interpretable in terms of our rational life.

Here consequently the Stoic view of life comes in sharp conflict with that of Epicurus. For Epicurus, man is set down in a universe which is an interplay of senseless atoms, and he exists as a creature who, though of slight powers and open to strange vicissitudes, is nevertheless within his humble sphere a free agent, bound by no loyalties beyond himself, and concerned only to make the most he can of his private life under the guidance of an unpretentious ideal of pleasure. The Stoic too is concerned in practice with the possibilities of his personal satisfaction. But these possibilities he proposes to arrive at, not by disregarding the cosmos which surrounds him, but by looking to this as the source of all true knowledge about himself. Instead of going his own way regardless of the greater powers of nature, it is his business as a rational being to discover how the universe is going, and adjust his own step to it. From this universe at large all human values spring. And man is accordingly not a stranger in the world, but the product of righteous forces which work themselves out, in part through him, but in any case inevitably and on a universal scale.

Before considering further what this ideal means concretely, a few words need to be added to complete the account of the general metaphysical theory of the school. The conception of the universe as a unitary whole, instead of as a collection of atomic elements, implies the reality of its rationality, or what Plato calls the Form. But the Stoic agrees with Aristotle in denying that the two things, matter and form, are at all separate; meaning exists *in* the world, not in a realm beyond it. Even Aristotle, however, had ended up with pure form; the Stoics get rid of the last trace of transcendentalism by reducing form itself to matter. The result is a materialistic pantheism. The world of material nature is the sole reality; but it is not dead matter. It is living, informed by a rational soul — is God. This soul of the world, the Logos, or rational principle, is everywhere present as a more active and subtle kind of matter, just as the human soul is present in the body directing it to rational ends; indeed what we call the human soul — *pneuma*, breath or spirit — is but a part of this greater world soul, participating in its rational qualities, and received back finally into the universal reason where its individuality is lost.

In opposition therefore to the explanation of the world processes by chance or mechanism, the Stoic conception is throughout teleological. Everything flows of necessity from the nature of the whole; and since that whole is Reason, everything has its place in an intelligible scheme. The combination of so thoroughly idealistic a tendency with materialism — a materialism which argues that an emotion, for example, is matter, since it would have no power to move a man unless it came in spatial contact with him — clearly gives rise to difficulties; and it shows the decline of first-rate philosophical insight that the Stoics were able to ignore these difficulties.

2. *The Ethical Ideal*. — With this general sketch of the Stoic metaphysics, we may turn back to their ethical conception. There are two words about which the Stoic ethics turns — *nature*, and *virtue;* and of the two the first is on the whole perhaps the more enlightening. It has appeared that, for the Stoic, Nature is a unitary whole in which every human act as well as every other physical event is subject to necessary laws. As a consequence natural living is connected not, as in the case of Epicurus, with individual desires and pleasures, but with the more general characteristics that belong to man as a component part of the one significant meaning of the world. The Stoics do not overlook the natural impulses; they are the starting-point of conduct. But they are not the source of *virtue;* from the standpoint of the good they are indifferent. Not only is it true that virtue does not arise except

as the natural capacities are subjected to reason, but it is this act of rational judgment and choice in which *alone* virtue consists. Only the good will, the rational attitude itself in its coincidence with the universal reason, makes a man virtuous. A particular desire may be *in accordance with* nature. But it is never so essential that it may not be dispensed with; and nothing is really *good* if we can get along without it.

Such a conception is connected with an innovation which the Stoics introduce into the psychology of Plato and Aristotle. Instead of making the feelings and emotions constitute a subordinate part or function of the soul standing over against the reason, they regard them rather as a disease, an imperfection, a disturbance of the reason itself. It follows that the emotions are not something to be regulated simply and held in check by the reason; they must be utterly rooted out. As a disease, emotion is not to be tolerated for a moment; if we give it ever so slight a foothold it is bound to grow and spread contagion. The true ethical ideal, therefore, is entire freedom from the emotions. It is not a question of tempering one's passions; that is to rest satisfied with being only a *little* mad, a *little* sick. The wise man must aim at perfect health of soul; he must have no passions at all. But may we not indulge in compassion for example, pity a friend in distress? Relieve our friend, by all means; but as for pity, no. Such a thing seems harmless; but as sure as we give way to it, we shall find it gaining strength and becoming ungovernable. Pity, too, is apt to make a man bungle his work, and thus actually to defeat its own end. It is true, so at least the later Stoics had to admit, that there are certain weaknesses of the flesh — the blush that rises unbidden to the cheek, the instinctive shrinking before pain and suffering — which I may not be able wholly to control; but these are no more than affections of the body, and need not touch the mind unless the mind itself shall so permit. An emotion in the strict sense is a disturbance of the mind; and over that the mind has full control, and may give or withhold its consent.

The truly virtuous life, then, will be a life that is free and undisturbed by the emotions; and that will only be possible as we refuse to allow our will to be coerced by those external things and events which lie outside the power of the mind itself. Let us recognize that only that is evil which we choose to regard as such; if we refuse to call it evil it may, indeed, harm our body, but it cannot touch the inner self. "Consider that everything is opinion, and opinion is in thy power. Take away then, when thou choosest, thy opinion, and like a mariner who has doubled the promontory, thou wilt find calm, everything stable, and a waveless bay." "Take away thy opinion, and then there is taken away the complaint: I have been harmed. Take away the complaint: I have been harmed, and the harm is done away." Instead of striving to win this and avoid that, let us rid ourselves of the *desires* which make things attractive or dreadful. It is the good fortune of the wise man not to need any good fortune. That only is a real evil which degrades the soul from its true dignity; and that only a good which enables the soul to stand fast in its integrity. "Soon thou wilt be ashes or a skeleton, and either a name, or not a name even. And the things which are much valued in life are empty and rotten and trifling, and like little dogs biting one another, and little children quarrelling and laughing and then straightway weeping." What is pleasure, for which men fight and die? Transitory, tiresome, sickly, it scarce outlives the tasting of it. "I am seeking," says Seneca, "to find what is good for a man, not for his belly. Why, cattle and whales have larger ones than he." Are we taken with a life of luxury and outward show? "As we sit at table, let us consider that this is but the dead body of a fish, that the dead body of a bird or of a pig; and again, that this Falernian is only a little grape juice, and this purple robe some sheep's wool dyed with the blood of a shellfish." Or do we work for fame, that future generations may praise us? Let us remember that men of after times will be exactly such as those whom now we despise and cannot endure, just as foolish and unthinking, just as short-lived. Let us then stand steadfast in the faith that nothing can harm us unless we ourselves open the gate to the enemy; that nothing is necessary save those inner possessions of which no one can rob us.

Such an ideal of character — the ideal of the wise man, or the sage — stands the chance however of becoming somewhat too stern and forbidding in its nature. In the rigor of their conception the Stoics seemed to make no allowance for the frailty of human nature. As in the later Christian doctrine, a man was either wholly saved or wholly lost, perfect and complete or else with no good thing in him; just as a stick is either straight or crooked, and there is no middle alternative. The man who is a hundred furlongs from Canopus, and the man who is only one, are both equally not in Canopus. For virtues are not many, but one, since all go back to the inner unity of the will which alone is good. If therefore the will is sound, the man possesses at one stroke all possible goods and perfections; if it is weak in one point it is weak in all, for no chain is stronger than its weakest link. The Stoics speak of the sage, accordingly, in the most extravagant terms; since all goods are one, he alone is just, wise, beautiful, brave, a king, an orator, rich, a legislator. So also there is no gradual progress toward virtue. The wise man becomes wise by a sudden conversion, which in a single moment bridges the gulf between total depravity and perfection. The world thus becomes divided between two classes — the sages, a scattered few, and the vast multitude of men, mostly fools. And the tendency was strong to make this division a source of Pharisaic pride, and to transfer the contemptuous disregard in which outer things were held to the men also who took delight in these things — that is, to mankind in general.

Time tended to soften somewhat the asperity of this attitude. The ideal sage, in his perfection, was too rare a phenomenon in the world, and the failure of the average Stoic to live up to the standard thus set was too obvious to himself and to his opponents alike; and so concessions necessarily were made. It had to be allowed that, after all, there are various grades of attainment, and that one is higher than another. So too it was found impossible, without too great paradox, to hold that everything in the world outside the good will is totally indifferent. Common sense will never admit that health and fortune, because they are more or less fortuitous and can at a pinch be dispensed with, are quite on a level with disease and penury. Accordingly, along with what is absolutely good, the

Stoics were led to make a distinction between those external things which tend to promote the good life and supply it with material, and those which have the opposite tendency; and it was admitted that, although the former are not good in the proper and ultimate sense, they yet are good in a secondary way, and relatively, the term "indifferent" being now applied to the third and more limited class of things which are recognized by common sense as having no important bearing on our lives. As a matter of fact, the assertion that pleasure and pain are absolutely indifferent and on an equality is clearly only a paradoxical overstatement of certain familiar truths apart from which it would carry no conviction at all. The truth that underlies it is, of course, that pain may be endured with cheerfulness by the brave man when it is inevitable, and even welcomed when it is a step toward some higher good; that pleasure is subordinate to character, and unworthy to engross the affections and to stand in the way of better things. And while the Stoic always retains his tendency to paradox, this more moderate attitude comes to be adopted also on occasion. The desirable thing is not to have the fire burn me — that I would willingly avoid if I could — but to refuse to let the pain of burning conquer me. Even positive pleasure is not wholly to be despised in so far as it follows virtue naturally and is not aimed at on its own account — "as in a tilled field, when ploughed for corn, some flowers are found amongst it, and yet, though these may charm the eye, all this labor was not spent in order to produce them."

3. *Social Philosophy.* — There is one further way in which the Stoic conception of Nature tends to set him in opposition to the Epicurean; it gave a sanction to society and its institutions for which Epicureanism has no counterpart. As an expression of universal law, man is related to his fellows essentially and fundamentally; sooner will one find anything earthy which comes in contact with no earthy thing than a man altogether separated from other men. To be sure, as states then were constituted, the Stoic might be excused from taking an active part in politics; but theoretically he was even in his private life still working for the public weal. "The services of a good citizen are never thrown away;

he does good by being heard and seen, by his expression, his gestures, his silent determination, and his very walk." Nor is this limited, as with the ancient Greek, to one's own particular state or city. "My nature," says the Emperor Aurelius, "is rational and social, and my city and my country, so far as I am Antoninus, is Rome, but so far as I am a man, it is the world."

This cosmopolitanism, which prided itself on the sentiment, I am first of all a man — *Homo sum* — was not indeed due to any very deep-seated feeling for humanity, and it did not need to carry any great sense of human obligation. As a matter of fact it does not always enable us in practice to draw a sharp line between Stoic and Epicurean. Epicurus' theory also had led to a cosmopolitanism of a sort; and the vagueness and generality of the Stoic's conception had some tendency to move toward a disparagement of particular social duties which at times approaches the individualism of his rival. But in theory there was a wide difference; whereas for Epicurus man is a citizen of the world simply because there is nothing that ties him to other men or to any particular community or state, the Stoic finds his justification precisely in such a connecting link. The consequence was an attitude of at least nominal piety toward all reputable forms of custom and institution. The natural logic of a deterministic pantheism was in the direction of an acquiescence in those established institutional values in which the universal reason has expressed itself — a tendency which, as Stoicism degenerated in becoming popularized, comes into the open as a disposition on the part of the Stoic preacher to act as an apologist for conventional morality and religion.

In this there lay, however, a certain difficulty for the Stoic position. The law of duty as it leads a man to play his part in a world in which Reason has been incarnated, and the law of duty as a man owes it to his inner self and to the integrity of will that is alone a good, do not seem sure of coinciding. It was his perception of the hollowness of all earthly things which first set the Stoic on his search for that steadiness and immutability in which the everyday notion of the good is lacking; and if the only good for man is thus the strength of mind that can make a willing assent to the universal

Reason a sufficient substitute for all lesser claims, what possible concern can he have with the way things turn out in the world of sense? Why should I aim at this or that partial result in a world which, if I view it in one light, is already all that God meant it to be, and which in another light would still, whatever happened, remain irrelevant to the one ideal of a mind fearless and unshaken?

The Stoics met the difficulty by taking both the demands as they stand and combining them. The universe is the expression of reason and of purpose; and in the natural constitution of man, and the natural order of society, we have the prophecy at least of what for man makes up the life of reason which the will is to adopt. In consequence he will live this life, accept the duties it imposes, co-operate in the universal enterprise. But none of these things in itself is *good;* that is a term which applies only to the right direction of the will itself. Very well, then, he will not call them good or set his heart upon them; he will not permit them to arouse desire or excite emotion. He will exercise his duties as a citizen, not from any sense of patriotism, but solely because it is the right thing to do. He will assume the responsibilities of a family because it is a human function to carry on the race, not out of any affection for wife or children. He will aim to do good to his fellow man, but only from a sense of duty. In general he will perform conscientiously the tasks which God by placing him in the world imposed upon him. But at the same time he will protect his own self-sufficiency by resolutely excluding from his mind all disturbing emotions and all desire to see things turn out in this way rather than in that; the outcome he will leave to God, dissociating himself meticulously from every concern except for his own inner poise of mind.

4. *Summary.* — Taken at its best, and more particularly in the person of some of its later representatives, Stoicism offers an ideal of life seldom surpassed for noble simplicity. "I will look upon death or upon a comedy," says Seneca, "with the same expression of countenance. I will submit to labors however great they may be, supporting the strength of my body by that of my mind. I will despise riches when I have them as much as when I have them not. Whether fortune comes or goes, I will take no notice of her. I will

view all lands as though they belong to me, and my own as though they belonged to all mankind. I will so live as to remember that I was born for others, and will thank nature on this account; for in what fashion could she have done better for me? She has given me alone to all, and all to me alone. Whatever I may possess, I will neither hoard it greedily nor squander it recklessly. I will think that I have no possessions so real as those which I have given away to deserving people. I never will consider a gift to be a large one if it be bestowed upon a worthy object. I will do nothing because of public opinion, but everything because of conscience. Whenever I do anything alone by myself, I will believe that the eyes of the Roman people are upon me while I do it. In eating and drinking my object shall be to quench the desires of nature, not to fill and empty my belly. I will be agreeable with my friends, gentle and mild to my foes. I will grant pardon before I am asked for it, and will meet the wishes of honorable men halfway. I will bear in mind that the world is my native city, that its governors are the gods, and that they stand above and around me criticising whatever I do or say. When either nature demands my breath again, or reason bids me dismiss it, I will quit this life, calling all to witness that I have loved a good conscience and good pursuits, and that no one's freedom, my own least of all, has been impaired through me." So Epictetus: "My man, as the proverb says, make a desperate effort on behalf of tranquillity of mind, freedom and magnanimity. Lift up your eyes at last as released from slavery. Dare to look up to God and say: Deal with me for the future as thou wilt, I refuse nothing that pleases thee; clothe me in any dress thou choosest. Who would Hercules have been if he had sat at home? He would have been Eurystheus and not Hercules. But you are not Hercules, and you are not able to purge away the wickedness of others. Clear away your own; from yourself, from your thoughts cast away, instead of Procrustes and Sciron, sadness, fear, desire, envy, malevolence, avarice, effeminacy, intemperance." "Never value anything as profitable to thyself which shall compel thee to break thy promise, to lose thy self-respect, to hate any man, to suspect, to curse, to act the hypocrite, to desire anything which needs walls and curtains." A God dwells in the breast of every good man; let us not disgrace the abode of divinity. Virtue needs no external rewards. "As a horse when he has run, a dog when he has tracked the game, a bee when it has made the honey, so a man when he has done a good act does not call out for others to come and see, but he goes on to another act, as a vine goes on to produce again the grapes in season." The life of virtue is all-sufficient; it fills the whole soul and takes away the sensibility of any loss. What matters it if a stream be interrupted or cut off if the fountain from whence it flowed be still alive? As the stars hide their diminished heads before the brightness of the sun, so afflictions are crushed and dissipated by the greatness of virtue, and all manner of annoyances have no more effect upon her than a shower of rain upon the sea.

To attain then this integrity of soul, to be able to meet life cheerfully and confidently without fearing anything it can do to us — this alone constitutes man's good; mere pleasures seem poor and worthless in comparison. We are in the world not to live pleasantly but to quit us like men. "In the morning when thou risest unwillingly, let this thought be present: I am rising to the work of a human being. Why then am I dissatisfied, if I am going to do the things for which I exist and for which I was brought into the world? Or have I been made for this, to lie in the bedclothes and keep myself warm? But this is more pleasant. Dost thou exist, then, to take thy pleasure, and not at all for action or exertion? Dost thou not see the little plants, the little birds, the ants, the spiders, the bees, working together to put in order their several parts of the universe? and art thou unwilling to do the work of a human being, and dost thou not make haste to do that which is according to thy nature?" So likewise rank and riches have no honest value. It matters not whence we come, but whither we go. For a man to spend his life in pursuit of a title, which serves only when he dies to furnish out an epitaph, is below a wise man's business. It is the edge and temper of the blade that makes a good sword, not the richness of the scabbard; and so it is not money and possessions that make a man considerable, but his virtue. "They are amusing fellows who are proud of things which are not in our power. A man says : I am better than you, for I possess much land, and you are wasting with hunger. Another says : I am of consular rank ; another : I have curly hair. But a horse does not say to a horse : I am superior to you, for I possess much fodder and much barley, and my bits are of gold, and my harness is embroidered ; but he says : I am swifter than you. And every animal is better or worse from his own merit or his own badness. Is there then no virtue in man only, and must we look to the hair and our clothes, and to our ancestors ?" Every man is worth just as much as the things about which he busies himself. Let our riches consist in coveting nothing, and our peace in fearing nothing.

Secure in the eternal possession of himself, a man can afford to despise the buffets of fortune, and can even welcome them, in the confidence that all things are working for his good. It does not matter what you bear, but how you bear it. Outward circumstances are not our masters ; where a man can live at all he can also live well. A wise man is out of the reach of fortune, and attempts upon him are no more than Xerxes' arrows ; they may darken the day, but they cannot strike the sun. "I must die. Must I then die lamenting ? I must go into exile. Does any man then hinder me from going with smiles and cheerfulness and contentment ? Tell me the secret which you possess. I will not, for this is in my power. But I will put you in chains. Man, what are you talking about ? Me in chains ? You may fetter my leg, but my will not even Zeus himself can overpower. I will throw you into prison. My poor body, you mean. I will cut your head off. When, then, have I told you that my head alone can not be cut off ?" Not even death to the wise man is a thing to dread ; like birth and all that the seasons bring, it is but one of the things which nature wills. "For as to children masks appear terrible and fearful from inexperience, we also are affected in like manner by events for no other reason. What is death ? A tragic mask. Turn it and examine it. See, it does not bite. The poor body must be separated from the spirit either now or later, as it was separated from it before." "Pass, then, through thy little space of time conformably to nature, and end thy journey in content, just as an olive falls off when it is ripe, blessing nature who produced it, and thanking the tree on which it grew." Life itself is neither good nor evil, but only a place for good and evil. This indifference the Stoics carried to the extent even of advocating the voluntary giving up of life by suicide if occasion seemed to call for it. When life is so questionable a good, why not rid ourselves of a troublesome burden? "The house is smoky and I quit it." "The door is open; be not more timid than little children, but as they say when the thing does not please them: I will play no longer, so do you, when things seem to you of such a kind, say: I will no longer play, and be gone. But if you stay, do not complain." [1]

5. *The Problem of Evil.* — Before bringing the account of Stoicism to a close there are two problems in particular that it still remains to mention briefly — problems which the requirements of their theory led the Stoics to give a special prominence. These are the problems of evil, and of human freedom. As has been said, the Stoic accepts the teleological explanation of the universe, as against the theory of unmeaning mechanism; to him it is self-evident that the world is framed in accordance with a rational purpose. Accordingly the world must be a perfect world; and this the Stoics attempted to establish by appealing to the harmony and beauty that is present in it, and the apparent adaptation of means to end, especially in organic life. Thus the peacock is made for the sake of its beautiful tail; horses are made for riding; sheep to supply clothing for man, and dogs to guard and help him; asses to carry his burdens. Such reasoning, however, unless a severe restraint was put upon it, was clearly in danger of descending to trivialities; and at its best there still remain the difficulties raised by the numerous cases where, especially if we take human life as the end of creation, the products of nature seem quite irrelevant or else positively harmful. So the Stoics were put upon their mettle to meet these objections, and still maintain the perfection of the universe.

In doing this they succeeded in bringing out a suggestion, at

[1] Quotations from Epictetus, Marcus Aurelius and Seneca.

least, of most of the considerations by which subsequent thought
has tried to vindicate the ways of God to man. As regards physical
evils, at any rate, they had already met the difficulty consistently,
even if paradoxically, by their denial that such things are evil at all.
"Many afflictions may befall a good man, but no evil, for contraries
will never incorporate; all the rivers of the world are never able to
change the taste and quality of the ocean." Or again, if we wish to
take it on ground somewhat less high, let us remember that we only
have to live each moment at a time. It is neither the future nor
the past that pains me, but only the present. If then I do not let
my thoughts embrace at once all the troubles I may expect to befall
me, but consider each occasion by itself, I shall be ashamed to
confess that there is in it anything intolerable and past bearing.
Meanwhile there are other more positive considerations. The conception of the world as a unity enables us to explain a seeming
imperfection by its relation to the larger scheme of things into
which it enters; a partial evil becomes a universal good. "Must
my leg then be lamed? Wretch, do you then on account of one
poor leg find fault with the world? Will you not willingly surrender
it for the whole? Know you not how small a part you are compared with the whole?" "If a good man had foreknowledge of
what would happen, he would coöperate toward his own sickness
and death and mutilation, since he knows that these things are
assigned to him according to the universal arrangement, and that
the whole is superior to the part." "But how is it said that some
external things are according to nature, and others contrary to
nature? It is said as it might be said if we were separated from
society; for to the foot I shall say that it is according to nature for
it to be clean; but if you take it as a foot, and as a thing not independent, it will befit it both to step into the mud, and tread on
thorns, and sometimes to be cast off for the good of the whole body;
otherwise it is no longer a foot. We should think in some such
way about ourselves also. What are you? A man. If you consider yourself as detached from other men, it is according to nature
to live to old age, to be rich, to be healthy. But if you consider
yourself as a man, and a part of a certain whole, it is for the sake

of that whole that at one time you should be sick, at another time take a voyage and run into danger, at another time be in want, and in some cases die prematurely. Why then are you troubled? Do you not know that as a foot is no longer a foot if it is detached from the body, so you are no longer a man if you are separated from other men?"

It is true that often this does not carry us very far practically, since we are unable to put ourselves at the point of view of the whole; and so we may be forced to fall back on the blind faith that nature can do no wrong. But sometimes also, and particularly when we take moral welfare into view, we can see *how* evil may work for good. As a master gives his most hopeful scholars the hardest lessons, so does God deal with the most generous spirits. In reality no one is more unhappy than the man whom no misfortune has ever befallen. How many are there in the world that enjoy all things to their own wish, whom God never thought worthy of a trial. If it might be imagined that the Almighty should take off his thought from the care of his whole work, what more glorious spectacle could he reflect upon than a valiant man struggling with adverse fortune? Calamity is the touchstone of a brave mind that resolves to live and die master of itself. Adversity is the better for us all, for it is God's mercy to show the world their errors, and that the things they fear and covet are neither good nor evil, being the common and promiscuous lot of good men and bad.

6. *The Problem of Freedom.* — The second problem is that which had to do with freedom, or free will. The whole ethical standpoint of the Stoics presupposed an insistence on the supreme reality of duty, and on the responsibility that goes along with duty. On the other side their metaphysics made of the human agent a cog in a universal system ruled everywhere by strict necessity. Their opponents were quick to point out the apparent contradiction, and to insist that no place was left for real freedom and responsibility. A reconciliation of freedom with determinism was accordingly a matter of some importance for them; and the result was a conception of freedom which has proved to be a lasting contribution

to philosophy. So conceived, freedom acts to be sure in accordance with necessity. But this necessity is an expression of man's
nature; in yielding to it I am yielding not to an outside force,
but to the law of my own being. And is not this, indeed, the only
view of liberty that will stand examination? "But you say: I
would like to have everything result just as I like, and in whatever
way I like. You are mad, you are beside yourself. Do you not
know that freedom is a noble and valuable thing? But for me
inconsiderately to wish for things to happen as I inconsiderately
like, this appears to me not only not noble, but even most base.
For how do we proceed in the matter of writing? Do I wish to
write the name of Dion as I choose? No; but I am taught to
choose to write it as it ought to be written. And how with respect
to music? In the same manner. If it were not so it would be of
no value to know anything, if knowledge were adapted to every
man's whim. Is it then in this alone, in this which is the greatest
and the chief thing — I mean freedom — that I am permitted
to will inconsiderately? By no means, but to be instructed is this:
to learn to wish that everything may happen as it does." "We
are born subjects, but to obey God is perfect liberty."

7. *Stoicism and Christianity.* — Stoicism, it will probably have
been apparent, offers in a number of ways points of contact with the
Christian religion, and in fact it played a part in the preparation
which rendered the triumph of Christianity possible. The conception of the omnipresence of God as *pneuma* or spirit, the novel
emphasis laid upon duty as the inner law of man's nature, the ideal
of a life of self-denial easily passing into an ascetic contempt for the
things of this world, are among the points of resemblance that will
suggest themselves. But the points of difference are equally apparent. While the God of the Stoics is primarily one of impersonal intelligence and power, the God of Christianity is a God of love. The
outlines of the Stoic conception are almost uniformly hard and un-
compromising; God looks after the perfection of the whole, but this
may or may not be compatible with the happiness of individuals.
The same harshness was carried over into the relations of man to
man; more truly, perhaps, the first fact is a reflex of the second.

Theoretically the Stoics, even the milder Stoics, recommend an insensibility which is hardly human. A wise man is not affected by the loss of children or friends. "To feel pain or grief for the misfortunes of others," says Seneca, "is a weakness unworthy of the sage; for nothing should cloud his serenity or shake his firmness."

It follows that Stoicism can only appeal as a reward to the sense of satisfaction in one's mere power of endurance. Christianity on the other hand is a religion of hope and consolation; while it holds to the necessity of rejecting the solicitations of the senses, it does not make this negation an end in itself but a means to a fuller life, in another world if not in the present one. This doctrine of immortality finds no real place in Stoicism; to the Stoic immortality is only a possible hypothesis which carries no special consolation with it, and which in any case means only an extension of life and not its eternity. For even if our self-identity continues for a time after death, the final overthrow of this world of ours is bound to come; and in the universal conflagration which will then take place, all finite souls will be reabsorbed into the world soul and lose their individuality.

Finally, Stoicism is primarily an ethics and not, like Christianity, a religion. The philosopher attains virtue by his own efforts; he looks to himself for help, not to God. The wise man, so the Stoic could say, is as necessary to Zeus as Zeus to the wise man. In one way he is even superior to God; God is beyond suffering evil, while the wise man is above it. God surpasses the good man in this only, that he is longer good; the good man can excel God in the patience with which he bears the trials of his mortal lot. The result is, at its best, a respect for oneself and one's own integrity which is wholesome and heroic; at its worst, a Pharisaic pride in one's individual achievement and a contemptuous disregard for weaker men. But in any case it is a creed only for exceptional natures; while it fostered ideals which proved a saving leaven, it was too intellectual and self-centered to regenerate society. In the need that was felt for something that should appeal not to the intellect or bare will alone but to the feelings and emotions likewise, and which should take man out of himself and reinforce his weakness through some higher power, ethical philosophy was gradually to be displaced by a religious philosophy.

LITERATURE

Marcus Aurelius, *Thoughts*.
Seneca, *Dialogues, On Benefits, On Clemency, Letters*.
Epictetus, *Discourses* and *Encheiridion*.
Cicero, *Philosophical Works*.
Plutarch, *Morals*.
Capes, *Stoicism*.
Bryant, *The Mutual Influence of Christianity and the Stoic School*
Zeller, *Stoics, Epicureans and Sceptics*.
Seth, *Study of Ethical Principles*.
Matthew Arnold, *Marcus Aurelius* (in *Essays*).
Jackson, *Seneca and Kant*.
Watson, *Life of M. Aurelius*.
Bruce, *Moral Order of the World in Ancient and Modern Thought*.
Murray, *The Stoic Philosophy*.
Stock, *Stoicism*.
Arnold, *Roman Stoicism*.
Bevan, *Stoics and Sceptics*.
Davidson, *The Stoic Creed*.
Wenley, *Stoicism*.

§ 15. *The Sceptics*

1. Before turning however to this next development, it is necessary to give a brief account of the other tendencies of the period we have been considering. Of these the most important is Scepticism. The first representative of Scepticism was *Pyrrho* of Elis (365–275 B.C.), a contemporary of Aristotle. Like Zeno and Epicurus, Pyrrho brought to philosophy a practical interest and bent. But instead of attempting to find satisfaction through the medium of a dogmatic system of belief, he thought it was just in this direction that inquietude and perplexity lay. For after all that men have philosophized, what agreement have they reached on the simplest questions? Each school has its own special answer, which differs from the answer given by any other school. Let us

recognize then that much thinking is a weariness to the flesh; that speculation only involves us in doubt and uncertainty; that every question may be argued equally well on either side, so that a final decision is impossible. Let us find peace of mind by acquiescing in our enforced ignorance, and regarding as indifferent to us all external things, since we cannot possibly know the truth about them. In later days stories were current of the way in which Pyrrho exemplified his own philosophy in practice — how for example he declined to trust his senses even to the extent of turning out for a wagon or a precipice, and so had to be rescued by his friends.

Pyrrho had no very great influence on the thought of his own day; the field was not yet ready for him. But as the period of originality in speculative thinking became more distant, a new sceptical reaction grew up against the dogmatism of the dominant schools. This reaction succeeded in finding a home temporarily in the Academy itself, where it was adopted in the first place chiefly as a weapon against the Stoics. The most important names in connection with the Middle Academy, as it is called, are those of *Arcesilaus* (315–241 B.C.), and his more brilliant successor *Carneades* (215–130 B.C.). By Carneades scepticism was carried over into the realm of ethics as well; and it is related that while on a political embassy to Rome he created a great sensation by arguing very eloquently in a public discourse in behalf of justice, and then the next day speaking with equal effect against it. The Academic doctrine had however a more positive side as well. Although certainty cannot be attained, yet practical needs require that there should be something to render decision possible. This the Academics tried to give in their doctrine of probability. A thing may not be capable of proof, but it still may be more probable than its opposite; and this logic of probability is for practical needs as good as demonstration. A third tendency in Scepticism, which considered that the Academy was still too dogmatic and so professed to go back to the more thoroughgoing doctrine of Pyrrho, is found among the so-called Empiricists, who are chiefly physicians. Of these the most important are *Aenesidemus* of Cnossus and *Sextus Empiricus*.

2. The arguments of the Sceptics may be divided roughly into two classes — those empirical proofs, drawn chiefly from sensation, which show the actual uncertainty and contradictoriness of our knowledge, and the more theoretical considerations that have to do with the nature of thought or reason. These arguments have become familiar at the present day, and may be reproduced briefly as follows: [1] —

There are, first, the differences in the organization of animals, and the consequent difference in the impressions which the same object makes upon them. What is pleasant to one is disagreeable to another; what is useful to one to another is fatal. Thus young branches are eagerly eaten by the goat but are bitter to mankind; hemlock is nutritious to the quail but deadly to man. So animals differ vastly in the degree of development of their faculties. The hawk is far more keen-sighted than man, the dog has a much acuter scent. Must it not be a different world then that reveals itself to different beings? and who is to decide which is the true world?

Among men themselves there is the same variety in the ways in which things affect them. According to Demophon, the steward of Alexander used to feel warm in the shade and to shiver in the sun. Andron the Argive travelled through the deserts of Libya without once drinking. Again one man is fond of medicine, another of farming, another of commerce. How are we to set up any standard in the midst of the confusion that meets us? Everything goes back to personal tastes, and about tastes there is no disputing.

Furthermore, look at the different ways in which the same object will appear to the different senses. An apple presents itself to the sense of sight as yellow, to the taste as sweet, to the smell as fragrant. Does not this very fact that each sense modifies the report which an object sends in so as to change its character entirely show that we never get the true object at all? Conceivably there might be countless other senses, and each of these would have just as much, or just as little, title to be believed as those we possess.

And in the human constitution there are continual changes going on which affect our whole view of things. Health, sickness, sleep,

[1] Taken largely from Diogenes Laertius' life of Pyrrho, Bohn's Classical Library.

waking, joy, grief, youth, old age, courage, fear, want, abundance, hatred, friendship, warmth, cold, ease or difficulty of breathing — all determine us to the most varied and contradictory notions about the real nature of facts. What are we to take as the normal state, where things appear in their truth? And what opinion can we have of a being whose powers and faculties can be so easily upset and confounded by the most trifling cause?

Consider next the matter of custom and tradition, and the effect which habit, education and environment have in determining a man's beliefs. In the face of this, how can we suppose that there is any absolute foundation of true or false, right or wrong? In one community certain customs rule, and everybody regards them as eminently right and natural. Pass into the next country and you will find these same customs condemned as vicious and absurd. The Persians do not think it unnatural for a man to marry his daughter; but among the Greeks it is unlawful. The Cilicians delight in piracy while the Greeks avoid it. Different nations worship different Gods, and worship them by different rites. And in the same country customs are all the while changing. "We see scarcely anything just or unjust that does not change quality in changing climate. Three degrees of higher latitude overturn all jurisprudence. A meridian decides the truth. Fundamental laws change; right has its epochs. Pitiable justice, bounded by a river or a mountain! Truth this side the Pyrenees, error that side." [1]

In the object, as well as in the subject, there are causes of confusion. Nothing is seen by us simply and by itself, but in combination either with air, or with light, or with moisture, or heat, or cold, or motion, or evaporation or some other power. Sounds, for example, are different according as the air is dense or rare. Purple exhibits a different hue in the sun, in the moonlight and by lamplight. A stone which one cannot lift in the air is easily displaced in the water. It follows that we cannot know positively the peculiar qualities of anything, just as we cannot distinguish the real properties of oil in ointment.

Another frutiful cause of uncertainty is the position, distance and

[1] Pascal, *Thoughts.*

spatial relations of objects. Objects that we believe to be large sometimes appear small; those that we believe to be square sometimes appear round; those that we fancy even appear full of projections; those that we think straight seem bent; those that we think colorless appear colored. A vessel seen at a distance seems stationary. Mountains at a distance look smooth, but when beheld close at hand they are rough. The sun on account of its distance appears small; and it has one appearance at its rise, and quite another at midday. The neck of the dove changes its color as it turns. Since then it is impossible to view things irrespectively of place and position, it is clear that their real nature is not known.

In the same way qualities differ according to quantities. The horn of the goat is black; the detached fragments of this horn are whitish. A moderate quantity of wine invigorates, while an excessive quantity weakens. Certain poisons are fatal when taken alone; in mixture with other substances they cure.

The frequency or rarity of a thing determines our view of it. Earthquakes excite no wonder among those nations with whom they are of frequent occurrence; nor does the sun astonish us, because we see it every day.

Finally, we cannot say anything about an object without involving, explicitly or implicitly, a comparison or relation with other things. Thus light and heavy, strong and weak, greater and less, above and below, right and left, are obviously only relative terms. In the same way a man is spoken of as a father, or brother, or cousin in relation to some other persons; day gets its title from its relation to the sun; and everything has its distinctive name in relation to human thought. We cannot strip off these relations and have any content left; and consequently all our knowledge is relative — never of the thing in itself.

If perception is incapable of giving us truth, so equally is thought; and the difficulties in the process of syllogistic reasoning are accordingly pointed out. And if neither sensation by itself, nor thought by itself, can attain to certainty, their combination is clearly in no better case. The whole matter is summed up in the discussion about the *criterion* of truth. Every demonstration depends on the validity of certain premises, and these must themselves in turn be established if the whole process is not to hang in the air.   Consequently, unless we go on forever establishing one truth by another, we are compelled to find somewhere a starting-point that is absolutely certain in itself.   But what way have we of recognizing such a truth?   The Sceptics of course deny that there is any criterion. Sensation will not give it, for sensations have been shown to be utterly unreliable.   Shall we say, with the Stoics, that it is the clearness and self-evidence with which a truth comes home to us, or its universal acceptance by mankind?   But universal agreement does not exist, and would prove nothing if it did; and we are often very clear and very positive about what turns out to be no truth at all.   The Sceptics went on to show in detail, and with much acuteness, the flaws in the reasonings and results of the dogmatic philosophers.   The most extensive account that we possess of the sceptical arguments is in a work by Sextus Empiricus entitled *Against the Mathematicians*.   In this it is interesting to note that, among other things, the idea of causality is subjected to a destructive criticism. It is this same problem which occupied the greatest of modern sceptics — David Hume.

§ 16. *The Scientific Movement. Eclecticism. Philo*

1. Meanwhile, in another part of the world, a very considerable intellectual activity had been going on which, although it lies outside the main movement of philosophy, deserves a brief mention. In Athens, which after its loss of political importance had become practically a University town, the speculative interest continued to be predominant; but elsewhere the scientific side of Aristotle's work was being carried on with a considerable degree of success.   Alexandria, in Northern Egypt, had been founded by the conqueror in the second half of the fourth century, and under the enlightened rule of the earlier Ptolemies it sprang to a place among the centers of the world.   What its position did for it commercially, the founding of the great University of Alexandria accomplished in other lines.   To this immense school, the greatest of ancient times, students came from all over the world.   Its magnificent equipment, its botanical

garden, observatory and anatomical building, its collection of animals from every land, and its great library, amounting at one time to seven hundred thousand volumes, gave a great impetus to scholarship and science. A series of eminent scientists made the Museum illustrious : the best known are the mathematician *Euclid*, and the astronomer *Ptolemy*, who gives his name to the system which maintained itself down to the time of Copernicus, and whose *Geography* was used in the schools of Europe for fourteen centuries. So also literature was encouraged and had a considerable development. It is true that, for the most part, there was no great originality shown ; still the very dependence on the past gave rise to valuable results in the creation of a new interest in literary and linguistic studies. The history of literature, the critical investigation of problems of style, and the study of language and grammar, were put upon something like a systematic basis. In other cities too, such as Rhodes, Antioch and Tarsus, similar schools sprang up, and became centers of an active intellectual life.

2. Meanwhile in the realm of speculative thought there is one more tendency to be noted. Scepticism was too negative to satisfy any save a few ; but it was not without an indirect effect even in wider circles. The criticism which it brought against all philosophies alike would, at least, tend to prick the conceit that in any one school the absolute truth was contained. And the necessary recognition of the many points of similarity between Stoic, Academic and Peripatetic, which constant discussion brought about, also helped to lessen their opposition. Just as, in the Macedonian and Roman empires, political and racial extremes were gradually worn away, and compromises accepted to the end that all men might dwell together in a practical unity, so the teaching of the various schools began to be brought together on a common basis from which the more extreme differences had been eliminated. At least this was true of all except the Epicureans, who continued to stand out as heterodox, and to whose mechanistic and hedonistic tendencies the other schools found themselves opposed on a common ground. This eclectic tendency was in particular due to the contact of Greek philosophy with the Romans. Themselves without any strong

theoretical interests, and caring for philosophy, if they cared for it at all, mainly for its practical ends, the Romans would in general have but little sympathy with subtle metaphysical distinctions. To them the disputes of the philosophers were likely to seem trifling and uncalled for, and capable of being easily settled by a little common sense; the pro-consul Gellius actually took upon himself to urge the Athenian philosophers to come to a compromise, and offered his own services as mediator. Of this syncretistic temper *Cicero* is the most eminent representative; without any great philosophic gifts himself, his chief service is as a popularizer of Greek ideas.

3. What has been said so far of Eclecticism has had in view chiefly the philosophy of the West. The same general attitude brought about another movement which proved of considerable importance — the union, namely, of Oriental elements with the stream of European thought. It was at Alexandria that this tendency crystallized. Among the inhabitants of Alexandria there were a large number of Jewish colonists, who by their activity and abilities had made themselves a power. Among these exiles the Hellenizing tendencies which, in opposition to orthodox Judaism, had very nearly won the day even in Palestine itself, had an opportunity to work out freely. As early as the third century a translation was made of the Hebrew scriptures into the Greek of the Septuagint, and a considerable literature sprang up in which Jewish views of life are modified by contact with Western ideas; some of this is preserved among the books of the Apocrypha.

When, in the second century before Christ, the influence of the University at Alexandria waned and many of the Greek professors left the city, the Hellenistic Jewish thought became the dominant intellectual force. And in *Philo*, a Jew of great learning and ability, a systematic attempt was made, about the beginning of the Christian era, to show the inner harmony between Plato and Moses, Jewish religious thought and Greek philosophy. This attempt gave evidence of some power of original thought, and influenced the future development alike of philosophy and of Christian doctrine. According to Philo's conception God, like the monarch in the Oriental state, stands apart from the world in an ineffable perfection, and has to be connected with actual things by a series of lesser but more intelligible forms which are thought of, sometimes as Platonic ideas, sometimes from the standpoint of the Old Testament angelology. These are somehow an offshoot from God's nature without actually belonging to it as its component parts. The conception has its most important consequence in Philo's doctrine of the Logos — the mediator of God's revelation of himself. The repugnance of the Hebrew scriptures to Greek ways of thinking was overcome by having recourse to an ingenious method of allegorical interpretation.

LITERATURE

Maccoll, *The Greek Sceptics.*
Zeller, *Stoics, Epicureans and Sceptics.*
Patrick, *The Greek Sceptics.*
Bevan, *Stoics and Sceptics.*
Cicero, *Philosophical Works* (Bohn's Library).
Schürer, *History of the Jewish People,* 5 vols.
Philo, *Works* (Bohn's Library).
Drummond, *Philo-Judaeus,* 2 vols.
Mahaffy, *Greek Life and Thought.*
Mahaffy, *Silver Age of the Greek World.*
Conybeare, *Philo.*
Pfleiderer, *History of the Philosophy of Religon.*

THE RELIGIOUS PERIOD

§ 17. *Introduction*

The tendency just described was in part accountable for, in part the outgrowth of, a new direction which was imparting itself to philosophic thought, and through which philosophy was passing from an ethical to a religious or theosophic basis. Even in quarters where the influence of the Orient was not specially in evidence this religious trend may be observed. Stoicism had, in particular, attempted to act the part of a substitute for religion, and to meet the needs which the national religion had lost any real capacity for satisfying. Alongside the priest, absorbed in the ceremonial and political duties of his office, the Stoic or Cynic philosopher was generally recognized as the real spiritual guide of his time. He occupied a position similar in many respects to that of the modern clergyman. Peculiarities of dress and appearance — his cloak and long beard — marked him off from the rest of men; he was appealed to for advice in difficult moral problems; a philosopher was attached to many of the Roman families as a sort of family chaplain; he was called in along with the physician at a death-bed. The discourses which he was accustomed to deliver had a close analogy to the modern sermon, and are indeed historically related to it.

In attempting thus to meet the new needs of the age, there resulted within Stoicism itself an appreciable change of tone. In the later Stoics, such as Marcus Aurelius, Seneca and Epictetus, we have a reaction against the logical subtilties and unprofitable formalism to which the Stoic sage had become very generally addicted, and a reaffirmation of the practical nature of philosophy; and in this reaffirmation the religious side receives an emphasis it had not had before. Nature takes on more the character of a God whose sons men are, and with whom they can enter into a relationship of love and gratitude. "We can be thankful to a friend for a few acres," says Seneca, "or a little money; and yet for the freedom and command of the whole earth, and for the great benefits of our being, as life, health and reason, we look upon ourselves as under no obligation. If a man bestows upon us a house that is delicately beautified with paintings, statues, gilding and marbles, we make a mighty business of it, and yet it lies at the mercy of a puff of wind, the snuff of a candle, and a hundred other accidents to lay it in the dust. And is it nothing now to sleep under the canopy of heaven, where we have the globe of the earth as our place of repose and the glories of the heavens for our spectacle?" In like manner a more human feeling toward our fellows connects itself with the same religious motive, and the Pharisaic opposition of the sage to the fool is tempered by the recognition of the universal brotherhood of man. How shall we despise one another? Are not Alexander the Macedonian and his groom alike parts of nature, and brought to the same level by death? Or why should we be angry with our fellow-men and blame them for their injurious and evil deeds? Nature is working in them with the same necessity as in every part of her domain, and we may as well be angry that thistles do not bring forth apples or that every pebble on the ground is not an Oriental pearl. The immortal gods are not vexed because during so long a time they must tolerate men continually; and they in addition take care of them in every way. Shall you, whose life is so brief, become wearied of enduring the wicked, and that too when you yourself are one of them?

Meanwhile the demand was growing more insistent for some cure for the ills of life more thoroughgoing than the current philosophy, even at its best, was offering. The age was filled with a sense of spiritual unrest. The corruption of the ruling class, the contrasts of luxury and misery, the insecurity of life and property, the sense of world weariness which marked the passing of moral enthusiasms, brought home to men the feeling that the world was growing old and that some catastrophe was impending. A new sense of sin and evil which outgrew the ability of Stoicism to cope with it was making its appearance; while the Stoic ideal of virtue, felt by bitter experience to lie beyond the reach of unaided human effort, lost its original appeal.

This sense of sin and of human insufficiency resulted in an immense impetus to the religious life, especially on its superstitious side. Adherents of the religions of the East poured into Rome, and gained converts and wealth on every side. Their ascetic practices, their fantastic mythologies, their mysterious purificatory rites, were grasped at eagerly. In a more articulate form the same tendencies found an expression in philosophy. The attempt at a combination of Eastern and Western thought from the Oriental side by the Jew Philo has already been referred to; and the same attempt was made by Greeks as well. A point of departure was secured by going back to some of those aspects of the previous philosophy which the more recent ethical development has neglected. The earliest attempt centers about the name of Pythagoras — a name which by reason of the mythical haze that surrounded it offered a convenient handle. A Neo-Pythagoreanism arose in Alexandria as a half-religious sect with ascetic tendencies; here belongs the name of the notorious religious teacher and wonder-worker, *Apollonius* of Tyana. It was to Plato however that the thought of the time more and more turned to lend authority to its philosophical speculations. In *Plutarch* we have a position, allied to that of the Neo-Pythagoreans, which appeals thus to Plato rather than to Pythagoras, though without any great depth of insight, and with an intermixture of mysticism and magic; and in the third century A.D. this Platonic influence culminates in what was to prove the last great system of Greek thought — Neo-Platonism.

LITERATURE

Seneca, Marcus Aurelius, Epictetus.
Apuleius, *Works* (Bohn's Library).
Lucian, *Dialogues*.
Plutarch, *Morals*.
Tredwell, *Life of Apollonius of Tyana*.
Mahaffy, *Greek World under Roman Sway*.

§ 18. *Plotinus and Neo-Platonism*

Plotinus (204–269 A.D.), of Lycopolis in Egypt, came to Rome about 244, and taught philosophy there for twenty-five years. He was a disciple, at Alexandria, of *Ammonius Saccus*, who is some-times reckoned as the founder of Neo-Platonism; but the latter's fame is dwarfed by that of his greater pupil. Plotinus had also come in contact with Persian ideas through having taken part in an expedition of the Emperor Gordian against that country, in which he barely escaped with his life. In Rome his success was pro-nounced, and he included an emperor and an empress among his disciples.

1. *The Doctrine of God.* — Neo-Platonism is a religious philoso-phy which connects itself closely with the consciousness of evil and the felt need for salvation. As such it presupposes naturally a certain dualism in the ethical life; and such a dualism always finds it easy to take on a more universal form. The consciousness of a moral struggle in ourselves tends to report itself metaphysically as a division of the world into a good principle and a principle of evil; we meet this in the religion of Persia for example, where the history of the world reduces itself to a contest between Ormuzd and Ahriman, God and the devil, light and darkness.

Now according to the psychology most widely current, the natural interpretation of evil in ourselves is by referring it to the dominance of the "lower" or more obviously physical appetites, and by finding the root of evil therefore in the body — that is, in matter. This way of thinking we come across almost everywhere. In some instances, as in the semi-Christian sect of the Manichaeans, it meets us in its most extreme form; and even where there is no desire to make the dualism absolute, as in the case of the more orthodox Christian teachings and in Neo-Platonism itself, the influence still makes its presence felt. Matter is felt somehow to be evil, and the flesh always and necessarily at war against the spirit. Salvation therefore lies not in regulating our bodily desires but in exterminating them, in outgrowing the life of the senses and leaving it behind while we find our blessedness in the pure life of the spirit.

Plotinus is said by tradition to have been ashamed that he had a body; he would never name his parents, or remember his birthday. The human side of life — its feelings, emotions, everyday activities — thus loses all its worth; it is as nothing to the soul, the real self. The sensuous life is a mere stage play — all the misery in it is only imaginary, all grief a mere cheat of the players.

To connect this with the doctrine of Plato was not a difficult task. If it does not represent the whole of Plato, or even the best part of him, still there is much in his writings that lends itself to such a mode of thought; he too had disparaged the life of sense, and had appeared to find the highest good in a transcendent world. But the Neo-Platonists left Plato far behind. Reality had still been for Plato the world of Forms, and the Forms are nothing except as they have an intellectual and rational status. But there is another way in which the mind might go to work in order to arrive at ultimate reality — by dropping all distinctions and determinate differences. And in Plotinus it is this latter tendency that gets the upper hand; on such a showing God becomes the infinite blank before which all human thought is powerless.

There is one way in which the claim that God is unknowable might be interpreted that carries no offence to the ordinary religious consciousness; it might only mean that God is far beyond our perfect comprehension. We cannot with our limited thought processes exhaust the depths of his nature; his goodness is unsearchable and his ways past finding out. At the same time the knowledge which we do possess, though not exhaustive, is so far as it goes felt to be real knowledge; the relations under which we see the truth are but a small part of all the relations that would constitute it for a perfect intelligence, but they nevertheless are valid in their own degree.

The other way is to insist that in God intelligence is itself literally transcended, that in his truth he is wholly unintelligible. We attain to him not by trying to make our knowledge more complete, but by giving up any attempt at comprehension, and allowing the distinct conceptions of the intellect to fade into the haze of an immediate identity of feeling. It is this latter path which mysticism takes. To know God it is not enough to get rid of the sensuous and the bodily life; we must get rid of the intellect as well. We must separate ourselves from all things and be alone; must cut loose from every definite idea that can occupy the mind. All we can say is that God is the ultimate unity; nay, we cannot say even so much as this, for in speaking of him as unity we are predicating an idea of him, and so are limiting his absoluteness. God transcends everything that we can say or think. We cannot say so much as that he exists, for he transcends existence. He does not live, for it is he who gives life. He is not good, for he stands above goodness. He neither knows anything, nor has anything of which he is ignorant, for knowledge has no meaning in connection with his nature. We recognize him only by a blind feeling of "something real," "as those who energize enthusiastically, and become divinely inspired, perceive indeed that they have something greater in themselves, though they do not know what it is." [1] The only truth is a negative truth; to reach him we must lay aside all positive attributes.

The result is that no intellectual processes will bring us into that immediate contact with God which is salvation; the ultimate method of religion is not thought, but mystic feeling. The Neo-Platonist does not to be sure, as some mystics have done, despise the intellectual life, and attempt by a single leap to reach the consummation of an identity with God. The cultivation of the intellectual insight is an essential preliminary task; for of all things mind is nearest to the divine source, and we must pass through it on our upward progress. But there remains a step still to be taken. "The wizard king builds his tower of speculation by the hands of human workmen till he reaches the top story, and then summons his genii to fashion the battlements of adamant, and crown them with starry fire." [2] The final goal is that ecstasy in which personality and thought and consciousness are left behind, and we melt to a oneness with the Absolute into which no shade of difference enters.

2. *The Relation of God and the World.* — But here we may seem to have reached a position inconsistent with the ethical dualism from

[1] Plotinus, V, 3, 14. [2] Vaughan, *Hours with the Mystics.*

which we started. If all distinctions are unreal and the One the sole reality, we have at a stroke blotted out the entire universe of our experience as less even than a dream; and with it has gone any difference between good and bad as well. The contradiction between the two standpoints is in fact an absolute one. But since each represents a motive which the Neo-Platonist is unwilling to abandon, he is forced to attempt a reconciliation; and to this adjudication of the quarrel between the monistic aspirations of metaphysics and religion and the dualism of the ethical experience, a good share of Plotinus' effort is directed.

In a general way he does this through a device which, though not novel, was here for the first time given a significant philosophical expression. There had been a rather frequent disposition in preceding attempts at a religious philosophizing to think that the gap between God and matter can be bridged over if we introduce a graduated scale of existence, connecting the two extremes by a series of smaller differences. In the Logos doctrine of Philo, the aeons of the Christian Gnostics, the demonology of the Neo-Pythagoreans, we have such an attempt to mediate between the supreme God and those facts of the material world which are thought to be unworthy of him. Theoretically of course there is no advantage which a small gap has over a large one; the difficulty is that there should be any gap at all. Still it is a help to the imagination if the transition can be made less noticeable. And the delegation of the responsibility for imperfection to some inferior grade of reality provides a makeshift for retaining, along with these imperfections, the notion of perfection also.

In Neo-Platonism this takes the form of a theory of Emanation. Finite existence is accounted for as a progressive falling away from an original perfection. It is the very nature of the Good that out of its superabundance it should overflow, until every possibility of good and every possible kind of perfection has been realized. We should of course guard against thinking of this as a partition of the original unity, for God is no sum of parts; he is an indivisible whole who in his giving still abides with no diminution of his essence. The process may more truly be compared to the gleaming of a bright body, to the radiation of the sun, to a cup which eternally overflows because its contents are infinite and cannot be confined within it. The figure of light is the one which on the whole is least inadequate. As light shines into the darkness, and illuminates it, without at the same time suffering in its own existence, so the workings of the Eternal One overflow from its central being without thereby lessening in any degree the reality of their source. And as the brightness of the light decreases continually in intensity until it loses itself in the surrounding darkness, so the power of the Absolute expresses itself in more and more diluted form in the hierarchy of the phenomenal world. This hierarchy is represented by the three stages of mind or rational spirit, soul and body. Each stage has a dual aspect. On the one hand it looks toward, and is constituted by, the truer reality in the scale of being above; it is an *imitation* of this, as the spoken words imitate or represent the thought in the mind. On the other hand, it itself overflows to carry on its measure of perfection to the next lower stage. The material world is the lowest stage of all — an image in an image, the shadow of a shadow.

And since now every series must have its limit, in the end we come to pure matter, Not-being, wherein is no reality at all. Pure matter is not a "thing"; it is difficult indeed to know just how to talk about it. While it can only be defined as a negative limit to the real, still absolute nothingness could hardly serve even as a limit; it must have some metaphysical validity at least, or gradations of value in existence would never intrude to make trouble for the philosopher. Verbally we may say that evil is no substantial fact standing over against the good as a positive constituent of the world; just in so far as a thing *is*, as it partakes of reality, it is good, and it is evil only in so far as it is *not*. But after all it is a positive sort of nothing; why otherwise should not all reality be wholly positive, as God is, and possess no lack? In the end a dualism still remains, however attenuated it may be.

It would be impossible here to attempt to follow the involutions of Plotinus' treatment of the problem of evil; it will be enough to note that he anticipates with great detail and subtlety all theodicies since his day. Whatever standing we may decide to give to pure matter as the negative principle of evil, Plotinus does not sympathize with those contemporary religions and philosophies which regarded this existing world as evil through and through; on the contrary, he has a large interest in explaining apparent evils away in the light of their participation in reality and perfection. For *all* reality, once more, is good *in so far as* it is real; even the body is bad not in its own right but because it fills the soul with pleasures and pains, and so turns the mind from its true object to a preoccupation with particular things. It is only when we touch absolute bottom in pure matter, pure want and insufficiency, the limit that has nothing left of perfection in it, that we get a genuine principle of evil. This infects to an extent — though only to an extent — the lower stage of material existence. Soul and intellect on the other hand are not evil at all; they merely represent varying grades of perfection, each perfect in its kind, though it may not be of the highest kind.

Such a naturalistic emphasis in Plotinus gets expression in what is the first systematic attempt at a metaphysics of beauty, or theory of aesthetics; beauty is the shining through of the spiritual reality in the lower forms whose truth it constitutes. And this naturalism tempers the ascetic tendencies in his philosophy. "To despise the world, and the gods, and other beautiful natures that are contained in it, is not to become a good man. He who loves anything is delighted with everything which is allied to the object of his love; for you also love the children of the father whom you love. But every soul is the daughter of the father of the universe." "His mind must be dull and sluggish in the extreme, and incapable of being incited to anything else, who, in seeing all the beautiful objects of the sensible world, all this symmetry and great arrangement of things, and the form apparent in the stars, though so remote, is not from this view mentally agitated, and does not venerate them as admirable productions of still more admirable causes." [1]

3. *The Process of Salvation.* — Meanwhile, however we may account for it, evil as a practical problem still remains with us; and

[1] Plotinus, II, 9, 16.

the final task of philosophy is to show how we may escape it and attain salvation. Here Plotinus has a clearer path. As the phenomenal world has its being through a falling away from the Absolute, so there persists in it a longing to return to its original perfection. This return forms the substance of the ethical and religious life. We must rid ourselves of the restrictions of matter and, rising above the realm of the particular and finite, retrace our steps toward God. In general, the process consists in penetrating to the universal ideas which underlie the world of phenomena, and so accustoming the soul to its proper food. "The soul perceives temperance and justice in the intellection of herself and of that which she formerly was, and views them like statues established in herself which through time have become covered with rust. These she then purifies, just as if gold were animated and, in consequence of being incrusted with earth, not perceiving itself to be gold, should be ignorant of itself; but afterward, shaking off the earth which adheres to it, should be filled with admiration in beholding itself pure and alone." [1] This is of necessity a gradual process. The soul is like "children who, immediately torn from their parents, and for a long time nurtured at a great distance from them, become ignorant both of themselves and their parents"; it must be prepared by degrees — through the contemplation of beautiful objects, beautiful sentiments, beautiful actions, beautiful souls — for the sudden burst of light which marks the final vision. "All that tends to purify and elevate the mind will assist in this attainment, and there are three different roads by which the end may be reached. The love of beauty which exalts the poet, that devotion to the one and that ascent of science which makes the ambition of the philosopher, and that love and those prayers by which some devout and ardent soul tends in its moral purity toward perfection — these are the great highways conducting to that height above the actual and the particular where we stand in the immediate presence of the infinite, who shines out as from the deeps of the soul." [2]

In all this the soul must be ever on its guard not to remain entangled in mere particulars; herein lies the relative imperfection

[1] Plotinus, IV, 7, 10.   [2] Vaughan, *Hours with the Mystics*.

of the life of moral conduct as an ultimate end. In a good deed
there is implicit a universal value; but it is only ascetic contemplation which is able to free this ideal fact from the unessentials in
which it is immersed. As Ulysses from the magician Circe, we must
flee to our native land. The love of God means the giving up of
all earthly loves. And when one has seen God face to face he cares
for no minor beauties. As one who, entering into the interior of the
adytum, leaves behind all the statues in the temple, or as those who
enter the sanctuaries purify themselves, laying aside their garments,
and enter naked, so should the soul approach its goal. "This
therefore is the life of the gods and of divine and happy men — a
liberation from all terrene affairs, a life unaccompanied with human
pleasures, a flight of the alone to the alone." An immortality in the
ordinary sense is a denial of true life; "a resurrection with body is
a transmigration from sleep to sleep, like a man passing in the dark
from bed to bed." The true goal is only reached when the soul loses
all thought, desire and activity, all individual life, in an ecstasy of
immediate union with God. "This is the true end of the soul, to
come into contact with his light, and to behold him through it, not
by the light of another thing, but to perceive that very thing itself
through which it sees." [1]   In this "darkness which transcends all
gnostic illumination" it does not see another, but becomes one with
God, absorbed, conjoining center with center.

4. *Later Neo-Platonism.* — The spiritualization of the world in
which Neo-Platonism results opened the way for an appeal to non-
physical agencies in the explanation of events which might easily
become fantastic; and among the successors of Plotinus this is
what took place. The world becomes a great hierarchy of souls —
Gods, demons, men, — and the mystical affinities and relationships between souls, which find expression in divination, astrology
and magical rites, tend to take the place of sober investigation.
Jamblicus, the founder of Syrian Neo-Platonism, has a special
connection with this tendency.

Historically this last outcome of Greek thought gets an importance through making itself the champion of Paganism in the now

[1] Plotinus, VI, 9, 11; III, 6, 6; V, 3, 17.

losing struggle which this was carrying on with Christianity. The struggle was wholly unsuccessful. The immediate future belonged to Christianity; philosophy could hope to survive, not by antagonizing it and joining forces with its rival, but by accepting the new contribution it was making. For a moment Paganism seemed to have a chance of success when the Emperor Julian, called by Christians the Apostate — a man trained in the school of the Neo-Platonists — attempted to reverse the verdict of history. But a half-sentimental regret for the beauty of the pagan past was no match for the living forces of the present; and at the death of Julian his plans came to nothing. The last refuge of Neo-Platonism was the Academy at Athens, in connection with which the name of *Proclus* is the most important. But in 529 A.D. the Academy was closed by order of the Emperor Justinian, the teaching of heathen philosophy was forbidden, and the philosophers driven into exile.

LITERATURE

Taylor, *Select Works of Plotinus*.
Vaughan, *Hours with the Mystics*.
Whittaker, *The Neo-Platonists*.
Bigg, *Neo-Platonism*.
Guthrie, *Plotinus*.
Inge, *The Philosophy of Plotinus*, 2 vols.
Fuller, *The Problem of Evil in Plotinus*.

§ 19. *Christianity. The Church Fathers. Augustine*

1. The new power which thus seemed to have supplanted the old was, in its inception, not a philosophy but a life. Questions of theory occupied the early disciples but little. Belief in God, and the influence of the personality of Christ in renewing the life of the soul, were the central features of the new religion; the evidences of acceptance with God were the fruits of love, peace, righteousness, and not a belief in any set of doctrines.

At the start Christianity had thus no conscious dependence on philosophical thought; and among many of the early fathers, as, for example, Tertullian, there was a disposition to be openly hostile to the encroachments of philosophy as likely to corrupt the purity and simplicity of faith in the gospel. Nevertheless if Christianity was to continue to expand, its coming under the influence of Greek forms of thought was a foregone conclusion. As converts began to come in from the Gentile world, they would bring with them inevitably their former modes of thinking. Some of them, like Justin Martyr, had been philosophers before they became Christians. They had sought for truth as Stoics, and Peripatetics, and Pythagoreans; and now that they had found the goal of their seeking in the religion of Christ they could hardly fail to look at this in terms of the problems they had previously been trying to solve, and to regard it as the true philosophy as well as the true life. The need for justifying their faith to the heathen world would lead them in the same direction.

In this there was of course some danger. In many cases the theoretical interest began to overshadow the practical and moral, even sometimes to displace it. By a very considerable body of Christians, the essential thing came to be looked upon not as a Christ-like character, but as a superior and esoteric knowledge (*gnosis*), in which the Christian tinge was sometimes merely nominal. This attempt by *Gnosticism* to capture the new religion in the interest of Graeco-Oriental philosophy constituted one of the earliest and gravest dangers to the Church, which was only averted after many years of controversy. But although the Gnostics were defeated, they left their mark upon their antagonists. The Church never went back to the primitive form of undogmatic Christianity which had represented its early type. It rejected such doctrines as were inconsistent with its genius; but it began, nevertheless, to lay greater stress upon doctrinal agreement and theoretical formulation.

For this work it had almost of necessity to make use of the intellectual tools which Greek philosophy had forged. There was a more conscious use of these in some cases than in others. In Alexandria, especially, where philosophical traditions were strong, there arose a school of philosophical theologians of which *Origen* (185–254) is the most important representative. These attempted with clear insight, and very considerable ability, to Platonize theology. And even when theology supposed it was dispensing with the help of philosophy it was still dependent upon it at every step. From one point of view this involved a loss. The substitution of dogma for the free spirit of devotion went along necessarily with a certain lowering of standards and misplacement of emphasis. But the change could hardly have been avoided if Christianity was to do the work it actually succeeded in doing. As time went on the character of the Church altered. It became, of course, larger and more unwieldy; and along with those who were genuinely permeated by the spirit of the gospel there began to flock to it, attracted by its growing success, a multitude of men who were only superficially affected by their new professions. Later on it was the Church which more and more was forced to assume many of the civil functions of society in order that anarchy might be averted. Under these conditions nothing but a strong ecclesiastical organization, and a definitely formulated creed, could have held the Church together as a catholic body. The Church creed preserved Christianity on a distinctly lower level than in primitive Apostolic times; but it did preserve it. The process of creating an orthodox body of doctrine was of course no immediate result; it extended through several centuries. During this time the Church had to meet and conquer numerous heresies — tendencies, that is, which afterward were pronounced heresies by their victorious opponents, though there were moments when it seemed that they might themselves conquer and be accepted as the orthodox opinion. In the long run, however, the Church was led to avoid such dogmas as were inconsistent with the work marked out for it, and to arrive at a basis of general agreement.

2. If we compare this resultant body of doctrine with the purely philosophical development of Neo-Platonism which falls within the same general period, we shall find both resemblances and differences. Both deal with the same general problems — with God and his relation to the world, with the nature of sin or evil, and with the way of salvation. They agree, furthermore, in that for both the path to God is not through the discursive exercise of reason but through an immediate revelation. But here they separate. For

the Platonist the revelation is one that comes directly to the philosopher in those moments of ecstasy when he merges with the divine. The claims of immediacy in the form of a direct experience of God are not lacking, it is true, in Christianity; and in Christian mysticism a direct Neo-Platonist influence continues down to modern times. But circumstances compelled the Church to put its emphasis on the fact of a single *historical* revelation. In the primitive Church, where conditions were freer and the spiritual life more spontaneous, a claim to inspiration was not uncommon, and prophets and apostles were numerous. But the farther Christianity got away from its original source, the more the need for some commonly accepted standard grew evident. That standard could be nothing but conformity with the teachings of Christ and his immediate disciples. Accordingly the insistence on the authority of a definite historical revelation in the past came to be more and more the position of the orthodox body of Christians. This was mediated at first by oral tradition; and then, as time made tradition less reliable, by a gradually formed canon of sacred writings that were believed to go back to Apostles and eye-witnesses. And when now the Montanists claimed the right to do what the early Church had done and to supplement this historical message by the immediate testimony of prophetic inspiration, the attempt was recognized as dangerously lawless and condemned as a heresy.

The problem of evil also reached its orthodox solution only after controversy. In the various heretical sects nearly every current answer to the problem was reproduced, down to the baldest dualism of the good and evil principle. The temptation to find the root of evil in matter was very strong. Nowhere was the antagonism between the life of the flesh and the life of the spirit more pronounced than in the experience of Christians, or the necessity more keenly felt of mortifying the deeds of the body for the salvation of the soul. But the central fact of the Incarnation, along with a feeling for the dignity and the infinitude of God, caused the Church to reject all attempts to regard matter as essentially evil. The stronger sense of sin which characterized the Christian consciousness kept it also from being satisfied with any doctrine of evil as mere privation or absence of reality.   Christianity found a solution, instead, in the moral realm, by having recourse to the freedom of the will.   God created all finite beings good, even the devil himself. But he gave them also the power of choice; and by falling away from God they have perverted this power to evil.   Evil is thus the fault of the creature, not of the creator.   It is true that along with this there was a good deal of practical dualism.   The tendency to regard the body as naturally evil and apart from God, and the consequent impulse to the ascetic life, gained a firm foothold in the Church, and became invested with an odor of superior sanctity. But this feeling did not succeed in getting itself expressed consistently in the form of dogma; on the contrary, in the doctrine of the resurrection of the body the Church definitely cut loose from the Neo-Platonic conception of blessedness as a complete emancipation from the bodily life.

By rejecting an ultimate dualism, Christianity was left the problem of explaining the existence of the world in its distinction from the absolute nature of God; and here also its attitude is opposed to that of Neo-Platonism.   In refusing to regard the world as independently and eternally real while at the same time denying that it either is a part of God himself or an emanation from his being, the Church had recourse to the theory of the *creation* of the world out of nothing.   In this way it can be looked upon as dependent wholly on God's power, and yet as not in any sense identical with him.   This latter or pantheistic standpoint the Church consistently frowned upon, in spite of the fact that the philosophical framework of its theology, in so far as it was taken from the Greeks, was all the time drawing it in that direction.   But counteracting this logical compulsion, and counteracting it for the most part successfully, there was another factor which the influence of Christianity had much to do with raising to a position of philosophical importance — the feeling for *personality*.

In early times the individual had been largely swallowed up in the community; the tribe or state had stood before his vision as supreme, and in comparison his own rights and importance were as nothing.   The Sophists had made a start toward breaking up this unity, and the same general tendency was being repeated in the Roman world. The early Roman, in a peculiarly pronounced way, lived his whole life with reference to the State, and made the glory of his country the main goal of his labor. But while the young and vigorous Republic might seem an end to which it was worth while for a man to devote his life, an Empire, luxurious and corrupt, where the will of a single man was supreme and that man often a monster of iniquity and madness, could hardly continue to supply a rational motive and ideal. At the same time the rule of Rome appeared too inevitable for any other and worthier national life to take its place. Accordingly the individual man was thrown back upon himself, and a demand was set up for a satisfaction that should come home to him personally and singly.

The hopelessness of the outlook, however, reported itself in the prevalent severity and rigor of the ideal. In Stoicism, and in the asceticism of the religious tendencies, there is the same inability to get much positive and hopeful content into life; since man must needs suffer let him make a virtue of necessity, and take what satisfaction he can in his power to do without. Such a conception was too negative to set in motion forces that should influence powerfully the life of mankind at large; the natural desire of men in general was for a warmer and more comforting ideal. Still it did help to deepen the feeling of individuality. It called forth a sense of power and responsibility in the man who thus was bending all his energies to the crushing out of his desires and passions; and by doing this it paved the way for a more positive meaning to personality.

Such a content to the individual life Christianity brought. Here also there was conflict and repression; but it was not repression that ended with itself. Man crushed out the old self only that God might enter. The feelings no longer were starved; they were set free and stimulated. And with this appeal to his emotional life, the value of man as such was felt in a way it had not been before. The conception of God as a potentate, to be approached only through rites and ceremonies which were primarily a state affair, gave place to the thought of him as a father in direct contact with his children. And when God could reveal himself directly to his humblest creature, when he loved him and desired his salvation, then not simply humanity in the large, but each individual man, became a thing of worth. Wherever this conception really came home to men, it worked an immediate change in all the current ideals of society. The artificial barriers of rich and poor, slave and free, noble and common, became a thing of no importance. A new respect for human life grew up amid the almost incredible callousness of the Roman world. Hope and confidence took the place of despair or of a forced unconcern; the goodness of God, and the worth of the human soul, must in the end lead to happiness.

With this new sense of personality and moral agency the vague pantheism of past philosophies, and the ultimate absorption of man's life in the divine life, was no longer felt to be satisfactory. Man is a being created in the image of God, who may, as the fact of sin reveals, even set himself in opposition to the God who made him. Personal immortality, which in Greek philosophy had for the most part either been rejected outright or held with much hesitation, becomes a fundmental article of the Christian creed. The same thing determines too the way we look at God. God also must be thought of not as a vague abstraction above all definite conceptions, the conception of personality included, but as himself a person. All things flow from him, not by any fatalistic law of necessity, but in accordance with his intelligent purpose and by an act of free creation.

3. The process by which, under the influence of such ideas as these, the fluid beliefs of the early Church were gradually shaped into a highly complex dogmatic system, belongs to the history of theology; here it will be enough to say a word about the last and greatest of the Fathers to whom this shaping was due. *Augustine,* Bishop of Hippo, marks the transition between the constructive period of Christian thought, and the long period of the Middle Ages when dogma had become fixed and stereotyped. Augustine is not only one of the great thinkers of the world, but he also has a particularly interesting personality — a personality of which we know a good deal through his own *Confessions.* He was born in Africa in 354 A.D. His mother was a woman of great strength of

character, and a devoted adherent of Catholic Christianity; and it came to be her one aim in life to see her son a Christian. For many years this wish did not seem likely to be fulfilled. Augustine's youth in the corrupt city of Carthage made him familiar with a life of dissipation; and the ambition which his brilliant intellectual gifts justified turned him to secular pursuits. He became a rhetorician, and after leaving Carthage practised for a time in Rome, and then in Milan. Meanwhile he had discovered an aptitude for philosophy, and had made himself familiar to a considerable extent with philosophic thought. At an early age he was attracted by the Manichaeans and their solution of the problem of evil. But from the first he felt the crudity of their metaphysics; and while it was some time before he was ready definitely to reject their doctrines, his further intellectual development carried him continually away from them. In Milan he came under the influence of Ambrose, whose preaching made a profound impression on him. Finally, after a violent struggle against the complete self-abnegation which seemed to him to be demanded by Christianity, he passed through an experience which led him once for all to abandon his old life. Thereafter, till his death as Bishop of Hippo in 430, he devoted his time and abilities wholly to the service of the Church and Catholic Christianity.

In Augustine we find two strains of thought opposing one another. As a philosopher — and he was a philosopher before he was a theologian — he anticipates in a remarkable way the standpoint of later thought. The modern movement, beginning with Descartes, which turns away from objective knowledge to the self as a clew for interpreting reality, finds its counterpart, often very exact, in Augustine's writings. Augustine even goes beyond Descartes by the emphasis he places on the nature of the self as active will, in opposition to the intellectualism which had characterized ancient philosophy. The freedom of the will, accordingly, assumes a prominent place in his earlier thought.

But in this purely philosophical tendency Augustine was too far in advance of his age to have any immediate effect. What the times demanded was something quite different. It was, therefore, the second tendency in Augustine which became the dominant and important one, both in its influence on the Church and in his own development. For the moment the need was for authority; and this authority the Church alone was in a position to exercise. The Roman mind was naturally of the legalistic type. It tended to think of God, not as working in a world akin to him by coming home to the lives and consciences of men, but as a judge and law-giver, promulgating a definite constitution and definite enactments, and holding men to obedience under pain of punishment.

Such a forensic conception made necessary a mediator between God and man — an institution which should act as a conservator of God's interests on earth. And this need for a Church possessing a clearly defined body of doctrine and having an authoritative legal status grew all the time greater the more the weakness of the Empire became apparent. This alone could preserve men from intellectual anarchy during a period which neither produced the ability, nor offered the external opportunity, for an attainment of truth by the individual; this alone could present the objective organization and the prestige to stand up against the social con-vulsions which were impending. Both of these things appealed powerfully to Augustine himself. He also had experienced the impotency of reason, and had passed from one stage of thought to another until he had reached at one time a more or less complete Academic scepticism. The ideal of a Church which offered an infallible system of doctrine, based on authority, and satisfying his religious needs, attracted him, as it has many others since. On the other hand the outer splendor and impressiveness of the Milan Church also affected a mind by nature ambitious and eager for a career. Accordingly when, as Bishop of Hippo, he himself had reached a position of authority, we find Augustine the philosopher giving way to Augustine the theologian, and devoting all the powers of his mind to the support of the Church whose authority he was to help establish securely for future ages.

This new standpoint involved more or less collision with the old. If the Church is to be the absolute mediator between God and man the emphasis can no longer rest on the subjective side, or on the idea of man as a free will. If God reveals himself directly in the consciousness of the individual, the importance of the Church as an organization becomes secondary. The doctrine that there is salvation only within the limits of the Church is a necessity if its authority is to be maintained. Augustine is not ready to deny the principle of free will; but he limits its application in such a way as practically to transform it into determinism. The first man Adam was, indeed, free; he had the power to choose what course he pleased. But having thus saved his general principle, Augustine can go on to deny freedom elsewhere. By his apostasy from God Adam corrupted human nature, and the race lost its power of free action. Henceforth man is predetermined to sin, and cannot possibly escape from its power save by the supernatural aid of God's grace. This grace comes only through the Church, by the rite of baptism. Accordingly the Church holds the key to salvation, and no one outside its organization can hope to escape the condemnation which his guilt deserves. Meanwhile if freedom is denied to man, it is asserted all the more emphatically of God. God chooses to save certain men, and damn others, solely because he wills to do so, without reference to any merit on their part.

In the *City of God*, Augustine formulates his view of the Church in the most elaborate philosophy of history that had so far been attempted. All history is regarded as a conflict between the earthly city which belongs to the children of the world, and the City of God, the Church — a drama to end in the final victory and felicity of the saints. Already Rome had been sacked by the Goths, and its pagan glory was drawing to an end. The prophetic vision of a triumphant theocracy filled Augustine's mind, and like many another prophecy it helped to bring about its own fulfilment. It is the Church which is to be the dominant factor in the next period of human history.

LITERATURE

Donaldson, *Critical History of Christian Literature and Doctrine*.
Bigg, *Christian Platonists of Alexandria*.
Allen, *Continuity of Christian Thought*.

Mansel, *Gnostic Heresies.*
Augustine, *Confessions, City of God.*
Harnack, *History of Dogma.*
Hatch, *Hibbert Lectures.*
Fisher, *History of Christian Doctrine.*
McCabe, *St. Augustine and his Age.*

II. THE MIDDLE AGES AND THE TRAN-
SITION TO MODERN PHILOSOPHY

THE MIDDLE AGES

§ 20. *Introduction*

Not long after Augustine's death the Roman Empire fell, and
we enter upon a new era in the history of the world and of
thought. What is the general character and significance of this
period?

1. *The Greek Element.* — Our modern thought is a compound
into which three main elements enter. Its framework, the concepts or ideas which it uses, come to us largely from the Greeks.
But philosophy is not simply an exercise of intellectual comprehension. It grows out of the needs of human life, and can only get its
final justification as it succeeds in organizing this and rendering
it effective. And here the Greeks may be said to have failed. All
the Greek philosophizing could not prevent the break-up of Greek
social and political life; indeed philosophy was one of the elements
that hastened this dissolution. And the Greeks had not the
necessary political genius to enable them to work out a practical
substitute for the forms that had proved inadequate.

2. *The Roman Element.* — This lack was supplied by the Roman
element. However he might be wanting in intellectual subtilty,
the Roman was prĕeminently fitted to impress upon the world the
value and the reality of government and law. The principle of
authority ran through his life — the authority of husband over
wife, of father over son, of master over slave, of state over citizen.
And while the outcome was often harsh and forbidding in appearance, yet the rule of blood and iron was the only means of reducing
the world to at least a measure of order.

The results of this genius for organization passed over to later times, even after the Empire itself had fallen. To the Roman is largely due that external framework of society and government without which the spiritual side of civilization would be impossible. The most important form in which this inheritance was transmitted was that combination of Roman practical efficiency with Greek philosophy which took the shape of Roman law. The Stoics in particular had reached the conception of a law of nature binding on all men alike, and of a consequent cosmopolitanism which recog- nized the essential equality of all men as expressions of the univer- sal reason working throughout the universe. This conception had important results by being brought into contact with practical legislation. As the power of Rome gradually extended there grew up, alongside the civil law, the so-called *jus gentium*, which governed her relation to those who were not citizens, and which it was the policy of Rome to make broad and tolerant in its provisions, leaving local customs as much as possible unchanged. In this way there arose, alongside the ordinary Roman procedure, the idea of a more common and universal law, which under the influence of Stoic thought assumed a position of special importance. As opposed to the particular and more or less conventional enactments due to local or temporary conditions, it came to be regarded as the law of nature, binding upon all by the original constitution of man's being, and recognized by him intuitively as such. This conception had a very considerable influence in rendering possible a more rational and scientific treatment of legislation ; in particular, it gave the theoretical basis for that codification of the laws of the Empire, represented in the Justinian and in other codes, which still remains the legal groundwork of our modern life.

3. *The Christian Element.* — The work of the Romans was thus the work of embodying in actual institutions the ideas which, for the Greek philosophers, had been largely theory. But while by their political genius they thus performed a service of the greatest value for later civilization, in one essential element they were lack- ing. Roman civilization tended to overbear the individual, and so to furnish no motive power for growth and progress ; in addition

man needed to be taught his proper worth, and be given an inspiration that should set him to work. This emphasis on the development of the personal life as the only security for stability and progress in society, Christianity, potentially at least, supplied. By its appeal to the feelings it set free latent forces in man's nature, and it created a new sense of the value of the individual life by relating it to the life of all men through their common relation to God. It is true this ideal was more or less unstable. It depended too exclusively on an appeal to the emotions, which necessarily lost something of their force as time went on; there was lacking the definite intellectual grasp, and the concrete institutional forms, to direct the emotional life and give consistency and permanency to its workings. Christianity needed therefore to be supplemented by the contributions which Greece and Rome had to offer. It took many centuries for this union to become effective, and often in the meantime the characteristic spirit of Christianity seemed on the point of dying out. But its influence never was completely lost even in the darkest ages, and under more favorable conditions it was destined to contribute to modern life and thought some of their most valuable features.

4. *The German Element.* — There is still a fourth element which enters into modern life — the Teutonic. The problem of the future was to create a new and more adequate ideal of human living. Conceivably the Roman world might have had within it the power to make a fresh start and assume this task. But historically this is not what happened. The German hordes which for some time had been pressing the Empire from the north became more and more threatening the more the vigor of the restraining forces was impaired. At last the exhaustion of the Empire became too great to hold them back any longer; in successive waves they overran the provinces, and Italy itself. Rome was captured, and the conquerors set up kingdoms of their own. If civilization was to be carried on at all, it could only be by the assimilation of this new material.

In point of fact the Teutons, though barbarians, had in them the possibilities of a development higher in some ways than any that

had preceded. Their most striking characteristic was a pronounced sense of individuality and love of freedom, along with a
simplicity of character and ruggedness of moral nature that furnished admirable soil for Christianity. Before however they could
realize their destiny a long period of training was required. It was
the special work of the Middle Ages to take the raw material at its
disposal and impress upon it the ideas and institutional forms that
could be rescued from the wreck of the ancient world. The time
was again to come when a radical criticism of beliefs and institutions
was possible and necessary, but this was still a long way off; that
when it came it did not result in more violent disturbances to
society was due, along with a difference in racial characteristics,
to the thoroughness with which the Middle Ages had done their
work of education.

§ 21. *The First Period. Scotus Erigena, Anselm, Abelard*

1. *The Church and the Barbarians.* — When Rome fell, the only
institution capable of standing for law and order was the Church.
Since this was divorced largely from the political state, it would
arouse no special antagonism on the part of the victors, while its
sanctity and external lustre were calculated to excite awe in the
minds of barbarians accustomed only to the rudest life. When the
Goths sacked Rome they still respected the Church, and offered it
the privilege of asylum; and during the period which followed it
was the Church that stood as a defence against anarchy. Stretching as it did throughout the Empire, with a strong internal organization, it at once set about the task of conquering the victors —
a task which it accomplished in a surprisingly short space of time.
The Germans, separated from the local associations of their own
religion, showed a readiness to accept the cult of a higher civilization in which there was so much to impress the senses, and which
displayed such skill in adapting itself to the people with whom it
had to deal. The Church begins, accordingly, the victorious career
which was to make it, not simply the arbiter of the intellectual
beliefs of the world, but, as a vast hierarchy centering in the Pope at

Rome, a great and at times the ultimate exponent of civil authority also, able to enforce its commands upon kings and emperors.

Meanwhile the intellectual life of antiquity seemed on the point of being eclipsed. In the centuries following the fall of the Empire the literature and culture of Greece and Rome became almost as if they had never been; outside the Church there was no leisure for such things, and inside the Church little inclination. All true wisdom was given in the Church creed — all that was necessary to salvation. Heathen learning and philosophy were useless, as heathen art was vicious, and if they were not regarded as positively un-Christian and so deserving to be rooted up and destroyed, they were at least a matter of indifference. "A report has reached us," writes Gregory the Great to the Bishop of Vienne, "which we cannot mention without a blush, that thou expoundest grammar to thy friends. Whereat we are so offended and filled with scorn that our former opinion of thee is turned to mourning. The same mouth singeth not the praises of Jove and the praises of Christ." Some slight respect for intellectual culture still persisted in the monasteries; but it was elementary, and chiefly ecclesiastical in type. Previous philosophy survived for the most part only as it filtered through the writings of the Fathers, who frequently were hostile to it. Of the works of Plato and Aristotle only the merest fraction was known, and this through translation and commentary.

2. *Scholasticism.* — When accordingly, about 900 A.D., a somewhat greater activity shows itself in the life of thought, this new intellectual interest takes a particular direction. Scholasticism has two main characteristics. It is, in the first place, a philosophy of dogmatic religion, assuming a certain subject-matter as absolute and unquestioned. The Church could not consistently allow freedom in the search for truth, since she herself already possessed the truth by an infallible revelation; the limits within which thought could move were necessarily strictly defined. Meanwhile a certain work was left for the intellect which was not obviously dangerous. This was the work of showing that the doctrinal content is also self-consistent and rational. Granting that dogma is to be taken as established, it yet might seem a pious task to show how,

when given, it is acceptable to the reason and capable of being justified by it. There was indeed danger in this, as the Church was later on to discover — the danger that the rational justification should become a requirement, and the dogma be measured by its standard and derive authority from it. But meanwhile to oppose the tendency would have been to oppose all intellectual life whatever, and this not even the Church would have been powerful enough to do successfully.

The most prominent characteristic of Scholasticism, then, is its function as a systematizer and rationalizer of religious dogma. And in connection with this there was another circumstance that largely determined its peculiar character. This was the barrenness of the material with which it had to work. The very considerable sum of concrete knowledge about the world which antiquity had collected had dropped out of existence for the Middle Ages. Instead of being able therefore to utilize the fruits of a rich human experience, the Schoolmen were compelled to deal very largely with abstractions. All they could do was to draw fine distinctions and work out logical implications from the most general statements about the world. And while to this task they often brought a surprising ability and acuteness, the lack of a worthy subject-matter was bound to vitiate their efforts and give to their speculations that air of unreality and triviality which strikes the modern mind so forcibly. "Surely," says Bacon — who to be sure is not a very sympathetic or impartial critic — "like as many substances in nature which are solid do putrify and corrupt into worms, so it is the property of good and sound knowledge to putrify and dissolve into a number of subtile, idle, unwholesome, and as I may term them, vermiculate questions, which have indeed a kind of quickness and life of spirit, but no soundness of matter or goodness of quality. This kind of degenerate learning did chiefly reign among the schoolmen, who, having sharp and strong wits and abundance of leisure, and small variety of reading, but their wits being shut up in the cells of a few authors, chiefly Aristotle their dictator, as their persons were shut up in the cells of monasteries and colleges; and knowing little history, either of nature or time, did out of no great quantity of matter, and infinite agitation of wit, spin out unto us those laborious webs of learning which are extant in their books. For the wit and mind of man, if it work upon matter, which is the contemplation of the creatures of God, worketh according to the stuff and is limited thereby; but if it work upon itself, as the spider worketh its web, then it is endless, and brings forth indeed cobwebs of learning, admirable for the fineness of thread and work, but of no substance or profit."

3. *Erigena. Realism and Nominalism.* — The first period of the scholastic philosophy may be taken as extending to about the twelfth century, and it is marked by a comparative degree of speculative freedom. After the long night of the intellect, men rediscovered the delights of reason with a feverish joy. The most trivial logical questions had the power of rousing an unbounded enthusiasm. And the naïve confidence in the accord of reason with dogma — a confidence which could not be shaken until experience had shown something of the direction in which reason was to lead — made possible a less guarded attitude than afterward could be allowed. It is true that in the case of the first great philosopher of the Middle Ages, *John Scotus Erigena* (about 810–880), the Church was already inclined to be on its guard. Nevertheless we find in not a few instances a frankness and boldness in the expression of entirely rationalistic opinions which indicates the absence of anything like the more effective censorship and control of a later period.

In general, the determining influence upon this period of philosophy was Plato. It was Plato, however, not at first hand, but through the medium of Neo-Platonism. Erigena was a native of Ireland, a country in which the best learning of the day had taken refuge; his scholarship was varied and profound for his time, and he possessed the unusual accomplishment of a knowledge of Greek. He was, therefore, fitted to bring about that first infusion of ancient thought which was to be repeated on a larger scale at each new step of advance down to the times of the Renaissance.

It was Erigena's revival of the transcendental standpoint of Neo-Platonism, with its graded hierarchy of existence, which was largely influential in shaping the course of what, as opposed to the more purely theological problems dealing with the interpretation of dogma, was to constitute the great philosophical problem of the Middle Ages.   This is the question as to the reality of universals — a question that goes back to Plato.   It divided the thinkers of the Middle Ages into three great schools — the Realists, the Nominalists, and those who tried to mediate between the two.   The Realists, who are represented by Erigena, take their stand with Plato, and declare that class terms are real — more real than individual things.   The more general a term is, the more reality it possesses; man is more real than particular men, the circle than particular circles.   The Nominalists, on the other hand, taking up the cause of common sense, denied that the concept, or class, has an existence of its own beyond the individuals which make up the class; it is these individuals that alone are real.   For extreme Nominalism, of which *Roscellinus* is one of the earliest representatives, the concept is absolutely nothing but a common name which can be applied to a number of particular things.

In ringing the changes upon this problem a good share of the philosophical energies of the Middle Ages is expended.   So far as the net result is concerned it is for us not very large.   The problem had been treated by the Greek philosophers with far more concrete knowledge and genuine insight; the Scholastics hardly did more than add some logical detail, and an elaborate philosophical terminology which has not proved an unmixed blessing.   There is however a significance which the controversy possesses apart from the questions of metaphysics that are directly involved.   It represents one aspect of the fundamental struggle between the dominant mode of thought of the Middle Ages, and the beginnings of the modern scientific and individualistic spirit which was to undermine the power of the Church and create a new civilization.

It was natural that the Church should be realistic.   The graded system of reality which absorbed the part in the whole, the less general in the more general, was a counterpart, in the intellectual world, of the hierarchy of the Roman ecclesiastical system, at the top of which the Pope stood supreme as the representative of the Church universal.   To admit that the individual alone is real, and not the class, would have been to deny that solidarity of the human race on which the whole Church doctrine of sin and redemption was based; it would have been to admit that particular persons and particular churches have reality while the one Holy Catholic Church is a mere name, and so that the mediation of the Church is unnecessary in religion.

Furthermore if Nominalism were true, and particular things alone were real, then consistently men's attention ought to be directed to such things, and secular and scientific interests, rather than religious and ecclesiastical ones, should hold the foremost place. Nominalism was the natural ally of the scientific spirit, even if this was not consciously present in the minds of the earlier Nominalists; and science is incompatible with an exclusive interest in personal salvation such as the Church endeavored to foster, and on the existence of which its authority rested. When it was worked out, moreover, Nominalism was bound to conflict with the whole principle of dogmatism. A dogma is a past generalization which is divorced from the correcting influence of new facts and taken as necessarily and absolutely true. With such traditional generalizations the Church was identified; it stood for authority rather than investigation — the authority of other people's experience in the past. To center attention on the particular facts out of which generalizations grow, and to maintain the superior validity of these facts, was to substitute the principle of private judgment.

In its earlier history Nominalism was not aware of all its implications. In taking its stand upon the common-sense denial that class terms have an objective existence apart from things, it supposed itself to be entirely orthodox; indeed it was able to retort the cry of heresy against its rival. Without doubt the logical tendency of Realism was in the direction of pantheism. If individuals exist only as members of the class and not in their own right, then the highest concept, God, is the sole reality, in whom alone all lesser facts — the world and man — have being. "God is everything that truly is," says Erigena; and again, "This is the end of all things visible and invisible, when all visible things pass into intellectual, and the intellectual into God, by a marvellous and unspeakable union." It is true that he adds, "yet not by any confusion or distinction of essences or substances"; but it is a question what he can really mean by this. In spite of the risk, however, the Church remained realistic. The need was still for a unifying force in opposition to disintegrating tendencies such as were present in feudalism for example. Realism alone supplied a theoretical basis for this, and Nominalism had accordingly to wait for a more favorable opportunity.

4. *Anselm.* — The typical exponent of Realism in the first period of the Middle Ages is *Anselm*. Born in Aosta in 1033, he was attracted to the famous monastery of Bec, in Normandy, by the name of Lanfranc, whom he afterward succeeded as Abbot. Later he was again made Lanfranc's successor as Archbishop of Canterbury under William the Red; and in this office, after a career marked by a number of vicissitudes which his conscientiousness and uprightness occasioned, he died in 1109. Anselm combines in a remarkable way a strong speculative bent with genuine piety, an unflinching acceptance of the orthodox creed, and a confidence that reason and revelation will lead to the same goal. With Anselm there is no question of doubting the doctrines of the Church; faith must always precede knowledge. In the last resort we do not reason in order that we may believe. We believe in order that we may know; the unbeliever who does not first perceive the truth by faith can no more arrive at an understanding of the truth than the blind man who does not see the light can understand the light. Our duty is therefore to accept the teachings of the Church in all sincerity and humility, and strive to comprehend them. If we succeed, we may thank God; if we do not, let us simply end our search and submit to God's will, instead of denying the dogma and allowing our reason to stray outside the limits which it sets.

Anselm is himself however fully convinced that the attempt will be successful. In the endeavor to make the objects of faith intelligible to reason he examines the fundamental doctrines of the Church, particularly the doctrines of the Trinity and the Atonement, in a way that deeply influenced subsequent theology. On the more distinctively philosophical side he is now remembered chiefly for his attempts to prove the existence of God. He threw himself into this problem with an intensity of earnestness which often made him go without food and sleep. The most characteristic result of his meditations was the famous ontological argument — an argument which has appealed to some of the greatest thinkers since Anselm's day, and which still retains an influence and a fascination. The argument is substantially as follows: We define God as a being than which nothing greater can be thought. Now there is in the mind the idea of such a being. But also such a being must exist outside the mind; if it did not, it would fail to be a being than which nothing greater can be thought, since a being with the added attribute of existence is greater than one merely in idea. Therefore God exists not merely in the mind, but also as a real existence outside the mind. The obvious criticism was seen by a contemporary of Anselm, a monk named Gaunilo; he points out that it bases itself solely upon the *idea* of perfection and the *idea* of existence, and does not prove anything whatever about an objective reality corresponding to these ideas of ours. To a convinced realist however, who starts from the superior reality of universals, the objection would probably not appear well founded.

5. *The Growth of Rationalism. Abelard and Conceptualism.* — The tendencies which in Anselm had been held in equilibrium could not, however, be expected to continue always to exist together in entire harmony. The rational and logical spirit, grown by exercise, was bound to show a disposition to break loose from its connection with theology and to set up on its own account. As against the ideal of a unified intellectual life in which reason acts as the obedient handmaid of the Church, three somewhat specialized attitudes can be distinguished in the thought of the day. On the one hand stood the theologians proper, who fell back upon authority and aimed simply to set forth the dogmas as they had been handed down from the Fathers. More or less in competition with this there was the growing interest in dialectical and logical skill for its own sake, apart from the service which it rendered to theology. Meanwhile a third attitude also was assuming some importance. Dissatisfied alike with the formalism of the theologians and with the abstract

rationalism of the philosophers, the more religious natures here and there, reverting to a tendency which had come down from the Neo-Platonists, found refuge in mysticism. This movement connects itself in particular with the abbey of St. Victor. Besides *Hugo of St. Victor* (1096-1140), and his followers *Richard* and *Walter, St. Bernard of Clairvaux* (1091-1153) may be mentioned as its best-known representative, though from a standpoint less philosophically grounded. By its cultivation of freedom and spontaneity in the religious life, mysticism had a part to play among the influences which later were to bring the Middle Ages to a close.

For the present, however, the growing rationalistic spirit was of special significance. This has its most remarkable representative in the famous *Abelard* (1079-1142). Abelard was the possessor of a typically French intellect — keen, clear cut, impatient of mysticism and obscurity; and his striking talents early gave promise of a brilliant career. He became a pupil of *William of Champeaux*, in Paris, but soon came into collision with his teacher, and defeated him so signally in argument that William's popularity waned and Abelard was the hero of the day. At the age of twenty-two he had opened a school of his own at Melun, and both here, and later on in Paris, was extraordinarily successful as a teacher. William was an extreme Realist, and in opposition to him Abelard took an intermediate position. Traditionally he has been regarded as the founder of Conceptualism; and while there is some doubt about his real teaching, it would seem to have approached at any rate to this position. Conceptualism is substantially identical with the more commonly received opinion about the nature of universal terms at the present day. The class term has no objective existence as such; it exists only as a thought, a concept in our minds. But neither is it a mere breath or word. There at least exists in the particular things a similarity or identity of qualities, through whose abstraction by a mental act the concept is formed; and to this extent it is objectively valid. Conceptualism in this sense was taken account of in the more moderate realism which later, in St. Thomas Aquinas, came to be the orthodox doctrine. It is granted that only in the mind does the universal appear in its full potentiality; but it exists implicitly as an essence in things themselves, and outside the mind it has an explicit existence also as an idea in the mind of God.

The clearness and independence of Abelard's mind showed itself in other fields as well. He brought the same rationalistic temper to subjects more directly connected with the dogmas of the Church. With rather surprising frankness he condemns the credulity which is willing to take beliefs on trust without a rational justification. "A doctrine is not believed," he declares, "because God has said it, but because we are convinced by reason that it is so." Doubt is no sin, as the Church had held; "by doubting we are led to inquire, and by inquiry we perceive the truth." He confesses to an admiration for the ancient philosophers, and finds expressed in them the essential doctrines of religion and morality; "Shall we people hell," he writes, "with men whose life and teachings are truly evangelical and apostolic in their perfection, and differ in nothing, or very little, from the Christian religion?" The attempt is made to establish a theory of ethics independent of dogmatic sanctions. Christianity itself Abelard regards as, fundamentally, the rehabilitation of the natural moral law which was revealed to the Greek sages also; that which in Christianity is mysterious and not open to rational interpretation he was inclined to minimize. This naturalistic tone appears in his treatment of the particular dogmas; the three persons of the Trinity, for example, are resolved into three attributes of God — power, wisdom and goodness — united in a single personality.

§ 22. *The Second Period. The Revival of Aristotle. Thomas Aquinas, Duns Scotus, William of Occam*

1. *Arabian Philosophy. The Crusades.* — Abelard's views were condemned by the Church; but this did not prevent the spread of the rationalistic and independent spirit. For a time it almost looked as if the Renaissance might be anticipated by several centuries. One factor in this was the influence of Arabian thought. While Europe had been asleep, learning had taken refuge among the Mohammedans. The works of Greek philosophy,

especially Aristotle's, were preserved and studied when they were known to Christian scholars only in the most fragmentary form. In the courts of the Eastern caliphs, and in the kingdom of the Moors in Spain, there came about a brief period of culture in which a considerable scientific activity went along with a vigorous, though not very original, philosophical revival. The most important name among the Arabian commentators and philosophers who influenced the later Scholasticism is that of *Averroës* (1126–1198).

The reception of this influence was made easier by a change which was beginning to come over the spirit of the age, and which was furthered in particular by the Crusades. These great religious wars had turned out quite otherwise than their promoters had anticipated. The religious results, from the standpoint of Catholicism, were almost nothing, while there were other consequences entirely opposed to the Church's desire. The men of Europe had their dormant wits effectually shaken by contact with other peoples, and by the novel experiences which their wanderings brought them. Christendom found to its surprise that those whom it had been accustomed to look upon with contempt as heretics were in reality a brave and warlike people, with many virtues of their own, and a civilization in some respects superior to that of Europe. Contact with them inevitably rubbed off to some extent the provincialism on which the hold of the Church depended in a measure; and the feeling of respect which the field of battle engendered facilitated an exchange of ideas. So also two other tendencies which were to weaken the power of the Church received a stimulus from the Crusades. The rivalry resulting from the coming together of men from every country in Europe brought to the surface a new sense of national spirit which was opposed to the pretensions of the Church. Furthermore, commercial activity was given an impetus owing to the necessity of transporting and provisioning the large armies of the Crusaders, as well as to the closer communication brought about between the East and the West, and the revelation of new luxuries and new wants. Both of these things tended to accentuate the new secular spirit as opposed to the religious.

Many of the conditions, accordingly, seemed to be favorable to a breaking away from the authority of the Church; and indeed on a small scale some of the features of the Renaissance were actually anticipated. The widespread interest in learning is shown in the rise of the great Universities, while in the court of Frederick the Second, more especially, a new culture was introduced which was as thoroughly pagan as that which characterized the Italian cities in the fifteenth and sixteenth centuries. To Frederick all religion was alike untrue, Mohammed and Christ alike imposters. But the movement was premature; it had no sufficient knowledge to back it, and the hold of the Church was still too great to be broken. The new forces were turned safely into ecclesiastical channels, and spent themselves in infusing fresh life into Scholasticism rather than in breaking away from it. The Church philosophy got possession of the Universities, where it remained intrenched even after a different spirit had come over the outer world; and the awakening was postponed for several centuries.

2. *The Revival of Aristotle. Aquinas.* — In turning the new tendencies to her own account the Church showed her usual astuteness. One chief incentive to the threatened revolution in the intellectual world was due to the opening for the first time to Europe of a knowledge of the real Aristotle, and the coming of its scholars into contact with a mind of the first order whose thinking was not specifically theological. It is the influence of Aristotle which is the dominant factor in the whole of the following period. At first the Church had been alarmed at the evident dangers involved in the situation, and it had tried to avert them by condemning Aristotle. But as the Greek text came to be known, and the pantheistic tinge which Aristotle had taken from his Arabian commentators was found not to be necessary to his interpretation, the attitude of the Church was altered. She began to realize that she had in Aristotle a possible instrument for her own ends. And so effectively did she use this that when, later on, the emancipation of the intellect was brought about, Aristotle instead of being the agent of that emancipation was the one chief obstacle against which the new spirit had to make war. By setting up the dictatorship of

Aristotle, the Church had set bounds to the intellect more effectually than she had ever been able to do by means of dogma. There had been no recognized authority in the realm of pure reason in the earlier Middle Ages, and accordingly, within the limits of certain dogmatic results, the reason had had free play. By establishing now the supreme authority of Aristotle in every sphere to which reasoning applies, and by interpreting Aristotle in her own way, a tool was at hand for holding the reason in check without at the same time denying it its rights. Even in matters of science the question was, not what does nature reveal, but what does Aristotle say; and when science began to emerge, the authority of the philosopher was actively used to check its growth. "My son," so according to an anecdote was the reply made to one who thought he had discovered spots on the sun, "I have read Aristotle many times, and I assure you that there is nothing of the kind mentioned by him. Be certain therefore that the spots which you have seen are in your eyes and not in the sun."

Following the work of such men as *Alexander of Hales*, *St. Bonaventure* and *Albert the Great*, the formulation of Scholasticism in Aristotelian terms was given its final shape at the hands of *St. Thomas Aquinas*, the Angelic Doctor (1225-1274), a pupil of Albert's, and one of the most comprehensive minds in the history of thought. Here by means of the Aristotelian concepts of matter and form, all existence is arranged in a hierarchical system in which the lower is subordinated to the higher — body to soul, matter to spirit, philosophy to theology, the secular power to the ecclesiastical — with a thoroughness and acuteness which left a lasting impression, and which settled what was practically to be the official philosophy of the Catholic Church. It is in Aquinas that the formula was at last attained which was to be accepted by the Church as the final statement of the relation that exists between philosophy and revelation, reason and faith. The naïve confidence in the ability of reason to justify the full content of religious belief had not been supported by experience. It came to be recognized that there are heights to which reason cannot possibly reach. The loftier truths of revelation belong to a sphere where reason is incompetent to decide; they are mysteries, to be accepted only on the ground of a faith in authority. But while the fields of reason and of faith are thus not coextensive, and while therefore philosophy cannot hope to make theology fully intelligible to the limited powers of the human mind, there need not for all that be any actual contradiction between the two. So far as it goes, reason is harmonious with faith; but there comes a point where it no longer is able to pass judgment, and here faith steps in as a more ultimate principle, which stands to the natural powers of the mind as their final consummation.

3. *Religion and Reason. The Revival of Nominalism.* — In the system of Aquinas the scholastic philosophy reached its culminating point; from this time on the interest centers in the emergence of those tendencies which finally were to undermine it, and introduce the modern period. It will be sufficient here to point out certain factors in this evolution.

The distinction which had now been clearly drawn between natural and revealed religion, reason and theology, was not of a nature to stop within the limits to which Aquinas had attempted to confine it. The notion of revelation as something above reason furnished a basis for a separation between the two realms which grew continually more pronounced. In accordance with this distinction religion comes to be taken as having a special organ — faith — with regard to which reason has nothing to say. In one form or other this has been a widely influential attitude down to the present day. To the man of religious interests who wishes to be undisturbed in his cherished beliefs, and who chafes at the violence which often seems to be done, not to these simply but to his reason likewise, by the attempt to bring the two together, it may seem a welcome relief to give up the whole endeavor to harmonize his knowledge with his faith, and be able to deny to reason the right to interfere in the separate province of religion. At the same time he gains for reason a free play in its own proper field, unchecked by the irritating feeling that it must continually be squared with some preconceived result. To-day, for example, it is common to find men securing for themselves the right to follow the leadings of science and still to retain the religious beliefs upon which science seems to cast doubt, by adopting the principle of a division of labor, according to which reason is to be allowed its validity, but only in the lower region of empirical phenomena. Even if it comes therefore to an apparent contradiction between scientific and religious truth, this contradiction means nothing; science does not pretend to absolute truth, and may still remain practically valid even if it does not square with truth in its final and transcendent form.

The intent of this is to save religion; but it is easy to see that the same attitude may just as well be adopted from a different motive. Especially in an age when religious authority is strong and requires evasion if thought is to have free scope, it may be seized upon as a pretext by men who have no concern for religion, and only want a chance to rationalize the universe. If revelation and reason are distinct, there can be no harm in pushing the conclusions of reason to any result, however extreme, since religion is not prejudiced thereby. This attitude found expression in the famous doctrine of the "twofold truth" — the doctrine, namely, that a thing might be true according to reason which was not true theologically, and *vice versa*. In the case of many who adopted this point of view in practice, there was no intention of undermining religion or the Church. Nevertheless the tendency was due at bottom to a demand for the emancipation of the reason from Church trammels, and this in the end was bound to weaken her authority. Aquinas' contention that certain doctrines are beyond discovery by the unassisted reason was gradually widened. The doctrines which natural theology, or rational thought, could attain to and defend successfully decreased in number, until, in William of Occam, even the arguments for the existence of God were held to be insufficient.

But when it has reached this point philosophy is no longer in any positive way a minister to theology as it had started out by being. It has become a mere critical inquiry into the nature of reason which ends in discrediting the capacity of knowledge for reaching ultimate truth, or for dealing with anything except the phenomenal world. This is, in one aspect, the meaning of a controversy which forms one of the central points about which the thought of the later Middle Ages turns — the question as to the primacy of the intellect or of the will. The Thomists, or followers of Aquinas, maintained the ancient doctrine that intellect is original and supreme, and that God's will is determined by his knowledge. Their opponents, who are represented by the Franciscans, *Duns Scotus* and *William of Occam* — Thomas was a Dominican, and a rivalry between the two orders intensified the philosophical rivalry — maintained, on the contrary, that if God's will is limited by an eternal truth then there is something above God which determines him. Accordingly God must be conceived as an absolutely free will; and therefore truth and falsehood, right and wrong, are nothing in themselves, but are established by God's voluntary act. On the practical side this means that religion is no longer identified with a reasoned statement of truth, but is a disposition of will, a moral life, which obeys the law of duty imposed on it by God's authority. If truth rests on the inscrutable will of God, it must of necessity be unknowable by the natural reason.

The only sphere which is left to reason is, accordingly, the lower or natural world which does not come in contact with the realm of ultimate reality. But when it has thus been forced to become purely naturalistic, reason is ready for a further step. Men cannot continue indefinitely to hold to truth which not only has no rational ground, but which actually is contradicted by all that human beings mean by reason. That which has reason on its side cannot fail in the long run to get an advantage; the subjects with which it deals are going to gain constantly in interest and in consequent reality. And if it has been admitted that reason confines us to the natural world from which all supersensible realities are excluded, then inevitably the conclusion will in time be drawn that this world is the only true one, and that supersensible realities do not exist. The supersensible world may still be handed over to theology to do with as it pleases, and there may be no open break so long as theology does not attempt to compete with scientific explanations; this, for instance, is Bacon's attitude later on. But to all intents and purposes theology has been dispossessed of all real rights. The tendency, therefore, of the doctrine of twofold truth was to confine philosophy to the physical world, and so to prepare the ground for science as the highest truth which we are capable of knowing.

The same tendency shows itself in the revival of Nominalism. The older Nominalism had failed because the age was still in need of the unifying authority of the Church, and Realism had been the philosophical justification of this authority. Aquinas was a Realist, although not of the more extreme type; and so also was Duns Scotus. But in William of Occam the nominalistic tendency becomes once more explicit. Individual things are the only realities; concepts have no existence *extra mentem*. Interpreted, this means that the period of authority is passing. Nominalism, by its insistence on the reality of particular things, justified the growing scientific spirit in its attention to facts rather than to dogmas. It justified the revolt of individuals against the ready-made generalizations of the past, and of nations against the absolutism of the Catholic Church. It was no longer therefore opposed to the needs of the age, but was in line with what was soon to become a dominant tendency.

4. *The Beginnings of Science.* — By itself the purely logical movement within Scholasticism would have had no great result; it needed to be reënforced by the concrete growth of knowledge. During the Middle Ages this was rendered impossible in any considerable degree. Some interest in science had been aroused through contact with the Mohammedans and an acquaintance with the works of Aristotle. But it was not encouraged either by the Church or by public opinion. The Church felt more or less clearly that the growth of knowledge was a menace to its own position; while to the popular mind too close a familiarity with the works of nature was supposed to argue an unholy connection with the powers of evil. Even the office of Pope did not prevent the possessor of unusual scientific knowledge from being looked on with suspicion, while a less influential man, like the monk *Roger Bacon* (1214–1294), was compelled to pay the full penalty for being in advance of his age. Bacon saw the problems of science with remarkable clearness, and his *Opus Majus* is a monument of industry. But as a result he only gained the popular name of being

a wizard and magician, while by the Church his work was condemned and he himself confined for many years as a prisoner in his cell. In spite of everything, however, the scientific spirit persisted and grew in strength; and when at last the conditions were ripe it suddenly attained a development which has been the means of determining the whole course of modern thought.

LITERATURE

Poole, *Illustrations of Thought in the Middle Ages.*
Adams, *Civilization in the Middle Ages.*
Duruy, *History of the Middle Ages.*
Emerton, *Medieval Europe.*
Townsend, *The Great Schoolmen of the Middle Ages.*
West, *Alcuin.*
Church, *St Anselm.*
Storrs, *Bernard of Clairvaux.*
Compayré, *Abelard.*
Laurie, *The Rise and Early Constitution of Universities.*
Vaughan, *Hours with the Mystics.*
Rashdall, *Universities of Europe in the Middle Ages,* 2 vols.
Deane, Translation of Anselm's *Proslogium, Monologium, Cur Deus Homo.*
De Wulf, *History of Medieval Philosophy,* 2 vols.
Lecky, *History of the Rise of Rationalism in Europe.*
Rickaby, Translation of Aquinas' *Summa Theologiae.*
Gardner, *John the Scot.*
McCabe, *Abelard.*
Vaughan, *St. Thomas of Aquin.*
Taylor, *The Medieval Mind.*
Thompson, *History of the Middle Ages.*
Gibson, *Philosophy of St. Thomas Aquinas.*
De Wulf, *Philosophy and Civilization in the Middle Ages.*
McKeon, *Selections from Medieval Philosophers.*
Grabmann, *Thomas Aquinas.*

TRANSITION TO MODERN PHILOSOPHY

§ 23. *The Renaissance. Bruno*

1. *The Renaissance and the Reformation.* — The necessary conditions for the introduction of the modern period were brought about by the great movement which, from its various aspects, is called the Renaissance, or the Revival of Learning, or the Reformation. It has already been seen that the influences bringing this about had been at work at least as early as the Crusades. From that time on society was gradually becoming transformed away from the ecclesiastical and toward the secular ideal. The growth of commerce and industry necessarily gave an emphasis to secular interests. The new social class which in consequence rose to importance alongside the nobles and the clergy tended to ally itself with the king in his struggles with the feudal lords, since only through a strong central authority could trade and industry be protected; and this joined with other influences in building up a new national spirit. Nations began with growing success to break away from ecclesiastical control, and to separate the civil power from the spiritual. Here the Nominalism of the later Scholastics threw in its lot with the new tendency, and we find Occam openly on the side of national authority in its conflicts with the Pope.

It was in Italy that the Renaissance first became an accomplished fact. Here the greater commercial activity, and the intense rivalry between the different cities, had been coincident with the rise of an aggressive and relatively unmoral individualism. As early as the fourteenth century the main features of the literary renaissance appear in Petrarch and Boccaccio. But it is from the year 1453 that the Renaissance is commonly dated. In that year Constantinople, the capital of the Eastern Empire, which had continued up to this time to maintain an ignoble existence, was taken by the

Turks. Many of the Greek scholars, driven from their country, took refuge in Italy. Here they found the soil prepared for them, and the result was immediate and revolutionary. The revelation of the real spirit of classical antiquity to men beginning to feel the possession of new powers of life and capacities of appreciation, and heartily sick of the dry and tasteless theological nourishment with which they had had to satisfy themselves, overturned all their old ideas. The shackles of the Church fell from their minds, and they turned back to the past with a passionate delight. A civilization sprang up which, as opposed to the religious civilization of the Middle Ages, was definitely pagan in its spirit — pagan not only in its love of beauty and literature and its delight in living, but also in its frank sensualism and egoism. The whole scale of values was shifted. "Men cared more for an old manuscript of the poets than for the prophets and apostles; for a Greek vase or statue than for temperance and holy living." A new zest for all that was human and beautiful found expression in a great period of artistic creation. Even the court of St. Peter's was paganized, and we have the spectacle of a series of Popes whose vices have made their names synonyms of infamy, but who nevertheless were accomplished scholars, artistic dilettantes, and patrons of art and learning. In philosophy nearly every system of ancient times was revived. Plato, the artist among philosophers, attracted a large following, and a Platonic Academy was founded in Florence. Other scholars set up Aristotle, interpreted not as he had been by the Church, but freely and naturalistically; while still others turned to Pythagoreanism and Neo-Platonism, to Stoicism, Epicureanism and Scepticism, and even to the earlier Greek schools.

Beyond Italy the Renaissance took on a somewhat different character. In Germany, where it was grafted on a type of mind naturally profounder and more religious, and where the religious life had already been deepened by the mysticism of Eckhart and Tauler and the Brethren of the Common Life, its most characteristic product was the Reformation of Luther; even Humanism in its German form, as typified in Erasmus and Melanchthon, shows strong religious sympathies. But the Reformation is an expression of the same revolt against authority. By its doctrine of justification by faith apart from any external mediation, and by its appeal to immediate Christian experience, it stood for individual freedom as against the pretensions of the Church.

Moreover along with these there went other and more external changes, which in a short space still further revolutionized the old order. The voyages of Columbus and Vasco da Gama, Balboa and Magellan, resulting, among other things, in the discovery of America and of the road to the Indies, changed the map of the world, and opened up vast possibilities which had not been dreamed of before. In quick succession there came also a series of inventions of world-wide significance. The discovery of gunpowder revolutionized the art of war, and put the common soldier and the noble on an equal footing; printing first made possible a generally diffused knowledge and culture; while the telescope laid open the structure of the heavens, and the compass enlarged the boundaries of the earth. All these changes furnished a powerful spur to the imaginative and creative spirit, to which the Elizabethan age in England bears special witness.

And, finally, there came forward to realize the new possibilities in the way of knowledge a brilliant group of scientists of the first magnitude — Tycho Brahe, Copernicus, Galileo, Kepler and others — whose investigations gave a firm foundation to those scientific methods and conceptions which were destined to enter into all future thought. In particular Copernicus, by shifting the center of the universe from our earth and making this but a point in a vast system, created a profound impression on men's imaginations, and perhaps more than any other single influence helped to cut the ground from beneath the narrow theological view of life which hitherto had dominated men's minds. God could no longer be conceived as having his local habitation in the heavens; the whole geography of the spiritual world was thrown into confusion, and the conception of God's relation to the universe transformed. In a word, a wholly new way of looking at the world emerged — the way of the modern man. Nothing could be more modern in tone, for example, than the essays of Montaigne; in their cool common sense, their cautious scepticism, their condemnation of superstition and religious fanaticism, and their wide spirit of toleration, they mark the complete emancipation of cultivated thought from ecclesiastical influences, and the secularization of human life and human interests.

2. *Bruno.* — Turning now to the way in which this enormous change is mirrored in philosophical theory, we may pass over the transition period briefly. At first, as has been said, men had been compelled to go back to the remoter past to get that concrete content the lack of which repelled them in the Middle Ages, but which they were not yet ready to supply from their own resources. But soon the mere renewal of ancient systems gave place to more original attempts. What is most characteristic of the Renaissance period in philosophy may be found in *Giordano Bruno.* Bruno was a Dominican monk, born near Naples in 1548. His fiery spirit and poetic temperament soon however put him out of sympathy with dogmatic and ascetic Catholicism. Persecuted in consequence by the Church, he passed a varied and unhappy life wandering from country to country — Switzerland, Germany, England, France, — but nowhere finding peace. At last he fell into the clutches of the Inquisition, and was burnt at the stake in Rome (1600).

In Bruno there are most of the elements that go to make the Renaissance period attractive. There is the ardent enthusiasm for nature and beauty; the revolt from asceticism and Scholasticism alike; the consciousness of a new and vaster universe suddenly laid open to man, and the confidence that it can be grasped without the long process of careful investigation whose necessity time was to show; and, finally, along with this, the inevitable ferment and unclearness of new ideas imperfectly apprehended. In his zeal for life Bruno goes back to the ancient Hylozoism. All nature is alive. A world soul permeates everything. The universe is a great organism, whose dwelling-place is the infinite reaches of space. To this emotional realization of the infiniteness and divineness of the natural world his eyes had been opened first by the Copernican theory. "By this knowledge we are loosened from the chains of a most narrow dungeon, and set at liberty to rove in a most august empire;

we are removed from presumptuous boundaries and poverty to the innumerable riches of an infinite space, of so worthy a field, and of such beautiful worlds." Nothing now is limited and restricted, and nothing is dead matter. As he looks forth on the world man comes in contact everywhere with a power akin to him, which is nearer to him than he is to himself, and yet which pulsates through the remotest regions of the heavens and informs all things. "It is not reasonable to believe that any part of the world is without a soul life, sensation and organic structure. From this infinite All, full of beauty and splendor, from the vast worlds which circle above us to the sparkling dust of stars beyond, the conclusion is drawn that there are an infinity of creatures, a vast multitude, which, each in its degree, mirrors forth the splendor, wisdom and excellence of the divine beauty." The stars have intellectual and sense life — "those sons of God who shouted for joy at the creation, the flaming heralds his ministers and the ambassadors of his glory, a living mirror of the infinite Deity."

Accordingly we must rid ourselves of the paltry thought that it is for us that all things are created. "Only one bereft of his reason could believe that those infinite spaces, tenanted by vast and magnificent bodies, are designed only to give us light, or to receive the clear shining of the earth." "If in the eyes of God there is but one starry globe, if the sun and moon and all creation are made for the good of the earth and for the welfare of man, humanity may be exalted, but is not the Godhead abased? Is this not to straiten and confine his providence? What! is a feeble human creature the only object worthy of the care of God? No, the earth is but a planet, the rank she holds among the stars is but by usurpation; it is time to dethrone her. The ruler of our earth is not man, but the sun, with the life which breathes in common through the universe. Let the earth eschew privilege; let her fulfil her course, and obey. Let not this contemplation dispirit man, as if he thought himself abandoned by God; for in extending and enlarging the universe, he is himself elevated beyond measure, and his intelligence is no longer deprived of breathing space beneath a sky meagre, narrow, and ill-contrived in its proportions. Dwellers in a star, are we not comprehended within the celestial plains, and established within the very precincts of heaven?" "This is that philosophy which opens the senses, which satisfies the mind, which enlarges the under-standing, and which leads man to the only true beatitude; for it frees him from the solicitous pursuit of pleasure, and from the anxious apprehensions of pain, seeing that everything is subject to a most good and efficient cause." [1]

In this conception of the universe there are two sides, both of which Bruno wishes to emphasize. On the one hand he insists upon the unity of the whole. Reality is an eternal spirit, one and indi-visible, and as such alone possesses truth; all things that appear are but images of this ultimate reality. "The heavens are a picture, a book, a mirror, wherein man can behold and read the form and the laws of supreme goodness, the plan and total of perfection." "From this spirit, which is One, all being flows; there is one truth and one goodness penetrating and governing all things. In nature are the thoughts of God. They are made manifest in figures and vestiges to the eye of sense; they are reproduced in our thoughts, where alone we can arrive at consciousness of true being. We are surrounded by eternity and by the uniting of love. There is but one centre from which all species issue, as rays from a sun, and to which all species return. There is but one celestial expanse, where the stars choir forth unbroken harmony. From this spirit, which is called the Life of the Universe, proceeds the life and soul of every-thing which has soul and life, the which life, however, I understand to be immortal, as well in bodies as in their souls, there being no other death than division and congregation." [2] But while now God is the whole, he also is a whole which is present in its complete-ness in each single part. He is in the blade of grass, in the grain of sand, in the atom that floats in the sunbeam, as well as in the bound-less All. Each man is a point in which the fulness of the Godhead is reflected; it represents the whole; it is the microcosm which in miniature reproduces the great macrocosm of the universe. With Bruno "man is a mirror within a mirror, and his perception of

[1] Taken from Frith, *Life of Bruno*, pp. 42–46, Paul, Trench, Trübner & Co.
[2] *Ibid.*, p. 278.

things is a reflection of nature, which is the reflection of the thought of God."

3. *Paracelsus.* — Evidently the return to nature in this its early form lends itself rather to a poetical glorification of the world, an imaginative interpretation which reaches its goal by a subjective leap, rather than to the sober attention to details which was needed before science could be established. The same tendency to prematureness showed itself in the form likewise of an interest in magic, astrology, alchemy and the search for the philosopher's stone. *Paracelsus* is the type of a host of men who sprang up all over Europe — men of enthusiasm for nature, and to some extent of good ideals, but men whose undisciplined imaginations led them beyond the bounds of sober thinking. Some valuable knowledge about the world did, it is true, result; in alchemy, in particular, the search for that which should turn everything to gold was the means of giving a start to the science of chemistry. But before real progress could be made these attractive but not very fruitful methods of magic and theosophy had, equally with the barren logic of the Schoolmen, to be definitely set aside.

LITERATURE

Burckhardt, *The Civilization of the Renaissance.*
Montaigne, *Essays.*
Cellini, *Autobiography.*
Owen, *The Sceptics of the Italian Renaissance.*
Vaughan, *Hours with the Mystics.*
Symonds, *Renaissance in Italy,* 7 vols.
Frith, *Life of Bruno.*
Smith, *Erasmus.*
McIntyre, *Giordano Bruno.*
Lindsay, *History of the Reformation.*
Boulting, *Giordano Bruno.*

§ 24. *Bacon*

1. *The Defects of the Existing Philosophy.* — The man who came forward to attempt this task was *Francis Bacon* (1561–1626). In Bacon's checkered career — a career ending in his disgrace and

removal from the Lord Chancellorship — there is rather too obvious a lack of any very delicate sense of personal honor and dignity to arouse an unqualified respect. Nor indeed as a thinker is Bacon deserving of the excessive admiration which it was once the fashion to bestow upon him. About the more ultimate questions of philosophy he has little to say; and even on the side of science and the world of nature his work is far from final. He continually promises more than he is able to perform. It was other men who were actually doing the things whose necessity Bacon was pointing out, and Bacon was not always able to recognize the value of their work; he never accepted the Copernican theory, for example. But in spite of these defects the work which he accomplished was an important one. What the times needed was not simply men to carry out practically the new methods of science in a detailed investigation of the world, but also some one with the breadth of vision to realize clearly and in a large way what these methods meant, to emphasize their relation to previous methods, and to set them in connection with some worthy end in terms of human life. For this task Bacon was well equipped. The catholicity of his scientific interests enabled him to keep in view and call attention to their more universal aspects. So too his reputation as a statesman lent to his words a special weight; while the gifts of a great writer, helped out by a wide learning, gave his exposition an impressiveness which much increased its influence.

Bacon starts with the recognition that philosophy has broken down and is in general disrepute. What is the reason for this, when other things are prospering? Take the mechanical arts — "they grow and perfect themselves daily as if enjoying a certain vital air, while philosophy, like a statue, is adorned and celebrated, but moves not. The former also are seen rude and commonly without proportion and cumbrous in the hands of their first authors, but afterward get new strength and aptness; the latter is in its greatest vigor with its first author, and afterward declines." This is a feeling about philosophy which frequently finds expression; and in Bacon's time it had a special justification. "The fable of Scylla is a lively image of the present state of letters, with the countenance and expression of a virgin above, the end in a multitude of barking questions, fruitful of controversy, and barren of effect." [1]

This unfortunate state of affairs has three main roots, three "distempers of learning": the first fantastical learning, the second contentious learning, and the last delicate learning. By delicate learning Bacon means the dilettante spirit which the Renaissance had made fashionable; here words usurp the place of substance, and matters of style and polished phrases are substituted for real weight of meaning. "Of this vanity Pygmalion's frenzy is a good emblem; for words are but the images of matter, and except they have life of reason and invention, to fall in love with them is all one as to fall in love with a picture." The second distemper is that which the Schoolmen represent, and the image of Scylla will stand for it. The first, or fantastical learning, is exemplified in the spirit that makes men run after old wives' tales, wonders, ghosts and miracles; or in a pseudo-scientific form gains credence for alchemy and natural magic.

From these three roots grow the numerous errors which infect philosophy; and of these Bacon names a long list. There is the extreme affecting either of antiquity or novelty, "whence it seemeth the children of time do take after the nature and malice of the father. For as he devoureth his children, so one of them seeketh to devour and suppress the others; while antiquity envieth there should be new additions, novelty cannot be content to add but it must deface. Antiquity deserveth that reverence that men should make a stand thereupon, and discover what is the best way; but when the discovery is well taken, then to make progression. And to speak truly, those times are the ancient times when the world is ancient, and not those which we account ancient by a computation backward from ourselves." Other errors, depending on this, take the form of a "distrust that anything should be now to be found out which the world should have missed and passed over so long time"; or the "conceit that of former opinions the best hath still prevailed and suppressed the rest, so that the result of new search will be nothing save to light upon exploded errors. The truth is, that time

[1] *Great Instauration*, Preface.

seemeth to be of the nature of a river or stream, which carrieth down to us that which is light and blown up, and sinketh and drowndeth that which is weighty and solid." To these we may add the premature formulation of knowledge which checks its growth; an extreme specialization; too much confidence in man's own wit and understanding apart from the contemplation of nature; an impatience of doubt and haste to assertion without due and mature suspension of judgment; a lazy content with discourses already made.

And, finally, there is the greatest error of all — "the mistaking or misplacing of the last or farthest end of knowledge. For men have entered into a desire of learning or knowledge, sometimes upon a natural curiosity and inquisitive appetite, sometimes to entertain their minds with vanity and delight, sometimes for ornament and reputation, sometimes to enable them to victory of wit and contradiction, and most times for lucre and profession; and seldom to give a true account of their gift of reason, to the benefit and use of men. As if there were sought in knowledge a couch whereupon to rest a restless spirit; or a tarasse for a wandering and variable mind to walk up and down with a fair prospect; or a fort or commanding ground for strife and contention; or a shop for profit or sale; and not a rich storehouse for the glory of the creator and the relief of man's estate. Howbeit I do not mean, when I speak of use and action, that end before mentioned of the applying of knowledge to lucre and profession; for I am not ignorant how much that divideth and interrupteth the prosecution and advancement of knowledge, like unto the golden ball thrown before Atalanta, which while she goeth aside and stoppeth to take up, the race is hindered. But as both heaven and earth do conspire and contribute to the use and benefit of man, so the end ought to be, for both natural and moral philosophies, to separate and reject vain speculations and whatsoever is empty and void, and to preserve and augment whatever is solid and fruitful." [1]

2. *The Aim of Philosophy.* — For Bacon, then, philosophy, in opposition to the practical barrenness of the Scholastics, has the

[1] *Adv. of Learning*, Spedding's ed., Vol. VI, pp. 117-135.

definite function of serving for the benefit and relief of the state and society of man — for a "restitution and reinvesting of man to the sovereignty and power, in that wheresoever he shall be able to call the creatures by their true name he shall again command them which he had in his first state of creation." [1] Such an ideal is pictured in the unfinished fragment of the *New Atlantis*. Here Bacon imagines an island, shut off from the rest of the world, and raised to a high point of felicity and civilization; and this is brought about simply by a systematic application of the human mind to a discovery of the secrets of nature, and the utilization of these for inventions intended to secure man's control over his environment. In a sort of scientific society called Solomon's House, this aim is carried out with a high degree of organization and efficiency; and Bacon gives rein to his imagination in anticipating all sorts of possible results of inventive skill, including the microphone and telephone, the flying machine and submarine vessels, to say nothing of several kinds of perpetual motion. This whole conception, it is to be observed, is thoroughly practical and secular. All speculative questions relating to God and his purposes, or to the ultimate destiny of man, are excluded from the realm of reason, and handed over to theology and faith. At most a contemplation of the world — and this is the true sphere of philosophy — may be made to refute atheism; but it can supply no positive content. To be sure, Bacon still is ready to acknowledge the truth of theology in its own sphere; but he deprecates any mingling of theology and reason. "If any man shall think by view and inquiry into sensible and material things to attain to any light for the revelation of the nature and will of God, he shall dangerously abuse himself. It is true that the contemplation of the creatures of God hath for end, as to the natures of the creatures themselves, knowledge, but as to the nature of God, no knowledge, but wonder, which is nothing else but contemplation broken off or losing itself. Nay, further, as it was aptly said by one of Plato's school, the sense of man resembles the sun, which openeth and revealeth the terrestrial globe, but obscureth and concealeth the celestial; so doth the sense discover natural

[1] *Interpretation of Nature*, Vol. VI, p. 34.

things but darken and shut up divine." [1]   Theology is grounded
only on the word of God, and not upon the light of nature ; to the
latter it may be but foolishness, as "that faith which was accounted
to Abraham for righteousness was of such a point as whereat Sarah
laughed, who therein was an image of natural reason."   Whether
this profession of faith in theology is altogether sincere may be a
matter of some doubt ; at any rate, the thing Bacon is most concerned with is, not to establish faith, but to free reason, and give it
full play in its proper sphere.   As reason has nothing to say about
the concerns of theology, so theology, on its side, must not meddle
in matters which do not belong to it.   The Bible is made to teach
religion, not science ; and to endeavor, as some have done, to build
a system of natural philosophy on Scripture is to seek the dead
among the living.

3. *Method of Induction.* — What now is the new method by
which Bacon looked to see human thought and life straightway
revolutionized?   In the first place it is empiricism, as opposed to
the syllogistic reasoning of the Scholastics.   Bacon thought that
"theories and opinions and common notions, so far as can be
obtained from the stiffness and firmness of the mind, should be
entirely done away with, and that the understanding should begin
anew plainly and fairly with particulars, since there is no other
entrance open to the kingdom of nature than to the kingdom of
heaven, into which no one may enter except in the form of a little
child." [2]   These prepossessions of which it is our first duty to rid
ourselves are what Bacon metaphorically calls Idols : — Idols of
the Tribe, or the predispositions which by the natural working of the
mind more or less beset every one ; Idols of the Cave, or individual
idiosyncrasies, due to mental and bodily structure, habits, education
or accident, which refract and discolor the light of nature ; Idols
of the Forum, or of language, "for men believe that their reason
governs words, but it is also true that words, like the arrows from a
Tartar bow, are shot back and react upon the mind" ; and Idols
of the Theatre arising from the dogmas of philosophers, so called
because all received systems are but "so many stage plays, repre-

[1] *Inter. of Nature,* Vol. VI, p. 29.   [2] *Novum Organum,* § 68.

senting worlds of their own creation after an unreal and scenic fashion." [1]

Abandoning these presuppositions, we are to begin with the particular facts, and only arrive at generalisations by a gradual process instead of at a single leap. The syllogism, on which the Schoolmen rely, is a useful instrument in certain cases, but it is incompetent to reach the truth of nature. Dealing as it does with words and ideas rather than with things, whenever these ideas happen to be vague, incomplete and not sufficiently defined — and this is usually the case — it falls at once to the ground. Let us abandon all such trifling with nature, and come to her with open minds to learn what she has to teach; let us "approach with humility and veneration to unroll the volume of creation, to linger and meditate therein, and with minds washed clean from opinions to study it in purity and integrity. For this is that sound and language which went forth into all lands, and did not incur the confusion of Babel; this should men study to be perfect in, and, becoming again as little children, condescend to take the alphabet of it into their hands, and spare no pains to search and unravel the interpretation thereof, but pursue it strenuously, and persevere even unto death."

Induction from empirical particulars is thus the general method of science. But induction must itself escape the perils that attend it as it has commonly been applied. What logic has had in a meager way to say of induction, as a mere enumeration of particulars, is vicious and incompetent. "To conclude upon an enumeration of particulars without instance contradictory is no conclusion, but a conjecture; for who can assure in many subjects, upon those particulars which appear of a side, that there are not others on the contrary side which appear not. As if Samuel should have rested upon those sons of Jesse which were brought before him, and failed of David, which was in the field." [2] True induction accordingly must not be in too great haste to generalize, but must consider carefully all opposing instances. It must not specialize and confine itself to a few objects but must be universal in its scope. It must

[1] *Novum Organum*, 39 ff.   [2] *Adv. of Learning*, Vol. VI, p. 265.

not be too ready to run after immediate utility, but must look for experiments that shall afford light rather than profit, "imitating the divine creation, which only produced light on the first day, and assigned that whole day to its creation, without adding any material work." And it must subject its data to the most careful experimental examination, "not following the common example of accepting any vague report or tradition for fact; so that a system has been pursued in philosophy with regard to experience, resembling that of a kingdom or state which would direct its councils or affairs according to the gossip of city and street politicians, instead of the letters and reports of ambassadors and messengers worthy of credit."

More definitely, the new method from which Bacon hoped so much was briefly this: After clearing the mind of presuppositions, the next step is to gather and carefully tabulate all possible knowledge of the facts of nature; for it is useless to clear the mirror if it have no images to reflect. These facts are not to be taken at haphazard, but are to be the result of careful and exact experiment, in which the natural imperfections of the senses are to be assisted by whatever instruments and processes may be necessary. Such a catalogue of facts Bacon himself started, and he expected that a determined and concerted effort on the part of men of science would soon render it practically exhaustive. The problem of science now is to discover what, following the scholastic terminology, Bacon calls the "forms" of things. Every "simple nature," that is, or ultimate quality, has a form, or essence, or law, which is always present where the quality is, and which, if it can be discovered, will always serve to superinduce the quality in any particular object. Suppose, then, that we wish to discover the form of a simple nature like heat. Using the tabulations we have made of all the cases in nature where heat appears, and, again, of cases where it is absent, we find by a process of comparison and exclusion what the form of heat must be. It cannot be weight, for example, for we find heavy bodies in both lists; nor can it be a host of other things for the same reason. And at last we hit upon *motion* as the one thing which always is present when heat is present, and absent when heat is absent. Finally, we may draw up a third list which represents the presence of the quality in varying degrees; and in this we ought to find the form presenting a similar variation. This is, in brief, Bacon's scientific method, though of course it admits of working out in greater detail, particularly in the way of formulating certain kinds of cases which are especially illuminating as test instances.

The results of Bacon's work were incommensurate with the promises he had held out. What he did was to call attention in an impressive way to the necessity for induction, experiment, and the empirical study of facts. But his great work remained at his death the mere sketch of a method which he had found it impossible to exhibit in its actual working; and he had not sufficiently understood the conditions of science to lay out a path for others. In particular, he was almost wholly blind to the important part which deduction plays in scientific inquiry. As he conceived it, Bacon's method was almost mechanical in its nature, leaving little to that scientific imagination and fertility of hypothesis which characterizes the great scientists. "Our method of discovering the sciences," he says, "is such as to leave little to the acuteness and strength of wit, and, indeed, rather to level wit and intellect. For as in the drawing of a straight line or accurate circle by the hand much depends upon its steadiness and practice, but if a ruler or compass be employed there is little occasion for either, so it is with our method." [1]

LITERATURE

Bacon, *Advancement of Learning; Novum Organum; De dignitate et augmentis scientiarum; New Atlantis.*

Fowler, *Bacon.*

Spedding, *Life and Times of Francis Bacon,* 2 vols.

Fischer, *Bacon and his Successors.*

Nichol, *Bacon,* 2 vols.

Church, *Bacon.*

Steeves, *Francis Bacon.*

Broad, *Philosophy of Francis Bacon.*

Taylor, *Francis Bacon.*

[1] *Novum Organum,* § 61.

§ 25. *Hobbes*

1. The deductive side of science, whose importance Bacon had overlooked, was emphasized by another Englishman, *Thomas Hobbes*. Hobbes, the son of a clergyman, was born at Malmesbury in 1588. After passing through the University of Oxford he became a tutor in the Cavendish family, with which he remained more or less closely connected throughout the course of a long life. In his earlier years he gave no special philosophical promise. He took no interest in the scholastic doctrines which still were taught at Oxford, but neither did he actively revolt against them; his tastes lay in a different direction. It was not till his fortieth year that an accidental event gave a new turn to his thought. Picking up a book on geometry, of which to that time he had been ignorant, he was greatly impressed by it. "It is impossible," he is reported to have said as he read the 47th proposition; and as he went back and traced the steps which led up to the proof of the proposition an interest was aroused which set him at once to the study of mathematics. Combined with a growing interest in the physical sciences, the outcome of this was a new philosophical standpoint.

Hobbes starts from the thesis that the cause of all events whatsoever can be reduced to *motion*, and thus can be made amenable to mathematical and deductive treatment. Philosophy is the reasoned knowledge of effects from causes and causes from effects; and since these are always motions, philosophy is the doctrine of the motion of bodies. Such an idea meant the freeing of science from esoteric natures, Aristotelian forms, and final causes, and its restriction to exact quantitative investigations. It is true Hobbes was only pointing out what was already the conscious method of his scientific contemporaries. Nor was he able to contribute to the history of science any results to be compared in value for a moment with theirs. He came to the study of mathematics too late ever to be master of it; and in his extended controversies with mathematicians of his day he committed himself to positions that were hopelessly in the wrong, as, for example, in his insistence on the possibility of squaring the circle. But Hobbes is not inter-

ested in scientific methods simply; he intends to assert a philosophical principle which is universal, and which results in an entirely
mechanical and materialistic metaphysics.   Not only is a mechanical explanation to be given to events in the material world, but the
same method is to be followed in psychology and sociology.   Consciousness likewise is a form of motion.   It is reducible, that is, to
changes in the nervous system; these changes are brought home to
us in what we call sensations, and by the combination of sensations
the entire life of consciousness is to be explained.   In the same way
the life of society, in turn, is a still more complex mechanism,
strictly determined, and so capable of being treated deductively.
In Hobbes' original plan a trilogy of works — *De Corpore, De
Homine* and *De Cive* — was to follow up these mechanical principles through all their workings.

2. As it happened, he was induced by the course of events to
change his original plan and produce the last part of his work earlier
than he had intended.   The occasion of this was the political
situation in England, which resulted in the beheading of Charles the
First and the exile of the Royalists.   Hobbes, by his connection
with the Cavendishes, was naturally in sympathy with the Royalist
party, and his social philosophy, on which his chief historical
importance rests, is meant to be a message for the times.   In this
his actual procedure is not in point of fact what his theory demands;
neither Hobbes nor any philosopher before or since has ever done
much toward accounting for the concrete facts of human life in
terms simply of the laws of motion.   What he does rather is to
attempt, not a mechanistic, but a "naturalistic" treatment of man
and society — to explain them, that is to say, on the basis of those
relatively simple desires and motives that most obviously pertain
to the human animal as a biological phenomenon.

Hobbes starts from the conception of man as naturally self-seeking and egoistic, and nothing more.   A man loves only himself; he
cares for others only as they minister to his own pleasure.   "If by
nature one man should love another as man, there is no reason why
every man should not equally every man."   This idea of human
nature Hobbes corroborates by various facts drawn from a cynical

observation of men's foibles. In a company, for example, is not each one anxious to tell his own story, and impatient of listening to others; and when one leaves, are not the rest always ready to talk over his faults? None of the reputable qualities and virtues are in truth disinterested; only in appearance do they have in view a good that is located outside the agent. Thus pity, or grief for the calamity of others, arises from the imagination that the like calamity may befall ourselves. Laughter is a "sudden glory" caused either by some sudden act of our own that pleases us, or by the apprehension of some deformed thing in another by comparison whereof we suddenly applaud ourselves. The value or worth of a man is his "price," or what would be given by another for the use of his power; honor and dishonor are the manifestations of this value, or the "opinion of power," whether just or unjust makes no difference. The "social" character of man in which philosophers had professed to find the origin of society has no existence; we seek society not for its own sake, but that we may receive some honor or profit by it. There is no disinterested satisfaction in social intercourse; "all the pleasure and jollity of mind consists in this, even to get some with whom comparing, it may find somewhat wherein to triumph and vaunt itself." [1]

This view of human nature Hobbes attempts to put on a scientific basis. The basis is physiological, and goes back to primitive movements of appetite or desire, and aversion. Objects of desire and aversion we are said to love or hate — desire and love being one and the same thing save that by desire we always signify the absence of the object, and by love most commonly its presence. Similarly such objects constitute what men call "good" and "evil." The feeling or appearance of appetite is pleasure, of aversion pain; or when they arise from a mental expectation of future consequences, they are known as joy and grief. Out of the simple passions all the other and more complex emotions are derivable. Thus appetite with an opinion of attaining is called hope; aversion with an opinion of hurt from the object, fear; aversion with hope of avoiding that hurt by resistance, courage; sudden courage, anger;

[1] *De Cive*, I. 2, 51.

grief for the discovery of some defect of ability, shame; and the like.

Now in a state of nature, where selfish characteristics rule unrestrained, the result must be a condition of continual warfare in which each man's hand is raised against his neighbor. All men will have an appetite for the same things, and each man's selfishness will lead him consequently to encroach upon his fellows whenever he has the opportunity. Under such conditions there is no satisfaction possible in life, no place for industry, navigation, commodicus building, knowledge of nature, arts, letters, society; what is worst of all, there is " continual fear and danger of violent death, and the life of man solitary, poor, nasty, brutish and short." Does any one doubt that this is what human nature, unrestrained, would lead to? "Let him therefore consider with himself," says Hobbes, "when taking a journey, he arms himself and seeks to go well accompanied; when going to sleep he locks his doors; when even in his house he locks his chests; and this when he knows there be laws and public officers armed to revenge all injuries shall be done him." [1]

It is the intolerableness of this state of things which gives rise to society and government. Society does not call into play any new or non-egoistic impulses; all social life springs either from poverty or vainglory, and it exists for glory or for gain. But it is found that selfishness can be gratified better by peace than by war. "The passions that incline men to peace are fear of death, desire of such things as are necessary to commodious living, and a hope by their industry to obtain them. And reason suggesteth convenient articles of peace upon which men may be drawn to agreement." [2] An enlightened self-interest will lead a man to see that it is vastly preferable for him to give up the abstract right to everything which he is strong enough to wrest from other men and keep, and to refrain from aggression upon their liberty, *provided* he is certain of securing a like immunity for himself. But this last is only possible on two conditions: First, all men alike must enter into the agreement to respect one another's rights; and, second, the carrying out of the compact must be guaranteed by the creation of a single power

[1] *Leviathan*, Ch. 13.   [2] *Ibid.*

sufficiently strong to enforce its demands upon individuals, since the only way to keep men to their contracts is by physical compulsion. "Covenants without the sword are but words, and of no strength to secure a man at all"; [1] witness the acts of nations, and the almost entire lack of good faith and honor in their dealings with one another, since here there is no such authority to compel them to live up to their promises.

For the sake then of peace and protection, men will be willing to hand over their individual rights and powers to one man or assembly of men — to submit their wills to a single will which they thus endow once for all with the supreme authority necessary to maintain order; and when such an agreement comes about, society and government succeed to the original state of anarchy. Men universally will find this to their advantage, for there is no one enough superior to his fellows to be secure against aggression. "For as to the strength of body, the weakest has strength enough to kill the strongest, either by secret machination or by confederacy with others that are in the same danger with himself." An even greater equality exists in natural gifts of the mind; "for there is not ordinarily a greater sign of the equal distribution of a thing than that every man is contented with his own share."

It follows as one consequence from this theory that "right" and "morality" are a creation of the state; they relate to man only in society, and not in his original solitude. By natural endowment man has nothing but instincts of self-seeking and self-preservation, and there is no limit to these except the power of gratifying them. Obligation, duty, right and wrong, have as yet no meaning. Duty only arises when there steps in an outside power to impose laws; and this power is the state. Right and wrong are thus identical with the commands and prohibitions of the state. "The desires and other passions of men are in themselves no sin; no more are the actions that proceed from those passions till they know a law that forbids them, which, till laws be made, they cannot know; nor can any law be made till they have agreed upon the person that shall make it." [2] A man can therefore have no individual morality that

[1] *Ibid.*, Ch. 17. [2] *Ibid.*, Ch. 12.

conflicts with these commands of his rulers; in making a claim to this he would be breaking the contract which gives rise to morality, and so be putting himself outside the pale of society in which alone the words have meaning.

So religion too must be a state affair; as the commonwealth is one person, it should exhibit to God but one worship. Hobbes takes for granted, as a corollary of his views of human nature, that each man will if left to himself attempt to force his own opinions on other men; and so a central authority is necessary, here as elsewhere, to keep men within bounds. Rights of conscience and of private judgment are on such a view irrelevant; religion is something not to be believed on reason, but accepted under orders. "For it is with the mysteries of our religion as with wholesome pills for the sick, which swallowed whole have the virtue to cure, but chewed, are for the most part cast up again without effect"; we must trust in him that speaketh though the mind be incapable of any notion at all from the words spoken. And who now is it that shall judge whether a revelation be from God? Evidently, unless we go back to private judgment again, not individuals, nor any arbitrary collection of individuals in a church, but only the commonwealth as a whole. Outward conformity to the worship of the established Church, and a profession of belief, is therefore a necessity of civil order. This is Hobbes' answer to the religious fanaticism in which the political troubles of his day had their more immediate source. Meanwhile, he is free to grant, it is only "conformity" with which the state is much concerned. It does not, because it cannot, constrain the minds of its citizens; in your own heart you may believe what you please if only you keep it to yourself. If this is thought disingenuous, Hobbes bids you remember that, in your profession of belief under compulsion, the king is really acting, not you, and so you are not responsible for the contradiction.

The practical issue of all this is that the will of the state — that is, of the king, or the authorities who represent the established government — is supreme, unlimited and inalienable, and that disobedience or rebellion is in every case unjustified. Nothing can release the subject from the duty of obedience. The contract is not between people and ruler, but is a covenant of the people with one another, to which the ruler is not a party; and accordingly no possible act of his can be a breach of contract and furnish an excuse for rebellion. Rebellion cannot be justified legally, because the sovereign is himself the source of law. It cannot be justified by natural rights which the subject possesses — to life, liberty, property — because the very possibility of the existence of government implies that the subject has freely signed these natural rights away. Nothing the sovereign can do to a subject can properly be called injustice. The king is acting by the authority given him by the people, and to complain of his act is to complain of oneself; if the subject dissents, he has already voluntarily made his dissent a crime. Does the king seize a man's property? He has property rights only with reference to others, not to the sovereign. The king is the recipient of power freely handed over to him, and once given this cannot be recalled. For what would such a recall mean? It would mean that society no longer exists, that no one remains to judge disputes, and that the original anarchy has returned; and any conceivable act of despotism on the part of the ruler is preferable to this.

3. The philosophy of Hobbes had shown a clear understanding of certain aspects of the scientific problem, but it was not altogether fitted to give the new impetus for which philosophy was waiting. In the first place its theory of knowledge was not wholly satisfactory. Hobbes had accepted Nominalism and denied the reality of universals; concepts are mere counters which the mind uses to reckon with, and represent no objective realities. So long as we keep to the empirical side of science, as Bacon did, there is not so obvious a difficulty in attributing reality simply to individual things. But trouble starts when, with Hobbes, we lay emphasis on deduction and mathematical law. For these laws themselves are concepts, or universals, and so instead of having the highest reality for science they would seem to have no reality at all.

In the second place Hobbes' materialism fails to give a very satisfactory account, in terms of his ultimate presuppositions, of the nature of those human facts of conscious experience which make up one of the great divisions into which phenomena fall. It is true that physical laws can be appealed to more or less successfully to account for the appearance and connection of mental phenomena; here Hobbes' position is an anticipation of modern physiological psychology. But as metaphysics it is crude. Matter and mind cannot be identified outright, and a sensation made literally the same thing as a motion of brain particles, except by a confusion of thought. It needed a clearer recognition of the distinctive character of consciousness, and an appreciation of the problems which its relationship to the material world involves, to bring about the rise of modern philosophy in its fullest sense.

LITERATURE

Hobbes, *On Human Nature; De Cive; Leviathan; De Corpore; Of Liberty and Necessity; De Homine.*

Sneath, *The Ethics of Hobbes.*

Bonar, *Philosophy and Political Economy.*

Robertson, *Hobbes.*

Patten, *Development of English Thought.*

Watson, *Hedonistic Theories.*

Stephen, *Hobbes.*

Woodbridge, *The Philosophy of Hobbes in Extracts and Notes collected from His Writings.*

Taylor, *Hobbes.*

Graham, *English Political Philosophy from Hobbes to Maine.*

III. MODERN PHILOSOPHY

§ 26. *Introduction*

1. Before proceeding to consider the more important modern philosophers it may be well to sum up briefly. It has been said that the task of the Middle Ages was primarily a task of *training*. Confronting the chaos brought about through the breakdown of ancient civilization, by centuries of authority, and in ways that were often harsh, crude and arbitrary, the Church had succeeded in instilling so thoroughly settled habits of thought and action that these remain a part of our inheritance to the present day. Such an attitude of unreasoning acceptance does not give play to man's highest powers. In the stress of conditions in the medieval period the specific contribution of Christianity — the bringing back of conduct to the inner personality, and the founding of all the outer life on the individual will and conscience — had a tendency to be obscured; and it has been the work of modern times to bring this once more to the front. But for whatever measure of success it has had in this undertaking the preceding centuries of authority should receive some credit. It was inevitable that before a new spirit of freedom and individuality should get a solid foothold there would first have to be a negative movement of revolt to clear the ground. Much the same situation had arisen before in what has been called the Greek Enlightenment; and there scepticism and the criticism of authority had helped bring about social disintegration also. That the same result did not follow now was due in part to the thoroughness with which the medieval period had done its work. Save in exceptional instances, the spirit of change was regulated and restrained in a way to prevent any violent catastrophes, and to substitute for revolution a process of gradual modification.

The history of modern thought is, in brief, the history of the way in which a life according to authority passes, through an intermediate period of protest and criticism, to an attempt at reconstruction along lines that should meet more successfully man's reasonable needs. Philosophy proper has its setting in this more fundamental change. It is only as man understands himself and the world in which he lives that he can move effectively for practical freedom; intellectual enfranchisement is a part of social progress. So we find modern thought taking two directions, according as it concerns itself primarily with the external world, or with the facts of human nature and the human mind. It is the attempted combination and reconciliation of these two motives, and the relating of them both to the life of man as a social being, which furnishes the main problems with which modern philosophy is engaged and the most general clue to its understanding.

2. It already has been said that one distinctive characteristic of modern thought is the way in which it bases itself upon the individual man. Its watchword is progress, and it is only through individual initiative that conscious progress can take place; so long as men receive their principles from external authority, these stand over against them as an unchangeable ideal to which they may not set themselves in opposition. In science, this individualism takes the form of free investigation and experiment, of a direct interrogation of nature uninfluenced by traditional opinions. In the world of human life it means the assertion of the right of private judgment, the privilege of criticising all the dogmas of religion and political authority, the setting up of the individual reason as the final court of appeal. Accordingly the first phase of modern thought takes the form of a scientific Rationalism — an appeal to reason that derives its method and criterion from the new scientific inquiry. From Descartes to Leibniz there is a period of ambitious metaphysical systems all having a close connection with physics and mathematics, and showing a firm confidence in the power of reason to discover the ultimate secrets of the universe.

3. But Rationalism had its dangers. In the reaction against authority and the past, reason came to mean man's private reason

in a rather too exclusive sense. It was reason in the form of certain principles, necessarily abstract, that were supposed to reveal their truth directly to the individual in his isolation from the life, experience and institutions of the race; the historical sense, the sense of perspective needed to correct the self-assurance of the critical intellect, was conspicuously lacking. With no regard for how beliefs and institutions had come into being, or what in their historical environment was the value which they possessed, men were accustomed to judge and to condemn, often in a supercilious and shallow fashion, everything that did not approve itself clearly to these narrow and abstract principles which they had set up as the ultimate criterion. Reason in this meaning tended inevitably to separate itself from other aspects of the human spirit, and became actively opposed to all feelings, aspirations and enthusiasms which could not meet its tests. Hence the emotionally cold and un-imaginative type which presents itself in the so-called Enlightenment of the eighteenth century.

4. Nor did the process stop with this. After being used as an instrument for getting rid of other beliefs, reason began to call itself in question. Ancient scepticism had already thrown doubt upon the powers of the human mind, and this scepticism had been revived by men like Montaigne and Pascal. One great fact however tended to prevent such an attitude from having much weight — the evident and marvellous success of science. So long as men were actually showing by the use of reason what undeniable results could be obtained, it needed more than a revival of ancient doubts to shake the hold of Rationalism. But a more profound and thorough-going criticism had been gaining headway. As the question was forced upon philosophy: What is the origin and sanction of these metaphysical principles that have been used so freely? the current of thought for the time being changes its direction, and becomes primarily a theory of knowledge. The result is that Rationalism was gradually undermined. Locke, the Englishman, institutes an inquiry into the origin of knowledge, and, true to the English traditions represented in Bacon, he finds this to be wholly empirical. Experience is the source of all we know; the innate and universal

ideas of reason on which the Rationalists had relied have no existence. But if this is true not only philosophy but science is affected
in so far as science pretends to anything like certainty. The result
is Scepticism, which reached its culminating point in David Hume.

5. Along this line it was impossible to go farther. Meanwhile
however another movement was preparing destined to give a new
turn to the thought of the age. In a measure Rousseau may be
taken as the precursor of this movement. Showing in himself
many of the distinctive faults of the preceding period, he yet set
himself in conscious opposition to it by an emphasis, one-sided
indeed, but perhaps unavoidably so, on some of the facts of human
life which Rationalism had neglected, more particularly the fact
of feeling. In France the negative side of his influence predom-
inated, and had its issue in the Revolution. But in Germany there
appeared men of genius who were prepared to receive from him a
more positive inspiration. The brilliant period of German literature that begins with Lessing and Herder, seizing on the vital part
of Rousseau, supplemented it in a way to create a new human standpoint. The thought of man as an integral part of the life of the
world instead of as just a separate individual; of God as an immanent spirit rather than a far-off abstraction; of beliefs and institutions as having their roots in history, and needing in consequence to
be judged in terms of their concrete setting; of the value of art and
religion, and the emotional side of life in general, as opposed to the
deification of the abstract reason — all these things were brought
in to renew and vitalize philosophy. They constitute the main
significance of that series of philosophical systems, from Kant to
Hegel, which makes this one of the outstanding periods in the
history of human speculation.

6. But German Idealism in its turn failed to fulfil the prophecies
of its more enthusiastic followers; the faith that in Hegel's books the
intelligible universe had come to final flower did not stand the test
of time. For one thing, Idealism through its primary concern with
the spiritual experience had run the risk of neglecting the equally
insistent facts of the physical world of science. Science meanwhile
was not standing still; another great scientific epoch, centering

about the notion of Evolution in particular, was transforming all along the line traditional ways of interpreting physical and human facts alike. With the notion of an absolute and timeless universe the principle of evolution clearly was out of step; and there were other reasons too for a reaction. The Idealist's sympathy had been with finality rather than with experiment and progress; he preferred to point out the reason implicit in things as they now exist instead of asking how they might be changed for the better. To this the reforming spirit of the new age could not but object. In consequence we find a variety of tendencies emerging which, while they lend themselves to no single picture, agree for the most part in repudiating the traditional Idealism; change takes the place of permanence, pluralism of a single ideal unity, individualism of social conservatism, experimentalism of metaphysics. And this conflict continues to the present day.

SYSTEMS OF RATIONALISM

§ 27. Descartes. The Cartesian School

1. *The Method of Philosophy.* — It is with *René Descartes* (1596–1650) that modern philosophy is generally thought of as beginning. There were several things that helped to give his philosophical doctrines this importance. In the first place they were based on a conscious method, and this method was an explicit recognition of the scientific spirit. At the same time the modern principle of individuality and subjectivity was fully recognized by Descartes; the existence of the self is the starting-point of his constructive effort, while the test of truth is the clearness with which truth justifies itself to the individual reason untrammeled by the past. Finally Descartes' dualism, the sharp difference he draws between mind and body with their irreconcilable attributes of thought and extension, was the almost necessary precondition of any satisfactory solution of a real difficulty here. By this separation science was left free to follow its bent in the physical universe, while at the same time the short-and-easy method of a philosophical materialism was seen to need reëxamination. If an immaterial reality exists alongside the material, the philosopher is compelled to face a wider problem than the purely scientific one; and the insistent need for some way of connecting the two worlds thereby is forced upon his notice. It is true the violence of the separation itself gave rise to difficulties. But until the two distinct points of view represented in the notion of matter on the one hand and of mind or spirit on the other were brought into relief, the whole philosophical problem was bound to suffer from confusion.

The interest of Descartes' life lies in the story of his mental history. He came from a well-to-do family and possessed through life an independent fortune, so that he was able to devote himself to the things that appealed most strongly to him. Educated in the Jesuit school of La Flêche, and led to believe that a clear and certain knowledge of all that was useful in life might be acquired by education, he had an extreme desire for learning. But his course of study completed, he soon found himself compelled to reconsider his opinion. "For I found myself involved in so many doubts and errors, that it seemed to me that I had derived no other advantage from my endeavors to instruct myself but only to find out more and more how ignorant I was. And yet I was in one of the most celebrated schools in Europe, where I thought there must be learned men if there were any such in the world. Moreover I knew what others thought about me, and I did not perceive that they considered me inferior to my fellow-students, albeit there were among them some who were destined to fill the places of our masters."

Descartes began to doubt, therefore, whether there existed in the world any such wisdom as he had been led to hope for, although he did not cease to think well of some of the scholastic pursuits if followed with discretion. Language and history, which bring us into contact with men of other times, are, like travelling, of great value. "It is well to know something of the manners of foreign peoples in order that we may judge our own more wisely. But if one spends too much time in travelling in foreign countries he becomes at last a stranger in his own; and when one is too curious to know what has been done in past ages he is liable to remain ignorant of what is going on in his own time." Eloquence, again, and poetry he held in high esteem; but he regarded both as the gifts of genius rather than the fruit of study.

"Above all I was delighted with the mathematics, on account of the certainty and evidence of their demonstrations; but I had not as yet found out their true use, and although I supposed that they were of service only in the mechanic arts, I was suprised that upon foundations so solid and stable no loftier structure had been raised; while, on the other hand, I compared the writings of the ancient moralists to palaces very proud and very magnificent, but which are built on nothing but sand or mud. I revered our theology, and as much as any one I strove to gain heaven; but when I learned, as an assured fact, that the way is open no less to the most ignorant than to the most learned, and that the revealed truths which conduct us thither lie beyond the reach of our intelligence, I did not presume to submit them to the feebleness of my reasonings, and I thought that to undertake the examination of them, and succeed in the attempt, required extraordinary divine assistance, and more than human gifts. I had nothing to say of philosophy save that, seeing it had been cultivated by the best minds for many ages, and still there was nothing in it which might not be brought into dispute, and which was, therefore, not free from doubt, I had not the presumption to hope for better success therein than others; and considering how many diverse opinions may be held upon the same subject and defended by the learned, while not more than one of them can be true, I regarded as pretty nearly false all that was merely probable. Then, as to the other sciences which derive their principles from philosophy, I judged that nothing solid could be built upon foundations so unstable. . . . And finally, as for the pseudo-sciences, I thought I was already sufficiently acquainted with their value to be proof against the promises of the alchemist, the predictions of the astrologer, the impostures of the magician, the artifices and vain boasting of those who profess to know more than they actually do know.

"For these reasons, so soon as I was old enough to be no longer subject to the control of my teachers I abandoned literary pursuits altogether, and being resolved to seek no other knowledge than that which I was able to find within myself or in the great book of the world, I spent the remainder of my youth in travelling, in seeing courts and armies, in mingling with people of various dispositions and conditions in life, in collecting a variety of experiences, putting myself to the proof in the crises of fortune, and reflecting on all occasions on whatever might present itself, so as to derive from it what profit I might. . . . It is true that, while I was employed only in observing the manners of foreigners, I found very little to establish my mind, and saw as much diversity here as I had seen before in the opinions of philosophers. So that the principal benefit I derived from it was that, observing many things which, although they appear to us to be very extravagant and ridiculous, are yet commonly received and approved by other great peoples, I gradually became emancipated from many errors which tend to obscure the natural light within us and make us less capable of listening to reason.   But after I had spent some years thus in studying in the book of the world and trying to gain some experience, I formed one day the resolution to study within myself, and to devote all the powers of my mind to choosing the paths which I must thereafter follow — a project attended with much greater success, as I think, than it would have been had I never left my country nor my books." [1]

"I was then in Germany, whither the wars, which were not yet ended there, had summoned me; and when I was returning to the army from the coronation of the emperor, the coming on of winter detained me in a quarter where, finding no one I wished to talk with, and fortunately having no cares nor passions to trouble me, I spent the whole day shut up in a room heated by a stove, where I had all the leisure I desired to hold converse with my own thoughts. One of the first thoughts to occur to me was, that there is often less completeness in works made up of many parts and by the hands of different masters than in those upon which only one has labored. . . .   And so I thought that the sciences contained in books, at least those in which the proofs were merely probable and not demonstrations, being the gradual accumulation of opinions of many different persons, by no means come so near the truth as the plain reasoning of a man of good sense in regard to the matters which present themselves to him.   And I thought still further that, because we have all been children before we were men, and for a long time of necessity were under the control of our inclinations and our tutors, who were often of different minds, and none of whom, perhaps, gave us the best of counsels, it is almost impossible that our judgments should be as free from error and as solid as they would have been if we had had the entire use of our reason from the moment of our birth, and had always been guided by that alone. . . . As for all the opinions which I had accepted up to that time, I was

[1] *Discourse upon Method*, Part I, Torrey's translation, Henry Holt & Co.

persuaded that I could do no better than get rid of them at once, in order to replace them afterward with better ones, or, perhaps, with the same, if I should succeed in making them square with reason. And I firmly believed that in this way I should have much greater success in the conduct of my life than if I should build only on the old foundations, and should rely only on the principles which I had allowed myself to be persuaded of in my youth without ever having examined whether they were true." [1]

What then Descartes resolved to do was to strip himself completely of all that he had formerly believed and start *de novo*, with the intention of admitting only that which was absolutely certain, in order to see if on this basis a system of philosophy might not be erected which should escape the uncertainties of the old. To do this he required a definite method of work; and as the old logic was unsuitable for the discovery of new truth, he drew up a code of rules for himself. "The first rule was, never to receive anything as a truth which I did not clearly know to be such; that is, to avoid haste and prejudice, and not to comprehend anything more in my judgments than that which should present itself so clearly and so distinctly to my mind that I should have no occasion to entertain a doubt of it. The second rule was, to divide every difficulty which I should examine into as many parts as possible, or as might be required for solving it. The third rule was, to conduct my thoughts in an orderly manner, beginning with objects the most simple and the easiest to understand, in order to ascend as it were by steps to the knowledge of the most composite, assuming some order to exist even in things which did not appear to be naturally connected. The last rule was, to make enumerations so complete, and reviews so comprehensive, that I should be certain of omitting nothing." [2]

The basis and suggestion of these rules of Descartes lies in mathematical reasoning. Briefly, the two steps involved are *intuition* and *deduction* — the only two ways open to man for attaining a certain knowledge of truth. By intuition is meant the immediate self-evidence with which a truth forces itself upon us,

[1] *Discourse upon Method*, Part II.
[2] *Ibid.*, Torrey's translation. p. 46

"the conception of an attentive mind so distinct and so clear that no doubt remains to it with regard to that which we comprehend." Most of our ideas are confused and obscure because we try to take in too much at once. He who is bent on including too many things at one look sees nothing distinctly; in the same way, he who in one act of thought would attend to many objects confuses his mind. So the first thing to do is to analyze out from our habitual thinking those clear and axiomatic principles whose certainty cannot be doubted. These clear axioms are what Descartes calls innate ideas. As they are necessary to give us any starting-point for our demonstration, and as they cannot be the result of empirical experience — since in that case they would not be certain and universal — they must represent primitive germs of truth which nature has planted in the human intellect, and which the mind is capable of finding within itself when it goes to work the right way. Having thus secured a starting-point in intuition, the next step is deduction — the process by which, through a series of steps each intuitively certain, we are able to reach new conclusions. Two ideas whose connection is not immediately self-evident may be shown to be connected through this string of intermediate intuitions; and if each step is in reality seen, as we take it, to be necessary, the conclusion has an equal certainty, and it too is an innate idea.

Now of all human knowledge mathematics is the clearest, and furnishes the most self-evident axioms. Descartes therefore will begin with mathematics, and by accustoming his mind to nourish itself on truths and not to be satisfied with false reasons, he will get himself in readiness for more ambitious efforts. So successful was this endeavor that in the course of a few months he found himself with a mastery over his science, and an ability to advance to new truths in it, which surprised and delighted him. Thinking, however, that it needed a riper age than his present twenty-three years before he should be capable of dealing with fundamental questions, he postponed the consideration of these until he should have gained a sufficient discipline.

2. *The Existence and Nature of the Self.* — At length, considering that his capacities are now matured. be sits down to the serious task

of ridding himself of all his false opinions in order to begin anew from the foundation. Now, "all that I have hitherto received as most true and assured I have learned from the senses, or by means of the senses. But I have sometimes found that these senses were deceivers, and it is the part of prudence never to trust entirely those who have once deceived us. But although the senses may deceive us sometimes in regard to things which are scarcely perceptible and very distant, yet there are many other things of which we cannot entertain a reasonable doubt, although we know them by means of the senses; for example, that I am here, seated by the fire, in my dressing gown, holding this paper in my hands, and other things of such a nature. And how can I deny that these hands and this body are mine? Only by imitating those crazy people whose brains are so disturbed and confused by the black vapors of the bile that they constantly affirm that they are kings while in fact they are very poor; that they are clothed in gold and purple while they are quite naked; or who imagine themselves to be pitchers, or to have glass bodies. But what! These are fools, and I should be no less extravagant if I should follow their example. Nevertheless I have to consider that I am a man, and that I fall asleep, and in my dreams imagine the same things, or even sometimes things less probable than these crazy people do while they are awake." It seems to me now, indeed, that my present state is different from dreaming. But then I remember that I have often had a similar illusion while asleep, so that there seems to be no certain mark by which the waking can be distinguished from the sleeping state.

"Let us, then, suppose that we are asleep, and that all those particular events — that we open our eyes, shake our heads, stretch out our hands, and such like things — are only false illusions; and let us think that perhaps neither our hands nor our entire bodies are such as we perceive them. Nevertheless we must at least admit that the things which we imagine in sleep are like pictures and paintings, which can only be formed after the likeness of something real and veritable. Accordingly these things in general — namely, eyes, head, hands, body — are not imaginary, but real and existent." At least we must suppose that the simple elements of which they are made up are real — corporeal being in general and its extension, the figure of things extended, their quantity or size, their number, and the like. Even if the compositions are illusions and the sciences which deal with them false, yet how can I doubt those elemental truths of which, for example, arithmetic and geometry treat — that two and three make five, or that a square always has four sides?

"Nevertheless I have long cherished the belief that there is a God who can do everything, and by whom I was made and created such as I am. But how do I know that he has not caused that there should be no earth, no heavens, no extended body, no figure, no size, no place, and that, nevertheless, I should have perceptions of all these things, and that everything should seem to me to exist not otherwise than as I perceive it? And even in like manner as I judge that others deceive themselves in matters that they know best, how do I know that he has not caused that I deceive myself every time that I add two to three, or number the sides of a square, or judge of anything still more simple, if anything more simple can be imagined?" He certainly does permit me to deceive myself at times; why may I not always be deceived? "I shall suppose, then, not that God, who is very good and the sovereign source of truth, but that a certain evil genius, no less wily and deceitful than powerful, has employed all his ingenuity to deceive me. I shall think that the heavens, the air, the earth, colors, figures, sounds, and all other external things, are nothing but illusions and idle fancies which he employs to impose upon my credulity. I shall consider myself as having no hands, no eyes, no flesh, no blood, as having no senses, but as believing falsely that I possess all these things. I shall obstinately adhere to this opinion; and if by this means it will not be in my power to arrive at the knowledge of any truth, at all events it is in my power to suspend my judgment." [1]

"I make the supposition, then, that all things which I see are false; I persuade myself that nothing has ever existed of all that my memory, filled with illusions, has represented to me; I consider that I have no senses; I assume that body, figure, extension, motion

[1] *Meditations,* I.

and place are only fictions of my mind. What is there, then, which can be held to be true? Perhaps nothing at all, except the statement that there is nothing at all that is true. But how do I know that there is not something, different from those things which I have just pronounced uncertain, concerning which there cannot be entertained the least doubt? Is there not some God, or some other power, who puts these thoughts into my mind? That is not necessary, for perhaps I am capable of producing them of myself. Myself, then! at the very least am I not something?

"But I have already denied that I have any senses or any body : nevertheless I hesitate, for what follows from that? Am I so dependent upon the body and the senses that I cannot exist without them? But I have persuaded myself that there is nothing at all in the world, that there are no heavens, no earth, no minds, no bodies; am I then also persuaded that I am not? Far from it! Without doubt I exist if I am persuaded, or solely if I have thought anything whatever. But there is I know not what deceiver, very powerful, very crafty, who employs all his cunning continually to delude me. There is still no doubt that I exist if he deceives me; and let him deceive me as he may, he will never bring it about that I shall be nothing so long as I shall think something exists. Accordingly, having considered it well, and carefully examined everything, I am obliged to conclude and to hold for certain that this proposition, *I am, I exist*, is necessarily true, every time that I pronounce it or conceive it in my mind."

The foundation of Descartes' philosophy, that through which he is to secure a firm foothold, is thus the *existence of the self* — an existence which is in no wise to be doubted, since even in this doubt the self appears. But what next is the nature of the self whose existence is so certain? I am accustomed to think of myself as made up of a body and a mind. As for my body, I commonly suppose I know what that is — it is something that possesses shape, can fill space so as to exclude other bodies, and can have sensations from outer impressions. But none of these attributes pertain to that self which is a necessity of thought. Suppose I admit the possibility of an evil genius who deceives me: then every one of these bodily attributes may be open to doubt. If now I turn to the soul, is there anything here that belongs to me intrinsically? Yes, there is the attribute of *thought.* So long as I think, so long certainly I exist, although so far as I can see I might immediately cease to exist if once I were to stop thinking. "I am, then, to speak with precision, a thing which thinks, that is to say, a mind, an understanding, or a reason — terms the significance of which was unknown to me before.

"But I am a truly existing thing; but what thing? I have said, a thing which thinks; and what more? I stir up my imagination to see whether I am not still something in addition. I am not this collection of members which is called the human body; I am not a thin and penetrating vapor diffused throughout these members; I am not a wind, a breath, a vapor; nor anything at all of all that I am able to picture or imagine myself to be, since I have assumed that all that is nothing at all, and that without changing this assumption I find that I do not cease to be certain that I am something.

"But what is it, then, that I am? A thing which thinks. What is a thing which thinks? Is it a thing which doubts, which understands, which conceives, which affirms, which denies, which wills, which wills not, which imagines also, and which perceives. Surely it is no small matter if all these things belong to my nature. But why do they not belong to it? Am I not that which even now doubts almost everything, which nevertheless understands and conceives certain things, which is assured and affirms these only to be true and denies the rest, which wills and desires to know more, which wills not to be deceived? . . . And I also certainly have the power of imagining; for although it might happen (as I have already supposed) that the things which I have imagined were not true, nevertheless this power of imagining does not cease really to exist in me and to form part of my thought. Finally, I am the same being which perceives, that is, which has the knowledge of certain things as if by the organs of sense, since in reality I see light, I hear noise, I feel warmth. But I have been told that these appearances are false, and that I am asleep. Granted; nevertheless, at least it is very certain that it appears to me that I see light, that I hear noise, and that I feel warmth; and it is just that which in me I call perceiving; and that, precisely, is nothing else than thinking. From this point I begin to know what I am with more clearness and distinctness than heretofore." [1]

The basis on which Descartes proposes to build is thus the undeniableness of "consciousness." This alone it is impossible to doubt; this alone comes home to me as a directly felt experience whose reality depends, not on an inference, but on the immediate fact of its being experienced. I may be mistaken about the object of my thought, but that casts no shade of doubt upon the thought itself and the immaterial "I" who thinks. I am, it is true, accustomed to suppose that things, bodies, are the one undeniable fact, and to overlook the thought by which these things are known. I see, for example, a piece of wax before me; can anything be more certain than this? "What, then! I who appear to conceive of this piece of wax with so much clearness and distinctness, do I not know myself not only with much more truth and certainty, but even with much more distinctness and clearness! For if I judge that the wax is, or exists, from the fact that I see it, certainly it follows much more evidently that I am, or that I exist myself, from the fact that I see it. For it may be that what I see is not in reality wax; it may also be that I have not eyes even to see anything; but it cannot be that while I see, or — what I do not distinguish therefrom — while I think I see, I who think am not something."

Cogito, ergo sum — here is one fact at least that cannot be denied; and from it, as an axiom, we now may start in order to get back again, with a new certainty, the wider reality which provisionally we have doubted. The test to be applied to those further truths we already know; they must approve themselves to us with the same clearness and certainty that goes with the perception of our own existence. What now is the process by which we are to make our way back to the world again?

3. *The Existence of God and of the World.* — The first step is the proof for the existence of God. This proof takes in Descartes more

[1] *Meditations.* II.

shapes than one, but it is sufficient here to state it in its simplest form. We find a great number of ideas in the mind. Some of these it seems to us come from our own nature, others from an external compulsion, while others, again, we regard as mere fictions which the mind has put together of its own invention. But what evidence is there that anything exists outside the mind to correspond to these ideas, apart from a natural tendency to believe which we have seen proves nothing?

The certainty we are after can, so Descartes thinks, be reached through the medium of the principle of causality. It is a thing manifest and self-evident by the same natural light which assured us of the existence of the self, that there must be in every cause at least as much reality as reveals itself in the effect; otherwise we should have a portion of the effect arising out of nothing. If there-fore in my mind there exists any single idea which evidently is too great to have originated from my own nature, then I can be sure that outside of me there is a commensurate cause. For the most part I discover nothing in my ideas which thus evidently requires more than my own nature to produce it; but to this there is one exception. I find in myself an idea of God as a substance infinite, eternal, immutable, independent, omniscient, omnipotent, by which myself and all other things have been created. Is it conceivable that attributes so exalted ever should have come from the imperfect and finite nature which I know my own to be? For the same reason it is impossible that the capacity for conceiving such an idea should have been derived ultimately from my parents, or from any other cause that falls short of the perfection of the idea itself. Accord-ingly I have bridged the gulf between myself and external reality; the real existence of God must be postulated as the only being great enough to account for the presence in me of this idea of God which indubitably exists.

And with the self and God established the rest is relatively easy. We were prevented from resting in our natural conviction that a material world exists beyond us by the final doubt whether a malignant power might not purposely be deceiving us. But the act of deception necessarily grows out of some defect, and cannot be attributed to the God whose perfection we have established. Accordingly this doubt must now be put aside and, *in so far as it is clearly conceived*, the reality of matter must be admitted; else God would be responsible for making us believe a lie.

4. *The Nature of Matter.* — Such in brief is the metaphysics by which Descartes supposed that, with the same certainty and clearness that are found in a geometrical proof, the essential features of a world philosophy can be established. It will be evident on consideration that the process of proof contains various assumptions which Descartes did not bring clearly into view, and which might be questioned more easily than he thought possible. But whether we consider his reasoning valid or not, there are two things which he had accomplished. He had set up the ideal of a method which, in intention at any rate, discarded all assumptions based on authority; and he also had marked out, with a precision not before attained, certain fundamental distinctions which subsequent philosophy was bound to take into account.

The point about which at the start this later development centers is the sharp distinction which Descartes had drawn between mind and matter — the two substances into which the world of experience is divided. The nature of mind, or soul, has already been considered; it is a thing which thinks. However we may regard the adequacy of this phrase to express the essential character of mind, at least it emphasizes the immaterial nature of consciousness, and makes it possible to avoid that confusion of the conscious life with the outer world which underlies alike the obscure hylozoism of earlier philosophers and the dogmatic materialism of more modern times. But when we come to ask about the corresponding attribute of matter, a difficulty will arise. The matter which the common man knows, and in which he feels a natural compulsion to believe, is matter as he sees, and hears, and touches, and tastes it — extended, colored, sonorous. Some of these qualities however, as for instance color, taste and sound, science is disposed to say are not original, but are secondary effects upon our sensibility which have no counterpart in the thing itself. Descartes meanwhile had found it possible to demonstrate that matter exists at all only by appealing to the veracity of God; and if some of the qualities in which God has led us to believe are demonstrably false, is not his whole case jeopardized?

Descartes saves himself by his theory of truth and falsity. When I judge, for example, that I see a red object, there are two things that enter in. There is, first, the fact that I have a sensation of redness; and this as a datum of immediate experience is a fact about which no doubt whatever is possible. But I may also go beyond this, and infer that the sensation has a counterpart in some actual quality out in space. But while I may be inclined to draw this inference, I do not need to do so; it is a matter of choice on my part, or of will. False judgments, then, are due to the fact that I go beyond the certain knowledge which I possess and draw conclusions that are not warranted; and for this I am responsible, not God. If God chooses to give us a knowledge that is less than perfect, it is nothing of which we can complain. And if, again, he has given us a power of willing which is unlimited, and which thus may extend beyond our knowledge, that also is no hardship. He would only be deceiving us if that were false which we see *clearly* and *distinctly* to be true. This supplies the criterion by which we are to distinguish between what we commonly, but erroneously, regard as the qualities of matter, and those qualities which really belong to it; we are to resist the unthinking inclination to judge hastily, and withhold our assent until the truth approves itself to us clearly and axiomatically.

In this way we shall find, Descartes thinks, that *extension* is the only quality that can be conceived clearly. That extension can be so conceived is evident from the fact that it is extension to which the truths of geometry, the clearest of all the sciences, apply. The other qualities, on the contrary, involve no such self-evident intuitions. They are like the sensation of hunger, which furnishes no knowledge, but only serves a utilitarian purpose by warning us of bodily needs. The essence of matter, consequently, is extension. It is infinite, and infinitely divisible; this last point involves a denial of the theory of atoms. Again, since space as extension is an attribute of matter. there is no such thing as empty space. By identifying matter with extension Descartes also is compelled to regard it as wholly passive; and so in order to get a foundation for science he has to introduce from the outside a new conception — that of motion. With matter and motion granted, we have all the data necessary for explaining the entire natural world in strictly mechanical terms.

5. *The Relation of Mind and Body.* — Meanwhile the merit that Descartes can lay claim to on the ground of clearness was counterbalanced by a resulting difficulty. If mind and matter are so totally different in their nature, how can they come together to form a single world? how in particular are they to react upon and affect each other, as apparently they do? The full stress of this problem did not at once make itself evident; but a beginning was made in connection with a point that became for Descartes himself a matter of some importance. It is in the human organism that matter and mind come into closest contact. Now the body is a part of the material world, and its actions ought logically to be subject to the same mechanical laws that govern other things. The compulsion that drove Descartes in this direction is shown in his famous doctrine of the automatism of brutes. "The greatest of all the prejudices we have retained from infancy is that of believing that brutes think. The source of our error comes from having observed that many of the bodily members of brutes are not very different from our own in shape and movements, and from the belief that our mind is the principle of the motions which occur in us — that it imparts motion to the body, and is the cause of our thoughts. Assuming this, we find no difficulty in believing that there is in brutes a mind similar to our own; but having made the discovery, after thinking well upon it, that two different principles of our movements are to be distinguished — the one entirely mechanical and corporeal, which depends solely on the force of the animal spirits and the configuration of the bodily parts, and which may be called corporeal soul, and the other incorporeal, that is to say, mind or soul, which you may define as a substance which thinks — I have inquired with great care whether the motions of animals proceed from these two principles, or from one alone. Now having clearly perceived

that they can proceed from one only, I have held it demonstrated that we are not able in any manner to prove that there is in the animals a soul which thinks. I am not at all·disturbed in my opinion by those doublings and cunning tricks of dogs and foxes, nor by all those things which animals do, either from fear, or to get something to eat, or just for sport. I engage to explain all that very easily, merely by the conformation of the parts of the animals." [1]

And if it is true that the life of animals can be explained without reference to intelligence, this is equally conceivable of the vast majority of the activities of men as well. In the *Tract on Man*, Descartes undertakes to show how, assuming the body to be nothing but a statue or machine of clay, the mere mechanical motion of parts is enough to account for what we call its life; "just as you may have seen in grottoes and fountains in the royal gardens, that the force alone with which the water moves, in passing from the spring, is enough to move various machines, and even to make them play on instruments, or utter words, according to the different arrangement of the pipes which conduct it. And indeed the nerves of the machine that I am describing to you may very well be compared to the pipes of the machinery of these fountains, its muscles and its tendons to various other engines and devices which serve to move them, its animal spirits to the water which sets them in motion, of which the heart is the spring and the cavities of the brain the outlets. Moreover, respiration and other such functions as are natural and usual to it, and which depend on the course of the spirits, are like the movements of a clock or a mill which the regular flow of the water can keep up. External objects which, by their presence alone, act upon the organs of its senses, and which by this means determine it to move in many different ways according as the particles of its brain are arranged, are like visitors who, entering some of the grottoes of these fountains, bring about of themselves, without intending it, the movements which occur in their presence; for they cannot enter without stepping on certain tiles of the pavement so arranged that, for example, if they approach a Diana taking a bath, they make her hide in the reeds; and if they pass on in

[1] *Letter to Henry More*, Torrey, p. 284.

pursuit of her, they cause a Neptune to appear before them who menaces them with his trident; or if they turn in some other direction, they will make a marine monster come out who will squirt water into their faces, or something similar will happen, according to the fancy of the engineers who construct them. And finally, when the *reasonable soul* shall be in this machine, it will have its principal seat in the brain, and it will be there like the fountain maker, who must be at the openings where all the pipes of these machines discharge themselves if he wishes to start, to stop, or to change in any way their movements." [1]

The last words of the quotation show however that Descartes was not ready to carry out his thesis to the final consequences. That would have been to deny altogether the influence of the will — of ourselves, in other words — upon our actions; and Descartes was not prepared to sacrifice this to suit a theory. Accordingly he admits that while our more habitual and reflex actions are due to mechanism alone, yet it also is possible for the mind to interfere and alter the motions of the body. The seat of this interaction he supposed to be a part of the brain known as the pineal gland. Here the animal spirits, or fine particles of the blood, whose entrance into the various nerves determines the body to one action or another, may be deflected by the influence of the soul, and so made the instrument by which the soul moves the body. It is this relationship of mind and body that justifies a distinction between two classes of conscious fact. The activity of the mind is the activity of pure thought. But the mind is also influenced by its connection with the body, and this gives rise to certain modes of consciousness — emotions, sensations and the like — which are of a lower order. For Descartes, as for most of the ancients, the high- est type of life is the intellectual life.

6. *The Cartesians. Occasionalism.* — The influence which Des- cartes exerted was immediate and profound. In France the most important names among the thinkers who professed themselves Cartesians are those of *Geulincx* and *Malebranche*. Only one point in connection with these men need be mentioned here. Descartes

[1] *Tract on Man*, Torrey, p. 278.

had admitted the fact of a mutual influence between the soul and the body, without going on to explain its possibility. With this his followers were not satisfied. The main difficulty lay for them in the question how, if matter and mind are so absolutely diverse in nature, there can be any such thing as an influence of one upon the other. The answer took the form which became known as Occasionalism. The difficulty of an interaction was admitted, and it was solved by falling back on the omnipotence of God. It is no power of the human mind that effects an alteration in the physical world, but a direct act of God; a particular exertion of the will does not move the human body, but *on occasion of* this act of will God intervenes, and changes the direction of the body in a way to secure the desired result. There is thus no need of any influence passing between the two unlike substances.

Occasionalism proved to be only a temporary stopping-place; but it showed the direction in which the logic of Descartes' standpoint was to lead. Descartes had left the world divided into three constituent parts — the two substances, mind and matter, and a third more ultimate reality, God. It was by appealing to this last reality that the separation could, it seemed, most naturally be overcome, if the distinction which Descartes had drawn was not again to be confused. Descartes himself had recognized this. Defining a substance as that which can be conceived through itself alone, he had seen that after all mind and matter are no true substances in the ultimate sense, since they are not to be conceived apart from God; so that in the strict meaning of the term only one substance — God — exists. On this showing Occasionalism had a glimpse of the true problem when it fell back on an appeal to God's power. But its solution remained an external one; the way to a more intimate connection between God and the world was brought to light by Spinoza.

LITERATURE

Descartes, *Discourse upon Method; Meditations; Principia Philosophiae; Emotions of the Soul.* Translations: Veitch (*Method, Meditations, Selections from the Principles*); Lowndes (*Meditations*); Torrey (*Selections*); Haldane and Ross (*Works*, 2 vols.).

Mahaffy, *Descartes*.
Fisher, *Descartes and his School*.
Huxley, *Methods and Results*.
Caird, *Essays on Literature and Philosophy*.
Smith, *Studies in the Cartesian Philosophy*.
Iverach, *Descartes, Spinoza and the New Philosophy*.
Haldane, *Descartes, His Life and Times*.

§ 28. *Spinoza*

Baruch Spinoza was a Portuguese Jew, born in 1632 in Amsterdam, where his parents had taken refuge from persecution.   On account of the scandal growing out of his heretical opinions, he was excommunicated from the synagogue in 1656, after vain efforts to bribe him to maintain at least an outward conformity.   So bitter was the feeling against him that an attempt was even made to get rid of him by assassination; and his opinions were hardly less objectionable to Christians than to Jews.   The latter portion of his life he spent in relative seclusion, supplying his very simple wants by grinding lenses, for which he earned a wide reputation.   His profound intellect and the beauty of his character attracted however a few friends and disciples.   His fame gradually extended, and he was offered at one time the chair of Philosophy at Heidelberg; but he preferred the liberty to hold without restriction his own beliefs and think his own thoughts.   Money possessed no greater attraction for him than fame and position.   The patrimony of which his sisters had attempted to deprive him he voluntarily relinquished, after first securing his title to it by a legal process.   He refused a present from the French king which a simple dedication would have brought to him.   An admirer, Simon de Vries, who proposed to leave Spinoza his property, was dissuaded by him in favor of the natural heir; and when the latter, after De Vries' death, fixed a pension which had been willed to Spinoza at five hundred florins, he declared the sum too great, and refused to take more than three hundred.   His own death occurred in 1677.

It is not easy to give a brief account of Spinoza's philosophy that shall at once be intelligible and do justice to its spirit.   Couched as it is in abstract and scholastic terms, and given the form of rigid mathematical demonstration, an understanding of the chain of close reasoning which constitutes his system calls for a somewhat technical acquaintance with metaphysics. Furthermore there are acknowledged inconsistencies in Spinoza's thought which complicate a systematic exposition. Without attempting this, accordingly, it will be enough to suggest in a general way what it is that Spinoza in his philosophy is trying to accomplish.

The estimates of Spinoza have been somewhat startling in their divergence. For a time he was very generally execrated as an atheist and a foe to religion; by others his philosophy has been thought to be so fundamentally religious that Novalis gave to him the name "God-intoxicated." Both these judgments represent factors in his thought that are necessary for its proper understanding. From the standpoint of orthodox theology there is no doubt that Spinoza is irreligious. He denies outright the personal God of the Christian, the government of the world according to purpose, and the freedom of the will. It is often difficult to distinguish his theory from a thoroughgoing naturalism which identifies God with the necessary laws of the physical universe. On the other hand Spinoza evidently supposes that he is vindicating the only worthy idea of religion; the ordinary conceptions he opposes as themselves in reality irreligious. God is the beginning and the end of his philosophy. This philosophy, in spite of its abstractness, is not meant in the last analysis to be merely theoretical or metaphysical. As the title — *Ethica* — of his most important book implies, it is practical, a philosophy of life and of redemption.

The central idea of Spinoza, and that which gave him much of his influence somewhat later on when the period of the Enlightenment was drawing to a close, is his recognition of the *unity* of things, not as an intellectual necessity alone, but as a requirement of religious feeling likewise. Descartes had split the world up into two substances distinct from each other, and a God separate from both alike. The Rationalism which took its rise from him tended still further to remove God from the world, until he became a mere far-away observer with scarcely any relation to his work. Such a separation was fatal in two ways. It emptied the idea of God of content, and so tended to render him superfluous; and it made it equally impossible to give any real explanation of the world of things. It was Spinoza's task to insist upon the close connection of God with the world, and to interpret all reality whatsoever in terms of his ultimate perfection.

The starting-point of Spinoza's thought is the perception of the unreality of finite things. Man begins by taking the world as a collection of independent persons and objects, each complete in itself and real in itself. But he soon discovers the futility of this. Intellectually he cannot stop with any object taken alone. He finds he is unable to understand it apart from its connections with other things; and he thus is led continually on from one relationship to another in an endless series. Nor, emotionally, can he rest his affections on the changing facts of the finite world. They are ever leaving him disappointed and disillusioned, and he craves some permanent and perfect object to satisfy his ideal demands. "After experience had taught me," Spinoza says in a passage which describes how he was led to philosophy, "that all the usual surroundings of social life are vain and futile, seeing that none of the objects of my fears contained in themselves anything either good or bad except in so far as the mind is affected by them, I finally resolved to inquire whether there might be some real good having power to communicate itself, which would affect the mind singly to the exclusion of all else; whether in fact there might be anything of which the discovery and attainment would enable me to enjoy continuous, supreme and unending happiness." Such happiness, he saw clearly, neither riches, nor fame, nor the pleasures of sense could give. "Further reflection convinced me that if I could really get to the root of the matter, I should be leaving certain evils for a certain good. I thus perceived that I was in a state of great peril, and I compelled myself to seek with all my strength for a remedy, however uncertain it might be; as a rich man struggling with a deadly disease, when he sees that death will surely be upon him unless a remedy be found, is compelled to seek such a remedy with all his strength, inasmuch as his whole hope lies therein; all the objects pursued by the multitude not only being no remedy that tends to preserve our being, but even act as hindrances, causing the death not seldom of those who possess them, and always of those who are possessed by them. All these evils seem to have arisen from the fact that happiness or unhappiness is made wholly to depend on the quality of the object which we love. When a thing is not loved no quarrels will arise concerning it, no sadness will be felt if it perishes, no envy if it is possessed by another, no fear, no hatred, in short, no disturbance of the mind. All these arise from the love of what is perishable, such as the objects already mentioned. But love toward a thing eternal and infinite fills the mind wholly with joy, and is itself unmingled with any sadness; wherefore it is greatly to be desired and sought for with all our strength." [1]

What is the end of philosophy then? It is the practical end of escaping from the fleeting show which the phenomenal world presents, since this gives no real felicity, and of finding blessedness by identifying ourselves with that true reality, without variableness or shadow of turning, which alone is worthy to call forth our love and able to satisfy it. And this object which alone approves itself to heart and intellect alike is the one eternal unity of the universe — a universe that embraces all things finite and that gives to them whatever reality they possess; in religious language, it is God. Instead of God being a hazardous inference from the undoubted reality of finite things, it is these latter which are doubtful; it is their insufficiency which leads us to the all-sufficient whole in which they have their being. For philosophy the starting-point is not from them, but from the one reality which alone is absolutely certain, and from which they are themselves to be deduced.

Stated in this general way Spinoza's aim, on the theoretical side, is that which nearly all philosophies have made their object; an understanding of the ultimate unity of things has been indeed the main reason for philosophy's existence. It remains to ask how successfully Spinoza accomplishes his task. What is the nature of God's connection with the world, and how far does it satisfy alike the head and the heart?

[1] *Improvement of the Intellect*, Elwes' translation, Vol. II, pp. 3–5.

I. SPINOZA'S METAPHYSICS

1. *Substance and Attributes.* — And first, a brief statement of the intellectual construction which Spinoza makes the basis of his ethical and religious conclusions.   Every fact that can exist must come under one of three heads: it is a substance, or an attribute, or a mode.   A substance is "that which is in itself, and is conceived by means of itself, that is, that the conception of which does not need to be formed from the conception of any other thing."   An attribute is "that which the understanding perceives as constituting the essence of substance."   A mode is a "modification of substance: in other words, that which is in, and is conceived by means of, something else."[1]   The term "mode," to put it more simply, stands for the whole list of particular and finite facts that make up our world — alike external things and inner states of consciousness.

But now Descartes had already seen that, strictly speaking, there is only a single substance.   Matter and mind are not conceivable in themselves, but can only be understood by reference to God; and Spinoza accordingly is consistent in reducing them from substances to attributes of the one substance, God.   Reality, then, is one, eternal, infinite.   On the one substance all things depend — attributes as its eternal essence, finite things as the modifications of these attributes.   Just as in geometry eternal truths about spatial relations are deduced from self-evident premises, so from the definition of God his attributes are to be derived, and, from these, other lesser truths.   The nature of the real and ultimate connections in the world is thus not that of cause and effect, but of logical dependence.

Spinoza's doctrine of substance opens up to him a solution of the problem which had occupied Descartes and the Cartesians — that which concerns the relation of mind and body.   Of the infinite number of attributes which belong to the nature of God we know only two — thought and extension.   On the surface these seem to be connected; an act of will apparently causes a bodily movement,

---

[1] *Ethics*, Pt. I. Def.   This and the following quotations are from Professor Fullerton's translation, *The Philosophy of Spinoza*, Henry Holt & Co.

while an external impression gives rise to a sensation or a feeling. On the other hand there are difficulties in understanding this interaction; Descartes had felt these difficulties, and they had led him to his belief in the automatism of brutes and the all-but automatism even of human beings. We cannot, for one thing, get any clear notion of how it is one substance can act upon another of a wholly different nature. And there is a more formidable difficulty still. If we follow out scientific method with entire consistency, we naturally are forced to look for the same physical explanation for our own bodily movements as for the movements of lifeless things; and this excludes a reference to acts of will, which have no place in the physical world. Occasionalism might seem to obviate the first difficulty, but it hardly touched the second.

Spinoza's doctrine of substance pointed him to a new solution. If the attributes of thought and extension are not two separate things, but only aspects of one and the same thing, they cannot interfere with or act upon each other; for a thing cannot interact with itself. Nevertheless a definite relation will exist between them, just because it is the same substance of which they both are attributes. That which in one light appears as a mode of extension or a physical fact will be, in another light, a mode of thought or fact of consciousness; and so the two modes will correspond, and an exact parallelism will hold between the attributes without the need that any interaction should take place.

In this way Spinoza justifies the claim of science to give an explanation of all physical events, including the actions of the human body, in purely physical terms. For each mode of thought a mode of extension will exist. But since there is no interaction, thought can only be explained by reference to the thought series, and extension by reference to other modes of extension, never the one by the other. "A mode of extension, and the idea of that mode, are one and the same thing, but expressed in two ways — a truth which certain of the Hebrews appear to have seen as if through a mist, in that they assert that God, the intellect of God, and the things known by it, are one and the same. For example, a circle existing in nature, and the idea — which also is in God — of this existing circle, are one and the same thing, manifested through different attributes; for this reason, whether we conceive nature under the attribute of extension or under that of thought, we shall find there follows one and the same order, or one and the same concatenation of causes, that is, the same thing. I have said that God is the cause of an idea, for instance the idea of a circle, merely in so far as he is a thinking thing, and of the circle merely in so far as he is an extended thing, just for the reason that the formal being of the idea of a circle can only be perceived through another mode of thinking as its proximate cause, that one in its turn through another, and so to infinity. Thus whenever we consider things as modes of thinking, we must explain the whole order of nature, or concatenation of causes, through the attribute of thought alone; and in so far as we consider them as modes of extension, we must likewise explain the whole order of nature solely through the attribute of extension." [1]

2. *The Nature of God.* — So much for a general statement. But now in what way is this ultimate substance — God — to be conceived? He is not the God of popular belief. Can he be thought of after the fashion of a man, with body, and mind, and the passions of men? Surely not. Is he a being who acts according to ends or purposes beyond himself? "I confess the doctrine which subjects all things to a certain arbitrary fiat of God, and makes them depend upon his good pleasure, is less wide of the truth than that of those who maintain that God does all things with some end in view. The latter appear to affirm that there is something external to God and independent of him, upon which, as upon a pattern, God looks when he acts, or at which he aims as at a definite goal. This is simply subjecting God to fate, and nothing more absurd than this can be maintained concerning God, who is the first and only free cause, as well of the essence of all things as of their existence." [2] Again, this doctrine denies God's perfection; for if God acts with an end in view he necessarily seeks something which he lacks. "Nor must I here overlook the fact that the adherents of this doctrine, who have chosen to display their ingenu-

[1] Pt. II, 7. Schol.   [2] Pt. I, 33, Schol. 2.

ity in assigning final causes to things, have employed in support of their doctrine a new form of argument, namely, a reduction, not *ad impossibile*, but *ad ignorantiam*, which shows that there was no other way to set about proving this doctrine. If, for example, a stone has fallen from a roof upon some one's head and has killed him, they will prove as follows that the stone fell for the purpose of killing the man. If it did not fall in accordance with God's will for this purpose, how could there have been a chance occurrence of so many circumstances? Perhaps you will answer, it happened because the wind blew, and the man had an errand there. But they will insist, why did the wind blow at that time? and why did that man have an errand that way at just that time? . . . And so they will keep on asking the causes of causes, until you take refuge in the will of God, that asylum of ignorance. So, again, when they consider the structure of the human body they are amazed, and because they are ignorant of the causes which have produced such a work of art, they infer that it has not been fashioned mechanically but by divine or supernatural skill, and put together in such a way that one part does not injure another. Hence it happens that he who seeks for the true causes of miracles, and endeavors, like a scholar, to comprehend the things in nature, and not, like a fool, to wonder at them, is everywhere regarded and proclaimed as a heretic and an impious man by those whom the multitude reverence as interpreters of nature and the gods." [1]

There are thus no final causes in nature; our popular notions are due to a wholly unjustifiable transference of our own conditions to God. Men are constituted with an impulse to seek their own advantage, and they do everything with some purpose in view that has reference to this. "Hence it happens that they always desire to know only the final causes of actions, and, when they have learned these, are satisfied. But if they cannot learn these from some one else, nothing remains for them to do but to turn to themselves, and have recourse to the ends by which they are wont to be determined to similar action; and thus they necessarily judge another's character by their own. Again, since they find in them-

[1] Pt. I, Appendix.

selves and external to themselves many things which, as means, are of no small assistance in obtaining what is to their advantage, as, for example, the eyes for seeing, the teeth for chewing, plants and animals for food, the sun for giving light, the sea for maintaining fish, and so on — this has led them to regard all the things in nature as means to their advantage. And knowing that these means have been discovered, not provided, by themselves, they have made this a reason for believing that there is some one else who has provided these things for their use. . . . Moreover, as they had never had any information concerning the character of such beings, they had to judge of it from their own. Hence they maintained that the gods direct all things with a view to man's advantage, to lay men under obligation to themselves, and to be held by them in the highest honor; whence it has come to pass that each one has thought out for himself, according to his disposition, a different way of worshipping God, that God might love him above others and direct all nature to the service of his blind desire and insatiable avarice. Thus this prejudice has become a superstition, and has taken deep root in men's minds; and this has been the reason why every one has applied himself with the greatest effort to comprehend and explain the final causes of all things. But while they sought to prove that nature does nothing uselessly (in other words, nothing that is not to man's advantage), they seemed to have proved only that nature and gods and men are all equally mad. Just see how far the thing has been carried. Among all the useful things in nature they could not help finding a few harmful things, as tempests, earthquakes, diseases and so forth. They maintain that these occur because the gods were angry on account of injuries done them by men, or on account of faults committed in their worship. And although experience daily contradicted this, and showed by an infinity of instances that good and evil fall to the lot of the pious and of the impious indifferently, that did not make them abandon their inveterate prejudice; they found it easier to class these facts with other unknown things of whose use they were ignorant, and thus to retain their present and innate condition of ignorance, than to destroy the whole fabric of their reasoning and think out a new one. Hence they assumed that the judgments of the gods very far surpass man's power of comprehension. This in itself would have been sufficient to hide the truth forever from mankind had not mathematics, which is concerned, not with final causes, but with the essences and properties of figures, shown men a different standard of truth." [1]

It is from these prejudices that all our judgments of worth in nature have sprung. "After men have persuaded themselves that everything that happens happens for their sake, they had to regard that quality in each thing which was most useful to them as the most important, and to rate all those things which affected them the most agreeably as the most excellent. Hence to explain the natures of things they had to frame the notions *good, evil, order, confusion, beauty* and *deformity;* and from their belief that they are free have arisen the notions of *praise* and *blame*, and *sin* and *merit.* . . . They have called *good* everything which conduces to health and to the worship of God, and *bad* everything that is unfavorable to these." In reality, good and evil indicate no positive element in things, considered, that is to say, in themselves. They are only modes of thinking, or subjective notions. One and the same thing can be at the same time good, bad, and indifferent. For example, music is good for the melancholy man, and bad for him who mourns; while for the deaf man it is neither good nor bad. "And as those who do not understand nature make no affirmations about things, but only imagine things, and take imagination for understanding, in their ignorance of things and of their nature they firmly believe that there is *order* in things. For when things are so arranged that, when they are represented to us through the senses, we can easily imagine them, and hence can easily think them over, we call them orderly; if the opposite be true, we say they are in disorder, or are *confused*. And since those things we can easily imagine are more pleasing to us than others, men place order above confusion — as though order had any existence in nature except in relation to our imagination — and they say that God created all things in order, thus unwittingly ascribing imagination to God. . . .

[1] Pt. I, Appendix.

So if the motion communicated to the nerves by objects represented through the eyes is conducive to health, the objects which cause it are called *beautiful;* those objects on the other hand that excite a contrary motion are called *ugly.* Again, those that move the sense through the nostrils are called odoriferous or stinking; those that move it through the tongue sweet or bitter, savory or unsavory, and so on. Finally, those that move the ears are said to give forth noise, sound or harmony; which last has driven men so mad that they believed even God takes delight in harmony. Nor are there wanting philosophers who have persuaded themselves that the motions of the heavenly bodies compose a harmony. All this sufficiently proves that every one has judged of things according to the condition of his brain, or, rather, has taken the affections of his imagination for things. Hence it is not surprising that so many controversies have arisen among men as we find to be the case, and that from these scepticism has resulted. For although men's bodies are in many respects alike, yet they have very many points of difference; and therefore what seems good to one seems bad to another, what seems orderly to one seems confused to another, what is pleasant to one is unpleasant to another. The sayings: 'Many men, many minds,' 'Every man is satisfied with his own opinion,' 'Brains differ as much as palates' — these are in everybody's mouth; and they sufficiently prove that men judge of things according to the condition of their brains, and rather imagine things than comprehend them. For had they comprehended things, all these proofs would, as mathematics bears witness, if not attract, at least convince them." [1]

None of the attributes of worth, then, which we are accustomed to assign to the world, have any real existence. All that we can say is that things are, and are necessarily. God did not create them for a purpose, nor could he have made them to be otherwise than we actually find them. To suppose that God is a free cause and able to prevent the things which follow from his nature from coming to pass, is the same as saying that God can prevent it following from the nature of a triangle that its three angles are equal

[1] Pt. I, Appendix.

to two right angles. We cannot ascribe to God will or intellect at all in the human meaning of the words. "If intellect or will do belong to God's eternal essence, each of these attributes must be taken in a sense very different from the common one. For there would have to be a world-wide difference between our intellect and will, and the intellect and will constituting God's essence, nor could they agree in anything except the name; just as the Dog, a constellation, agrees with dog, an animal that barks." [1]

But if God has neither passions, nor purposes, nor intellect, nor will, nor moral worth, what content are we to assign to him? There is no doubt that Spinoza seems often to be trying to conceive of reality, after the manner of the scientist, as a great system of natural law; the scientific view forms at any rate the positive basis for his criticism of religion and teleology. On this positive side, "science touched with emotion" perhaps comes closest to characterizing his general attitude. But does even science have any final truth as an account of the divine? Or is God after all in his essence anything more than abstract substance, of which we can say nothing whatever that is definite?

3. *God and the Finite World.* — Such a question brings out a real difficulty in Spinoza's philosophy. He wants, undoubtedly, a substance that shall find a place for, and give an explanation to, the reality of the phenomenal world; this world is what we start from, and undeniably it possesses reality of a kind, even if its reality is imperfect and incomplete. That the process of abstraction does not lead to reality he was well aware; the abstract man is not more but less real than particular men, and only represents the fact that these have certain elements in common. But for all that, in his actual procedure, the eternal facts with which he identifies reality show a tendency to become just such abstractions; to use Hegel's figure, Spinoza's Absolute is the lion's den to which all tracks lead and from which none return.

And even if Spinoza had been always true to the ideal of reality as law rather than as mere substance, he still had an unsolved problem in the fact of imperfection and contingency. By the

[1] Pt. I, 17, Schol.

geometrical method we can at best only get truths which, though derived, are as absolute and as eternal as the God on whose definition they depend; the theorem of geometry is as true and adequate as the axioms on which it is based. But what then of the inadequate and false ideas represented in Spinoza's modes? Whence comes our phenomenal knowledge of ourselves and of the world? Such false ideas can never be arrived at by a method that gives only truth. To put it in another way, our inadequate notions of the world and the contingent modes of extension which these represent either have an existence or they have not. If they have an existence they are a part of God, since nothing exists outside of him; and then how can they be otherwise than as they are for God — eternal and adequate? Or, if they have no existence at all, how do we come to talk about them as if they did exist? The fact is that by no possibility can Spinoza connect the world of appearance, of finite modes, of existence in time, with the true and eternal (timeless) reality of God, and of those derivative truths, equally eternal, that can be deduced from him. Logically he ought, it would seem, to have denied the finite world outright, as his spiritual predecessor Parmenides had done; but he had far too much respect for facts and science to permit of this. Indeed the whole purpose of his philosophy is to show how man, from being a mere part of the phenomenal world, can escape from its finiteness and attain true felicity.

2. THE DOCTRINE OF SALVATION

1. *Human Bondage.* — It has appeared that, according to Spinoza, the unsatisfactoriness of life is due to the fact that our affections are set, not upon an object that is eternal and unchanging, but upon transitory and imperfect things. If the object of our love were without variableness it would lay to rest our passions, and impart to life something of its own calm and steadfastness. But because we love that which has no constancy and no true reality we are in a continual turmoil of emotions; we hate, and envy, and fear, are exalted and depressed, take even our pleasures feverishly, and never know what peace is like. Subjection to the emotions

then, and an ignorance of our true end — the former growing out of the latter — are the elements which constitute human bondage.

The further justification of this is found in a naturalistic psychology of the human life. It will doubtless seem to moralists generally most strange, Spinoza writes, "that I should endeavor to treat by a geometrical method the vices and follies of man, and to desire by a sure method to demonstrate those things which these people cry out against as being opposed to reason, or as being vanities, absurdities and monstrosities. The following is my reason for doing so: Nothing happens in nature which can be attributed to any vice of nature; for she is always the same and everywhere one — so that there must be one and the same method of understanding the nature of all things whatsoever, that is to say, the universal laws and rules of nature. The effects therefore of hatred, anger, envy, considered in themselves, follow from the same necessity and virtue of nature as other individual things; they have therefore certain causes through which they are to be understood, and certain properties which are just as worthy of being known as the properties of any other thing in the contemplation alone of which we delight. I shall therefore . . . consider human actions and appetites just as if I were considering lines, planes or bodies."

In pursuit of this end Spinoza starts by defining the essence of life as *self-preservation* — the tendency of each individual thing to persist in its own being, to welcome all that tends to increase this, and oppose and reject whatever tends to limit it. When this act of self-assertion depends wholly on ourselves we have what Spinoza calls an *action;* when it depends in part upon what lies beyond ourselves it is a *passion.* How is this distinction between actions and passions to be understood?

The answer goes back to the two ways of regarding the human mind implied in Spinoza's metaphysics. If we take our phenomenal knowledge about the world, the particular states of our empirical consciousness, we have what Spinoza has called modes. Now such finite facts are not complete in themselves or open to a fully adequate explanation; each is causally dependent on another finite fact, and this again on another, and so on ad infinitum. Thus in the physical realm any bodily change depends, not on the nature of the body alone, but on the body as affected by another mode — that is, upon the interaction between the body and the outside world; and the antecedents of this interaction can never be completely followed out. The same thing is true of the modes of thought, or ideas, which correspond to bodily modes. Accordingly our supposed adequate knowledge of objects is nothing of the sort. When we think we perceive an external object, what we really have is a sensation representing a state of our own body — a state which is caused by the interaction between the real object and our sense organs, and which consequently, by reason of its being a product of two factors, is a true representative of neither of them. This is the old doctrine of the relativity of sense perception which goes back to Protagoras. All our sense knowledge is, therefore, inadequate and confused.

But there is another way of looking at the human mind. Besides being a collection of finite modes, our minds are also a constituent part of God's nature, since everything whatever that exists exists in God. In their essence therefore, their inmost truth and reality, our ideas may be viewed " under a certain form of eternity "; and when thus viewed they no longer are inadequate. The distinction between actions and passions, then, goes back to the distinction between adequate thought which has its full explanation in the mind itself as this is identical in its essence with God, and inadequate thought which depends on the mind as a collection of finite modes each getting what explanation it is capable of by reference to an infinite series of other finite facts. We are never fully active except as we think truly and see things as they are in God; for it is in thought that the essence of our nature lies. "The desires which follow from our nature in such a way that they can be comprehended through it alone, are such as are referred to the mind in so far as it is conceived as consisting of adequate ideas. The other desires, however, are not referred to the mind except in so far as it conceives things inadequately, and their strength and growth must be defined, not as human power, but as that of the things that are outside us. Hence the former are properly called actions, the latter passions;

for the former always indicate our power, the latter, on the contrary, our impotence and fragmentary knowledge." [1]

But the mind strives to persevere in its being, and is conscious of this its endeavor, not only in so far as it has clear and distinct ideas, but also in so far as it has confused ideas. And here comes in Spinoza's doctrine of the emotions. For typically an emotion is just a confused idea, or a passion. The body can be affected in many ways by which its power of acting is increased or diminished; modifications of the body and their corresponding ideas through which either of these results is brought about are what we call emotions. A passion in which the mind passes to a greater degree of perfection is pleasure; one in which it passes to a lesser degree of perfection is pain. By reference to the three elements — desire, pain, pleasure — all the varied emotions are to be defined. Thus, love is pleasure accompanied by the idea of an external cause; hate is pain accompanied by a similar idea. Derision is pleasure which has its source in the fact that we conceive something we despise to be in the thing we hate. Hope is inconstant pleasure arising from the idea of something future or past, of the event of which we have some doubt. Despair is pain arising from a thing present or past, regarding which cause for doubt has been removed; and so on. In general, "an emotion which is called a passion of the soul is a confused idea, through which the mind affirms the energy of existence possessed by its body, or any part of it, to be greater or less than it was before, and through the presence of which the mind itself is determined to this thought rather than to that." [2]

The attainment of true freedom has accordingly two sides. It is an escape from the emotions, and it is an escape from inadequate and false ideas: and these two things are one. True blessedness is thus the blessedness of knowledge. "Hence it is of the utmost service in life to perfect the understanding or reason as far as we can; and in this one thing consists man's highest felicity. Indeed, blessedness is nothing but that very satisfaction of the soul which arises from an intuitive knowledge of God. But to perfect the understanding is only to comprehend God, his attributes, and the

[1] Pt. IV, Appendix II.　　　　　[2] Pt. III, Fullerton, p. 152.

actions that follow from the necessity of his nature.   Wherefore the ultimate aim of the man who is controlled by reason, that is, the highest desire with which he strives to restrain all the others, is that which impels him to conceive adequately himself and everything that can fall within the scope of his understanding." [1]   That alone is good which is conducive to knowledge; that which hinders and diminishes it is bad.

Meanwhile we should note that the emotions, for Spinoza, continue to be real parts of human nature, and not, as the Stoics had thought, a mere disease of the mind to be eradicated.   It is from the *bondage* of the emotions we are to free ourselves, not from the emotional life itself.   Emotions are bad in so far as they are *passions*.   But to activity also there belongs its appropriate emotional side which constitutes an integral part of the good life, and which takes on the one hand the form of strength of mind, and on the other that of nobility and generosity.   Thus temperance, sobriety, presence of mind in danger, are a species of strength of mind, or of the desire by which each man endeavors to preserve his own being according to the dictate of reason alone; while moderation and mercy are forms of a similar rational desire to help and to join to himself in friendship other men.

What in other words Spinoza wishes to maintain is the need for getting rid of emotional disturbances that are depressing, devitalizing and obstructive, and for cultivating instead a cheerful and expansive mood.   For pleasure and cheerfulness are *life*, while pain and sorrow are always bad and work against improvement; and we cannot promote life by checking its exuberance.   We grow by fixing our minds on the possibilities of active achievement and positive good, not on evils and deficiencies.   Whereas the sick man eats what he dislikes from a fear of death, a man in health enjoys his food; and in consequence he reaps more benefit than if he feared death and directly desired to avoid it.   This is why pity, repentance and humility are for Spinoza motives to be avoided.   They mean a lowering of vitality, a movement away from perfection; they concentrate attention on our weakness and make us blind to

[1] Pt. IV, Appendix IV.

our true strength.   Repentance is doubly bad; for he who repents is weak, and is conscious of his weakness.   Man's good lies with the positive forces that liberate his energies.   Vice is impotence, and can be cured only by new accessions of power; and power means pleasure, cheerful serenity, buoyancy.   It is because knowledge brings us into contact with larger reaches of existence, expands the soul and increases its power of action and enjoyment, that it constitutes a good.   Knowledge is thus not to be conceived just as passionless intellect; we cannot separate knowledge from emotion, if by emotion we understand a pleasurable sense of vital function.

   2. *Human Freedom.* — This, in general terms, is the outcome of Spinoza's philosophy; it may be well however to consider the process a little more closely.   And at first sight it might seem that freedom is impossible in Spinoza's system, since necessity rules in this from first to last.   It has been seen that all things follow necessarily from the nature of God; an event is called contingent only in relation to the imperfection of our knowledge.   And of course the life of man does not fall outside this necessity.   Is it said that we know by experience that it is within the power of the mind alone to do many things solely by its own decree — to speak, for example, or to be silent as it chooses?   "But surely the condition of human affairs would be much more satisfactory if it *were* as much within man's power to be silent as to speak.   But experience gives sufficient and more than sufficient proof of the fact that there is nothing less under a man's control than his tongue, nor is there anything of which a man is less capable than of restraining his impulse.   This is the reason most persons believe that we are free only in doing those things to which we are impelled by slight desires, for the impulse to do such things can be easily checked by the memory of some other thing of which we often think; but that we are by no means free in doing those things to which we are impelled by strong emotion which cannot be checked by the memory of some other thing.   But for their experience of the fact that we do many things which we afterward regret, and that we often, when we are harassed by conflicting emotions, see the better and follow the worse, nothing would prevent them from believing that we are always free in our

actions. Thus the infant believes that it desires milk of its own
free will, the angry child that it is free in seeking revenge, and the
timid that it is free in taking to flight. Again, a drunken man
believes that he says of his own free will things he afterward, when
sober, wishes he had left unsaid; so also an insane man, a garrulous
woman, a child, and very many others of the sort, believe they
speak of their own free will, while nevertheless they are unable to
control their impulse to talk. Thus experience itself shows, no less
clearly than reason, that men think themselves free only because
they are conscious of their actions, and ignorant of the causes which
determine them. It shows, moreover, that the mind's decisions
are nothing but its impulses, which vary with the varying condition
of the body." [1]

We cannot, therefore, escape from the necessary facts of existence; reality is what it is, and we cannot make it different. But
this is bondage *only* when we rebel against it, and set up in its stead
private and arbitrary ends. We shall find freedom — the only true
freedom — in knowing the truth and accepting it. We are not
under constraint because we are subject to law, but because we are
subject to our own ignorance and passions. God is perfect freedom,
not because he can act arbitrarily, but because he acts solely from
the laws of his own nature and under no compulsion; there is
nothing external to him that can determine him to act.

Now emotions, since they are passions rather than actions, represent such an influence of external things. But the road to salvation
already has appeared. We can overcome the emotions by *understanding* them, by ridding ourselves of our confused ideas and seeing
everything in its innermost truth as a *necessary* fact. Everyday
experience will show us how potent an effect the recognition of the
necessity of things has upon our attitude toward them. To aim at
the impossible is a sure source of perturbation and discontent. But
if I once see that it *is* impossible I no longer make myself unhappy
about it; the mind accepts the inevitable and its vain struggles
cease. "The more the knowledge that these things are necessary is
brought to bear upon individual things which we imagine more

[1] Pt. III, 2, Schol.

distinctly and vividly, the greater is the power of the mind over the emotions. To this fact experience itself bears witness. We see sorrow at the loss of some good thing mitigated as soon as the man who has lost it perceives that he could not have preserved it in any possible way. Thus we see, also, that no one pities an infant because it cannot speak, walk or reason, and because, in a word, it lives so many years, as it were, without the consciousness of self. But if most persons were born as adults and only one here and there as an infant, then every one would pity infants, for then we should regard infancy itself, not as a natural and necessary thing, but as a defect or fault of nature."

Spinoza goes on to show the ways in which the emotions can in practice be controlled by the superior force, permanence, frequency and harmony which are characters belonging to true knowledge, and which enable it to hold the mind against false and inadequate ideas. These all go back ultimately to that which constitutes the chief power of adequate ideas — their relation to the idea of God. Everything alike can be referred to the idea of God, since he is the truth of all things; and when it is thus referred, we have at hand an instrument whose force is irresistible for overcoming the emotions. For the philosopher, convinced that all events, including human actions, are the outcome of the necessity of the divine nature, nothing merits contempt, hatred, pity; he has simply to understand them as a part of the whole of things, not to judge them. He will lay aside all private and selfish aims and merge himself in the great life of the whole, to whose will he will bow without repining, and find thereby joy and peace. Once know and accept things as they are in God, and the warring desires and passions which distract us will pass away; the motives which look large to us now in our ignorance will lose their power. "Griefs and misfortunes have their chief source in an excessive love of that which is subject to many variations, and of which we can never have control. No one is solicitous or anxious about anything unless he love it; nor do injustices, suspicions, enmities and so forth arise, except from the love of things of which no one can really have control. Thus we easily conceive what power clear and distinct knowledge, and especially that third kind of knowledge the foundation of which is the knowledge of God and nothing else, has over the emotions; if it does not, in so far as they are passions, absolutely remove them, at all events it brings it about that they constitute the least part of the mind. Furthermore, it begets love toward that which is immutable and eternal, and which we really have within our power — a love which, consequently, is not stained by any of the defects inherent in common love, but can always become greater and greater, and take possession of the greatest part of the mind, and affect it everywhere." [1]

This is very different from the love of God which religion ordinarily inculcates. The God of positive religions is a God of the imagination, an individual like ourselves who loves and hates, is angry and jealous, and acts by an arbitrary will. In consequence all the defects of human love enter into our relations to him, and love may easily pass into hate. But no one can hate the eternal and necessary order of nature. This love toward God cannot be stained either with the emotion of envy or of jealousy, but is the more intensified the greater the number óf men we conceive bound to God by the same bond of love. "We can show in the same way that there is no emotion directly opposed to this love capable of destroying it. Hence we may conclude that this love toward God is the most unchangeable of all the emotions, and cannot, in so far as it is referred to the body, be destroyed except with the body itself."

In the final stage of this process of emancipation we have already gone beyond mere practical rules of life to something more ultimate, which gives its peculiar tinge to Spinoza's whole thought. From the falsity of ordinary opinion we have passed by the power of discursive reason to adequate ideas; but there is a higher kind of knowledge still. Reason is not merely our individual reason working under conditions of time; it is also eternal, freed from all restrictions, a part of the infinite intellect of God. And the same truths which we have gained laboriously by processes of reasoning may also take on another form, the form of an immediate flash of

[1] Pt. V, 20, Schol.

intuition in which they are seen to flow directly from the one Truth — God. From this third kind of knowledge springs the highest possible satisfaction of the mind. "The more of this kind of knowledge any one possesses, the clearer is his consciousness of himself and of God, that is, the more perfect and blessed is he." "From this third kind of knowledge necessarily springs the intellectual love of God. For from this kind of knowledge springs pleasure accompanied by the idea of God as cause, that is, a love of God not in so far as we imagine him as present, but in so far as we comprehend God to be eternal." "And this intellectual love of the mind toward God is the very love of God with which God loves himself, not in so far as he is infinite, but in so far as he can be expressed by the essence of the human mind considered under the form of eternity; that is, the intellectual love of the mind toward God is a part of the infinite love with which God loves himself. From this we clearly comprehend in what our salvation, or blessedness, or freedom, consists; to wit, in an unchangeable and eternal love toward God, that is, in the love of God toward men. This love or blessedness is in the sacred Scriptures called glory." [1]

To recapitulate, how does this doctrine of freedom contribute to the service of life? "First, it is of value in that it teaches us that we act according to God's decree, and are participants in the divine nature; and this the more, the more perfect the actions we perform, and the better we comprehend God. Hence this doctrine not only sets the soul completely at rest, but also teaches us in what our highest felicity or blessedness consists, to wit, only in the knowledge of God, which leads us to do only those things that love and piety recommend. Thus we see clearly how far from a true estimate of virtue are those who expect God to honor them with the highest rewards for their virtue and good actions, as though for the extremest slavery — as if virtue and the service of God were not felicity itself, and the completest freedom. Second, it is of value in that it teaches us how to behave with regard to those things which depend upon fortune and which are not within our power, that is, with regard to those things that do not follow from our nature. It

[1] Pt. V, 31, Schol.; 32, Cor.; 36, and Schol.

teaches us, namely, to look forward to and endure either aspect of fortune with equanimity, just because all things follow from the eternal decree of God, by the same necessity with which it follows from the essence of a triangle that its three angles are equal to two right angles. Third, this doctrine is of service to social life in that it teaches to hate no one, to despise, to ridicule, to be angry at no one, to envy no one. It is of service, further, in that it teaches each one to be content with what he has, and to aid his neighbor, not from womanish pity, partiality or superstition, but solely under the guidance of reason, according to the demands of the time and the case. Fourth, this doctrine is of no little advantage to the state in that it shows how citizens ought to be governed and led; namely, not so as to act like slaves, but so as to do freely what is best." [1]

"And even if we did not know our mind to be eternal, we should nevertheless regard as of the highest importance piety and religion. The belief of the multitude appears to be otherwise. Most men seem to think that they are free just in so far as they are permitted to gratify desire, and that they give up their independence just in so far as they are obliged to live according to the precept of the divine law. Piety, then, and religion, and all things without restriction that are referred to greatness of soul, they regard as burdens; and they hope after death to lay these down, and to receive the reward of their bondage, that is, of piety and religion. And not only by this hope alone, but also and chiefly by fear — the fear of being punished after death with dire torments — are they induced to live according to the precept of the divine law so far as their poverty and feebleness of soul permit. If men had not this hope and fear, but if on the contrary they thought that minds perished with the body, and that for the wretched, worn out with the burden of piety, there was no continuance of existence, they would return to their inclination, and decide to regulate everything according to their lusts, and to be governed by chance rather than by themselves. This seems to me no less absurd than it would seem if some one, because he does not believe he can nourish his body with good food to

[1] Pt. II, 49. Schol.

eternity, should choose to stuff himself with what is poisonous and deadly; or, because he sees that his mind is not eternal or immortal, should choose on that account to be mad and to live without reason. Blessedness is not the reward of virtue, but virtue itself; nor do we rejoice in it because we restrain the desires, but, on the contrary, because we rejoice in it we are able to restrain the desires." [1]

"With this I have completed all that I intended to show regarding the power of the mind over the emotions, and the freedom of the mind. From what I have said it is evident how much stronger and better the wise man is than the ignorant man who is led by mere desire. For the ignorant man, besides being agitated in many ways by external causes, and never attaining true satisfaction of soul, lives as it were without consciousness of himself, of God, and of things, and just as soon as he ceases to be acted upon ceases to be. While, on the contrary, the wise man, in so far as he is considered as such, is little disturbed in mind, but, conscious by a certain eternal necessity of himself, of God, and of things, he never ceases to be, but is always possessed of true satisfaction of soul. If indeed the path that I have shown to lead to this appears very difficult, still it may be found. And surely it must be difficult since it is so rarely found. For if salvation were easily attained, and could be found without great labor, how could it be neglected by nearly every one? But all excellent things are as difficult as they are rare." [2]

LITERATURE

Spinoza, *Improvement of the Intellect, Ethics, Theologico-Political Treatise, Political Treatise*. Translations: Elwes (*Works*, 2 vols.); White (*Ethics* and *Tractatus*); Fullerton (*Selections from Ethics*).

Pollock, *Spinoza*.

Martineau, *Study of Spinoza*.

Martineau, *Types of Ethical Theory*.

Caird, *Spinoza*.

Caird, *Essays on Literature and Philosophy*.

Iverach, *Descartes, Spinoza and the New Philosophy*.

[1] Pt. V, 41 and Schol.; 42.   [2] Pt. V, 42, Schol.

Joachim, *Study of the Ethics of Spinoza.*
Duff, *Spinoza's Political and Ethical Philosophy.*
Graham, *English Political Philosophy from Hobbes to Maine.*

§ 29. *Leibniz*

The temperament and life history of *Gottfried Wilhelm Leibniz* are as far as possible removed from those of his predecessor. Born in Leipsic in 1646, he early showed a remarkable genius which took the whole world as its field. In mathematics, where he is celebrated as being one of the discoverers of the differential calculus; in law, civil and international; in history (he was employed to write the memoirs of the family of his patron, the Duke of Hanover); in religious controversy, and in philosophy proper, he stood among the foremost men of his time. This universality of mind enabled him to do justice to the varied interests which philosophy has to serve, and made his system a gathering-point for most of the important motives that had entered into its past development.

The practical side of Leibniz' nature was another factor that influenced his theoretical views. He was no mere thinker, like Spinoza, but a man of the world, in the midst of, and taking a part in, the life of his day. His legal training early gave him an entrance into politics, and either as writer or diplomatic agent he was connected with many of the important events of the period. This practical training perhaps emphasized his tendency to mediate between opposing views; the spirit which led him to attempt to get at the truth in all philosophies is that which reveals itself also in his political aims — for example, in his endeavor to heal the differences between Protestants and Catholics by drawing up a compromise on which both could unite. To the labor which his political offices involved we may add the effort to secure the establishment in Germany of learned societies, or Academies, by which the results of the new scientific spirit should be conserved and applied to human ends. This bore fruit during Leibniz' own lifetime in the Berlin Academy.

1. *The Nature of Substance.* — The more general aspects of Leibniz' philosophy can best be brought out by comparing them

with the solution which Spinoza had offered. The main emphasis in Spinoza had been upon the unity of the world, a unity which was to bring together the factors Descartes had left separate — mind, matter and God. For Leibniz also this was the ultimate goal of philosophy; but it had been purchased at what seemed to him too great a price. For apparently it left no place for the genuine reality of individuals — men and things. A man of practical affairs, individuals were to Leibniz indubitably real, and no theory which failed to account for their reality seemed tenable. He was not satisfied, either, with Spinoza's rejection of teleology or purpose; the very essence of practical life consists in working for ends, and no theory which disparages ends is likely to seem adequate to the practical man. At the same time Leibniz felt the need, as Spinoza had done, for a more intelligible unity to things than Descartes had shown the way to; and he accepted, also, the relative validity at least of that strictly mechanical view of the physical world which Spinoza's parallelism had been designed to justify. How in the light of these truths could justice still be done to the world of finite things, and to human intelligence and freedom?

The answer which Leibniz gave was made possible through a reconstruction of the idea of substance, both mental and material. Descartes had defined matter as *extended* substance. This had involved the assumption that it is passive and inert, and able to receive motion only from the outside. Leibniz was led by various motives to substitute, for extension, *power of resistance* as the essential quality of matter. In this way the notion of passive matter is replaced by what is essentially the modern scientific conception of matter as energy, or force. A substance is a being capable of action; and since we find individual things exerting force, the substantiality of which they had been deprived by Spinoza in favor of his single ultimate substance has now to be restored to them. Furthermore, these substantial units to which extended matter reduces itself cannot be themselves extended. We cannot find anything really ultimate and indivisible in the atoms of the physicists; whatever is still material, however small it may be, is still capable of being further divided. In order to get a true indivisible unit we need to leave behind the extended altogether.

And from this new standpoint there is opened up the possibility of removing the absoluteness of that distinction between matter and mind upon which Descartes had insisted. If the essence of matter is extension, then it has no point of contact with the mental life; it is, indeed, the opposite of thought. Spinoza had tried to avoid the dualism by referring both thought and extension to a single substance. This however involves self-contradiction; it means asserting that the same substance is both extended and unextended. But when now, instead of extension, we characterize matter as *force*, a means of connection will appear. For force has its analogue in the conscious life; corresponding to the activity of matter there is conscious activity, or will. Indeed are there any positive terms in which we can describe the nature of force unless we conceive it as identical with that conscious activity which we know directly in ourselves? The notion of matter has thus been entirely transformed. Instead of its being a passive lump of extended substance, extension is merely the phenomenal way in which matter appears to us. Actually what we call matter is a host of unextended centers of force, whose activity is at bottom, when we interpret it, a spiritual or perceptual activity. The reality of the world is not matter, but *monads*.

In order however to complete the picture, the concept of mind has also to suffer a partial transformation. According to Descartes, the essence of mind is thought; and Leibniz also retains a tendency to this intellectualism. But the conception of mind which hitherto had ruled is vastly enlarged by Leibniz. Below the threshold of our clear consciousness there is, he thinks, a dark background of obscurer consciousness, *petites perceptions*, unconscious mental states. The existence of these Leibniz proves by various considerations. "For a better understanding of the *petites perceptions* I am wont to employ the illustration of the moaning or sound of the sea, which we notice when we are on the shore. In order to hear this sound as we do, we must hear the parts of which the whole sound is made up, that is to say, the sounds which come from each wave, although each of these little sounds makes itself known only in the confused combination of all the sounds taken together, that is to say, in the moaning of the sea, and no one of the sounds would be observed if the wave which makes it were alone. For we must be affected a little by the motion of this wave, and we must have some perception of each of these sounds, however little they may be; otherwise we should not have a perception of a hundred thousand waves, for a hundred thousand nothings cannot make something. We never sleep so profoundly as not to have some feeble and confused feeling, and we should never be wakened by the greatest noise in the world if we had not some perception of its beginning, which is small, just as we should never break a cord by the greatest effort in the world if it were not strained and stretched a little by less efforts, though the small extension they produce is not apparent." [1]

And in this new conception we have a means of still further lessening the gap which in appearance exists between what we know as mind, and the blind workings of force in material nature. This is done through the principle of *continuity*, which is another of the watchwords of Leibniz' philosophy. According to this principle, there are no breaks in nature; things shade into one another by infinitely small gradations. This means that there is a continuous series from the lowest monads up to the highest which we call souls, or spirits. Every monad alike lives a thought life, a life of perceptual activity. But the clearness of this thinking differs so widely as to seem at the two extremes almost a difference in kind. The thought which constitutes the life of the material monads is confused and turbid; compared with our own it is like a swoon or dreamless sleep. What we call souls, on the contrary, are monads in which this confused thought has come to at least a partial awareness of itself. Even in man a large part of the soul life still remains obscure. This relatively is the case with sense perceptions, and it is because the life of sense is thus confused that we see the world as material and not for what it really is — a collection of immaterial beings whose nature differs only in degree from ours.

---

[1] *New Essays*, p. 371. This and the succeeding quotations are taken from Latta's translation, Clarendon Press.

To sum up, reality consists of an infinite host of individual beings, or monads, representing countless different grades of development. Those lower in the scale are what we call matter; those more highly developed are souls; while highest of all are self-conscious minds, or spirits. The inner nature of these monads is describable in terms of force; or, in its more ultimate interpretation, of an active life consisting in various degrees of conscious perception or of thought. "In the smallest particle of matter there is a world of creatures, living beings, animals, entelechies, souls. Each portion of matter may be conceived as like a garden full of plants, and like a pond full of fishes. But each branch of every plant, each member of every animal, each drop of its liquid parts, is also some such garden or pond. Thus there is nothing fallow, nothing sterile, nothing dead in the universe; no chaos, no confusion save in appearance, somewhat as it might appear to be in a pond at a distance, in which one would see a confused movement, and, as it were, a swarming of fish in the pond, without separately distinguishing the fish themselves." [1]

2. *Preëstablished Harmony.* — By this time we may seem to have been carried to the opposite pole from Spinoza, and in establishing the reality of individuals to have lost the unity which is to bind them together. And the way in which Leibniz goes on to describe the life of the monads seems to make the problem more desperate still. Each monad, as a center of force, has the principle of its life and development contained wholly in its own nature. Instead of being, like the matter of Descartes, passive and so influenced only from without, it is never influenced from without at all. It has a perfect independence as regards the influence of all other created things. "Each spirit being like a world apart, sufficient to itself, independent of every other created thing, involving the infinite, expressing the universe, is as lasting, as continuous in its existence, and as absolute as the very universe of created things." [2] How indeed is a purely external influence thinkable? How could a thing act in response to an outer influence unless it were its own nature so to act — unless, that is, it had the active principle of its movement already in itself? Each monad thus lives its own life independ-

[1] *Monad.*, 66, 67, 69.   [2] *New System*, p. 316.

ently of every other monad. It is shut up to the possibilities of its own nature, and develops solely in accordance with its own laws; it has no windows through which anything can enter or go out. And yet, as a matter of fact, the different monads must somehow be related and take account of other monads in their actions, in order to make possible the ordered Cosmos that results.

The explanation lies in the two words — Preëstablished Harmony. It is true that each monad is a thing by itself, uninfluenced by any other monad. Nevertheless there is a real unity in the world; it is the unity of a plan or purpose which the world reveals, and which has its source in the mind of God. With reference to one another the monads are indeed windowless; they develop in accord with principles immanent in their own being. But they are not absolutely isolated. There is a higher reality on which each depends and a higher purpose that it serves; and it is this which explains why, in spite of being isolated, the monads yet show so intimate a correspondence. For it is with reference to the universal plan that the nature of each monad is constituted at the start. The course of development that is to make up the life of each is determined originally with the whole universe of other monads in view; and so simply by following its own course, without interference from outside, it yet runs parallel to, and reflects, the development which is going on independently in other monads.

This is illustrated by Leibniz in a simile. "I will say that this concomitance which I maintain is comparable to several different bands of musicians or choirs, playing their parts separately, and so placed that they do not see or even hear one another; which can nevertheless keep perfectly together by each following their own notes, in such a way that he who hears them all finds in them a harmony that is wonderful, and much more surprising than if there had been any connection between them." [1] The nature of the correspondence Leibniz expresses in the statement that each monad, although windowless, nevertheless at each stage of its existence *mirrors*, from its special point of view, the life of all the rest, just as in the physical realm each movement involves every other move-

[1] *Letter to Arnauld*, Latta, p. 47.

ment in the universe. This last is indeed only the other side, the phenomenal aspect, of the former fact. So one might come to know the beauty of the whole universe in each soul, if he could unfold all that is enfolded in it from the start.

This conception of preëstablished harmony has a particular application to one specific problem — the relationship of mind and body. Of course what we call a body is, for Leibniz, not actually material, but a group of monads of the less developed sort. Every "soul" or higher monad has such a group of inferior associates with which it stands in a specially close connection. These, by the law of their nature, tend to subordinate themselves to the central and ruling soul; and in this way they constitute what appears to us phenomenally as a body. "These principles have given me a way of explaining naturally the union, or rather the mutual agreement, of the soul and the organic body. The soul follows its own laws, and the body likewise follows its own laws; and they agree with each other in virtue of the preëstablished harmony between all substances, since they are all representations of one and the same universe." [1]

This is expressed in the famous figure of the clocks. Suppose two clocks or watches which perfectly keep time together; this may happen in three ways. The first way is by a direct mechanical influence of one upon the other; this is the usual conception of the relation between body and soul. The second way of making two clocks, even though they be bad ones, keep together, would be to put them in charge of a skilled workman who should regulate them from moment to moment — this, again, is the theory of Occasionalism. Finally, the third way would be to make the two clocks at first with such skill that we could be sure of their corresponding accurately for all the future. This is the way of preëstablished harmony — "a contrivance of the divine foreknowledge, which has from the beginning formed each of these substances in so perfect, so regular and accurate a manner, that by merely following its own laws, which were given to it when it came into being, each substance is yet in harmony with the other, just as if there were a

[1] *Monad*, 78

mutual influence between them, or as if God were continually put-ting his hand upon them."[1] This notion of a constant inter-vention implies indeed a conception of God that is unworthy of him. Surely his skill is not so limited that he could not make a mechanism that would run forever, and so must wind up his watch from time to time to prevent its running down; the more he has to mend it and set it right, the poorer a mechanic it shows him to be.

The reality of the world is thus, once more, the life of a multitude of immaterial beings, each developing its own nature along lines with which it is impossible that other monads should interfere, but nevertheless standing in relation to a universal plan, which finds its complete summing up in the one ultimate being — God. On God the monads severally depend, and this dependence enables them to act in harmony with the rest of the world, and to mirror its course ideally in themselves. And this suggests too, in a general way, what the universal purpose is, in so far as it is possible for us to fathom it. Development consists in making actual for each monad the possibilities of its own nature, or, since thought constitutes its nature, it consists in getting rid of confused perceptions, and attain-ing to the true ideas which lie concealed in the muddy depths of our primitive experience. The goal of life is to see things truly as they exist for God. In such an insight man's true freedom lies. Of course Leibniz cannot admit freedom as the fiat of an arbitrary will. The monad's nature is given at the start, and the course of its development is fixed; each present state of its being is alike a con-sequence of its preceding states and the determining condition of its future. But man is free in the sense that it is the law of his own nature that determines him, and not something from outside. He is free to realize himself in his completeness; and in so far as con-fusedness gives place to clear thought and he comes to understand the reasons for his conduct, this freedom becomes conscious and actual. Through knowledge the soul is truly active, truly a law to itself.

3. *The World of Freedom.* — And by this fact of freedom we are taken out of the realm of phenomena and related to the purposes of

[1] *Third Explanation*, p. 331.

God and to the moral universe. "Among other differences which exist between ordinary souls and spirits there is also this: that souls in general are living mirrors or images of the universe of created things, but that spirits are also images of the Deity or Author of nature himself, capable of knowing the system of the universe and to some extent of imitating it, each spirit being like a small divinity in its own sphere. It is this that enables spirits to enter into a kind of fellowship with God, and brings it about that in relation to them he is not only what an inventor is to his machine (which is the relation of God to other created things), but also what a prince is to his subjects, and indeed what a father is to his children. Whence it is easy to conclude that the totality of all spirits must compose the City of God, that is to say, the most perfect state that is possible, under the most perfect of monarchs. This City of God, this truly universal monarchy, is a moral world in the natural world, and is the most exalted and most divine among the works of God; and it is in it that the glory of God really consists, for he would have no glory were not his greatness and his goodness known and admired by spirits. It is also in relation to the divine City that God specially has goodness, while his wisdom and his power are manifested everywhere."[1]

It thus appears that for Leibniz the mechanical view of the world and the teleological, like mind and body, are not inconsistent or competing, but are rather two aspects of the same thing. The scientific aspect of the world, in terms of its physical relationships, is authoritative in its own field; there can be no interference with its laws, since the inner reality of which scientific laws are a phenomenal transcript is determined from the start. But to the philosopher, as distinct from the scientist, there is a further question that presents itself. Granted that any event can be referred to strictly necessary causes, why is it that the whole constitution of the universe should be what actually it is and not be something different? To answer this question we must go behind appearance to reality — to the inner life of the monads, and the moral purpose which is being realized in the lives of those monads who have

[1] *Monad.*, 83-86.

attained to spiritual self-consciousness. Such an underlying purpose has no quarrel with mechanism. "Things lead to grace by the very ways of nature, and this globe, for instance, must be destroyed and renewed by natural means, at the very time when the government of spirits requires it for the punishment of some and the reward of others." [1]

This conception of purpose is connected also with another important doctrine. There are for Leibniz two different kinds of truths — necessary truths, and contingent. Necessary truths follow with logical certainty. They are eternal and unalterable, and even the will of God cannot make them other than they are; they fall under the logical law of contradiction, and their opposite is unthinkable. But it is only abstract truths that thus are necessary. When we come on the other hand to empirical truths of fact, or of existence, there is no apparent necessity involved; so far as we can see, the course of the world might have been wholly different from what it actually has been. The particular facts of the world, therefore, are contingent, and all we can do is to find for them some *sufficient reason*.

Now this sufficient reason depends ultimately on purpose, or on a relationship to moral ends. Our particular world is only one among an infinite number that would have been possible had God so willed; why, then, should it exist rather than any other? Simply because God has chosen to create, not any world at random, but the best world he found it possible to create. Among all the possibilities which pass before his vision, God sees that only one combination of events will result in the greatest possible good and the least possible evil; and his supreme wisdom and perfection lead him to choose this and make it actual, in preference to any other of the possibilities which, apart from the question of better or worse, would have an equal right to exist. "The whole matter may be likened to certain games in which all the spaces on a board are to be filled up according to definite rules, so that unless you make use of some ingenious contrivance you find yourself in the end kept out of some refractory spaces. and compelled to leave empty more spaces

[1] *Monad.*, 88.

than you intended, and some of which you might otherwise have filled." [1] In a like manner the problem for God is, how to get a world representing the greatest possible amount of reality, the highest physical and moral perfection; and this "best of all possible worlds" which we find existing is the result.

Such a conception involves a solution of the problem of evil, which Leibniz works out most elaborately in his *Theodicy*. What appears to us as evil is only a necessary incident in the life of the whole, which, if we could but see it from the standpoint of the whole, we should recognize as necessary to the highest perfection. "And, indeed, as the lawyers say, it is not proper to judge unless we have examined the whole law. We know a very small part of eternity, which is immeasurable in its extent; for what a little thing is the record of a few thousand years which history transmits to us! Nevertheless from so slight an experience we rashly judge regarding the immeasurable and eternal, like men who, having been born and brought up in prison, or perhaps in the subterranean salt mines of the Sarmatians, should think that there is no other light in the world than that of the feeble lamp which hardly suffices to direct their steps. If you look at a very beautiful picture, having covered up the whole of it except a very small part, what will it present to your sight however thoroughly you examine it (nay, so much the more the more closely you inspect it), but a confused mass of colors, laid on without selection and without art? Yet if you remove the covering and look at the whole picture from the right point of view, you will find that what appeared to have been carelessly daubed on the canvas was really done by the painter with very great art. The experience of the eyes in painting corresponds to that of the ears in music. Eminent composers very often mingle discords with harmonies so as to stimulate and, as it were, to prick the hearer, who becomes anxious as to what is going to happen, and is so much the more pleased when presently all is restored to order, just as we take pleasure in small dangers or risks of mishap merely from the consciousness of our power or our luck, or from a desire to make a display of them; or, again, as we delight in the show of danger that

[1] *Ultimate Origination of Things*, p. 341.

is connected with performances on the tight rope, or sword-dancing; and we ourselves in jest half let go a little boy, as if about to throw him from us, like the ape which carried Christiern, king of Denmark, while still an infant in swaddling clothes, to the top of the roof, and then, as in jest, relieved the anxiety of every one by bringing him safely back to his cradle. On the same principle sweet things become insipid if we eat nothing else; sharp, tart, and even bitter things must be combined with them so as to stimulate the taste. He who has not tasted bitter things does not deserve sweet things, and indeed will not appreciate them. This is the very law of enjoyment, that pleasure does not have an even tenor, for this begets loathing and makes us dull, not happy." [1]

We cannot therefore judge a so-called evil by itself. It may either be necessary to avoid still greater evils, or it may be justified as a condition of attaining some positive good that far outweighs it, as the general of an army will prefer a great victory with a slight wound to a condition without wound and without victory. Even if in quantity the evil could be shown to surpass the good, yet the latter would still make up for this in quality; the glory and perfection of the blessed are incomparably greater than the misery of the damned, since the excellence of the total good in the lesser number exceeds the total evil in the greater number. From all this it follows that we cannot lay the blame for evil upon God. God is responsible for realities only in so far as they are positive and perfect; evil is not a positive but a negative fact, resulting from the necessary imperfection and limitation of finite creatures. It is with them as with a loaded vessel, which the river causes to move more or less slowly according to the weight it carries; its speed depends upon the river, but the retardation which limits this speed comes from the load.

4. *Theory of Knowledge.* — It remains to mention briefly one other important phase of Leibniz' thought. Nearly fifty years after his death there was published for the first time a work of his entitled *New Essays on the Human Understanding*. This contained an acute examination of Locke's theory of knowledge; and so it brings

[1] *Ibid.*, p. 346.

Leibniz into direct connection with the problem which was presently to become the main problem of philosophy. As Locke's theory still remains to be considered, Leibniz' criticism can only be noticed here in a cursory way.

Locke's general position, to anticipate, was briefly this: all our knowledge comes from sense experience, and there are no such things as innate ideas. The mind is a blank tablet. Images impress themselves upon it from external objects, and such images form the basis of all our knowledge. Leibniz opposes this whole conception. He does not, indeed, consider it necessary to hold that universal truths exist clearly and consciously in the mind at birth; he can agree with Locke that, in point of time, sensations will come first. But such universal knowledge exists *implicitly*, involved in the sensations themselves, although it is only brought to consciousness by the gradual clearing up of this originally confused sense experience. Leibniz' doctrine of *petites perceptions* enables him to understand how a thing may be in the mind, in an undeveloped way, even when we do not seem to be conscious of it. And universal ideas *must* be there implicitly, or we never should have them at all. No universal and necessary truth can possibly come from mere sensations. "The senses never give anything but instances, that is to say, particular or individual truths. Now all the instances which confirm a general truth, however numerous they may be, are not sufficient to establish the universal necessity of this same truth; for it does not at all follow that what has happened will happen again in the same way." [1]

In general, then, Leibniz goes back to a wholly different conception of the mind from that which Locke holds. Locke practically ignores the reaction of the mind itself in knowledge; for Leibniz this is the one essential thing. The mind is not a passive recipient of ideas; reality would not exist for it were it not already active in sensation and disposed to some specific outcome. Instead of its being true that everything is due to the influence of outer objects, in reality there is nothing due to this. According to Leibniz' theory of monads, the entire life develops solely from

[1] *New Essays*, p. 302.

within by the laws of its own nature; and so sensations are themselves innate. It is thus absolutely necessary in a theory of knowledge to take first of all into account the mind itself, with its native character, natural inclinations, powers, dispositions. "Accordingly I have taken as illustration a block of veined marble, rather than a block of perfectly uniform marble, or than empty tablets, that is to say, what is called by philosophers *tabula rasa*. For if the soul were like these empty tablets, truths would be in us as the figure of Hercules is in a block of marble, when the block of marble is indifferently capable of receiving this figure or any other. But if there were in the stone veins which should mark out the figure of Hercules rather than other figures, the stone would be more determined toward this figure, and Hercules would somehow be, as it were, innate in it, although labor would be needed to uncover the veins, and to clear them by polishing and thus removing what prevents them from being fully seen." [1]

LITERATURE

Leibniz, *Discourse on Metaphysics; New System; New Essays on the Human Understanding; Theodicy; Monadology; Principles of Nature and Grace.* Translations: Latta (*Monadology*, etc.); Duncan (*Selections*); Langley (*New Essays*); Montgomery (*Discourse on Metaphysics, Correspondence with Arnauld, Monadology*).

Merz, *Leibniz.*

Dewey, *Leibniz' New Essays.*

Russell, *A Critical Exposition of the Philosophy of Leibniz.*

[1] *Ibid.*, p. 366.

THE GROWTH OF EMPIRICISM AND THE ENLIGHTENMENT

§ 30. *Locke*

The name of *John Locke*, the founder of the new Empiricism which Leibniz had attacked in the *New Essays*, stands for what has been most characteristic in English philosophical thought down almost to the present day. Locke was born in Somersetshire in 1632 — a period marked by the beginning of the struggles of the parliamentary party against Charles the First. He was sent to Oxford, where however the academic spirit was still too much dominated by Scholasticism to arouse much interest in his mind. Later he received an appointment at the University, and continued for a number of years in more or less close connection with it. In 1666 he met Lord Ashley, afterward Earl of Shaftesbury, and one of the greatest of the statesmen of Charles the Second's reign. With him Locke entered into a lasting friendship. This intimacy brought him into contact with public life, and finally compelled him, on the fall of his patron, to seek refuge in Holland; here he stayed five years, returning to England on the accession of William of Orange. For the remainder of his life he was the most considerable intellectual force in England, and was responsible in no small degree for shaping the policy of the new government. He died in 1704.

Locke's attention was first directed to the field of philosophy by a chance incident. "Were it fit to trouble thee with the history of this essay, I should tell thee that five or six friends meeting at my chamber, and discoursing on a subject very remote from this, found themselves quickly at a stand by the difficulties that rose on every side. After we had awhile puzzled ourselves without coming any nearer a resolution of those doubts which perplexed us, it came into my thoughts that we took a wrong course, and that before we set ourselves upon inquiries of that nature it was necessary to examine our own abilities, and see what objects our understandings were or were not fitted to deal with. This I proposed to the company, who all readily assented; and therefore it was agreed that this should be our first inquiry. Some hasty and undigested thoughts on the subject I had never before considered, which I set down against our next meeting, gave the first entrance into this discourse; which having been thus begun by chance, was continued by entreaty, written by incoherent parcels, and after long intervals of neglect resumed again as my humor or occasion permitted; and at last, in a retirement where an attendance on my health gave me leisure, it was brought into that order thou now seest it." [1]

It is characteristic of the sober thoroughness which distinguished Locke that it was twenty years before this design was finally completed and the book given to the world. Indeed until he was nearly sixty years old he had published nothing. It was not till after his return from exile that his principal works appeared. His writings include three *Letters on Toleration*, two *Treatises on Government*, *Thoughts on Education*, *The Reasonableness of Christianity*, and the *Essay on the Human Understanding*.

In all these works the same general aim is to be found — to show the futility of empty verbiage, and an acquiescence in traditional assumptions which take the place of honest intellectual effort and inquiry. In opposition to this it strives to make men use their own minds, not upon words but upon real facts, to the intent that they may be freed from the weight of the past and attain to a rationally grounded liberty. The method by which Locke thought to accomplish this result was by demolishing the undue pretensions which the human intellect is wont to make for itself. However competent the mind may prove to be for dealing with homely matters of fact and experience, when it aspires to a dogmatic certainty about higher things it is in reality making use of words to which no definite and verifiable ideas correspond. The *Letters on Toleration* vindicate man's right to religious freedom just on this ground, that it is absurd to force all men dogmatically to adopt one

[1] *Essay*, Epistle to the Reader, Vol. I, p. 118, Bohn's Library.

particular belief when the foundations of our knowledge of the things which theology pretends to teach are so unsubstantial. The *Treatises on Government*, similarly, defend the freedom of the citizen in the state on the homely and intelligible basis of expediency or utility, in opposition to the unreasoning faith, resting on blind tradition, which expresses itself in the theory of a divine right of kings. Here Locke made himself the spokesman of the Revolution of 1688, by arguing that government is simply a means for serving the best interests of the people governed. As with Hobbes, government is based upon a contract; but it is a contract into which the monarch enters under strictly limiting conditions, and it has none of the rigidity for which Hobbes had argued. To retain old forms unchanged when circumstances have altered is to defeat the very purpose of the state; if at any time the ruler is untrue to his trust, and the advantages for the sake of which he was given power are no longer forthcoming, authority reverts to the people, and revolution is justified.

These same practical aims, in behalf of freedom and reasonableness, and against tradition, irrationality and restrictive forces, underlie the *Essay* also. In it Locke attempts a philosophical justification of the practical interests to which he is devoted. He comes to an examination of the powers of the human mind in order primarily to get a weapon against political superstitions, traditional dogmas, empty words divorced from things, and a sentimental and unreasoning " enthusiasm." "The commonwealth of learning is not at this time without master-builders, whose mighty designs in advancing the sciences will leave lasting monuments to the admiration of posterity. But every one must not hope to be a Boyle or a Sydenham; and in an age that produces such masters as the great Huygenius, and the incomparable Mr. Newton, it is ambition enough to be employed as an under-laborer in clearing the ground a little, and removing some of the rubbish that lies in the way to knowledge; which certainly had been very much more advanced in the world if the endeavors of ingenious and industrious men had not been much cumbered with the learned but frivolous use of uncouth, affected or unintelligible terms, introduced into the sciences and there made an art of, to that degree that philosophy, which is nothing but the true knowledge of things, was thought unfit or incapable to be brought into a well-bred company and polite conversation. . . . To break in upon the sanctuary of vanity and ignorance will be, I suppose, some service to human understanding." [1]

I. THE SOURCE OF KNOWLEDGE

1. *The Aim of the Essay.* — With this end in view, what Locke will attempt will be to "consider the discerning faculties of a man as they are employed about the objects which they have to do with. And I shall imagine I have not wholly misemployed myself in the thoughts I shall have on this occasion, if, in this historical, plain method, I can give any account of the ways whereby our understandings come to attain those notions of the things we have, and can set down any measures of the certainty of our knowledge or the grounds of those persuasions which are to be found amongst men, so various, different and wholly contradictory." [2] "If by this inquiry into the nature of the understanding I can discover the powers thereof, how far they reach, to what things they are in any degree proportionate and where they fail us, I suppose it may be of use to prevail with the busy mind of man to be more cautious in meddling with things exceeding its comprehension ; to stop when it is at the utmost extent of its tether ; and to sit down in a quiet ignorance of those things which, upon examination, are found to be beyond the reach of our capacities. We should not then perhaps be so forward, out of an affectation of a universal knowledge, to raise questions and perplex ourselves and others with disputes about things to which our understandings are not suited and of which we cannot frame in our minds any clear or distinct perceptions, or whereof (as it has perhaps too often happened) we have not any notions at all." [3]

Nor have we any right to complain of this limitation. "How short soever their knowledge may come of an universal or perfect

[1] *Essay*, Epistle to the Reader, Vol. I, p. 121.   [2] Bk. I. Chap. I, 2.   [3] Bk. I, Chap. I, 4

comprehension of whatsoever is, it yet secures their great concern-
ments that they have light enough to lead them to the knowledge
of their Maker and the sight of their own duties. Men may find
matter sufficient to busy their heads and employ their hands with
variety, delight and satisfaction, if they will not boldly quarrel with
their own constitution, and throw away the blessings their hands
are filled with because they are not big enough to grasp everything.
We shall not have much reason to complain of the narrowness of
our minds if we will but employ them about what may be of use to
us; for of that they are very capable : and it will be an unpardon-
able as well as childish peevishness if we undervalue the advantages of our knowledge, and neglect to improve it to the ends for
which it was given us, because there are some things that are set
out of the reach of it. It will be no excuse to an idle and untoward
servant who would not attend his business by candlelight, to plead
that he had not broad sunshine. The candle that is set up in us
shines bright enough for all our purposes. . . . It is of great use to
the sailor to know the length of his line though he cannot with it
fathom all the depths of the ocean. It is well he knows that it is
long enough to reach the bottom at such places as are necessary to
direct his voyage, and caution him against running upon shoals
that may ruin him." [1]

2. *No Innate Ideas*. — This then is the purpose of the Essay —
to destroy false pretensions of knowledge by showing, through a
careful examination of the facts of consciousness, how our ideas
originate, and what are the criteria for distinguishing real knowledge from that which is illusory. But before Locke can enter on
this there is a preliminary matter which he must discuss in order
to clear the way. This is the supposed existence of *innate ideas*.
"When men have found some general propositions that could not
be doubted of as soon as understood, it was a short and easy way to
conclude them innate. This being once received, it eased the lazy
from the pains of search, and stopped the inquiry of the doubt'
concerning all that was once styled innate. And it was of no small
advantage to those who affected to be masters and teachers to make

[1] Bk. I. Chap. I, 5, 6.

this the principle of principles, 'that principles must not be questioned': for having once established this tenet, that there are innate principles, it put their followers upon a necessity of receiving some doctrines as such; which was to take them off from the use of their own reason and judgment, and put them on believing and taking them upon trust without further examination, in which posture of blind credulity they might be more easily governed by and made useful to some sort of men who had the skill and office to principle and guide them. Nor is it a small power it gives one man over another to have the authority to be the dictator of principles and teacher of unquestionable truths, and to make a man swallow that for an innate principle which may serve to his purpose who teacheth them." [1]

It is a matter therefore not only of theoretical but of very great practical interest to determine whether we really have ideas of this kind. For this reason Locke sets out with an attempt to prove that there are no such things as innate ideas. "It is an established principle amongst some men that there are in the understanding certain innate principles; some primary notions, κοιναὶ ἔννοιαι, characters, as it were, stamped upon the mind of man, which the soul receives in its very first being and brings into the world with it. It would be sufficient to convince unprejudiced readers of the falseness of this supposition if I should only show how men, barely by the use of their natural faculties, may attain to all the knowledge they have without the help of any innate impressions, and may arrive at certainty without any such original notions. For I imagine any one will easily grant that it would be impertinent to suppose the ideas of colors innate in a creature to whom God hath given sight and a power to receive them by the eyes from external objects; and no less unreasonable would it be to attribute several truths to the impressions of nature and innate characters when we may observe in ourselves faculties fit to attain as easy and certain knowledge of them as if they were originally imprinted on the mind. But because a man is not permitted without censure to follow his own thoughts in the search of truth when they lead him ever so

[1] Bk. I, Chap. IV, 24.

little out of the common road, I shall set down the reasons that made me doubt of the truth of that opinion, as an excuse for my mistake if I be in one." [1]

Now what are the arguments for the existence of such ideas? First, there is the great argument from the universal assent of mankind. But it is necessary at the start to dispute the supposed facts. "I shall begin with the speculative, and instance in those magnified principles of demonstration, 'whatever is, is,' and 'it is impossible for the same thing to be and not to be'; which, of all others, I think have the most allowed title to innate. But yet I take liberty to say that these propositions are so far from having a universal assent that there are a great part of mankind to whom they are not so much as known."

"For, first, it is evident that all children and idiots have not the least apprehension or thought of them, and the want of that is enough to destroy that universal assent which must needs be the necessary concomitant of all innate truths; it seeming to me near a contradiction to say that there are truths imprinted on the soul which it perceives or understands not, imprinting, if it signify anything, being nothing else but the making certain truths to be perceived. For to imprint anything on the mind without the mind's perceiving it seems to me hardly intelligible."

"But that I may not be accused to argue from the thoughts of infants and to conclude from what passes in their understandings before they express it, I say next, that these two general propositions are not the truths that first possess the minds of children, nor are antecedent to all acquired and adventitious notions; which, if they were innate, they must needs be. . . . The child certainly knows that the nurse that feeds it is neither the cat it plays with nor the blackmoor it is afraid of; that the wormseed or mustard it refuses is not the apple or sugar it cries for, this it is certainly and undoubtedly assured of : but will any one say it is by virtue of this principle, 'that it is impossible for the same thing to be and not to be,' that it so firmly assents to these and other parts of its knowledge? He that will say children join in these general abstract speculations with

[1] Bk. I, Chap. II, 1.

their sucking bottles and their rattles may perhaps with justice be thought to have more passion and zeal for his opinion, but less sincerity and truth, than one of that age." [1]

To avoid the difficulty it may be said that men know these truths when they come to the use of the reason. As a matter of fact, however, the time of coming to the use of the reason is not necessarily the time we come to know such maxims; and even if it were it would not prove them innate. "For by what kind of logic will it appear that any notion is originally by nature imprinted in the mind in its first constitution, because it comes first to be observed and assented to when a faculty of the mind which has quite a distinct province begins to exert itself?" It is equally irrelevant to say that they are assented to as soon as they are proposed and understood. "By the same reason, all propositions that are true and the mind is capable of ever assenting to may be said to be in the mind and to be imprinted: since if any one can be said to be in the mind which it never yet knew, it must be only because it is capable of knowing it, and so the mind is of all truths it ever shall know." If such an assent be a mark of innateness, then "that one and two are equal to three, that sweetness is not bitterness, and a thousand the like must be innate." "Nay, thus truths may be imprinted on the mind which it never did nor ever shall know; for a man may live long, and die at last in ignorance of many truths which his mind was capable of knowing, and that with certainty. So that if the capacity of knowing be the natural impression contended for, all the truths a man ever comes to know will, by this account, be every one of them innate, and this great point will amount to no more but only to a very improper way of speaking, which, whilst it pretends to assert the contrary, says nothing different from those who deny innate principles. For nobody, I think, ever denied that the mind was capable of knowing several truths." [2]

In a similar way Locke goes on to show that there are no innate practical or moral principles; there are none which are universally received by all men. An examination of moral customs will show that there is no rule of right and justice which is not openly violated

[1] Bk. I. Chap. II, 4, 5. 24, 25.   [2] Bk. I, Chap. II, 5, 14.

by some nation, and the violation approved by the public conscience. The general resemblance in the conceptions of virtue in
different countries, and the general approval of it, are due to the
fact, not that virtue is innate, but that it is profitable. Finally, to
clinch the argument, Locke points out that no proposition can be
innate unless the ideas of which it is composed are innate also.
"Whatever we talk of innate principles, it may with as much probability be said that a man hath £100 sterling in his pocket and yet
denied that he hath either penny, shilling, crown or other coin out
of which the sum is to be made up, as to think that certain propositions are innate when the ideas about which they are can by
no means be supposed to be so";[1] and this last can be shown to be
the case with the ideas made use of in all the propositions for
which any claim to innateness has been made.

3. *All Knowledge from Experience.* — With innate ideas out of
the way, Locke can go on to the positive part of his work. Here
there are two main divisions. The first has to do with the way in
which we may be supposed to come by our ideas, since they are not
born in us. Meanwhile when an idea once is in the mind, its mere
existence there still does not involve the question of truth or
validity; this last arises only in connection with the relation of
ideas to one another, and so constitutes a separate inquiry.

To the first of these problems the answer is simple and unambiguous. "Every man being conscious to himself that he thinks, and
that which his mind is applied about whilst thinking being the ideas
that are there, it is past doubt that men have in their minds several
ideas, such as are those expressed by the words whiteness, hardness, sweetness, thinking, motion, man, elephant, army, drunkenness and others. It is in the first place, then, to be inquired how
he comes by them. . . . Let us then suppose the mind to be white
paper, void of all characters, without any ideas; how comes it to be
furnished? Whence comes it by that vast store which the busy
and boundless fancy of man has painted on it with an almost endless
variety? Whence has it all the materials of reason and knowledge?
To this I answer in one word, from experience; in that all our

[1] Bk. I, Chap. IV, 19.

knowledge is founded, and from that it ultimately derives itself. Our observation, employed either about external sensible objects, or about the internal operations of our minds perceived and reflected on by ourselves, is that which supplies our understandings with all the materials of thinking. These two are the fountains of knowledge from whence all the ideas we have, or can naturally have, do spring." [1]

The source of our knowledge of external objects is Sensation; while the other fountain, the perception of the operations of our own mind within us as it is employed about the ideas it has already got, is called Reflection. "These, when we have taken a full survey of them and their several modes, combinations and relations, we shall find to contain all our whole stock of ideas." "These alone, so far as I can discover, are the windows by which light is let into this dark room; for methinks the understanding is not much unlike a closet wholly shut from light, with only some little opening left to let in external visible resemblances, or ideas of things without: would the pictures coming into such a dark room but stay there and lie so orderly as to be found upon occasion, it would very much resemble the understanding of a man in reference to all objects of sight and the ideas of them." [2] "Thus the first capacity of human intellect is that the mind is fitted to receive the impressions made on it, either through the senses by outer objects, or by its own operations when it reflects on them. This is the first step a man makes toward the discovery of anything, and the groundwork whereon to build all those notions which ever he shall have naturally in this world. All those sublime thoughts which tower above the clouds and reach as high as heaven itself take their rise and footing here; in all that good extent wherein the mind wanders, in those remote speculations it may seem to be elevated with, it stirs not one jot beyond those ideas which sense or reflection has offered for its contemplation." [3] Ideas can, it is true, be combined in various novel ways; but every element in these complex ideas still comes to us from one of the two sources. "It is not in the power of the most exalted wit or enlarged understanding, by any

<hr />

[1] Bk. II, Chap. I. 1. 2.   [2] Bk. II, Chap. XI, 17.   [3] Bk. II, Chap. I, 24.

quickness or variety of thought, to invent or frame one new simple idea in the mind, not taken in by the ways before mentioned; nor can any force of the understanding destroy those that are there." If then we can analyze a supposed idea into these simple components we have the means of testing it, and of ridding ourselves of the domination of mere words to which no ideas correspond.

4. *Simple Ideas.* — In order to make his thesis good, accordingly, Locke is bound to give an account of the whole stock of our ideas, arrange and classify them, and show that there is none whose origin in experience cannot be clearly demonstrated. The most general division will be into Simple and Complex Ideas — the elements of our thought which come to us passively through sensation and reflection, and the various combinations which these may assume. Upon simple ideas Locke does not have to dwell very long. They are subdivided into ideas which come into our minds from one sense only, those which come from more senses than one, those that are had from reflection only, and those that are suggested to the mind by all the ways of sensation and reflection. Sounds, colors, tastes and smells, solidity, heat and cold, are examples of the first class. Belonging to the second division are ideas of space or extension, figure, rest and motion, which are received both through sight and touch. By reflection we get the ideas of perception and of volition. The final division includes such notions as pleasure, pain, power, existence, unity and succession. Thus pleasure or pain join themselves to almost all our ideas, both of sensation and reflection; the idea of unity is suggested by whatever we can consider as one thing, whether a real being or an idea; power is involved alike in the ability which we find in ourselves to move the various parts of our bodies and in the effects which material objects have on one another. The four classes include all the possible ingredients of our knowledge. "Nor let any one think these too narrow bounds for the capacious mind of man to expatiate in, which takes its flight farther than the stars and cannot be confined by the limits of the world, that extends its thoughts often even beyond the utmost expansion of matter and makes excursions into the incomprehensible inane. It will not be so strange to think these few simple ideas

sufficient to employ the quickest thought or largest capacity if we consider how many words may be made out of the various composition of twenty-four letters, or if we will but reflect on the variety of combinations that may be made with barely one of the above-mentioned ideas, viz., *number*, whose stock is inexhaustible and truly infinite." [1]

Before going on to speak of complex ideas, one point calls for special mention. Besides their existence in the mind, many of these simple ideas are also referred to the external world, where they are supposed somehow to belong to things. Color, for example, is commonly regarded as at once a sensation, and an attribute of objects. In order to avoid confusion between the mental existence of ideas and those physical facts which are supposed to give rise to them, it is well to call the latter, not ideas, but *qualities*. Meanwhile among these there is one important distinction. Certain qualities are entirely inseparable from a body, whatever its state; these are called original or primary qualities, and include solidity, extension, figure, motion and number. "Secondly, such qualities which in truth are nothing in the objects themselves but powers to produce various sensations in us by their primary qualities, *i.e.*, by the bulk, figure, texture, and motion of their insensible parts, as colors, sounds, tastes, etc., these I call secondary qualities."

Now whereas "the ideas of primary qualities of bodies are resemblances of them, and their patterns do really exist in the bodies themselves, the ideas produced in us by these secondary qualities have no resemblance of them at all. There is nothing like our ideas existing in the bodies themselves. They are, in the bodies we denominate from them, only a power to produce those sensations in us; and what is sweet, blue or warm in idea, is but the certain bulk, figure, and motion of the insensible parts in the bodies themselves. Flame is denominated hot and light, snow white and cold, and manna white and sweet, from the ideas they produce in us, which qualities are commonly thought to be the same in those bodies that those ideas are in us, the one the perfect resemblance of the other, as they are in a mirror; and it would by most men be judged very extravagant

[1] Bk. II, Chap. VII, 10.

if one should say otherwise. And yet he that will consider that the same fire that at one distance produces in us the sensation of warmth does at a nearer approach produce in us the far different sensation of pain, ought to bethink himself what reason he has to say that this idea of warmth which was produced in him by the fire is actually in the fire, and his idea of pain, which the same fire produced in him the same way, is not in the fire. Why are whiteness and coldness in snow, and pain not, when it produces the one and the other idea in us; and can do neither, but by the bulk, figure, number, and motion of its solid parts? The particular bulk, number, figure, and motion of the parts of fire or snow are really in them, whether any one's senses perceive them or not, and therefore they may be called real qualities, because they really exist in those bodies; but light, heat, whiteness or coldness, are no more really in them than sickness or pain in the manna. Take away the sensation of them, let not the eye see light or colors nor the ears hear sound, let the palate not taste nor the nose smell, and all colors, tastes, odors and sounds, as they are such particular ideas, vanish and cease, and are reduced to their causes, *i.e.*, bulk, figure and motion of parts."[1]

5. *Complex Ideas.* — We have seen that, according to Locke, of the simple ideas the mind cannot possibly frame one until it has been presented by experience. "If a child were kept in a place where he never saw any other but black and white till he were a man, he would have no more ideas of scarlet or green than he that from his childhood never tasted an oyster or a pineapple has of those particular relishes." So far the mind has been passive. But also it has power, after it has received these simple ideas, to act upon them in various ways. "The acts of the mind wherein it exerts its power over its simple ideas are chiefly these three: 1. Combining several simple ideas into one compound one, and thus all complex ideas are made. 2. The second is bringing two ideas, whether simple or complex, together, and setting them by one another so as to take a view of them at once without uniting them into one, by which way it gets all its ideas of relations. 3. The third is separating them from all other ideas that accompany them in their real existence;

[1] Bk. II, Chap. VIII, 10, 15.

this is called abstraction, and thus all its general ideas are made." [1]

All possible combinations of ideas can be brought under three heads: Modes, Substances, and Relations. Modes are "complex ideas which, however compounded, contain not in them the supposition of subsisting by themselves, but are considered as dependencies on, or affections of, substances; such as are ideas signified by the words triangle, gratitude, murder, etc." Of these modes there are two kinds. Simple modes are those which are "only variations or different combinations of the same simple idea, without the mixture of any other; as a dozen or score, which are nothing but the ideas of so many distinct units added together." Mixed modes are compounded of simple ideas of several kinds; for example "beauty, consisting of a certain composition of color and figure causing delight in the beholder."

"Secondly, the ideas of Substances are such combinations of simple ideas as are taken to represent distinct particular things subsisting by themselves, in which the supposed or confused idea of substance, such as it is, is always the first and chief. Thus if to substance be joined the simple idea of a certain dull whitish color, with certain degrees of weight, hardness, ductility and fusibility, we have the idea of lead." "Thirdly, the last sort of complex ideas is that we call Relation, which consists in the consideration and comparing one idea with another." [2] Such are the ideas of cause, of spatial and temporal relations, of identity and diversity, and the like. From this point of view Locke goes on to show, in detail, that all the terms of which metaphysics has made so much, and which have been thought to be too exalted to have grown out of everyday experience — even the idea of God itself — can be brought back to perfectly definite simple ideas in so far as they have any meaning at all.

6. *Criticism.* — Before going on it may be well to suggest briefly certain limitations that attach to Locke's discussion. Locke has a straightforward thesis to establish. He intends to show that we have no knowledge which does not arise in connection with sense

---

[1] Bk. II, Chap. XII, 1.   [2] Bk. II, Chap. XII, 4-7.

experience — in other words, that we do not come into the world with ready-made truths in our minds. And if this is his sole contention, it may be granted he has made his point. But is this really the most important point at issue? Might not a judicious opponent be content to admit that all truths come to our knowledge only in the course of experience, and still maintain that there are certain truths which may properly be called innate?

Take for example the supposed truth that every event must have a cause. There is a sense in which this is derived from experience; it could not very well be supposed to be in the mind of any one who had not witnessed instances of causation. But in spite of this, if it really is true that *every* event *must* have a cause, in the future as well as in the past, we plainly are going beyond the bare facts of experience in such a statement. All that *mere* experience could possibly tell us would be, that certain particular events in the past have had a cause. There is thus a distinction between a truth's coming to consciousness in connection with experience, and the claim that it is wholly summed up in the experience in connection with which it appears. If consequently there are truths that are *necessarily* and *universally* true, they must, it would seem, be due to some capacity of the mind involving more than a collection of its past experiences. Locke himself admits the existence of such truths, in what he says about causation for example. We are called on therefore to define more closely than Locke has done what the vague word "experience" really means; and this was left to Locke's successors, particularly to Hume and Kant.

2. NATURE AND EXTENT OF KNOWLEDGE

1. *Nature and Degrees of Knowledge.* — Having examined the source of our ideas, it still remains to consider what these ideas tell us in the way of truth. Now "since the mind, in all its thoughts and reasonings, hath no other immediate object but its own ideas, which it alone does or can contemplate, it is evident that our knowledge is only conversant about them. Knowledge, then, seems to be nothing but the perception of the connection and agreement, or disagreement and repugnancy, of any of our ideas. In this alone it

consists. Where this perception is, there is knowledge; and where it is not, there, though we may fancy, guess or believe, yet we always come short of knowledge." [1]

The varying certainty and clearness of our knowledge lies in the different way of perception the mind has of the agreement or disagreement of its ideas. Sometimes " the mind perceives the agreement or disagreement of two ideas immediately by themselves, without the intervention of any other; and this we may call intuitive knowledge. Thus the mind perceives that white is not black, that a circle is not a triangle, that three are more than two. . . . This part of knowledge is irresistible and, like bright sunshine, forces itself immediately to be perceived as soon as ever the mind turns its view that way; and leaves no room for hesitation, doubt or examination, but the mind is presently filled with the clear light of it. He that demands a greater certainty than this demands he knows not what, and shows only that he has a mind to be a sceptic without being able to be so." The next degree of knowledge is where the mind perceives the agreement or disagreement of any of its ideas, but not immediately; this is demonstrative knowledge. "Thus the mind being willing to know the agreement or disagreement in bigness between the three angles of a triangle and two right ones, cannot by an immediate view and comparing them do it. In this case the mind is fain to find out some other angles to which the three angles of a triangle have an equality; and, finding those equal to two right ones, comes to know their equality to two right ones." [2] A third degree of certainty which also passes, though with less justification, under the name of knowledge, will be considered presently in connection with sensitive knowledge.

2. *Knowledge of Real Existence.* — Meanwhile, if knowledge is only of the connection between our own ideas, does it not become thereby subjective, arbitrary and unreal? Locke is himself not unaware that this constitutes a problem. "It is evident that the mind knows not things immediately, but only by the intervention of the ideas it has of them. Our knowledge therefore is real only so far as there is a conformity between our ideas and the reality of

---

[1] Bk. IV, Chap. I, 1, 2.   [2] Bk. IV, Chap. II, 1, 2.

things.   But what shall be here the criterion?   How shall the mind, when it perceives nothing but its own ideas, know that they agree with things themselves?" [1]   Later on the question here raised attains a preëminent importance, and leads to strange results. Locke fails however to appreciate its full difficulty, and slips over it rather easily.   It never occurs to him to doubt that there is a real world, and that we can know it at least to an extent.   And so, apparently in defiance of his own previous definition, he goes on to a different conception of knowledge — the agreement of our ideas with the real things to which they refer.   We may have an assurance or conviction that such a reality exists to which our ideas correspond;   and it is only in this case that we have knowledge which is *real* as well as certain.

It is true there is one kind of knowledge that in a sense might be termed real, not because it agrees with an external archetype, but because it makes no pretence of referring to anything beyond itself. "All our complex ideas, except those of substances, being archetypes of the mind's own making, not intended to be the copies of anything nor referred to the existence of anything as to their originals, cannot want any conformity necessary to real knowledge." [2]   All our abstract knowledge, as opposed to that which deals with concrete facts — and most of the statements of necessary truth are thus abstract — is concerned with such ideas.   Mathematics is a case in point; in mathematics we are dealing only with ideas which we ourselves have formed, and whose truth is entirely independent of whether or not there happen to be any real objects in the world.   But such knowledge is after all not *strictly* real;   there is no disagreement only because there is no object with which to disagree.   When we turn to ideas of *substances*, however, a new factor enters.   This is the idea of *real existence*, which brings us back to real knowledge in the stricter sense.

There are three kinds of substances of which we may have a real knowledge.   We have the knowledge of our own existence — of the self — by intuition;   we perceive it so plainly and so certainly that it neither needs, nor is capable of, any proof.   Of the existence of

[1] Bk. IV, Chap. IV, 3.   [2] Bk. IV. Chap. IV, 3.

God we have a demonstrative knowledge. The proof of God is, briefly, this: We know that something exists, since we are sure of our own existence; and we know, also, that something must have existed from eternity, since we are intuitively certain that bare nothing can no more produce any real being than it can be equal to two right angles. Again, it is evident in the case of any derived being that it must have received everything it possesses from the reality from which it is derived. Since therefore we possess powers, perception, knowledge, all these things must be present in still greater measure in the eternal reality from which we spring; and we thus can be assured that a supremely powerful, knowing and intelligent being exists. Otherwise there must have been a time when there was no such thing as knowledge; and in that case it never could have come into being at all.

Finally, we can have a knowledge of material things through sensation; which if it fails of being as sure as our knowledge of ourselves and of God, is still practically certain. "For I think nobody can, in earnest, be so sceptical as to be uncertain of the existence of those things which he sees and feels." This assurance is confirmed by various arguments. First, it is plain that these perceptions are produced in us by exterior causes affecting our senses, since those to whom any organ is lacking never have the ideas belonging to that sense. The organs themselves, it is clear, do not produce them; for then the eyes of a man in the dark would produce colors, and his nose smell roses in the winter. In the second place, there is a manifest difference between ideas from sensation, and ideas from memory. If I turn my eyes at noon toward the sun I cannot avoid the ideas which the light or sun then produces in me, whereas I can at pleasure recall or dismiss ideas of the sun that are lodged in memory; and this points to an exterior cause for the former. Again, our senses corroborate one another. "He that sees a fire may, if he doubt whether it be anything more than a bare fancy, feel it too, and be convinced by putting his hand in it; which certainly could never be put into such exquisite pain by a bare idea or phantom." So that "this evidence is as great as we can desire, being as certain to us as our pleasure or pain, *i.e.*, hap-

piness or misery; beyond which we have no concernment, either
of knowing or being." [1]

3. *Limitations of Our Knowledge of the External World.* — But
granting it is proved we have a knowledge of the existence of
material things, we still have to ask how far this knowledge extends
— how adequate it is. Now our simple ideas, to begin with them,
are adequate; they may not be actual copies of material qualities,
but they are necessarily and truly connected with them in the order
of nature. "Since the mind, as has been showed, can by no means
make to itself these simple ideas, they must necessarily be the
product of things operating on the mind in a natural way, and
producing therein those perceptions which by the wisdom and will
of our Maker they are ordained and adapted to. From whence it
follows that simple ideas are not fictions of our fancies but the
natural and regular productions of things without us really operating upon us, and so carry with them all the conformity which is
intended or which our state requires; for they represent to us things
under those appearances they are fitted to produce in us. Thus
the idea of whiteness or bitterness as it is in the mind, exactly
answering that power which is in any body to produce it there,
has all the real conformity it can or ought to have with things
without us." [2]

When it comes to a knowledge of complex substances the case is
otherwise. We may combine ideas, and refer them to a substance,
when as a matter of fact they are not actually found together in
that substance; or we may leave out qualities which ought really
to be there; or, again, we may attribute to the connection in the
substance of its simple qualities a necessity which this does not
possess. If we have actually found certain simple qualities going
together, we have a real knowledge of their coexistence in nature
in this particular case. But we have practically no insight into the
reason for the connection, and so our knowledge hardly goes farther
than our empirical acquaintance with the particular instances;
necessity, for the most part, belongs only to abstract ideas. "Some
few of the primary qualities have a necessary dependence and

[1] Bk. IV, Chap. XI, 3–8.   [2] Bk. IV, Chap. IV, 4.

visible connection one with another, as figure necessarily supposes extension. Yet there are so few of them that we can by intuition or demonstration discover the coexistence of very few of the qualities that are to be found united in substances. Thus, though we see the yellow color and, upon trial, find the weight, malleableness, fusibility and fixedness that are united in a piece of gold, yet because no one of these ideas has any evident dependence or necessary connection with the others, we cannot certainly know that where any four of these are the fifth will be there also, how highly probable soever it may be." [1]

"In fine, then, when our senses do actually convey into our understandings any idea, we cannot but be satisfied that there doth something at that time really exist without us which doth affect our senses, and actually produce that idea which we then perceive; and we cannot so far distrust their testimony as to doubt that such collections of simple ideas as we have observed by our senses to be united together do really exist together. But this knowledge extends as far as the present testimony of our senses employed about particular objects that do then affect them, and no farther. For if I saw such a collection of simple ideas as is wont to be called man existing together one minute since, and am now alone, I cannot be certain that the same man exists now, since there is no necessary connection of his existence a minute since with his existence now; by a thousand ways he may cease to be since I had the testimony of my senses for his existence." [2]

4. *Probable Knowledge.* — So much for our certain knowledge. Fortunately however we do not have to depend upon demonstration for a great part of the affairs of life. "The understanding faculties being given to man, not barely for speculation, but also for the conduct of his life, man would be at a great loss if he had nothing to direct him but what has the certainty of true knowledge; for that being very short and scanty, as we have seen, he would be often utterly in the dark, and in most of the actions of his life perfectly at a stand, had he nothing to guide him in the absence of clear and certain knowledge. He that will not eat till he has

[1] Bk. IV, Chap. III, 14. [2] Bk. IV, Chap. XI, 9.

demonstration that it will nourish him, he that will not stir till he infallibly knows the business he goes about will succeed, will have little else to do but to sit still and perish."[1]   Accordingly Locke goes on to consider the grounds of *probability*, which in brief are these: "First, The conformity of anything with our own knowledge, observation and experience.   Secondly, The testimony of others, vouching their observation and experience.   In this is to be considered, (1) The number.   (2) The integrity.   (3) The skill of the witnesses.   (4) The design of the author, when it is a testimony out of a book cited.   (5) The consistency of the parts, and circumstances of the relation.   (6) Contrary testimonies."[2] Among the beliefs accepted on testimony, those based on revelation have, Locke thinks, a peculiarly high degree of assurance.   Nevertheless this always falls short of intuitive or demonstrative certainty, and therefore it can never prevail if it comes in conflict with truths of the latter kind.

5. *Ethics.* — A word remains to be said about Locke's ethical theory.   He never works this out in much detail, but it has nevertheless an importance for the history of ethics, since it may be regarded as a starting point for the utilitarianism which is peculiarly characteristic of moral philosophy in England.   Good and evil are for Locke nothing but pleasure and pain, or what occasions or produces pleasure or pain for us.   On this showing moral good and evil reduce themselves to the "conformity or disagreement of our voluntary actions to some law, whereby good or evil is drawn on us by the will and power of the lawmaker; which good and evil, pleasure or pain, attending our observance or breach of the law by the decree of the lawmaker, is that we call reward and punishment." The true ground of morality is thus the will and law of a God "who sees men in the dark, has in his hands rewards and punishments, and power enough to call to account the proudest offender."[3] Locke thinks that in this way, with the certainty of God's existence granted, ethics can be made a demonstrative science.

[1] Bk. IV, Chap. XIV, 1.
[2] Bk. IV, Chap. XV, 4.
[3] Bk. II, Chap. XXVIII. 5; Bk. I, Chap. III, 6.

LITERATURE

Locke, *Essay concerning Human Understanding; Treatises on Government; Thoughts on Education; Reasonableness of Christianity.*
Russell, *Selections.*
Fowler, *Locke.*
Fraser, *Locke.*
Curtis, *Outline of Locke's Ethical Philosophy.*
Green, *Introduction to Hume.*
Bourne, *Life of John Locke.*
Alexander, *Locke.*
Gibson, *Locke's Theory of Knowledge.*

§ 31. *Berkeley*

The philosophy of Locke was, for the most part, a clearing up and systematization of our common-sense beliefs. It proposed to itself no metaphysical subtilties, nor did it think it possible to attain to any great amount of absolute and ultimate knowledge. The present facts of sense, however, it did not doubt; and these, eked out by probability, seemed to it quite sufficient to answer all the practical needs of life. But Locke had set forces at work which did not stop with him. There were contradictions and difficulties present in his thought which he did not perceive, but which could not long be overlooked. One such difficulty has been noticed in his theory of knowledge. Technically he had limited the possibility of knowledge to a perception of the connections between ideas; but at once he had gone on to add to this the agreement of ideas with a reality which is no idea of ours at all. It was from this point that a movement started which was, in the end, to cast doubt on all knowledge whatsoever.

George Berkeley, on whom the mantle of Locke fell, was an Irishman, born in 1685. He entered Dublin University in 1700. His intellectual subtilty, his enthusiastic and imaginative temperament, and an attractive personality, soon won for him a high reputation among his intimates. His zeal for knowledge is illustrated in the story related of him that, after attending an execution with some companions, he induced his friends to suspend him from the ceiling that he might experience the sensation of strangling; he was cut down only after he had become unconscious.

It was in his early college days that the vision came to him of the new principle by which he hoped to revolutionize philosophy; and his chief work — *A Treatise on the Principles of Human Knowledge* — was published in his twenty-fifth year. The relative novelty of his thesis — the denial of the independent existence of matter — prevented an immediate recognition; but his acute reasoning, and the beauty of his literary style, gradually overcame the prejudice which the paradoxical nature of his position at first aroused. In 1713 Berkeley visited London, where he became acquainted with the brilliant literary circle of Queen Anne's reign. After some time spent in travel, he returned to England to carry out a great philanthropic scheme which for the next few years filled his thoughts. This was the idea of establishing in America the foundation of a higher and purer civilization than he found at home, through the instrumentality of a university which he proposed to start in the Bermudas. The plan was at once too noble and too visionary to appeal much to English politicians; but his enthusiasm and eloquence finally won the day, and he secured a grant from Parliament of £20,000. In 1728 he sailed for America, landing in Rhode Island; and here he spent the next three years in quiet and study, waiting for his plans for the university to be carried out. With Berkeley off the ground, however, the natural disinclination to the scheme reasserted itself; and convinced at last that the grant was never to be paid, Berkeley returned to England. Here he received an appointment as Bishop of Cloyne, in Ireland. His last appearance was in connection with a somewhat fantastic controversy about the merits of tar water, in which Berkeley, partly on experimental, partly on philosophic grounds, was convinced that he had found a panacea for physical ills, and which his interest in the welfare of humanity urged him to promote with his usual fire. His last work — *Siris* — combines the praises of tar water with some of the most profound of his philosophical reflections. He died in 1753.

1. *Unthinking Matter Does Not Exist.* — Of the two sides to Berkeley's doctrine, the negative and the positive, it was the first

that made the deepest impression on his age and on the future course of philosophy. His main thesis may be stated in his own words: "It is evident to any one who takes a survey of the objects of human knowledge, that they are either ideas actually imprinted on the senses, or else such as are perceived by attending to the passions and operations of the mind, or, lastly, ideas formed by help of memory and imagination. . . . But besides all that endless variety of ideas or objects of knowledge, there is likewise something which knows or perceives them, and exercises divers operations, as willing, imagining, remembering, about them. This perceiving, active being is what I call MIND, SPIRIT, SOUL, or MYSELF. . . . That neither our thoughts, nor passions, nor ideas formed by the imagination, exist without the mind, is what everybody will allow. And it seems no less evident that the various sensations, or ideas imprinted on the sense, however blended or combined together (that is, whatever objects they compose) cannot exist otherwise than in a mind perceiving them. I think an intuitive knowledge may be obtained of this by any one that shall attend to *what is meant by the term 'exist' when applied to sensible things*. The table I write on I say exists, that is, I see and feel it; and if I were out of my study I should say it existed, meaning thereby that if I was in my study I might perceive it, or that some other spirit actually does perceive it. There was an odor, that is, it was smelt; there was a sound, that is, it was heard; a color or figure, and it was perceived by sight or touch. That is all I can understand by these and the like expressions. For as to what is said of the absolute existence of unthinking things, without any relation to their being perceived, that is to me perfectly unintelligible. Their *esse* is *percipi;* nor is it possible they should have any existence out of the minds of thinking things which perceive them. It is indeed an opinion strangely prevailing amongst men, that houses, mountains, rivers, and in a word all sensible objects, have an existence, natural or real, distinct from their being perceived by the understanding. But with how great an assurance and acquiescence soever this principle may be entertained in the world, yet whoever shall find in his heart to call it in question may, if I mistake not, perceive it to involve a manifest contradiction. For what are the fore-mentioned objects but the things we perceive by sense? And what do we perceive besides our own ideas or sensations? And is it not plainly repugnant that any one of these, or any combination of them, should exist unperceived?"

"Some truths there are so near and obvious to the mind that a man need only open his eyes to see them. Such I take this important one to be, viz., that all the choir of heaven and furniture of the earth, in a word all those bodies which compose the mighty frame of the world, have not any subsistence without a mind — that their *being* is *to be perceived or known;* that, consequently, so long as they are not actually perceived by me, or do not exist in my mind or that of any other created spirit, they must either have no existence at all, or else subsist in the mind of some Eternal Spirit — it being perfectly unintelligible, and involving all the absurdity of abstraction, to attribute to any single part of them an existence independent of a spirit." [1]

This accordingly is what Berkeley starts in to prove — the nonexistence of an unspiritual, unthinking matter. Far from admitting that this is a paradox, Berkeley insists that he is only going back to, and justifying, the beliefs of common sense, in opposition to the confusion in which philosophers have involved the question. "Upon the whole," he says, "I am inclined to think that the far greater part, if not all, of those difficulties which have hitherto amused philosophers and blocked up the way to knowledge, are entirely owing to themselves — that we have first raised a dust, and then complain we cannot see." The root of the trouble lies in the supposition, universally made, but entirely false, that we can have such things as *abstract ideas*. In reality, every possible idea must be a particular concrete fact of consciousness, or an image, with definite characteristics which we can discover and describe. If there is no such image discoverable, we are wrong in supposing that we have any idea at all; we deceive ourselves by taking words for ideas. Once get free from the bondage of words, and represent to ourselves concretely the things we are talking about, half the difficulties of philosophy will be solved. "In vain do we extend

[1] *Treatise*, §§ 1, 2, 3, 4, 6.

our view into the heavens and pry into the entrails of the earth, in vain do we consult the writings of learned men, and trace the dark footsteps of antiquity — we need only draw the curtain of words to behold the fairest tree of knowledge, whose fruit is excellent, and within the reach of our hand."

With this preliminary warning, we may turn to our conception of matter — matter, that is, regarded as independent of mind or consciousness. The simple test is, Can we represent to ourselves what we mean by matter in this sense? or is it just a word which we use without any understanding behind it? It is on this that Berkeley rests his whole case. If we can tell what we mean by the existence of objects in abstraction from the fact of their being perceived, very well; if we cannot, then we are merely fooled by words, and must, if we are consistent, go back to the position of common sense and hold that matter is nothing but the very things we see, feel and hear — that is, the collections of ideas which make up the experience of perception.

"But, say you, though the ideas themselves do not exist without the mind, yet there may be things like them whereof they are copies or resemblances, which things exist without the mind in an unthinking substance. I answer, an idea can be like nothing but an idea, a color or figure can be like nothing but another color or figure. If we look but never so little into our own thoughts, we shall find it impossible for us to conceive a likeness except only between our ideas. Again, I ask whether those supposed originals or external things, of which our ideas are the pictures or representations, be themselves perceivable or no? If they are, then they are ideas, and we have gained our point; but if you say they are not, I appeal to any one whether it be sense to assert a color is like something which is invisible, hard or soft like something which is intangible, and so of the rest."

Every quality, then, which we can attribute to an object may be reduced to a sensible quality, or a sensation; and nothing can be like a sensation and still be absolutely different from what a sensation is, namely, conscious and immaterial. If any one objects to this conclusion, let him consider that, in the case of the majority of the qualities of matter, it is a conclusion already generally admitted. "They who assert that figure, motion, and the rest of the primary or original qualities do exist without the mind in unthinking substances, do at the same time acknowledge that colors, sounds, heat, cold, and such like secondary qualities do not." But now, in the first place, the fact that primary and secondary qualities exist inseparably in conjunction shows that, if the latter exist only in the mind, the same thing must be true of the former also. "For my own part, I see evidently that it is not in my power to frame an idea of a body extended and moving but I must withal give it some color or other sensible quality which is acknowledged to exist only in the mind. In short, extension, figure and motion, abstracted from all other qualities, are inconceivable. Where therefore the other sensible qualities are, there must these be also, to wit, in the mind, and nowhere else." [1]

Furthermore, the very same arguments that prove secondary qualities subjective apply equally to the primary. Thus for instance it is said that heat and cold are affections only of the mind, and not at all patterns of real beings existing in the corporeal substances which excite them; "for the same body which appears cold to one hand seems warm to another. Now why may we not as well argue that figure and extension are not patterns or resemblances of qualities existing in matter, because to the same eye at different stations, or eyes of a different texture at the same station, they appear various, and cannot therefore be the images of anything settled and determinate without the mind? Again, it is proved that sweetness is not really in the sapid thing because, the thing remaining unaltered, the sweetness is changed into bitter, as in case of a fever or otherwise vitiated palate. Is it not as reasonable to say that motion is not without the mind since, if the succession of ideas in the mind become swifter, the motion, it is acknowledged, shall appear slower, without any alteration in any external object?" [2]

But, it may be said, the essence of matter is not the qualities, but a substratum, or substance, which lies behind these and supports them. The qualities may be only subjective ideas; but you can-

[1] § 10. [2] § 14.

not get rid of the substantial existence underneath them. Now in the first place, *if* the qualities are ideas, they cannot subsist in an unperceiving substance. But what of this concept of substance itself? Locke had already criticised the notion, and had come to the conclusion that it is a purely negative idea; it is a "something we know not what," on a par with the mythical tortoise which for the Indian thinker holds up the world. Berkeley goes on to subject the idea to a still more vigorous criticism. "Let us examine a little the description that is given us of matter. It neither acts, nor perceives, nor is perceived; for this is all that is meant by saying it is an inert, senseless, unknown substance, which is a definition entirely made up of negatives excepting only the relative notion of its standing under or supporting. But then it must be observed that it supports nothing at all, and how nearly this comes to a description of a *nonentity* I desire may be considered. But, say you, it is the *unknown occasion* at the presence of which ideas are excited in us by the will of God. Now I would fain know how anything can be present to us which is neither perceivable by sense nor reflection, nor capable of producing any idea in our minds, nor is at all extended, nor hath any form, nor exists in any place. The words 'to be present,' when thus applied, must needs be taken in some abstract and strange meaning, and which I am not able to comprehend." "You may, if so it shall seem good, use the word 'matter' in the same sense as other men use 'nothing,' and so make those terms convertible in your style. For after all that is what appears to me to be the result of that definition — the parts whereof, when I consider with attention either collectively or separate from each other, I do not find that there is any effect or impression made on my mind different from what is excited by the term 'nothing.'" "It is a very extraordinary instance of the force of prejudice, and much to be lamented, that the mind of man retains so great a fondness, against all the evidence of reason, for a *stupid, thoughtless Somewhat*, by the interposition of which it would, as it were, screen itself from the Providence of God, and remove it farther off from the affairs of the world." [1]

[1] §§ 68, 75, 80

A material substance is accordingly unthinkable. Moreover, it would be of no possible use to us if we had it. "Though we give the materialists their external bodies, they by their own confession are never the nearer knowing *how* our ideas are produced; since they own themselves unable to comprehend in what manner body can act upon spirit, or how it is possible it should imprint any idea in the mind. Hence it is evident the production of ideas or sensations in our minds can be no reason why we should suppose matter or corporeal substances, since *that* is acknowledged to remain equally inexplicable with or without this supposition. . . . In short, if there were external bodies, it is impossible we should ever come to know it; and if there were not, we might have the very same reasons to think there were that we have now. Suppose — what no one can deny possible — an intelligence, without the help of external bodies, to be affected with the same train of sensations or ideas that you are, imprinted in the same order, and with like vividness in his mind. I ask whether that intelligence hath not all the reason to believe the existence of corporeal substances, represented by his ideas and exciting them in his mind, that you can possibly have for believing the same thing? Of this there can be no question; which one consideration were enough to make any reasonable person suspect the strength of whatever arguments he may think himself to have for the existence of bodies without the mind." [1]

To reiterate the main point, an unthinking matter does not exist, simply because it is inconceivable. "I am content to put the whole upon this issue: If you can but conceive it possible for one extended movable substance, or, in general, for any one idea, or anything like an idea, to exist otherwise than in a mind perceiving it, I shall readily give up the cause. And as for all that compages of external bodies you contend for I shall grant you its existence, though you cannot either give me any reason why you believe it exists, or assign any use to it when it is supposed to exist. I say, the bare possibility of your opinion's being true shall pass for an argument that it is so. But, say you, surely there is nothing easier than for me to imagine trees, for instance, in a

[1] §§ 19, 20.

park, or books existing in a closet, and nobody by to perceive them. I answer, you may so, there is no difficulty in it; but what is all this, I beseech you, more than framing in *your* mind certain ideas which you call books and trees, and at the same time omitting to frame the idea of any one that may perceive them? But do not you yourself perceive or think of them all the while? This therefore is nothing to the purpose; it only shows you have the power of imagining or forming ideas in your mind, but it does not show that you can conceive it possible the objects of your thought may exist without the mind. To make out this, it is necessary that *you* conceive them existing unconceived, or unthought of, which is a manifest repugnancy. When we do our utmost to conceive the existence of external bodies, we are all the while only contemplating our own ideas. But the mind, *taking no notice of itself*, is deluded to think it can and does conceive bodies existing unthought of or without the mind, though at the same time they are apprehended by or exist in itself." [1]

2. *God as the Cause of Our Ideas.* — So much for the negative argument. But if we were to stop here few persons, probably, would be convinced. Is there, we ask, no reality of any sort outside our own fleeting ideas? Can we say nothing beyond the fact that these ideas come and go? Certainly we can; and this brings us to the more constructive side of Berkeley's theory. In addition to the mere existence of ideas, there are two very important characteristics of our sense experience — its inevitableness, and its orderly coherence. "Whatever power I may have over my own thoughts, I find the ideas actually perceived by sense have not a like dependence on my will. When in broad daylight I open my eyes it is not in my power to choose whether I shall see or no, or to determine what particular objects shall present themselves to my view." [2] So too sensations have a steadiness, order and coherence; they are not excited at random, as those ideas which are the effect of the human will often are, but in a regular train or series. Let us then keep in mind these two conclusions: First, my ideas evidently require some cause beyond my own will; and, second, this cause

[1] §§ 22, 23. [2] § 29.

cannot be an unthinking matter — a word to which we have seen no positive notion corresponds. Nor, clearly, can the ideas be the cause one of another; "all our ideas, sensations, notions, or the things which we perceive, are visibly inactive — there is nothing of power or agency included in them."[1]

Is there then, we have to ask, any other sort of reality known to us, apart from passive ideas, to which we may have recourse? Yes; in addition to ideas we know *ourselves*, or *spirits*. As opposed to ideas, a spirit is a substance. "Besides all that endless variety of ideas or objects of knowledge, there is likewise something which knows or perceives them, and exercises divers operations, as willing, imagining, remembering about them";[2] and that this substance which supports or perceives ideas should itself be an idea, or like an idea, is evidently absurd. Instead of being passive, as ideas are, it is active. "All the unthinking objects of the mind agree in that they are entirely passive, and their existence consists only in being perceived; whereas a soul or spirit is an active being, whose existence consists, not in being perceived, but in perceiving ideas, and thinking."[3] We have no knowledge of any reality that is not one of these two sorts — *spirits*, or *ideas*. "The former are active, indivisible substances; the latter are inert, fleeting, dependent beings, which subsist not by themselves, but are supported by, or exist in, minds or spiritual substances."[4] We have to be sure no idea or image of a spirit — here Berkeley on his own showing may seem to be getting into difficulties. But we do have a *notion* of it, which prevents it from being a nonentity.

And now Berkeley's theory is ready for him. "We perceive a continual succession of ideas; some are anew excited, others are changed or totally disappear. There is, therefore, some cause of these ideas whereon they depend, and which produces and changes them. That this cause cannot be any quality, or idea, or combination of ideas, is clear already. It must therefore be a substance. But it has been shown that there is no corporeal or material substance. It remains, therefore, that the cause of ideas is an incor-

[1] § 25.
[2] § 2.
[3] § 139.
[4] § 89.

poreal, active substance, or spirit." [1] And since our own private will is not equal to the task, there must be some other Will that produces ideas in us — namely, God. Our ideas, to repeat, must have an objective cause. But instead of looking for this in an unthinking and unthinkable matter, why not have recourse to a reality of the same type as that we know already in the knowledge of ourselves?

In this hypothesis, we have everything that is needed to account for the objectivity, order, significance and necessity of our ideas. The objection that, if things are only ideas, we ought to be able to create a world to suit ourselves, is wholly without point; there stands a power over against us which, in sensation, determines the order our ideas shall follow. But such a controlling spirit will satisfy all the conditions. What we call the connection of qualities in things, or the laws of nature, stands only for this: that by the divine power one sensation is made to serve to us as a sign that we may, if we wish, get other concurrent sensations, or that other sensations are about to follow. "The connection of ideas does not imply the relation of *cause* and *effect*, but only of a *mark* or *sign* with the *thing signified*. The fire which I see is not the cause of the pain I suffer upon my approaching it, but the mark that forewarns me of it. In like manner the noise that I hear is not the effect of this or that motion or collision of the ambient bodies, but the sign thereof." This gives us a sort of foresight which enables us to regulate our actions for the benefit of life; and we cannot reasonably ask for more. "That food nourishes, sleep refreshes, and fire warms us; that to sow in the seedtime is the way to reap in the harvest; and, in general, that to obtain such or such ends such or such means are conducive — all this we know, not by discovering any necessary connection between our ideas, but only by the observation of the settled laws of nature, without which we should be all in uncertainty and confusion, and a grown man no more know how to manage himself in the affairs of life than an infant just born. And yet this consistent uniform working, which so evidently displays the goodness and wisdom of that Governing Spirit whose Will

[1] § 26.

constitutes the laws of nature, is so far from leading our thoughts to him that it rather sends them wandering after second causes." [1]

3. *Answers to Objections.* — Having stated his theory, Berkeley goes on to anticipate the objections that will be brought against it. First, it will be objected "that by the foregoing principles all that is real and substantial in nature is banished out of the world, and instead thereof a chimerical scheme of *ideas* takes place. All things that exist exist only in the mind, that is, they are purely notional. What therefore becomes of the sun, moon and stars? What must we think of houses, rivers, trees, stones? Are all these but so many chimeras and illusions of fancy? To all which I answer, that by the principles premised we are not deprived of any one thing in nature. Whatever we see, feel, hear, or any wise conceive or understand, remains as secure as ever. There is a *rerum natura,* and the distinction between realities and chimeras retains its full force. . . . The only thing whose existence we deny is that which *philosophers* call matter, or corporeal substance. And in doing this there is no damage done to the rest of mankind, who, I dare say, will never miss it." [2] The phrase "greater reality" has no meaning except as it indicates the superiority of certain ideas over others in vividness, coherency and distinctness; and in this sense the sun that I see by day is the real sun, and that which I imagine by night is the idea of the former. This also is an answer to the objection that there is a great difference between real fire, for instance, and the idea of fire, between dreaming or imagining oneself burnt, and actually being so. If real fire, we may further note, "be very different from the idea of fire, so also is the real pain which it occasions very different from the idea of the same pain; and yet nobody will pretend that real pain really is, or can possibly be, in an unperceiving thing, or without the mind, any more than its idea." [3]

Again, "it will be objected that we *see* things actually without or at a distance from us, and which consequently do not exist in the mind; it being absurd that those things which are seen at the distance of several miles should be as near to us as our own thoughts." [4]

[1] §§ 65, 31. 32.
[3] § 41.
[2] §§ 34, 35.
[4] § 42.

In reply to this, Berkeley calls attention to the fact that in dreams, also, we seem to see things at a distance, which yet have no reality outside the mind; but he has a more adequate answer still. For in his famous *New Theory of Vision* he had already attempted to prove that we do not *see* distance at all; all we receive through the senses is sensations of color and touch. When one says that a thing is at a distance, what he unconsciously means is that, in order to touch the thing, he foresees he would have to experience certain locomotive or muscular sensations, more or less numerous according to the distance from him at which the thing is placed. Vision is thus a "language" in which, by an arbitrary connection, one sensation (of color) stands as a sign for another (of movement).

Or do we object that, on this view, things are annihilated and created anew every time we shut and open our eyes? Once more Berkeley asks: Why call this absurd, if we can get absolutely no notion of what a thing can be when it is not perceived? And if it is "thought strangely absurd that upon closing my eyelids all the visible objects around me should be reduced to nothing, yet is not this what philosophers commonly acknowledge when they agree on all hands that light and colors, which alone are the proper and immediate objects of sight, are mere sensations that exist no longer than they are perceived?" [1] And so Berkeley goes on with various other objections; and although he does not meet them all with complete success, there is very little that has since been urged against him which he does not anticipate more or less clearly.

Let us sum up once more. "Ideas imprinted on the senses are real things, or do really exist — this we do not deny; but we deny that they can subsist without the minds which perceive them, or that they are resemblances of any archetypes existing without the mind, since the very being of a sensation or idea consists in being perceived, and an idea can be like nothing but an idea. Again, the things perceived by sense may be termed external with regard to their origin — in that they are not generated from within by the mind itself, but imprinted by a Spirit distinct from that which perceives them. . . . It were a mistake to think that what

[1] § 46.

is here said derogates in the least from the reality of things. It is acknowledged, on the received principles, that extension, motion, and in a word all sensible qualities, have need of a support, as not being able to subsist by themselves. But the objects perceived by sense are allowed to be nothing but combinations of those qualities, and consequently cannot subsist by themselves. Thus far it is agreed on all hands. So that in denying the things perceived by sense an existence independent of a substance or support wherein they may exist, we detract nothing from the received opinion of their *reality*, and are guilty of no innovation in that respect. All the difference is that, according to us, the unthinking beings perceived by sense have no existence distinct from being perceived, and cannot therefore exist in any other substance than those unextended, indivisible substances, or *spirits*, which act and think and perceive them ; whereas philosophers vulgarly hold the sensible qualities do exist in an inert, extended, unperceiving substance which they call *matter*, to which they attribute a natural subsistence exterior to all thinking beings or distinct from being perceived by any mind whatsoever, even the eternal mind of the Creator." [1]

4. *The Consequences of the Theory for Religion.* — And now for some of the further advantages which Berkeley's system is to bring. In the first place, it will banish at once from philosophy a number of difficult questions about which men have puzzled their heads and wasted their time to no purpose. Such questions as these, "whether corporeal substance can think," "whether matter be infinitely divisible," and "how it operates on spirit," as well as all the problems that arise from assuming the real existence of space, are set aside at once as meaningless. A still more far-reaching result has to do with the consequences for religion. For Berkeley's interest in philosophy is largely a religious interest ; and it seems to him that he has, in his Immaterialism, a potent weapon against the atheism of his day. It takes away the ground, in the first place, from Scepticism. "So long as we attribute a real existence to unthinking things, distinct from their being perceived, it is not only impossible for us to know with evidence the nature of any real

[1] §§ 90, 91

unthinking being, but even that it exists. Hence it is that we see philosophers distrust their senses and doubt of the existence of heaven and earth, of everything they see or feel, even of their own bodies." [1] If by matter I mean however that which I actually perceive by the senses, it is as impossible for me to doubt this as it is to doubt my own being.

And as the doctrine of matter "has been the main pillar of Scepticism, so likewise, on the same foundation, have been raised all the impious schemes of Atheism and Irreligion. . . . All these monstrous systems have so visible and necessary a dependence on it that, when this cornerstone is once removed, the whole fabric cannot choose but fall to the ground, insomuch that it is no longer worth while to bestow a particular consideration on the absurdities of every wretched sect of Atheists." [2] Do we ask for proof of God? It lies immediately before us, and is just as certain as the proof of our neighbor's existence. For as we do not see directly the very self of another man, but only certain bodily movements which stand as signs of what is present in his mind, so is not nature a Divine Visual Language in which God speaks to us, a system of signs which, by their order and coherency, tell indubitably of a Mind behind them?

"It seems to be a general pretence of the unthinking herd that they cannot *see* God. Could we but see him, say they, as we see a man, we should believe that he is, and believing obey his commands. But alas, we need only open our eyes to see the Sovereign Lord of all things with a more full and clear view than we do any one of our fellow-creatures. A human spirit or person is not perceived by sense, as not being an idea; when therefore we see the color, size, figure and motions of a man, we perceive only certain sensations or ideas excited in our own minds; and these being exhibited to our view in sundry distinct collections, serve to mark out unto us the existence of finite and created spirits like ourselves. Hence it is plain we do not *see* a man — if by *man* is meant that which lives, moves, perceives and thinks as we do — but only such a certain collection of ideas as directs us to think there is a distinct principle

[1] § 88. [2] § 92.

of thought and motion, like to ourselves, accompanying and repre-sented by it. And after the same manner we *see* God; all the difference is that, whereas some one finite and narrow assemblage of ideas denotes a particular human mind, whithersoever we direct our view we do at all times, and in all places, perceive manifest tokens of the Divinity: everything we see, hear, feel, or anywise perceive by sense being a *sign* or *effect* of the power of God, as is our per-ception of those very motions which are produced by men." [1]

By any true definition of language, therefore, God speaks to us as directly as one man to another. "Since you cannot deny that the great Mover and Author of nature constantly explaineth himself to the eyes of men by the sensible intervention of arbitrary signs which have no similitude or connection with the things signified, so as, by compounding and disposing them, to suggest and exhibit an endless variety of objects, differing in nature, time and place; thereby informing and directing men how to act with respect to things dis-tant and future, as well as near and present. In consequence, I say, of your own sentiments and concessions, you have as much reason to think the Universal Agent or God speaks to your eyes, as you can have for thinking any particular person speaks to your ears." [2]

"It is therefore plain that nothing can be more evident to any one that is capable of the least reflection than the existence of God, or a Spirit who is intimately present to our minds — producing in them all that variety of ideas or sensations which continually affect us, on whom we have an absolute and entire dependence, in short, 'in whom we live, and move, and have our being.' That the dis-covery of this great truth, which lies so near and obvious to the mind, should be attained to by the reason of so very few, is a sad instance of the stupidity and inattention of men, who, though they are surrounded with such clear manifestations of the Deity, are yet so little affected by them that they seem, as it were, blinded with excess of light." [3]

[1] § 148.
[2] *Alciphron*, Fourth Dialogue, Fraser, *Selections*, p. 271.
[3] *Treatise*, § 149.

5. *Sensation and Reason.* — If we follow the line of main emphasis in Berkeley's theory of knowledge, it would seem to have led us to the position that we can know only our own ideas. As a matter of fact this does not fully represent his belief. There was for him, as has been seen, knowledge of other reality as well. "We may be said to have some knowledge or *notion* of our own minds, of spirits and active beings, whereof in a strict sense we have not ideas." [1] And as Berkeley's thought developed he came to lay more stress on the intellectual framework of experience by which we rise to truth and God, and less upon sensations. "We know a thing when we understand it; and we understand it when we can interpret or tell what it signifies. Strictly the sense knows nothing." [2] But his entire consistency here is perhaps a little dubious. Most commonly he seems to speak as if the point from which we start, in knowledge, were a mass of unrelated sensations, and as if from these, by mere "experience," we finally arrive at their interpretation as the language of a divine Author. But if such a starting-point were granted, should we ever be in a position to reach, not merely this conclusion, but any conclusion at all? Could we be assured of the existence of any reality beyond the ideas themselves — the reality of God, or even that of other men? At any rate the logic of this "new way of ideas" needed a more critical examination than Berkeley was prepared to give. It was necessary that the consequences of empiricism and sensationalism — the consequences, that is, of the attempt to reduce experience to a congeries of separate sensations — should be carried out to their final issue. It was this work which Hume accomplished, and which constitutes his great significance in the history of thought.

LITERATURE

Berkeley, *New Theory of Vision; Principles of Human Knowledge; Three Dialogues between Hylas and Philonous; Alciphron; Siris.*
Fraser, *Selections.*
Fraser, *Berkeley.*
Fraser, *Berkeley and Spiritual Realism.*

[1] § 89. [2] *Siris*, § 253.

Huxley, *Critiques and Addresses.*
Mill, *Essays.*
McCosh, *Realistic Philosophy.*
Tower, *Relation of Berkeley's Later to his Earlier Idealism.*
Johnston, *The Development of Berkeley's Philosophy.*

§ 32. *Hume*

David Hume was a Scotchman, born in Edinburgh in 1711. His character was a mixture of the most kindly tolerance and good nature with shrewdness and a penetrating critical insight — an insight somewhat deficient however on the idealistic and imaginative side. Here is his own estimate of himself: "To conclude historically with my own character, I am, or rather was (for that is the style I must now use in speaking of myself, which emboldens me the more to speak my sentiments); I was, I say, a man of mild disposition, of command of temper, of an open, social and cheerful humor, capable of attachment but little susceptible of enmity, and of great moderation in all my passions. Even my love of literary fame, my ruling passion, never soured my temper, notwithstanding my frequent disappointments. My company was not unacceptable to the young and careless, as well as to the studious and literary; and as I took a particular pleasure in the company of modest women, I had no reason to be displeased with the reception I met with from them. In a word, though most men, anywise eminent, have found reason to complain of calumny, I never was touched or even attacked by her baleful tooth; and though I wantonly exposed myself to the rage of both civil and religious factions, they seemed to be disarmed in my behalf of their wonted fury. My friends never had occasion to vindicate any one circumstance of my character and conduct; not but that the zealots, we may well suppose, would have been glad to invent and propagate any story to my disadvantage, but they could never find any which they thought would wear the face of probability." Hume died in 1776.

1. *The Analysis of Knowledge.* — It has already been said that the significance of Hume's philosophy lies in the way in which he carries the empirical and sensationalistic tendencies in the thought

of Locke and Berkeley to their logical conclusion. He starts with a psychology which follows in general that of his predecessors, except that it is more unambiguous and thoroughgoing. Every possible object of knowledge is reducible either to an impression or an idea. "The difference between these consists in the degrees of force and liveliness with which they strike upon the mind and make their way into our thought or consciousness. Those perceptions which enter with most force and violence we may name *impressions;* and under this name I comprehend all our sensations, passions and emotions as they make their first appearance in the soul. By *ideas* I mean the faint images of these in thinking and reasoning; such, for instance, are all the perceptions excited by the present discourse excepting only those which arise from the sight and touch, and excepting the immediate pleasure or uneasiness it may occasion. I believe it will not be very necessary to employ many words in explaining this distinction. Every one of himself will readily perceive the difference betwixt feeling and thinking." [1]

There is another division among ideas which also is self-evident — that between simple and complex ideas. This last division tends to qualify to an extent the statement that ideas resemble or are copies of impressions. "I observe that many of our complex ideas never had impressions that corresponded to them, and that many of our complex impressions never are exactly copied in ideas. I can imagine to myself such a city as the *New Jerusalem*, whose pavement is gold and walls are rubies, though I never saw any such. I perceive, therefore, that though there is in general a great resemblance betwixt our *complex* impressions and ideas, yet the rule is not universally true that they are exact copies of each other. We may next consider how the case stands with our *simple* perceptions. After the most accurate examinations of which I am capable, I venture to affirm that the rule here holds without any exception, and that every simple idea has a simple impression which resembles it, and every simple impression a correspondent idea. That idea of red which we form in the dark, and that impression which strikes our eyes in sunshine, differ only in degree, not in nature." [2] Since

[1] *Treatise of Human Nature*, Bk. I, Pt. I, 1. [2] *Ibid.*

therefore complex ideas go back ultimately to simple ones, we may still affirm that the two species of perception are exactly corre-spondent. Accordingly we are led to the general conclusion that all our simple ideas in their first appearance are derived from simple impressions which they copy.

Impressions and ideas are thus the sole contents of the human mind, all of them going back originally to impressions. In order then to establish the reality of any supposed fact, we must be in a position to point out the definite, concrete impression which it is, or reproduces. "Since nothing is ever present to the mind but per-ceptions, and since all ideas are derived from something ante-cedently present to the mind, it follows that it is impossible for us so much as to conceive or form an idea of anything specifically different from ideas and impressions. Let us fix our attention out of ourselves as much as possible; let us chase our imaginations to the heavens, or to the utmost limits of the universe: we never really advance a step beyond ourselves, nor can conceive any kind of existence but those perceptions which have appeared in that nar-row compass. This is the universe of the imagination, nor have we any idea but what is there produced." [1]

2. *Criticism of the Self.* — Now on these principles it of course follows that, as Berkeley had pointed out, there can be no such thing as a material substance. "I would fain ask those philosophers who found so much of their reasonings on the distinction of sub-stance and accident, and imagine we have clear ideas of each, whether the idea of *substance* be derived from the impressions of sensation or reflection. If it be conveyed to us by our senses, I ask, which of them, and after what manner? If it be perceived by the eyes, it must be a color; if by the ears, a sound; if by the palate, a taste; and so of the other senses. But I believe none will assert that substance is either a color, or sound, or a taste. The idea of substance must therefore be derived from an impression of reflection, if it really exist. But the impressions of reflection resolve themselves into our passions and emotions, none of which can possibly represent a substance. We have, therefore, no idea of

[1] Bk. I, Pt. II, 6.

substance distinct from that of a collection of particular qualities, nor have we any other meaning when we either talk or reason concerning it. The idea of a substance is nothing but a collection of simple ideas that are united by the imagination, and have a particular name assigned them." [1]

But is it possible to stop here? Berkeley had insisted that we cannot know material substance. But he had supposed that *spiritual* substance — the self, or soul — we can know; and it was by using the self as an instrument that he was enabled to build up his positive theory of reality. But once again we have to ask, What is the positive impression on which the idea of self, or spirit, is based? Berkeley had himself admitted that there is no such impression. The self is not an idea; we only have a *notion* of it, which can be represented by no definite image. But in that case the self, or spiritual substance, has no more foundation than material substance; both must go together.

"I desire those philosophers who pretend that we have an idea of the substance of our minds to point out the impression that produces it, and tell distinctly after what manner that impression operates, and from what object it is derived. Is it an impression of sensation or of reflection? Is it pleasant, or painful, or indifferent? Does it attend us at all times, or does it only return at intervals? If at intervals, at what times principally does it return, and by what causes is it produced?" [2]   "There are some philosophers who imagine we are every moment intimately conscious of what we call our SELF; that we feel its existence and its continuance in existence, and are certain, beyond the evidence of a demonstration, both of its perfect identity and simplicity. . . . For my part, when I enter most intimately into what I call *myself* I always stumble on some particular perception or other, of heat or cold, light or shade, love or hatred, pain or pleasure. I never can catch *myself* at any time without a perception, and never can observe anything but the perception. When my perceptions are removed for any time, as by sound sleep, so long am I insensible of *myself*, and may truly be said not to exist. And were all my perceptions

[1] Bk. I. Pt. I, 6.   [2] Bk. I. Pt. IV, 5, Selby-Bigge's edition, p. 233.

removed by death, and could I neither think, nor feel, nor see, nor love, nor hate after the dissolution of my body, I should be entirely annihilated, nor do I conceive what is further requisite to make me a perfect nonentity. If any one, upon serious and unprejudiced reflection, thinks he has a different notion of *himself*, I must confess I can reason no longer with him. All I can allow him is that he may be in the right as well as I, and that we are essentially different in this particular. He may, perhaps, perceive something simple and continued which he calls *himself*, though I am certain there is no such principle in me.

"But setting aside some metaphysicians of this kind, I may venture to affirm of the rest of mankind that they are nothing but a bundle or collection of different perceptions, which succeed each other with an inconceivable rapidity, and are in a perpetual flux and movement. The mind is a kind of theater where several perceptions successively make their appearance, pass, re-pass, glide away, and mingle in an infinite variety of postures and situations. There is properly no *simplicity* in it at one time, nor *identity* in different, whatever natural propension we may have to imagine that simplicity and identity. The comparison of the theater must not mislead us. They are the successive perceptions only that constitute the mind; nor have we the most distant notion of the place where these scenes are represented, or of the materials of which it is composed." [1]

3. *Criticism of the Idea of Cause.* — No doubt the common belief in an identical self needs somehow to be accounted for. Before attempting this however we shall need to turn first to another — on the whole the most important — of Hume's contributions to philosophy. There are certain all-pervading relationships, in addition to the relation to a self, which appear to bind our ideas together so as to constitute what we know as knowledge; these also need to be critically analyzed in order to make sure they are legitimate and can be carried back to definite impressions. And of these by far the most important is the relation of cause and effect. The necessity attaching to the causal relationship had throughout

[1] Bk. I, Pt. IV, 6, p. 251

conditioned Berkeley's advance from the mere existence of ideas to his conception of the world as a universal and rational system of signs dependent upon God. And he had found, as he thought, a basis for causation in that free activity of Spirit which is not, indeed, picturable to the imagination, but which is rationally intelligible. Can this now be justified?

Again there is the same inexorable demand: what is the impression from which the idea of causation is derived? "Let us cast our eye on any two objects which we call cause and effect, and turn them on all sides, in order to find that impression which produces an idea of such prodigious consequence. At the first sight I perceive that I must not search for it in any of the particular *qualities* of the object; since, whichever of these qualities I pitch on, I find some object that is not possessed of it, and yet falls under the denomination of cause and effect."[1] The idea must then be derived from some *relation* among objects. Now when I examine the matter, I find two such relations clearly present — *contiguity*, and *succession*. But these do not exhaust what I mean by causation; an idea may be contiguous or prior to another without being considered as its cause. There is still something to be added — the idea of *necessary connection*. But what is the nature of this necessary connection, and where is the impression from which it is derived? The more we consider it the more puzzling the question appears. Search as I will, the only relations between objects that I discern are "those of contiguity and succession, which I have already regarded as imperfect and unsatisfactory. Shall the despair of success make me assert that I am here possessed of an idea which is not preceded by any similar impression? This would be too strong a proof of levity and inconstancy, since the contrary principle has been already so firmly established."[2]

Let us then turn from the question for the moment and take up two related questions, in the hope that these may incidentally throw some light on the matter in hand. First, for what reason do we pronounce it *necessary* that everything whose existence has a beginning should also have a cause? Secondly, why do we conclude

[1] Bk. I, Pt. III, 2, p. 75.   [2] Bk. I, Pt. III, 2, p. 77.

that such and such particular causes must *necessarily* have such and such particular effects? what is the nature of that inference we draw from the one to the other, and of the belief we repose in it?

Hume disposes of the first question by denying that the necessity exists. "Here is an argument which proves at once that the foregoing proposition is neither intuitively nor demonstrably certain. . . . As all distinct ideas are separable from each other, and as the idea of cause and effect are evidently distinct, 'twill be easy for us to conceive any object to be non-existent this moment, and existent the next, without conjoining to it the distinct idea of a cause or productive principle. The separation therefore of the idea of a cause from that of a beginning of existence is plainly possible for the imagination; and consequently the actual separation of these objects is so far possible that it implies no contradiction nor absurdity, and is, therefore, incapable of being refuted by any reasoning from mere ideas; without which 'tis impossible to demonstrate the necessity of a cause." [1] Accordingly we shall find upon examination that every demonstration which has been produced for the necessity of a cause is fallacious and sophistical.

If the belief in the necessity of a cause does not go back to an intuitive or demonstrative truth, it will have to come from observation and experience. How then does experience give rise to such a principle? Hume finds it convenient to consider this in the less general form: why do we believe that any particular cause will necessarily be followed by some particular effect? And the only possible reason is that we have found this effect as a matter of fact to follow in the past. "Thus we remember to have seen that species of object we call *flame*, and to have felt that species of sensation we call *heat*. We likewise call to mind their constant conjunction in all past instances. Without any farther ceremony we call the one *cause*, and the other *effect*, and infer the existence of the one from that of the other."

"Thus in advancing, we have insensibly discovered a new relation betwixt cause and effect when we least expected it. This relation

[1] Bk. I, Pt. III, 2.

is their *constant conjunction*. Contiguity and succession are not sufficient to make us pronounce any two objects to be cause and effect, unless we perceive that these two relations are preserved in several instances. We may now see the advantage of quitting the direct survey of this relation, in order to discover the nature of that *necessary connection* which makes so essential a part of it. . . . Having found that, after the discovery of the constant conjunction of any objects, we always draw an inference from one object to another, we shall now examine the nature of that inference, and of the transition from the impression to the idea. Perhaps 'twill appear in the end that the necessary connection depends on the inference, instead of the inference's depending on the necessary connection." [1]

First, then, is the transition which inference involves due to the reason, or to the mere association of ideas in the imagination? If reason determined us, it could only be in the form of a conclusion from the premise that nature is uniform, or that instances of which we have had no experience must resemble those of which we have had experience. But this is something it is entirely impossible to establish, even with probability. The inference must therefore be an affair of the imagination. At first this seems unlikely, in view of the strength of belief when compared with that which attaches to the mere fancies of the imagination. Hume is thus led to a consideration of the nature of *belief*. And he finds that the only difference between an idea which we believe, and a mere fancy, lies in the superior force and liveliness of the former. A belief is something more than the bare existence of an idea. It is a particular manner of forming an idea. And the same idea can only be varied by a variation of its degree of force and vivacity.

What is it, then, that makes the idea in question so lively that I believe in it? The answer goes back to the general principle that any present impression has the power, not only of transporting the mind to such ideas as are related to it, but also of communicating to them a share of its own force and vivacity. The "cause" stands for such a present impression; and the peculiar strength of belief which

[1] Bk. I, Pt. III, 6, p. 87.

attaches to the causal inference is due to the fact that, by constant conjunction, the relation has acquired the force of *custom*, or habit.

As all objective knowledge, in so far as it goes beyond present impressions, is based upon causation, custom accordingly is what governs all our thinking, and custom only. "Thus all probable reasoning is nothing but a species of sensation. 'Tis not solely in poetry and music we must follow our taste and sentiment, but likewise in philosophy. When I am convinced of any principle, it is only an idea which strikes more strongly upon me. When I give the preference to one set of arguments above another, I do nothing but decide from my feeling concerning the superiority of their influence. Objects have no discoverable connection together; nor is it from any other principle but custom that we can draw any inference from the appearance of one to the existence of another." [1]

Returning now to the idea of necessary connection, we may sum up Hume's argument briefly: So long as I regard one instance of causation only, I cannot discover anything beyond the relations of contiguity and succession. "I therefore enlarge my view to comprehend several instances, where I find like objects always existing in like relations of contiguity and succession. At first sight this seems to serve but little to my purpose. The reflection on several instances only repeats the same objects, and therefore can never give rise to a new idea. But upon farther inquiry, I find that the repetition is not in every particular the same, but produces a new impression, and by that means the idea which I at present examine. For, after a frequent repetition, I find that, upon the appearance of one of the objects, the mind is *determined* by custom to consider its usual attendant, and to consider it in a stronger light upon account of its relation to the first object. It is this impression, then, or *determination*, which affords me the idea of necessity." [2]

Such a conclusion amounts to neither more nor less than this: that what we call power, or force, or causal efficiency, exists not at all in *objects*, but only in the *mind*. In a discussion in which we need not follow him, Hume shows how all attempts to give a positive content to these terms, as objective realities, have failed. Once

[1] Bk. I, Pt. III, 8, p. 103. [2] Bk. I, Pt. III, 14, p. 155.

more, there must be some impression discoverable somewhere if the term is to represent anything real; and there is nothing in objects to give rise to this impression. "Since the idea of power is a new original idea, not to be found in any one instant, and which yet arises from the repetition of several instances, it follows that the repetition *alone* has not that effect, but must either *discover* or *produce* something new which is the source of that idea." Clearly the repetition of like objects in like relations of succession and contiguity *discovers* nothing new in any of them; and it is equally certain that this repetition *produces* nothing new in the objects themselves or in any external body. "These ideas, therefore, represent not anything that does or can belong to the objects which are constantly conjoined. But though the several resembling instances which give rise to the idea of power have no influence on each other, and can never produce any new quality *in the object*, yet the *observation* of this resemblance produces a new impression *in the mind*, which is its real model. For after we have observed the resemblance in a sufficient number of instances, we immediately feel a determination of the mind to pass from one object to its usual attendant, and conceive it in a stronger light upon account of that relation. This determination is the only effect of the resemblance, and therefore must be the same with power or efficacy, whose idea is derived from the resemblance. The several instances of resembling conjunctions lead us into the notion of power and necessity. These instances are in themselves totally distinct from each other, and have no union but in the mind which observes them and collects their ideas. Necessity, then, is the effect of this observation, and is nothing but an internal impression of the mind, or a determination to carry our thoughts from one object to another. . . . Necessity is something that exists in the mind, not in objects; nor is it possible for us ever to form the most distant idea of it considered as a quality in bodies."

"I am sensible that, of all the paradoxes which I have had or shall hereafter have occasion to advance in the course of this treatise, the present one is the most violent, and that 'tis merely by dint of solid proof and reasoning I can ever hope it will have admission and overcome the inveterate prejudices of mankind. . . . The contrary notion is so riveted in the mind, that I doubt not but my sentiments will be treated by many as extravagant and ridiculous. What! the efficacy of causes lie in the determination of the mind! As if causes did not operate entirely independent of the mind, and would not continue their operation even though there was no mind existent to contemplate them or reason concerning them. Thought may well depend upon causes for its operation, but not causes on thought. . . . I can only reply that the case here is much the same as if a blind man should pretend to find a great many absurdities in the supposition that the color of scarlet is not the same with the sound of a trumpet, nor light the same with solidity. If we have really no idea of a power or efficacy in any object, or of any real connection betwixt causes and effects, 'twill be to little purpose to prove that an efficacy is necessary in all operations. We do not understand our own meaning in talking so, but ignorantly confound ideas which are entirely distinct from each other. I am, indeed, ready to allow that there may be several qualities, both in material and immaterial objects, with which we are utterly unacquainted; and if we please to call these *power* or *efficacy*, 'twill be of little consequence to the world. But when, instead of meaning these unknown qualities, we make the terms of power and efficacy signify something of which we have a clear idea, and which is incompatible with these objects to which we apply it, obscurity and error begin then to take place, and we are led astray by a false philosophy. This is the case when we transfer the determination of the thought to external objects, and suppose any real intelligible connection betwixt them; that being a quality which can only belong to the mind that considers them." [1]

4. *Origin of a Belief in the External World.* — In discussing the nature of causation, we have found it difficult always to avoid falling in with the popular notion, and speaking of objects as if they existed outside the mind. It is time to recall the fact, however, that in reality it is only our own ideas that we can directly know. And since the principle of causation has now been resolved into

[1] Bk. I, Pt. III, 14, pp. 163–168.

mere expectation due to custom, there is to all appearance no way left ever of getting outside these purely subjective facts of consciousness. It remains to ask accordingly how men ever came to think that it is otherwise. How out of a flux of unrelated feelings, never repeated, do we evolve an independent world of identical things and identical selves?

Briefly, Hume's answer is something as follows: "We may observe that 'tis neither upon account of the involuntariness of certain impressions, as is commonly supposed, nor of their superior force and violence, that we attribute to them a reality and continued existence which we refuse to others that are voluntary and feeble. For 'tis evident our pains and pleasures, our passions and affections, which we never suppose to have any existence beyond our perception, operate with greater violence, and are equally involuntary, as the impressions of figure and extension, color and sound, which we suppose to be permanent beings. The heat of a fire, when moderate, is supposed to exist in the fire; but the pain which it causes on a near approach is not taken to have any being except in the perception." [1]

This explanation being rejected, we must search for some other hypothesis. And Hume finds it convenient to divide the question into two: what is the cause of our belief, first, in the *continued* existence of objects, and, second, in their *distinct* or separate existence? As regards the first of these, a little examination will disclose that all those objects to which we attribute a continued existence have a peculiar *constancy;* or, if they change, they show a *coherence* in their changes. "These mountains, and houses, and trees which lie at present under my eye, have always appeared to me in the same order; and when I lose sight of them by shutting my eyes, or turning my head, I soon after find them return upon me without the least alteration. My bed and table, my books and papers, present themselves in the same manner, and change not upon account of any interruption in my perceiving them." So too "when I return to my chamber after an hour's absence, though I find not my fire in the same situation in which I left it, still I am

[1] Bk. I, Pt. IV, 2, p. 194.

accustomed in other instances to see a like alteration produced in a like time, whether I am present or absent."

And if we inquire how this constancy and coherence of certain impressions goes about to produce so extraordinary an opinion as that of the continued existence of body, the answer is found in a peculiar tendency of the imagination. "When we have been accustomed to observe a constancy in certain impressions, and have found that the perception of sun or ocean, for instance, returns upon us after an absence or annihilation with like parts and in a like order as at its first appearance, we are not apt to regard these interrupted perceptions as different (which they really are), but on the contrary consider them as individually the same, upon account of their resemblance." "This resemblance is observed in a thousand instances, and naturally connects together our ideas of these interrupted perceptions by the strongest relation, and conveys the mind with an easy transition from one to another. An easy transition, or passage of the imagination, along the ideas of these different and interrupted perceptions, is almost the same disposition of mind with that in which we consider one constant and uninterrupted perception. The thought slides along the succession with equal facility as if it considered only one object; and therefore confounds the succession with the identity." It is from this propensity that there arises the fiction of the continued existence of objects; which is intended to disguise as much as possible the interruption of our ideas, and enable us to gratify our inclination to regard them as identical. The same thing comes about from the side of coherence. "The imagination, when set into any train of thinking, is apt to continue even when its object fails it, and, like a galley put in motion by the oars, carries on its course without any new impulse. Objects have a certain coherence even as they appear to our senses; but this coherence is much greater and more uniform if we suppose the objects to have a continued existence; and as the mind is once in the train of observing an uniformity among objects, it naturally continues till it renders the uniformity as complete as possible."

But while the imagination has thus a strong tendency to regard objects as identical and possessing a continued existence, must not our reason, just as soon as we consider the matter, tell us this is not the case? Since our perceptions, and objects, are one and the same thing, the actual interruption of our ideas is always there to contradict the propensity for imagining them continuous. Instead however of rejecting this last opinion, as logically they should have done, men have striven to retain both beliefs; and a conflict has necessarily been the result. "In order to set ourselves at ease in this particular we contrive a new hypothesis, which seems to comprehend both these principles of reason and imagination. This hypothesis is the philosophical one of the *double existence* of perceptions and objects; which pleases our reason in allowing that our dependent perceptions are interrupted and different, and at the same time is agreeable to the imagination in attributing a continued existence to something else, which we call *objects*. This philosophical system, therefore, is the monstrous offspring of two principles which are contrary to each other, which are both at once embraced by the mind, and which are unable mutually to destroy each other. Not being able to reconcile these two enemies, we endeavor to set ourselves at ease as much as possible by successively granting to each whatever it demands, and by feigning a double existence where each may find something that has all the conditions it desires." [1] In a somewhat similar way Hume goes on to account for the fiction of a substantial soul underlying our ideas.

5. *Scepticism.* — And so we have reasoned ourselves into a frame of mind where the solid fabric of the world dissolves like a dream before our eyes, or passes into a kaleidoscopic unreality of change. But can we really accept this result? Is it possible honestly to believe it? No; Hume admits that no one will be permanently convinced. As long as our attention is bent upon the subject, the philosophical and studied principle may prevail; but the moment we relax our thoughts nature will display herself, and draw us back to our former belief in the reality of permanent and identical things. And yet if our reason tells us that actually the contrary opinion is

[1] Bk. I, Pt. IV, 2, pp. 194–198, 215.

true, must we not of necessity follow its leading? But what *is* belief? nothing, once more, but the liveliness and force with which an idea strikes us. Reason thus furnishes no assured test; indeed reason has peculiar disadvantages of its own. The moment we have set to work to reason, then a doubt as to the validity of our reasoning is possible, nay, is forced upon us. This we must justify by a new argument, and this in turn by another; and all the time we are getting farther and farther away from those clear and immediate impressions on which the possibility of belief depends, until at last there remains nothing of the original probability however great we may suppose it to have been, and however small the diminution by every new uncertainty. Our immediate and instinctive beliefs yield to our reason, which for the moment carries with it the greater vividness. But the more refined and intricate reasoning becomes, the less this vividness of belief can belong to it; and the moment the mind relaxes we swing back to our natural opinions. The mind is in a strait 'twixt the two; now one is uppermost, and now the other.

Is, then, absolute scepticism the final word of philosophy? Are we to refuse to believe at all by reason of the dilemma in which we find ourselves? "Should it here be asked me whether I sincerely assent to the argument which I seem to take such pains to inculcate, and whether I be really one of those sceptics who hold that all is uncertain and that our judgment is not in *any* thing possessed of *any* measure of truth and falsehood, I should reply that this question is entirely superfluous, and that neither I nor any other person was ever sincerely and constantly of that opinion. Nature, by an absolute and uncontrollable necessity, has determined us to judge as well as to breathe and feel. Whoever has taken the pains to refute the cavils of this *total* scepticism has really disputed without an antagonist, and endeavored by arguments to establish a faculty which nature has antecedently implanted in the mind and rendered unavoidable. My intention then in displaying so carefully the arguments of that fantastic sect is only to make the reader sensible of the truth of my hypothesis that all our reasonings concerning causes and effects are derived from nothing but custom, and that belief is more properly an act of the sensitive than of the cogitative part of our natures." [1]

The result of Hume's inquiry is, accordingly, not to destroy belief — that is an impossibility — but to do away with the false assumption of its certain and demonstrable character. We believe, not because we can prove our opinions, but because we cannot help believing. If we are of the opinion that "fire warms or water refreshes, 'tis only because it costs us too much pains to think otherwise." Our belief is due to custom and instinct, not to reason. Since this is so, we can never fully guard ourselves against the assaults of scepticism. "This sceptical doubt, both with respect to reason and the senses, is a malady which can never be radically cured, but must return upon us any moment, however we may chase it away and sometimes may seem entirely free from it. 'Tis impossible upon any system to defend either our understanding or our senses, and we but expose them farther when we endeavor to justify them in that manner. As the sceptical doubt arises naturally from a profound and intense reflection on those subjects, it always increases the farther we carry our reflections, whether in opposition or in conformity to it. Carelessness and inattention alone can afford us any remedy. For this reason I rely entirely upon them; and take it for granted, whatever may be the reader's opinion at this moment, that an hour hence he will be persuaded there is both an external and an internal world." [2]

"I am first affrighted and confounded with that forlorn solitude in which I am placed by my philosophy. When I look abroad I foresee on every side dispute, contradiction, anger, calumny and detraction. When I turn my eye inward I find nothing but doubt and ignorance. All the world conspires to oppose and contradict me; though such is my weakness that I feel all my opinions loosen and fall of themselves when unsupported by the approbation of others. Every step I take is with hesitation, and every new reflection makes me dread an error and absurdity in my reasoning."

"After the most accurate and exact of my reasonings I can give no reason why I should assent to it, and feel nothing but a *strong*

[1] Bk. I, Pt. IV, 1, p. 183. [2] Bk. I, Pt. IV, 2, p. 218.

propensity to consider objects *strongly* in that view under which they appear to me. The memory, senses and understanding are all of them founded on the imagination, or the vivacity of our ideas. Yet if we assent to every trivial suggestion of the fancy, beside that these suggestions are often contrary to each other, they lead us into such errors, absurdities and obscurities that we must at last become ashamed of our credulity."

"But on the other hand, if the consideration of these instances make us take a resolution to reject all the trivial suggestions of the fancy and adhere to the understanding, that is, to the general and more established properties of the imagination, even this resolution, if steadily executed, would be dangerous, and attended with the most fatal consequences. For I have already shown that the understanding, when it acts alone and according to its most general principles, entirely subverts itself, and leaves not the lowest degree of evidence in any proposition either in philosophy or common life."

"Most fortunately it happens that, since reason is incapable of dispelling these clouds, nature herself suffices to that purpose, and cures me of this philosophical melancholy and delirium, either by relaxing this bent of mind, or by some avocation and lively impression of my senses which obliterate all these chimeras. I dine, I play a game of backgammon, I converse, and am merry with my friends; and when, after three or four hours' amusement, I return to these speculations, they appear so cold and strained and ridiculous that I cannot find in my heart to enter into them any farther." [1]

6. *Ethics.* — The Humian scepticism plays only a subordinate rôle in the second or ethical side of Hume's philosophy, except in so far indeed as this avoids any appeal to absolute principles such as scepticism has undermined. Hume starts as an empiricist from the undoubted fact that men do pass moral judgments; there are a number of things in conduct and character which call forth their esteem — justice, honesty, gratitude and the like. Supposedly there must be some common quality in all these things to explain why the same judgment is applied to them; and the first task of an

[1] Bk. I, Pt. IV, 7. A condensed quotation, taken from Aikins' *Philosophy of Hume*

ethical theory is accordingly to discover the nature of this common attribute.

Now among the virtues certain social qualities rank high; and some part at any rate of the merit assigned to such virtues comes from their general *utility*. In the case of some of them utility is the *sole* cause of our moral approbation. This is true for example of fidelity, truthfulness and chastity; these we should hardly call by the name of virtue except for their useful consequences, although as a result of habit we often forget the consequences and accept them as if they were good in their own right. A similar inquiry will show that the same thing is true in the case of the more fundamental virtues also — humanity, benevolence, friendship — which are not merely a means to some further end, but which call forth an immediate admiration and affection; here equally their usefulness will be found to play an important rôle as a source of our regard.

In so far Hume might appear to be saying what the Utilitarians were later on to say more explicitly — that the morality of an action is due to its contribution to the general happiness. And in point of fact it is the humanitarian emphasis that is strongest in his pages; a large part of his purpose is to show, in opposition to philosophers, like Hobbes, who had set out to reduce every human motive to self-love, that there is an original capacity in man for being affected directly by happiness other than his own. Thus the usefulness which we approve in a socially meritorious action is not that which affects ourselves, but usefulness to the persons who are benefited by the act; at times even, as in the case of a brave or generous deed performed by an adversary, we may approve conduct actually prejudicial to ourselves.

As Hume goes on, however, it appears that his first suggestion as to the nature of the common quality needs to be amended; social utility is not after all the one thing common to every form of merit, though it is the most important. Along with things that are socially useful we ascribe merit to other human characteristics; we approve qualities that are useful to the individual alone apart from social consequences, as well as those that are merely agreeable, to ourselves or to others. Thus industry, frugality, presence of mind, call forth disinterested approval irrespective of their general effect upon society. And the outcome is that, empirically, the distinguishing mark of a virtue is to be looked for in something more ultimate than utility, whether social or individual — in the fact, namely, that the quality in question *pleases* us. Accordingly the final definition runs as follows : a virtue is whatever mental action or quality gives to the spectator the pleasing sentiment of approbation. The essence of virtue lies in the feeling it excites directly in the perceiving mind.

This leaves one thing to be accounted for ; how does it happen that we are able, contrary to the claims of a "selfish" ethics, to get pleasure from a feeling that exists, not in ourselves, but only in another person's mind? Hume replies by saying that this is made possible through *sympathy*. We are so constituted that when we recognize the existence of a feeling in another man, this has a natural tendency to excite a similar feeling in ourselves ; and to the contagious property which happiness or misery thus possess of spreading beyond their own boundaries, we are to attribute that capacity for taking an interest in the pleasures and pains of other men to which a very large proportion of the virtues owe their existence, and which makes it quite unnecessary to call in the indirect effect on my own pleasure in terms of self-love. This last may constitute a secondary motive ; but for this it already presupposes an original disposition toward desiring the happiness of others, as the pleasure we get from food presupposes hunger.

Against Hume's ethical doctrine a general objection may of course be brought similar to that brought against his metaphysics — that it destroys the objective validity of the ethical judgment by reducing it to the mere presence of a feeling in some particular person's mind. Hume does not deny this ; and in his earlier and less popularly written book on ethics, the *Treatise*, he seems rather to enjoy stating his doctrine in a way to call attention to its unorthodox character. Virtue and vice, he tells us, are not qualities in objects, but principles in the mind ; so that in calling an action vicious we mean nothing but that from the constitution of our human nature we have a feeling or sentiment of blame in the contemplation of it. But here again his scepticism is theoretical rather than practical. He does not really mean to cast doubt on moral beliefs; he is simply asking what, on the assumption of their general validity, they actually amount to. Their justification may be no more than that we find them existing empirically as parts of human experience. But they are not "relative" in a merely individualistic sense; whatever the range of variation, the facts still show a substantial identity of judgment, pointing to an "eternal frame and constitution" of our animal nature.

7. *The Opponents of Hume.* — The thoroughgoing nature of Hume's sceptical conclusions held in itself the promise of a new epoch. So long as the impulse to knowledge exists in man he cannot easily rest content with such an outcome. Nor can society be satisfied with so insecure a basis. Already religious, political and moral faiths had been weakened for educated men by hostile criticism; but a confidence in the power of reason to reach grounded truth had hitherto remained to steady them — a confidence which received its most powerful support from the notable success of science. If however that same empirical study of facts on which men prided themselves really carried with it the logical conclusions which Hume maintained, then reason itself was no longer to be depended on. And with reason, science too must fall, all its certainty and necessity vanish, and man's knowledge reduce itself to a mere expectation that things will happen as they have been wont to happen in the past, with no surer ground for this assurance than the bare fact that we are accustomed so to believe.

The attempt to go behind Hume's premises, and to correct the presuppositions which led to his sceptical conclusions, was made independently by two philosophers. The first was the Scotchman *Thomes Reid*, who found the root of the trouble in the "new way of ideas" — the supposition, namely, that it is only with our own ideas that we come in contact. Instead of our being, as Hume maintained, shut up to the knowledge of our own sensations, Reid took his stand on what he held to be the belief of common sense — the belief that we have an immediate intuition of external reality as such. And we have a similar intuition of several universal truths, such as the principle of causation, which represent not mere ideas, but the original constitution of the human mind by which our empirical experience can be regulated and judged. Reid was the founder of a considerable school — the so-called Scottish school — which has had a strong influence on English thought, and which is represented by such men as *Dugald Stewart* and *Sir William Hamilton*. But Reid's merits have almost been lost sight of in the fame of a much greater thinker. This was the German philosopher, *Kant*. It was Hume who helped set Kant on the track of a conception which was to revolutionize philosophy. First, however, it will be necessary to speak briefly of certain other aspects of the period just considered, and to note the beginnings of a further influence which also was to find philosophical expression in Kant.

LITERATURE

Hume, *Treatise of Human Nature; Essays; Inquiry concerning Human Understanding; Inquiry concerning Principles of Morals; Natural History of Religion; Dialogues concerning Natural Religion.*
Aikins, *Selections.*
Huxley, *Hume.*
Knight, *Hume.*
Green, *Introduction to Hume.*
McCosh, *Scottish Philosophy.*
Seth, *Scottish Philosophy.*
Hyslop, *Hume's Ethics.*
Fraser, *Thomas Reid.*
Orr, *David Hume and His Influence in Philosophy and Theology.*
Elkin, *Hume.*
Calderwood, *David Hume.*
Laurie, *Scottish Philosophy in its National Development.*

§ 33. *The Enlightenment. Deism. The Ethical Development*

1. *The Spirit of the Enlightenment.* — In considering the course of philosophical development from Descartes to Hume we have thus far been concerned chiefly with its more technical and theoretical side. But it has another aspect also, of which it is important to get some understanding. This concerns the way in which, along

with other influences, it affected the general life and culture of the times, so as to give to this a distinct and peculiar character. The result is what is known as the period of the Enlightenment; and this may now be considered more briefly.

The Renaissance had been the product of a great wave of enthusiasm which for the time had seemed to be carrying everything before it. To the fresh forces which had been revealed in man nothing seemed impossible; cold caution, a sober criticism of the mind and its powers, an understanding of the historical conditions in which the new movements had their root, were felt to be unnecessary in the flush of victorious anticipation.

But as the impetus slackened a different attitude began to be in evidence. As the dreams of an Eldorado and of unlimited gold which had inspired the early voyages of discovery gave place to the hardships of a new land to be conquered and settled, so the confident faith in new spiritual powers grew more dim as time advanced. Metaphysical interests began to lose their attraction. Men in general were not indeed ready to accept the Pyrrhonism of such thinkers as Montaigne and Pascal; but the sceptical spirit was beginning to tell. Perhaps after all man was not made to know the ultimate truth of the universe; certainly his attempts so far had not met with the success that had been hoped. Meanwhile there were things close at hand which he might know. Let him turn from transcendental inquiries, and busy himself with the human interests which alone are really vital; the proper study of mankind is man.

And there was plenty to be found here demanding his attention. Along with the spiritual revolution that had come about, there had been inevitable changes in the structure of society as well. But these changes had been unconscious rather than premeditated. Many of the medieval institutions, ecclesiastical and feudal, still persisted as a dead weight against which the new ideals had to strive. So too the old beliefs for which the Church stood — beliefs which the thinkers of the Renaissance had contemptuously discarded — had by no means lost all of their vitality; and these allied themselves with reactionary tendencies in the social and political world to oppose any further change. Even the Renaissance itself added something to the problem; just as chivalry had degenerated into the caricature of itself which Cervantes ridiculed, so as the enthusiasm of the Renaissance died away it left behind extravagances and excrescences which needed to be cleared away.

The resulting period to which the name of the *Enlightenment* has been generally assigned belongs especially to the eighteenth century. The distinctive features of the Enlightenment are a certain lack of imagination, a hatred of vague enthusiasms and of misty ideals and ideas, a determination to apply the test of a severely critical reason to everything and to reject whatever will not stand the test, and the constant reference in all this, as the court of final appeal, to the one undoubted fact — the individual man exercising his rational powers of understanding, and possessed of inalienable rights which society is bound to respect. The outcome is a type of thought which may not enlist our sympathies very deeply, but which nevertheless had an important work to do. Let us consider once more the situation which confronted it. After the long period of the Middle Ages man had once more become conscious of himself; he had recognized, by the sudden bloom within him of unexpected powers, that he was not merely a member of society or of the Church, not merely one to take orders from some higher power whether man or God, but a free spirit who could sit in judgment upon whatever was offered him for his acceptance, and could demand that the world meet his cravings for a full and satisfying life. But the grip of vested interests was too strong to be broken all at once; a period of conflict had first to intervene. The process at the start necessarily was critical and negative. First it must be shown what man is *not*; he must be freed from the restraints which the past had laid upon him, must be set up over against society, and religion, and even moral law, as having a nature not to be coerced by anything external. Such a work was done by the Enlightenment, and done so thoroughly that the conception of the individual which it worked out is the dominant conception down to the present day. The result was one-sided. It gave the individual his rights indeed; but in trying to make him independent of the concrete environment which institutions represent it tended to empty his life of much of its actual content. It was the task of the period that followed to make the attempt to remedy this one-sidedness and abstractness without giving up the gains which the Enlightenment had won.

The weapon of the Enlightenment, as has been remarked, was primarily the critical intellect — severe, dispassionate, destructive, with little of light and warmth in it. Any sympathetic appreciation of the relative value which the ideas and institutions of the past might claim — what we now call the historical sense — was in the thinkers of the Enlightenment almost wholly lacking. It is not very strange that this should be the case. They were engaged in fighting that which had the weight of authority on its side, and which was far from being disposed itself to be conciliatory. Nor perhaps could there have been a better weapon against the great mass of unreasoning traditional beliefs than the unsympathetic logical intellect, tinged with ridicule, and appealing to those hard facts which common sense can appreciate without difficulty, and which have an obvious bearing on the more solid and practical interests of human life. We may be inclined now to find fault with the contemptuous rejection of whatever cannot be compressed within the limits of a clear-cut formula — in particular, what we call the *feeling* side of life. But the Enlighteners had a justification for their attitude. If men can be allowed to fall back upon feeling, that is the end of argument. What we need is clear ideas, something that can be grasped and defined. Feeling confuses thought; and, furthermore, since it tends first of all to gather around those things which custom has made familiar, it is the mainstay of that opposition to progress which it was the function of reason to demolish. The consequence was, however, that the thought of the Enlightenment was rather superficial; to realize its defects we have only to turn to one of its classical expressions in English literature — Pope's *Essay on Man*. Sundering himself as he did from the life of the race and the historical background which had shaped his own opinions as truly as the ones he criticised, judging everything by the test of an individual logic, it is not strange that the man of the Enlightenment should often have shown a very unenlightened attitude toward beliefs he did not share, and have revealed a constitutional blindness to some of the deeper aspects of the human spirit.

In its characteristic features the Enlightenment took its rise in England. From England it influenced the France of Voltaire and the Encyclopedists, where it had a peculiarly brilliant development. Germany was less affected; here the influence of Leibniz continued to be dominant, but Leibniz as systematized by Wolff in a highly rationalistic system from which the most valuable elements had dropped out. It was from this school that Kant, the philosopher of the new era, was to spring.

2. *The Deistic Movement.* — As regards England it will be enough, in addition to what has already been said in connection with Locke, to notice two movements — the growth of Deism, and the development of ethical theory. Deism was an attempt to get rid of the irrational elements in Christianity. It starts from a desire to explain away the mysteries of Church dogma, and to show that between revelation and reason there is no contradiction. Thus in Locke it calls men back from theology to the simplicity and reasonableness of the New Testament, whose one essential article of faith is the Messiahship of Christ. Revelation is not for the purpose of adding any mysteries of faith, but serves only the practical end of convincing men, through its miracles, of the simple truths of the Gospel.

But soon the emphasis on the reasonableness of revelation passed into the feeling that, if reason alone is competent to reach God, revelation is superfluous. Accordingly the attempt to rationalize the Bible narratives and doctrines gave place to the much simpler attitude of hostility, which admitted their irrationality and made the most of it. Over against revealed religion there was set the Deistic creed of so-called Natural Religion, whose outcome was to remove God more and more from the actual world and the immediate life of men. Such a creed had little content beyond the belief in a God who made the universe and set it in motion, and who has laid down certain laws of conduct for men in the moral law; of this natural and rational religious philosophy positive religions are only corruptions. Of course this precluded any sympathetic

appreciation of their historical meaning or of a possible truth underlying their imperfect statements of doctrine; historic religions are
due to the selfish cunning of priests and rulers, and are to be
attacked with every weapon at command.

Among the more important English Deists are Toland, Collins,
Tindal, Chubb and Morgan. On the whole Deism had but little
success in maintaining itself against the champions of revelation;
it represented indeed a position of unstable equilibrium. As it
opposed the Biblical account of God's dealings with the world on
the ground of their inconsistency with his goodness and justice, it
was compelled to assume that the same criticism did not apply
to the workings of Nature, where alone it could look for God. This
found expression in the shallow optimism of the period, and the
dictum that whatever is, is right. The opponents of Deism found
little difficulty in showing that the objections it brought against the
God of revelation could be turned with equal effect against its own
God of nature — a line of argument which was worked out most
effectively in Bishop Butler's famous *Analogy of Religion*.

3. *The Development of Ethical Theory.* — The effect of the Deistic
movement was to reduce religion for the most part to a life of moral
conduct. Indeed this was where practically the emphasis was
laid even by those theologians who stood as opponents of Deism;
for the unimaginative temper of the age, the deeper aspects of the
religious experience had but slight appeal. From this emphasis
there arose however one important consequence. The attempt to
find for morality a foundation independent of theology brought
about the first development of ethical theory on a large scale in
modern times; and to the chief phases of this development we may
now turn briefly.

The starting-point of English ethics is Hobbes and his selfish
theory of human nature. This naturally called forth strong
opposition, and nearly all the succeeding moralists have Hobbes
more or less directly in view. Among the earlier theorists, the
motive is particularly apparent in *Richard Cumberland*. Cumberland denies that man is wholly selfish, and adds to egoistic motives
social and benevolent affections also, which are equally original.

Man is social in his nature, and finds a direct satisfaction in doing good to others apart from the indirect benefits he may hope to gain. Moreover there is a necessary connection between individual and social welfare which makes it impossible to secure individual happiness except by subordinating oneself to the good of mankind. This connection is decreed by God, who thus supplies the ultimate ground for the obligation to perform those benevolent acts which the welfare of mankind demands, and in which morality consists.

Other attempts to give to ethics a rational foundation are represented by Cudworth, Clarke and Wollaston. *Ralph Cudworth* — a Platonist — had recourse to innate ideas of reason. *Samuel Clarke* attempted to find a criterion in the notion of conformity to the fitness or harmony of things — a relation which, like mathematics, is capable of being known as self-evident, and which is even independent of the will of God. With *William Wollaston*, who was influenced by Clarke, this takes the form of saying that a wrong act is ultimately a false judgment, or a lie. A rational being should act in accordance with the true relations of things; and it is because his act implicitly denies this truth that it is wrong. Thus the murderer acts as though he were able to restore life to his victim; the man who is cruel to animals declares by his act that the creature is a being devoid of feeling; he who refuses charity denies in practice the condition of the poor to be what it actually is. What of course Wollaston really means is, not that the refusal of charity is literally a lie, but that charity is a necessary form of social relationship which a lack of benevolence contradicts.

More important than any of the preceding names is that of *Lord Shaftesbury*. Shaftesbury's special contribution to a theory of ethics centers about his doctrine of the "moral sense" — a doctrine which later, in the form of "conscience," was to dominate English ethics on its more reputable side. He starts, as Cumberland had done, from a denial of the adequacy of self-love as a sufficient human motive; though it is not so much Hobbes that Shaftesbury has in mind as it is the more orthodox opinion which sought to uphold the majesty of God by making obedience the test of virtue, and which was led in consequence to deprecate the natural human qualities of kindliness, fair-mindedness and simple goodness, and to urge the fear of hell and the hope of heaven as the truly Christian motives. "There is," Shaftesbury writes, "no more of rectitude, piety and sanctity in a creature thus reformed than there is meekness or gentleness in a tiger strongly chained, or innocence and sobriety in a monkey under the discipline of the whip." Why does a man admire benevolence, and detest arrogance and injustice? Simply because, unless he is corrupted by bad habits and opinions, he cannot help it. "A common honest man whilst left to himself and undisturbed by philosophy and subtle reasonings about his interest, gives no other answer to the thought of villainy than that he cannot possibly find in his heart to set about it, or conquer the natural aversion he has to it." "No sooner are actions viewed, no sooner the human affections and passions discovered, than straight an inward eye distinguishes, and sees the fair and shapely, the amiable and admirable, apart from the deformed, the foul, the odious or the despicable." There is in such human traits an inherent attractiveness, appropriateness, harmony, proportion, order, to which something within our breasts responds directly; we know that they are good and admirable not by argument, but through the deliverance of an immediate inner feeling, or moral sense. This is, for morality, what good taste is in manners, or the artistic sense in art; a gentleman does not argue about the difference between decency and indecency, or a true artist need to resort to reasoning in order to tell beauty from ugliness.

As an actual fact we are not dealing here with mere analogies; in essence the three things are really one. To philosophize, in a just signification, is but to carry good breeding a step higher. For the accomplishment of breeding is to learn what is decent in company or beautiful in art; and the sum of philosophy is to learn what is just in society, and beautiful in nature and the order of the world. There is a beauty and deformity as well in actions, minds and tempers as in figures, sounds or colors; indeed it is here that the highest beauty will be found. Beauty does not lie in matter as such, but in the forms and proportions which mind impresses on it; and what mind creates in material of its own essence instead of in alien clay and stone must therefore take first rank. If anyone sees fit to deny that certain forms of character are in themselves admirable and lovable while others are by nature calculated to inspire hatred and disgust, this is not proof that such distinctions are not real, but only the revelation that he himself is lacking in the good taste or moral sense which belongs to a normal human nature.

These quotations perhaps will indicate sufficiently where Shaftesbury's chief emphasis is placed. The content of virtue is found by him first of all in its social character; and at times accordingly he seems to speak the language of the ardent humanitarian. But actually it is not the love of man which chiefly motivates his thought; as a matter of fact man and his works appear to him so seldom of a sort to call forth our spontaneous admiration and respect that they constitute a real stumbling-block for his theory. "All is delightful, amiable, rejoicing, except in relation to man only and his circumstances, which seem unequal." Strictly speaking, virtue is not the love of man; it is the love of order and beauty in society. The admirableness and beauty of the moral virtues rests not on the feelings singly, but on the part they play in a larger scheme; they are beautiful because they are "natural" — a necessary part of the ideal order of the world. This is how Shaftesbury proposes to reconcile self-interest with benevolence. In so far as they are "according to nature" even the private passions and affections are necessary and good; but they fulfil their natural function only as they subordinate themselves, not to the needs of the individual organism simply but to a still wider good — the welfare and prosperity of the species. Nothing can in the end justify our approval apart from the general system wherein it fills a place. And of this system even society itself is but a fragment. The final source of the attraction which excellence possesses is found not in any particular quality, but in the Whole. The beauty which lends validity to the moral life is due to the contribution which the ethical virtues make to the general order; it rests on the enthusiastic contemplation of the universe as a perfect whole in which all things praise God, and apparent evils are transformed into instruments of a higher good.

The recognition that sentiment plays an important part in determining the objects of our moral approval was taken up by other ethical thinkers of the period. *Francis Hutcheson*, Shaftesbury's most important follower, brought to the notion of a moral sense a careful and laborious psychological analysis in what was the most thorough and systematic treatment of moral theory that had yet appeared. We have already met a somewhat similar point of view in Hume. And as Hutcheson had systematized Shaftesbury, so Hume's account of sympathy as the source of a disinterested moral feeling was carried farther by *Adam Smith*, the great economist and author of the *Wealth of Nations*. Smith attempted to show that sympathy is the solvent of practically all the problems of ethics. The starting-point of morals is the ability to put ourselves imaginatively in the place of another man, and to feel an emotion called forth by an identical situation. When the sentiment thus aroused in us is approximately the same as that which we observe in our neighbor, the perception of this is the occasion of a pleasure, and we are said in consequence to enter into sympathy with, or approve, his emotional attitude. Next, having once had this experience with reference to others, we come to realize that they likewise are adopting the same attitude toward ourselves; and thereupon there is set up in our own breast a reflection of the impartial appraisal with which they view us, and we come to judge our own motives and feelings as a disinterested public might. This impartial spectator and umpire, this "man within the breast" who stands apart from our more impassioned and less reflective selves and views them as outsiders would view them, is the psychological source of the moral sense, for which we need therefore invent no special faculty.

The notion of a moral sense assumes another form, and one more congenial to the moral traditions of the English mind, in *Bishop Butler*. Conscience, the central fact in Butler's ethics, is not to be sure mere feeling; it is a form of reason. It is not however reason in its wider sense, but a special form of reason located in a special faculty, and carrying with it an emotional appeal as well.

Butler's most significant contribution is connected with his psychology of desire. We do not aim at pleasure, as the hedonists commonly had assumed; we aim at *objects*. What we need to take our start from is the conception of man as made up of active impulses that call for satisfaction in more or less determinate ways; pleasure accompanies the exercise of these faculties, but is in no wise responsible for them in the first place. And such being the case, there is no *a priori* reason why we should expect the objects that gratify an impulse to be confined within the limits of the self and its private ends or feelings. The fact plainly is that other people may be interesting to us on their own account and their welfare made an object of immediate desire, just as we desire food because we are hungry and not because we aim at pleasant feeling directly.

Moreover, self-love is something more than a mere spontaneous expression of impulse. Every satisfaction of desire does gratify the self. But to constitute self-love as a rational motive there has to be added to the idea of the particular objects which excite desire a further idea — the idea of the self as regulating the expression of desire; and this is a secondary product of *reflection*. Reflection is equally necessary to constitute the rational motive of benevolence. Accordingly there is no reason why self-love and benevolence may not really be motives as distinct as to experience they seem to be. Every motive must no doubt be interested in the sense that it would not constitute a motive were it not connected with some human satisfaction; but to say that it therefore must be "selfish" is an abuse of language. On the other hand all the original instincts without exception are disinterested if we mean by this that they do not have the self and its happiness consciously in view. The outcome is that happiness is not dependent on self-love. It consists in the enjoyment of those objects which are by nature suited to our several particular appetites, passions and affections; so that if self-love were wholly to engross us to the exclusion of every other principle, the sources of happiness would in reality be dried up.

Meanwhile human nature is not just a collection of faculties;

it is an organic whole. There must then be some principle of subordination; and this Butler finds in Conscience. In general, conscience performs the Platonic service of assigning the various elements of human nature to their proper place in the system of the good life; it is an additional principle of reflection, distinguishable alike from the primary instincts and affections and from the secondary motives of benevolence and self-love, which as a monitor stands above all other human faculties and, by approving or condemning, passes on their relative rank and value.

In opposition to this more orthodox development the tendency that was to have the most important consequences for later ethics took a different turn, to which the name utilitarianism has come to be attached. Psychologically such a tendency goes back to Hobbes and his common-sense view that pleasure is the end at which man aims; but instead of taking pleasure in its private sense, as the Greek hedonists had done, it substitutes the conception of the *general* happiness. This utilitarian principle had had a part to play in nearly all the ethical theories that have just been mentioned; but its logical implications had been obscured somewhat by other motives. It has met us in a more explicit shape in Locke, where it took on a theological form, the motive for the obligation we are under to work for the general good being looked for in God's will and power. Following Locke, this theological utilitarianism found expression in *William Paley's* famous definition of virtue; virtue consists in "seeking the happiness of mankind, in obedience to the will of God, and for the sake of everlasting happiness." Utilitarianism had to be secularized, however, and lose its theological props, before it was suited to the temper of the following century. This was done by a series of thinkers who start from Jeremy Bentham. Bentham's earlier work belongs to the eighteenth century, and he shows some of the salient characteristics of the Enlightenment; but it will be better to postpone what needs to be said about him to a later point.

LITERATURE

Berkeley, *Alciphron.*
Stephen, *English Thought in the Eighteenth Century.*
Cairns, *Unbelief in the Eighteenth Century.*
Locke, *The Reasonableness of Christianity.*
Butler, *Analogy of Religion, Sermons on Human Nature.*
Collins, *Butler.*
Selby-Bigge, *British Moralists.*
Shaftesbury, *Characteristics of Men, Manners, Opinions, Times.*
Fowler, *Shaftesbury and Hutcheson.*
Mackintosh, *On the Progress of Ethical Philosophy during the Seventeenth and Eighteenth Centuries.*
Patten, *Development of English Thought.*
Albee, *History of English Utilitarianism.*
Hibben, *Philosophy of the Enlightenment.*

§ 34. *The French Enlightenment. Voltaire and the Encyclopedists. The Materialists. Rousseau. Lessing and Herder*

1. *The French Enlightenment.* — The results of the English Enlightenment were introduced into France by *Voltaire*, who had been influenced by Locke during a sojourn in England. This influence took root in a brilliant circle of Frenchmen who, from their connection with the new Encylopedia which was to embody the knowledge that mankind had so far attained, were known as the Encyclopedists. Connected more or less closely with this enterprise were such men as Diderot, d'Alembert, Voltaire, Holbach, Turgot, Montesquieu, Helvetius and others. In addition to some positive scientific achievements, the French Enlightenment directed its weapons, as in England, against the popular religious beliefs which seemed to it to be irrational and harmful. But by reason of conditions in France, where the forces of obscurantism were much more strongly entrenched, the strife took on here a far sharper and more virulent tone. Against the intolerance and oppression of a corrupt clergy who used the instrument of traditional belief to block all efforts at reform, Voltaire and the Encyclopedists stood out as the deadliest foes. They set themselves, with every resource

of scientific knowledge, clear reasoning and biting wit, to discredit the foundation on which the influence of their opponents rested. It is this unceasing and fearless hatred of injustice which gives to the figure of Voltaire heroic proportions, in spite of his intellectual limitations and personal faults.

Such a practical aim determined also to a considerable extent the course which the French Enlightenment was to take. As a weapon against a real and dangerous foe, Hume's scepticism was too fine spun, too far from common sense, to appeal to the French reformers. As against Berkeleyan idealism, the more significant side of the French Enlightenment tended, in the fight against tradition, to a thoroughgoing and consistent scientific view of the world — that is, to Materialism — without bothering itself very much about theoretical difficulties. In the beginning, indeed, the Enlightenment was Deistic; it still held to natural religion, and to a somewhat vague and remote Deity who stands as the original source of the world. But such remnants of a religious faith were not very deep-seated, and they quickly tended to disappear as naturalism and sensationalism were carried out to their logical results. *Lamettrie*, in his *L'Homme Machine*, reduces man, as Descartes had reduced the animal, to a mere automaton — a body governed by purely physical laws. The innumerable facts which show the close dependence of the mind on bodily conditions were marshalled with much skill, and the conscious life reduced wholly to sensations dependent on bodily processes. This sensationalism was worked out theoretically by *Condillac*, who supposes a statue endowed simply with the sense of smell, and then tries to show how all the mental faculties can be evolved out of this. Condillac did not draw the ultimate consequences of this sensationalism; but other men stood ready to perform the task. *Helvetius*, in particular, carries the same principle into the practical and moral realm; the sole motive of our acts is egoism and self-interest, and the most exalted virtues can be explained as a result of self-love and a desire for pleasure.

These movements are summed up in *Holbach* in his *System of Nature*, where they take a form which is genuinely impressive.

Materialism becomes a grim gospel — a gospel of freedom from superstition and oppression. To Holbach's almost fanatical earnestness religion, and the tyranny of rulers which is buttressed by religion, seem the source of all human woes. The God of wrath and cruelty for which the Church had too often stood can only be banished by doing away with God altogether, and substituting Nature with its unbending laws. Truth and religion are unalterably opposed. "Nature invites man to love himself, incessantly to augment the sum of his happiness; religion orders him to love only a formidable God who is worthy of hatred, to detest and despise himself, and to sacrifice to his terrible idol the sweetest and most lawful pleasures. Nature bids man consult his reason and take it for his guide; religion teaches him that this reason is corrupted, that it is a faithless, truthless guide, implanted by a treacherous God to mislead his creatures. Nature tells man to seek light, to search for the truth; religion enjoins upon him to examine nothing, to remain in ignorance. Nature says to man: 'Cherish glory, labor to win esteem, be active, courageous, industrious'; religion says to him: 'Be humble, abject, pusillanimous, live in retreat, busy thyself in prayer, meditation, devout rites, be useless to thyself and do nothing for others.' Nature tells children to honor, to love, to hearken to their parents, to be the stay and support of their old age; religion bids them prefer the oracle of their God, and to trample father and mother under their foot when divine interests are concerned. Nature commands the perverse man to blush for his vices, for his shameless desires, his crimes; religion says to the most corrupt: 'Fear to kindle the wrath of a God whom thou knowest not; but if against his laws thou hast committed crime, remember that he is easy to appease and of great mercy; go to his temple, humble thyself at the feet of his ministers, expiate thy misdeeds by sacrifices, offerings, prayers.' Nature says to man: 'Thou art free, and no power on earth can lawfully strip thee of thy rights'; religion cries to him that he is a slave condemned by God to groan under the rod of God's representatives. Let us recognize the plain truth, that it is these supernatural ideas that have obscured morality, corrupted politics, hindered the advance of the sciences, and extinguished happiness and peace even in the very heart of man." [1]

We must banish then the mists of prejudice, and inspire man with courage and respect for his reason; it is only thus he can find a remedy against the evils into which fanaticism has plunged him, and throw off the fetters by which tyrants and priests everywhere succeed in enchaining the nations. There is but one truth, and it can never harm us. This " truth " which is to do away with evils is the truth of science. "Let man cease to search outside the world in which he dwells for beings who may procure him a happiness that nature refuses to grant; let him study that nature, let him learn her laws, let him apply his discoveries to his own felicity, let him undergo without a murmur the decrees of universal force." Matter and motion alone exist. Mind is nothing but an occult term that accounts for nothing. All things alike are necessary and subject to mechanical law. Order, purpose, beauty, are merely subjective. Man, instead of being that for whom all things were created, is entirely unimportant, an insect of a day. Necessity rules in the moral as in the physical world; the particles of dust and water in a tempest or a whirlwind, and an individual in the stormy movements of a revolution, move by the same necessity. There is no difference between the man who throws himself out of a window and the man whom I throw out, except that the impulse acting in the second comes from without, the other from within his own mechanism.

And behind this there lies in particular the motive which foreshadows the coming Revolution — the sense of social inequalities and injustice which call for drastic political changes. Let the great multitude of the oppressed shake off the idle prejudices through which whole nations are forced to labor, to sweat, to water the earth with their tears, merely to keep up the luxuries and corruption of a handful of insensates, a few useless creatures; let them demand the rights which Nature gives them. As government only derives its powers from society, for whose sake alone it exists, society may at any time revoke these powers if it seems to its advantage to do so. It may change the form of government, extend or limit the

[1] Quoted from Morley's *Diderot,* p 370

power intrusted to its rulers, over whom it retains a supreme authority by the immutable law of nature that subordinates the part to the whole.

2. *Rousseau.* — Meanwhile there had appeared within the circle of the Enlightenment a remarkable person who was destined to be the forerunner of a new and important movement. For a time he had cast in his lot with the Encyclopedists, and had contributed to that enterprise. But as the incompatibility of their standpoint with his own grew more apparent to him, he became sharply antagonistic to the whole principle of Rationalism.

This man was *Jean Jacques Rousseau*, a Swiss of French descent, born in Geneva in 1712. In his *Confessions* we have a record of his life and character given with a fidelity and frankness hardly surpassed in literature. Rousseau, to put it in a word, was a sentimentalist. He was a man with an extraordinary capacity for feeling combined with a weakness of will that was abnormal — a father who while preaching fervidly the duty of each mother to suckle her children left his own to the tender mercies of a public asylum without taking the trouble even to keep track of them; a philanthropist filled with love for mankind who yet could not live with any one by reason of his vanities and caprices and his irritable sensitiveness. "He has only felt," says Hume, "during the whole course of his life. He is like a man who was stript not only of his clothes, but of his skin, and turned out in that situation to combat with the rude and boisterous elements." His vagaries sometimes reached a point little short of madness. Nevertheless, in part by his very extravagances, he was able to make an impression on the artificial age in which he lived of which a more balanced nature might have been incapable. He died in 1778.

Before considering the influence of Rousseau, it may be well to stop for a moment and sum up again the results which the Enlightenment had accomplished. That which stands out most clearly in the whole movement is its Individualism. Now before man can be an intelligent shaper of his own destiny he must first recognize himself, his rights and powers, in independence of the more or less arbitrary environment that surrounds him, and that stands for the past rather than the future. The Enlightenment brought this recognition into sharp relief. But in doing this it ran the risk of going to the opposite extreme. From the conception of man simply as a dependent part of the world, subject to authority, it passed to the conception of him as a self-centered unit complete without reference to other things. By human convention all sorts of relations might be superinduced upon a man. But these are arbitrary, and for the most part unjustifiable; to get at the real man we must strip them all away. Society, instead of being a natural expression of needs of man's nature, is only an arbitrary contract which men make for the sake of certain external advantages. It may be a necessity if these are to be attained; but still in many ways it is a lamentable curtailing of the privileges men enjoy by nature. Naturally, on such a showing, there could be no recognition of the organic way in which man and his powers are rooted in the past life of the race; and there seemed no reason consequently why institutions might not be thrown off at any moment — that was what the French Revolution tried to do — and a start made entirely *de novo*.

To the new idealism which in Germany was to endeavor to correct the one-sidedness of the eighteenth century the relation of Rousseau was indirect rather than fully conscious. In many ways he was himself a child of the Enlightenment; few indeed have given the principle of individualism a sharper expression. The whole burden of his message is summed up in the phrase "a return to nature"; let us do away with all the artificial conventions and restrictions of society and go back to the simple life of primitive man, when each human being, a free creature with tranquil spirit and healthy body, was at liberty to develop his own nature without let or hindrance. Civilization is nothing but slavery, a huge series of blunders which carry us ever farther from the right path. "So long as men were content with their rustic huts, so long as they confined themselves to stitching their garments of skin with spines or fish bones, to decking themselves with feathers and shells and painting their bodies in different colors, to perfecting and adorning their bows and their arrows — in a word, so long as they only applied themselves to works that a single man could do and to arts that had no need of more hands than one, they lived free, healthy, good and happy so far as their nature would allow, and continued to enjoy among themselves the sweetness of independent intercourse. But from the moment one man had need of the help of another, the moment they perceived it was useful for one person to have provisions for two, equality disappeared, property was introduced, labor became necessary, and the vast forests changed into smiling fields which had to be watered by the sweat of men, and in which slavery and wretchedness were soon seen springing up and growing ripe with the harvests." The working of metals and agriculture, the acquirement of property, the growth of civil society, are successive steps in the process of enslavement. "The first man who, having enclosed a piece of ground, bethought himself of saying, This is mine, and found people simple enough to believe him, was the true founder of civil society. How many crimes, wars, murders, what miseries and horrors would have not been spared the human race by one who, tearing up the stakes, or filling the ditch, should have called out to his fellows: Beware of listening to this impostor; you are lost if you forget that the earth belongs to no one, and that its fruits belong to all." [1] All subsequent history has consisted in deepening the artificial inequalities which here got a foothold. They can only be overcome by an entire reconstruction. The supposed proofs that civilization represents a development are merely specious. The science and culture in which the Enlighteners took such pride, instead of being self-evident proofs of our superiority to the past are just another example of unfounded prejudice; examined, they will be seen to have no meaning whatever in terms of human welfare. They only serve to heighten the corruption of the age; men were far better off before the sciences arose. This in brief is the argument of Rousseau's two earliest treatises — the *Discourse on the Sciences and the Arts*, and the *Discourse on the Origin and the Bases of the Inequality among Men.*

In his more sober moments, however, Rousseau did not really intend to deny the value of the social life altogether; he only meant

[1] *Discourse on Inequality.* Quoted from Morley, *Rousseau*, I, p. 166.

to place it on a different basis. The thing against which he protested was the notion that there was anything of real worth in a civilization which consisted simply in a high intellectual culture, and in the development of the arts and sciences and inventions depending on the intellect — that is, in the current ideal of Rationalism. For the conception of man as first of all intellect — cold, unimpassioned, critical reason — he held the utmost detestation. In opposition to the Lockian psychology which makes man's life a mere play of ideas, Rousseau insisted on the *unity* of the self; and this essential and very inmost man is — not intellect, but — *feeling*.

It was in his revelation, to a world incrusted with artificiality, of the power and beauty of sentiment or feeling, that the essence of Rousseau's contribution lay. For there was in feeling, on the one hand, a unifying force to set against the analytic understanding. The emotional outgoing toward nature and sympathy toward man is the revelation of an essential kinship with other things, which only needed to find a more adequate statement to give a new turn to human thought. Rousseau was quite conscious of this constructive side of his message. I hate, he says, this rage to destroy without building up; and again: To liberate a man, it is not enough merely to break his chains. So, too, feeling supplies a motive power which is needed for setting man at work to realize himself, and to remedy things instead simply of criticising them. This new emphasis is at work throughout Rousseau's philosophy, influencing it even when it seems to approach closest to Rationalism. Thus his conception of religion is still an abstract Deism; but it is suffused with a glow of emotion which is the promise of something more adequate to man's religious needs, and which enables him to assert that he is the only man of his age who really believes in God. It was because the materialism of his contemporaries offered him a world with which he could come into no emotional relation that he felt so strongly about it. Religion is an affair of the heart, not of the head. It does not depend on a belief in tradition and what some other man has said; "Is it simple or natural that God should have gone in search of Moses to speak to Jean Jacques Rousseau?" Nor can it be reasoned out beyond the reach of scepticism. But conscience and feeling are as real as reason. "I believe in God as fully as I believe in any other truth, because to believe or not to believe are the things in the world that are least under my control; because, when my reason is wavering, my faith cannot rest long in suspense; because, finally, a thousand motives of preference attract me to the side that is most consoling, and join the weight of hope to the equilibrium of reason."

And equally on the side of social theory, where Rousseau's chief importance lies, the claims of feeling tend continually to carry him on to a conception of man more adequate than the narrowly individualistic one. This makes him, first of all, the apostle of the common man, in whom are represented those simple and fundamental traits of humanity which appeal to Rousseau, and which go deeper than rank or any other external and artificial advantage. "It is the common people who compose the human race; what is not the people is so trivial that it is not worth taking into account. Before one who reflects, all civil distinctions disappear; he sees the same passions, the same feelings, in the clown as in the man of note and reputation; he only distinguishes their language, and a varnish more or less elaborately laid on."

And this democratic feeling is continually on the point of passing into a conception of man's relation to society which is quite the opposite of Rousseau's starting-point, though it is true such a conception fails to get any very clear and unambiguous expression. Like Hobbes and Locke before him, Rousseau bases society on a contract, by which men agree, for certain advantages, to give up the unrestricted individual freedom that belongs to them by nature. At times such a contract seems to be put in the form of an historical event. But Rousseau does not insist upon this aspect of it; in reality it stands rather for a statement of the conditions necessary to give social life a rational and just foundation, in opposition to theories which carry it back to force or mere status. In spite of his earlier utterances, and the echo of these in the famous words with which the *Social Contract* opens — Man is born free, and is everywhere in chains — Rousseau is far from thinking that the life of the noble savage is the true ideal. Rather, he recognizes explicitly that only in society does man truly live at all. "What man loses by the social contract is his natural liberty, and an unlimited right to anything that tempts him which he can obtain; what he gains is civil liberty, and the ownership of all that he possesses." A morality is given to his actions which they lacked before. "His faculties exercise and develop, his ideas expand, his sentiments become ennobled, his whole spirit is elevated to such a point that, if the abuse of this new condition did not often degrade him below that from which he came, he ought to bless without ceasing the happy moment which took him from it forever, and which has made of a dull stupid animal an intelligent being — a man." [1]

The problem is, then, to substitute for an abstract and primitive freedom a substantial and moral one; for a natural equality, a political equality. This is accomplished through a contract in terms of which each one is to sink his private will in the general will, the will of the whole. The permanent value of Rousseau's conception lies in his tendency to regard this at bottom, not merely as a giving up of rights for the sake of external advantages — life and security — but rather as a discovery of one's true and permanent self. He is on the point, at least, of recognizing that the individual, capricious will is not the real man after all; that the true self is not antagonistic to, but inclusive of one's fellows, and so can have a chance to develop only in society. Each individual may, as a man, have a particular will, contrary to or unlike the general will which he has as a citizen; his particular interest may speak to him quite differently from the common interest. But this latter really represents him more adequately than the former. When the individual is constrained to obey the general will by society he is not being enslaved, but is being "forced to be free" — forced to resist the temptation to sacrifice his lesser to his larger self.

With Rousseau, it must once more be admitted, this is hardly more than a suggestion; and when he goes on to connect it with his governmental machinery he tends to give it too external an interpretation to do justice to his deeper thought. Concretely, the

[1] Bk. I, 8. Harrington's translation, G. P. Putnam's Sons.

general will is the resultant of a popular vote, in which every citizen participates. "Take from these same wills the plus and the minus which destroy each other, and there will remain for the sum of the differences the general will." [1] Such a vote, on a matter of general principle — and with reference to an individual application of a principle the general will cannot pronounce — does away with private interests by making the question entirely abstract. Each individual, inasmuch as he will consider that the law he is passing is going to apply to himself, will vote for that which seems to him abstractly the best, in order to get in his own case the advantages that derive from it. "Why is the general will always right, and why do all desire constantly the happiness of each, unless it is because there is no person who does not appropriate to himself the word 'each,' and who does not think of himself while voting for all?" [2] Each submits necessarily to the conditions he imposes on others ; "it is for the sake of not being killed by an assassin that we consent to be killed if we become assassins." Of course in attempting to legislate for a particular case this common interest no longer exists, and private interests have a chance to assert themselves : that is why the general will can only act in the case of legislation that is entirely general in character.

It still is natural to ask, however, how such a majority rule can represent the general will if this latter is really to be defined as identical with the true will of the individual. Must not the result be contrary to the will of the man who votes against it, and so not an expression of himself but an enslavement? Rousseau has an answer to the difficulty, though it is not a very satisfactory one. The citizen consents to all the laws, even those which are passed in spite of him ; for when he votes, what is asked him is "not whether he approves the proposition or whether he rejects it, but whether or not it conforms to the general will. Each one in giving his vote gives his opinion upon it, and from the counting of the votes is deduced the declaration of the general will. When however the opinion contrary to mine prevails, it shows only that I was mistaken, and that what I had supposed to be the general will was not

[1] Bk. II, 3.   [2] Bk. II, 4.

general. If my individual opinion had prevailed I should have done something other than I had intended, and then I should not have been free." [1] This is ingenious; but it is unlikely always to satisfy the man who finds himself in a minority.

3. *Lessing and Herder.* — In France it was the negative side of Rousseau's teaching that chiefly influenced his contemporaries, and it presently was to issue, in an extreme form, in the doctrinairism of the French Revolution. In Germany however the more positive tendencies implicit in his thought were appreciated, and they proved to be a large factor among the influences that were to bring about one of the great periods of intellectual development in the history of the world. Germany, possessed hitherto of only a scanty literature, and, apart from Leibniz, of hardly any philosophy worthy the name, suddenly blossomed forth in a literature and a philosophy of the first magnitude. In both of these the same principle is at work; both stand for a rediscovery of the value of the life of spirit, as opposed alike to the authority of the Middle Ages and to the intellectualism of the Enlightenment. A fresh sense for the possibilities of human life shows itself in the undisciplined eagerness of the *Sturm und Drang* period for personal realization in every variety of experience. Restrained and regulated by the sense of artistic proportion which the new appreciation of Greek art had made at home in Germany through the labors of Winckelmann and Lessing, a way of looking at things sprang up which had almost nothing in common with the typical outcome of the Enlightenment. "We could not understand," says Goethe, in speaking of the impression which Holbach's *System of Nature* made upon himself and his associates, "how such a book could be dangerous. It appeared to us so dark, so Cimmerian, so deathlike, that we could scarcely find patience to endure its presence."

Through the medium of this expansion of the sympathies, history came to take on a new significance. In *Lessing's* case the concern is chiefly with the historical development of religion. For the Rationalist, as has been said, there had been no middle ground between the truth of a religion on the basis of reason, and its falsity and consequent origin in fraud and priestcraft. Lessing sees that the dilemma is an unreal one. Absolute truth, indeed, we cannot know; but also there is no absolutely false. Early religions are steps in the progressive revelation by which God educates mankind; the true religion of reason can only come as the result of a long process leading up to it, and so positive religions have a relative justification. This is the lesson of the *Education of the Human Race;* and it marks a decisive break from the Enlightenment.

In like manner there is implied a different view of God. God is no longer a being set apart from the life of the world; he is to be seen actually present and at work in nature, in the course of human events, in the heart of the spiritual experience, which all have their reality and unity in him. Now of all philosophers, it was Spinoza who had insisted most strongly on the unity and immanence of God. And as Spinoza had failed of any great immediate influence because he was so far removed from the temper of the Enlightenment, so now at last he comes into his own. It is Spinoza, with his ἔν καὶ πᾶν, who is preëminently the philosopher of the German literary movement. A God distinct from the world is unendurable to the new feeling for the beauty of the universe and the significance of the inner life. There is nothing to satisfy us in a God who "sat like a scrupulous artist beating his brains, and making plans, comparisons, rejections and selections, who played with worlds as children with soap bubbles till he gave preference to the one which pleased him most"; who, "in the great Inane of primeval, inactive eternity, has his corner where he contemplates himself, and probably ponders on the project of another world."

The conception of development which, by Lessing, is applied to the history of religion, is extended by *Herder* to the whole life of man. The thought that everything matures by a gradual and natural process pervades the whole of Herder's work. A beginning is made of a science of language by regarding this, not as a thing of divine origin or a manufactured product, but as an organic growth. The same sympathetic insight leads Herder to take a special interest in primitive poetry and folk-lore, which the artificial taste of the preceding age had passed by with scorn. And in his *Ideas for the Philosophy of the History of Mankind* the attempt is made to bring the whole course of human development under the conception of a unitary process.

LITERATURE

Rousseau, *Émile; Social Contract; Confessions.*
Morley, *Voltaire.*
Morley, *Diderot and the Encyclopedists.*
Morley, *Rousseau.*
Bosanquet, *Philosophical Theory of the State.*
Caird, *Essays on Literature and Philosophy.*
Davidson, *Rousseau and Education according to Nature.*
Lessing, *Education of the Human Race, Nathan the Wise.*
Herder, *Ideas for the Philosophy of the History of Mankind.*
Hibben, *Philosophy of the Enlightenment.*
Höffding, *J. J. Rousseau and his Philosophy.*

GERMAN IDEALISM

§ 35. *Kant*

Immanuel Kant was born in Königsberg in 1724, and spent his life without leaving his native province. He became Professor of Philosophy at the University of Königsberg in 1770. His *Critique of Pure Reason*, published in 1781, raised him to the foremost position among living philosophers, but his growing fame did not serve to alter his manner of life. His simple habits grew more and more regular and methodical as he grew older, and his interests limited themselves more exclusively to his abstract speculations. Heine's description of him is frequently quoted: —

"The life of Immanuel Kant is hard to describe; he has indeed neither life nor history in the proper sense of the words. He lived an abstract, mechanical, old-bachelor existence, in a quiet, remote street in Königsberg, an old city at the northeastern boundary of Germany. I do not believe that the great cathedral clock of that city accomplished its day's work in a less passionate and more regular way than its countryman, Immanuel Kant. Rising from bed, coffee-drinking, writing, lecturing, eating, walking, everything had its fixed time; and the neighbors knew that it must be exactly half-past four when they saw Professor Kant, in his gray coat, with his cane in his hand, step out of his house door and move toward the little lime-tree avenue which is named, after him, the Philosopher's Walk. Eight times he walked up and down that walk at every season of the year: and when the weather was bad his servant, old Lampe, was seen anxiously following him with a large umbrella under his arm, like an image of Providence. Strange contrast between the outward life of the man and his world-destroying thought. Of a truth, if the citizens of Königsberg had had any inkling of the meaning of that thought they would have shuddered before him as before an executioner. But the good people saw nothing in him but a professor of philosophy; and when he passed at the appointed hour they gave him friendly greetings — and set their watches."[1]

1. *The Nature of Kant's Problem.* — It is difficult in a brief space to give an approximate notion, even, of the nature of the revolution which Kant was the means of bringing about in philosophy. Roughly it may be said that this centers about two points in particular; and of these the one it will be convenient to consider first is the new conception of experience and of thought which it involves.

We have seen that Hume had dissolved the reality of the world into a host of unrelated feelings, or sensations, which summed together compose the human mind. But is this a tenable conception? Must there not be relating activities of the mind, not themselves feelings, brought to bear upon the material of sense before feelings can form a true experience or even themselves be objects of our knowledge? If mere sensations were the sole reality would not each be shut up in its own skin, totally cut off from the rest of the world? As a matter of fact, however, sensations are not thus isolated; somehow or other they get related. They are experienced not as a collection of isolated units but as an interconnected and orderly whole; they enter into a *unified* consciousness, which thus is something more than the mere sum of them taken together.

There is a term of which Kant makes a great deal of use in the *Critique* — the term *synthetic*. A synthetic judgment is one which goes beyond the meaning of the subject term, and binds to this some new idea not already contained there; as when, for example, I see my dog running across the field and, adding to the idea of dog a new qualification, I say, "My dog is chasing a rabbit." On the other hand if I say, "A dog is an animal," I am only making explicit an idea already contained in the concept " dog," and my judgment is analytic. We may say, then, using this terminology, that there is to experience a *synthetic* side for which Hume does not account. The relatedness of sensations, the unity which binds them together,

[1] Quoted from Royce's *Spirit of Modern Philosophy.*

is a new element which cannot be extracted from the isolated sensations themselves. To know two sensations together implies a state of consciousness which is not simply another sensation; for if it were, how could it ever serve as a connecting link? It would only add another term to be combined. Before sensations can be known, even in the simple relations of resemblance or of contiguity in time or space, they must be brought into a unified consciousness which thus is no mere additional sense fact, but an intellectual synthesis presupposed in every possibility of experience.

Kant, then, has pointed out that for the possibility of real knowledge it is necessary to presuppose a certain framework of thought relationships over and above the sense content to which Hume had reduced knowledge. It follows that the part which thought plays in connection with the objects of knowledge has to be conceived in a new and special way. Commonly in the past the relation of thought to its object had been understood in terms of the relation of a copy or reproduction to its prototype. For Kant, on the contrary, the relation is *constitutive*. The world, in so far as it is a *known* world, is an actual construct of thought. Any object to be known must enter into the world of knowledge, the thought world; and therefore between thought and its object there is no separateness, but an identity. To be real, to be objective, is to have a fixed place in this system of thought, not to exist beyond it. An object *is* only as it is for knowledge; and so it is actually built up out of these intellectual relationships which Kant had pointed out. It is this that makes experience no mere string of subjective feelings, but an ordered and orderly world of things.

For Kant, accordingly, the Cartesian principle which gives to consciousness, or the self, the fundamental place in the interpretation of the world is reasserted in a new form. The world is not an objective fact independent of us, to be defended or criticised as such. It is the product of the laws of our own understanding, acting of course in no arbitrary way, but in accordance with fixed and definite principles which are not peculiar to our separate individuality. Human experience, in this comprehensive sense, gives the point of view for the interpretation of everything that we can know; between the world, and ourselves, there is an inner identity.

Such briefly is the general presumption underlying Kant's thought; we may turn now to a somewhat more specific statement. Kant's chief problem centers about a fact to which already reference has several times been made, and which is most easily understood by going back to Hume. Kant had been originally an adherent of the school of Wolff, who had attempted to systematize the philosophy of Leibniz. But he soon had become dissatisfied with this. Wolff was a rationalist of the extremer type. He had the completest confidence that, by the use of abstract principles of reason, we can attain a demonstrative knowledge of ultimate verities. Kant found himself constantly less able to share this confidence; the more he thought, the more difficulty he found in the way of applying the *a priori* method of geometry to the problems with which philosophy is concerned. Is truth not attainable at all then? this Kant was not willing to admit. For a time indeed he tried to take refuge in empiricism. But Hume had revealed to him the outcome of empiricism — the overthrow of all knowledge whatsoever.

Now the main problem that had engaged Hume — the problem of causation — will suggest the nature of Kant's difficulty. Here is a supposed truth without which it had abundantly appeared that philosophers, to say nothing of scientists, could make no headway at all. But whence does the idea of causation come? It cannot be derived from experience and still retain its necessity; Hume had shown this clearly. With the difficulties in the rationalistic explanation Kant already was familiar. Here is a point accordingly which neither of the rival schools had found itself able satisfactorily to clear up.

"There can be no doubt whatever that all our knowledge begins with experience. By what means should the faculty of knowledge be aroused to activity but by objects which, acting upon our senses, partly of themselves produce ideas in us, and partly set our understanding at work to compare these ideas with one another, and, by combining or separating them, to convert the raw material of our sensible impressions into that knowledge of objects which is called experience? In the order of time, therefore, we have no knowledge prior to experience, and with experience all our knowledge begins.

"But although all our knowledge begins *with* experience, it by no means follows that it all originates *from* experience. For it may well be that experience is itself made up of two elements, one received through impressions of sense, and the other supplied from itself by our faculty of knowledge on occasion of those impressions. It is, therefore, a question which cannot be lightly put aside, but can be answered only after careful investigation, whether there is any knowledge that is independent of experience, and even of all impressions of sense. Such knowledge is said to be *a priori*, to distinguish it from *empirical* knowledge which has its sources *a posteriori*, or in experience. The term *a priori* must, however, be defined more precisely in order that the full meaning of our question may be understood. We say of a man who undermines the foundations of his house that he might have known *a priori* that it would fall; by which we mean that he might have known it would fall without waiting for the event to take place in his experience. But he could not know it completely *a priori;* for it is only from experience that he could learn that bodies are heavy, and must fall by their own weight when there is nothing to support them. By *a priori* knowledge we shall therefore, in what follows, understand, not such knowledge as is independent of this or that experience, but such as is *absolutely* independent of all experience. Opposed to it is empirical knowledge, or that which is possible only *a posteriori*, that is, by experience.

"Evidently what we need is a criterion by which to distinguish with certainty between pure and empirical knowledge. Now experience can tell us that a thing is so and so, but not that it cannot be otherwise. Firstly, then, if we find a proposition that, in being thought, is thought as necessary, it is an *a priori* judgment; and if, further, it is not derived from any proposition except one which is itself necessary, it is absolutely *a priori*. Secondly, experience never bestows on its judgments true or strict universality, but only the assumed or comparative universality of induction; so that, properly speaking, it merely says that so far as our observation has gone there is no exception to this or that rule. If therefore a judgment is thought with strict universality, so that there can be no possible exception to it, it is not derived from experience, but is absolutely *a priori*. Necessity and strict universality are, therefore, sure criteria of *a priori* knowledge, and are also inseparably connected with each other."

Necessary and universal judgments go beyond experience — so far Hume and Kant are agreed. But whereas Hume had stopped here and had said that *therefore* such judgments do not exist as valid knowledge, Kant reverses the argument. We cannot explain knowledge by denying its reality; if there are universal truths which everybody admits, the only thing to do is to accept these as our data, and then go on to explain their possibility. "Now, it is easy to show that in human knowledge there actually are judgments that in the strictest sense are universal, and therefore pure *a priori*. If an example from the sciences is desired, we have but to think of any proposition in mathematics; if an instance from common sense is preferred, it is enough to cite the proposition that there can be no change without a cause. To take the latter case, the very idea of cause so manifestly implies the idea of necessary connection with an effect, that it would be completely lost were we to derive it, with Hume, from the repeated association of one event with another that precedes it, and were we to reduce it to the subjective necessity arising from the habit of passing from one idea to another." [1] To give up the splendid results of science is, in particular, quite out of the question; if therefore we cannot be content to accept a theory that takes away their foundations we must search further, and ask ourselves what conditions are required to serve as a secure basis for these results which every one admits. How, in other words, is it possible to pass a judgment which does not simply state the results of what we have learned in the past but which adds to our knowledge, and which yet, in spite of the fact that it goes beyond what we have already experienced, can be said to be, not probably, but necessarily and universally true?

[1] *Critique of Pure Reason*, Introduction, Watson's translation, pp. 7–10, Henry Holt & Co.

There is another important consideration to be noted. "There is a sort of knowledge that even quits the field of all possible experience, and claims to extend the range of our judgments beyond its limits by means of conceptions to which no corresponding object can be presented in experience. Now it is just in the province of this sort of knowledge, where experience can neither show us the true path nor put us right when we go astray, that reason carries on those high investigations the result of which we regard as more important than all that understanding can discover within the domain of phenomena. Nay, we are even willing to stake our all, and to run the risk of being completely deluded, rather than consent to forego inquiries of such moment, either from uncertainty, or from carelessness and indifference. These unavoidable problems, set by pure reason itself, are *God*, *freedom*, and *immortality*, and the science which brings all its resources to bear on the one single task of solving them is *metaphysic*."

"Now one might think that men would hesitate to leave the solid ground of experience, and to build an edifice of truth upon knowledge that has come to them they know not how, and in blind dependence upon principles of which they cannot tell the origin, without taking the greatest pains to see that the foundation was secure. One might think it only natural that they would long ago have raised the question how we have come into possession of all this *a priori* knowledge, and what may be its extent, its import and its value. But the fact is that a part of this knowledge — mathematical knowledge for instance — has so long been established as certain that we are less ready to suspect the evidence for other parts, although these may be of a totally different nature. Besides, when we are once outside the circle of experience we are sure not to be contradicted by experience; and so strong is the impulse to enlarge our knowledge, that nothing short of a clear contradiction will avail to arrest our footsteps. Now such contradiction may easily be avoided, even where we are dealing with objects that are merely imaginary, if we are only careful in putting our fictions together. Mathematics show us by a splendid instance how far a science may advance *a priori* without the aid of experience. It is true that by it objects and conceptions are considered only in so far as they can be presented in perception; but it is easy to overlook the limitation because the perception in this case can itself be given *a priori*, and is therefore hard to distinguish from a mere idea. Deceived by this proof of the power of reason, we can see no limits to the extension of knowledge. So Plato forsook the world of sense, chafing at the narrow limits it set to our knowledge, and, on the wings of pure ideas, launched out into the empty space of the pure understanding. He did not see that with all his efforts he was making no real progress. But it is no unusual thing for human reason to complete its speculative edifice in such haste that it forgets to look to the stability of the foundation." [1]

The new philosophy, then, as opposed to all previous thought, is a *critical* philosophy; it is a criticism of the faculty of knowledge. In the past metaphysics has been the battle-ground of endless conflicts. "There was a time when Metaphysic held a royal place among the sciences, and if the will were taken for the deed, the exceeding importance of her subject might well have secured to her that place of honor. At present it is the fashion to despise Metaphysic, and the poor matron, forlorn and forsaken, complains like Hecuba, *Modo maxima rerum, tot generis natisque potens — nunc trahor exul, inops*. At first the rule of Metaphysic, under the dominion of the dogmatists, was despotic. But as the laws still bore the traces of an old barbarism, intestine wars and complete anarchy broke out, and the sceptics, a kind of nomads, despising all settled culture of the land, broke up from time to time all civil society. Fortunately their number was small, and they could not prevent the old settlers from returning to cultivate the ground afresh, though without any fixed plan or agreement. At present, after everything has been tried so they say, and tried in vain, there reign in philosophy weariness and complete indifferentism, the mother of chaos and night." [2]

The trouble lies in the very nature of dogmatism. It is due to the attempt of reason to advance *without any previous criticism* of its

---

[1] *Critique of Pure Reason*, Introduction, Watson's translation, p. 11.
[2] Preface, Max Müller's translation.

own powers. Such a dogmatic employment of reason can lead only to groundless assertions to which other assertions equally specious may always be opposed, the inevitable result being scepticism. The same defect, accordingly, taints dogmatism and scepticism alike; the only remedy is, neither to dogmatize, nor to raise equally ungrounded doubts, but to subject the nature of reason to a sober investigation in order to determine what it can, and what it cannot, hope to accomplish. This is entirely different from scepticism. Hume "ran his ship ashore for safety's sake on scepticism, whereas my object is rather to give it a pilot, who, by means of safe astronomical principles drawn from a knowledge of the globe, and provided with a complete chart and compass, may steer the ship safely." [1]

2. *How Are Necessary Judgments Possible?* — With this general introduction, we may go on to consider in what the special nature of Kant's results consists. Once more, there are two main questions which he sets before himself. The first is to show the conditions which render possible those synthetic, *a priori* judgments whose validity, in opposition to Hume, he proposes to defend. The second is to show what light the answer to this problem will throw on the validity of those further *a priori* judgments which pretend to carry us into the supersensible world, and upon which metaphysics has relied to prove the existence of God and other ultimate truths. We shall consider these in their order.

A distinction has already been drawn between two elements of our experience. In addition to the sense material to which Hume had reduced all the conscious life, there must also be certain relating activities of the mind itself. Necessary and *a priori* truths will evidently depend upon this latter factor. "That element in the phenomenon which corresponds to sensation I call the *matter*, while that element which makes it possible that the various determinations of the phenomenon should be arranged in certain ways relatively to one another is its *form*. Now, that without which sensations can have no order or form cannot itself be sensation. The matter of a phenomenon is given to us entirely *a posteriori*;

[1] *Prolegomena*, Introd.

but its form must be *a priori* in the mind, and hence must be capable of being considered by itself apart from sensation."[1]

Of these forms of experience there are two sorts. In the first place, the sensuous basis of experience does not come to us as absolutely raw material. It presents itself, in sense perception, as already related in two ways — in *space*, and in *time*. It is on such a "form of sensibility" that the possibility of geometrical truths rests. A long time before he reached the final standpoint represented in the *Critique of Pure Reason*, Kant had come to the conclusion that space and time are not objective realities, but are only the subjective ways in which we cognize realities which in themselves are non-spatial and non-temporal.

Meanwhile for experience as we know it it is not enough that the sensuous data should appear simply in the forms of space and time. Within that framework they must be subjected to other — intellectual — relationships, in order to constitute a world of definite things. What then are the essential *intellectual* elements which go to make up experience? Without following Kant into the details of this deduction it is enough to say that, by a laborious process, he arrives at a certain number of these which he groups under four heads — quantity, quality, relation and modality. We can say, that is, necessarily and universally, and quite prior to experience, that any particular experience will be quantitative; that it will possess a certain degree of intensity; that every change involves a permanent substance as a background; that all changes take place in accordance with the law of cause and effect; and so forth.

And now we come back once more to the main question; how is it possible to pass such judgments that go beyond experience? The answer is, in brief: because otherwise experience itself would be impossible. The necessity lies, not in things, but in ourselves. "In metaphysical speculations it has always been assumed that all our knowledge must conform to objects; but every attempt from this point of view to extend our knowledge of objects *a priori* by means of conceptions has ended in failure. The time has now come to ask whether better progress may not be made by supposing that

[1] *Critique of Pure Reason*, p. 20, First Ed.

objects must conform to our knowledge. Plainly this would better agree with the avowed aim of metaphysic to determine the nature of objects *a priori*, or before they are actually presented. Our suggestion is similar to that of Copernicus in astronomy, who, finding it impossible to explain the movements of the heavenly bodies on the supposition that they turned round the spectator, tried whether he might not succeed better by supposing the spectator to revolve, and the stars to remain at rest. Let us make a similar experiment in metaphysic with *perception*. If it were really necessary for our perception to conform to the nature of objects, I do not see how we could know anything of it *a priori;* but if the sensible object must conform to the constitution of our faculty of perception, I see no difficulty in the matter." [1]

Such is Kant's own statement of the matter; it may be well however to consider a little further just what he means. Kant finds the necessity he is in search of, to repeat, not as something in nature, which is then reproduced and known in our experience, but as something in experience which itself constitutes what we know as nature. Suppose we take a geometrical truth; how can we say, absolutely and without exception, that the sum of the angles of any triangle will equal two right angles? So long as it is a matter simply of our mental content, we might get certainty by the mere fact of holding steadfastly to one fixed meaning, and not allowing it to change or become confused. But how do we know that the world of actual things will conform to these geometrical ideals of ours? Not from experience; that might tell us that the proposition was true of all the objects we had examined in the past, but not that it would prove to be true of the next one we might happen to meet. Things can only come into our experience one by one; and by this process we can only tell the facts about the particular cases we have ʾ cross up to date, not about the rest, which as yet have not ʾ contact with us. The necessity, that is, in so far as *we* ʾcessity, cannot lie in reality as it exists in itself apart ʾce; for since we cannot grasp the whole of infinite ʾ since it is the conviction of a necessary connection *in our experience* that is to be justified, the coming of reality piecemeal into experience gives us no ground for asserting anything whatever about that which still is left outside. What follows, then? Simply this once more: that if we grant the validity of necessary judgments at all, it must be founded on the nature of our experience itself, and not on the nature of an external reality. Things, that is, must be subject to the laws of mathematics because they can only become things, for us, by taking on that spatial form on which the truths of geometry are based. They must conform to the structure of the mind, whose nature it is to cast everything into spatial relationships before they can become actual objects of our knowledge. If, then, our experience is of such a nature that nothing can enter into it without taking on a particular form, then we can say, with certainty, that everything, in the future as well as in the past, must have just this form and no other. We can pass, in other words, a necessary, synthetic judgment *a priori;* and on no other condition can we do so. No matter what may be true of reality beyond experience, we can be perfectly sure that, for us, everything in experience will exemplify the truths of geometry, because unless it succeeds in taking on the spatial form on which geometry is based it will not become part of our experience at all, but will remain for us non-existent.

In the same way we are to account for those other necessary judgments — the intellectual ones. How can we be sure that every effect must have a cause, or that there must always be a permanent substance underlying change? Simply because our intellectual machinery is so constituted that it will take no grist which does not adapt itself to these particular forms of substance and causality. A necessary judgment is possible for the reason that we are not judging about things in themselves, but about the necessary connection of elements in our own experience; and we could have nothing that it would be possible to call "experience" if it were not for certain necessary forms of relationship between the elements of which it is constituted. In other words, if I am to be an intelligent being, and have an experience which also is intelligible, this experience must be to a certain degree coherent. If it is to be *my* experience, it must be a unity; I must somehow be present through it all, binding its parts together into a whole. To have any coherency in my life it is not enough that fleeting sensations should exist. It is necessary also that I should be able to recognize these, and so that they should stand for objects that are identical and permanent; and a permanent object already involves the category of substantiality. In the same way the different objects, if they are to form part of a single experience, must be reciprocally connected with one another as members of a common world; and, again, the past and future must have some intelligible and necessary relation, since they also are parts of a single experience in every point of which I find myself equally present: and so we need the categories of reciprocity and causality as tools which the self necessarily requires to help it unify its life. Beyond our experience these categories may not apply: but since it is only such elements of reality as will fit the mould in which our intellectual nature is cast that in any wise concern us, we can take the laws as absolute. It is not, then, nature which imposes its necessity on us; it is we who give laws to nature. The truths of the rationalist are not revelations of existence beyond; they reveal, instead, our own intellectual make-up. They are the *forms* of experience, as over against its content.

It will be evident that, as against this view, Locke's criticism of innate ideas has no force. We have, says Locke, no innate idea of causality, for example, because many people have never in all their lives thought of the proposition that every effect must have a cause. This Kant would have no objection to admitting; if we mean the *conscious recognition* of the principle, that is a particular psychological fact in our minds which may arise only late in life, or conceivably never at all. But in another sense — as a form of thought — the principle has been at work from the very start. Every time I look to find the explanation of something that has happened, every time I connect two things together, I am implicitly making use of the causal relation. And it is this existence which it has as a necessary form of synthesis, not the conscious recognition which may or may not be attained by any particular individual, whose *a priori* character Kant is vindicating.

3. *No Knowledge beyond Experience.* — The Critical Philosophy, then, is an attempt to find out how it happens that our knowledge can hold good of the real world; and the answer is, that these real things are themselves constituted by the relationships which make up knowledge. It is essential to bear in mind that this implies a different conception of the nature of objectivity and reality from the common one. The world of which Kant is talking is nothing but the world as it forms a part of the content of human experience and knowledge. When Kant says that our thought constitutes nature he does not mean, therefore, that the universe which we are wont to think exists eternally, and out of which we as transient beings have sprung, first gains the right to be by coming under subjection to certain rules which our mind imposes — that we create all that is, as the subjective idealist might maintain. To the objective world in this sense — the eternal and fundamental background which we are ready to believe exists alongside and beyond any experiencing of ours — he has so far no reference at all; the world he has been talking about is the orderly content of knowledge within human experience itself. On the other hand Kant does not doubt that beyond this a more ultimate reality does actually lie. And it remains to ask what if anything we have a right to say about this ultimate world — the world of things-in-themselves.

And here we have reached those metaphysical convictions to which reference earlier was made. Philosophy has in general not been content to stop with the endless process of phenomena in space and time. It tries to get beyond this infinite regress to the ultimate unconditioned reality on which finite things depend, and by doing so to find a basis for those ideas in which it wishes to believe — God, freedom, immortality. So it postulates behind the changing content of experience a unitary and substantial soul; the infinite world process it tries to grasp in its completeness as a unity; and, finally, the totality of existence, self and world, it attempts to render conceivable through the idea of God. Is now this attempt to understand in final terms the nature of real existence one that can successfully be carried out?

Kant answers that it is not. The phenomenal world we know.

But the real, the noumenal world is closed to our theoretical under-standing. And the reason lies in what has been found to be the nature of knowledge. The rationalists had supposed that thought is an independent faculty able to reach truth by its own unaided exercise. Kant thinks he has shown, on the contrary, that thought is only one element or aspect of knowledge. For any concrete act of knowledge thought and sense are both alike required; and this indissoluble connection of thought with the material of sense defeats the claims of rationalism to grasp reality. Sense material alone is blind and unordered; it is not experience at all in an objective sense. But thought equally is helpless by itself; it is empty, an abstract form which has to have a content before it is objectively valid.

The result is that when we try to apply the categories of the understanding beyond the data of things in time and space — beyond the phenomenal world — we are involved in inevitable illusion. To endeavor to pass to an unconditioned whole by the use of ideas that apply only to the conditioned objects within experience is to leave experience behind, since without the concrete filling which sense supplies experience has no meaning; and in con-sequence the validity of our categories lapses. It is the entire function of causation, for example, to bind together the elements of what otherwise would be the chaotic world of sense particulars; and with such a function it naturally can have no power to carry us outside the world of finite causes and effects to a reality which has itself no cause. "The light dove, piercing in her easy flight the air and perceiving its resistance, imagines that flight would be easier still in empty space." The effort is of course in vain; of the nature of things-in-themselves we must always remain, intellectually at any rate, in complete ignorance.

Kant goes on to subject these ideas supposed to have a standing in the realm of ultimate reality to a destructive criticism. The abstract unity of consciousness, which alone the fact of experience necessitates, has nothing in common with the substantial soul of metaphysics, all of whose qualities are nevertheless derived from it, quite illegitimately of course. Again, when in reasoning about the external world we try to escape from the conditions of experience, the illegitimacy of our endeavor appears in the antinomies into which we fall. With equal force we may argue that the world is limited in time and space, and that it is unlimited; that every compound substance in the world consists of simple parts, and that no compound thing consists of simple parts; that there does, and that there does not, exist an absolute First Cause at the end of the finite series. The arguments on both sides, so Kant thinks, are logically sound; and the fact that they nevertheless refute each other shows that we have entered a realm where we do not belong, and where in the nature of the case truth is not to be attained by logic. "Both parties beat the air and fight with their own shadows, because they go beyond the limits of nature, where there is nothing they can lay hold of with their dogmatical grasp. They may fight to their heart's content; the shadows which they are cleaving grow together again in one moment, like the heroes in Valhalla, in order to disport themselves once more in these bloodless contests."[1] And, finally, the ordinary arguments for God's existence — the ontological argument, the argument from causation, and the argument from design — are critically examined and found wanting. Starting from a set of particular finite facts which enter into an infinite series of relationships with other facts, it is quite impossible to rise to a knowledge of their absolute and unconditioned ground, for the reason, once again, that all the ideas by which we attempt to go beyond particular facts are intended to apply only to relations *between* particulars.

So much, on the negative side, for these "Ideas of Reason" — God, the universe, the soul. They tell us nothing of ultimate truth, because they have left behind the sense content which alone gives to the forms of thought validity and renders knowledge possible. All the wrangling of philosophers arises "simply from our filling the gap due to our ignorance with paralogisms of reason, and by changing thoughts into things and hypostasizing them. On this an imaginary science is built up both by those who assert and those who deny, some pretending to know about objects of which no

[1] *Critique of Pure Reason*, p. 756, Müller's translation.

human being has any conception, while others make their own representations to be objects, all turning round in a constant circle of ambiguities and contradictions. Nothing but a sober, strict and just criticism can free us from this dogmatical illusion which, through theories and systems, deceives so many by an imaginary happiness. It alone can limit our speculative pretensions to the sphere of possible experience, and this not by a shallow scoffing at repeated failures, or by pious sighs over the limits of our reason, but by a demarcation made according to well-established principles, writing the *nihil ulterius* with perfect assurance on those Herculean columns which Nature herself has erected in order that the voyage of our reason should be continued so far only as the continuous shores of experience extend — shores which we can never forsake without being driven on a boundless ocean which, after deceiving us again and again, makes us in the end cease all our laborious and tedious endeavors as perfectly hopeless." [1]

But are these ideas nothing but pure illusion then? If they are, how does it happen that the human mind continually swings back to them? In conclusion Kant goes on to show that there is a relative value and validity which the ideas may still possess. They are not merely arbitrary; they stand for an impulse that is ineradicable. The desire to grasp things as a whole is one which the reason never can forego. But since it is an aim that cannot be realized, the value of the ideas can only be a *regulative* value *within* experience, not one that results in objective knowledge. The Ideas of Reason stand as an ideal toward which knowledge is directed, and which, by keeping constantly before the mind the fact that any particular synthesis of knowledge is still imperfect, reminds us that we must not stop content as if we had already reached the goal. But the ideal of a perfect unity thus is *only* an ideal; it never can be summed up and completed.

4. *Freedom and God as Postulates of the Moral Life.* — So much for the outcome of the Critical Philosophy; is it possible to rest satisfied with it? Certainly it seems to leave us without any of the knowledge that has been considered most desirable by philosophy

[1] *Critique of Pure Reason*, p. 395, Muller's translation.

in the past; the very conception of a noumenal world beyond the confines of our human experience is no more than problematical — a mere x to which no object corresponds. Even so, Kant thinks, there is one real gain. If we cannot prove the existence of a God, we have at least excluded the possibility of disproving him. If our knowledge is only phenomenal, reason can have no more right to deny that such a reality exists than to affirm it; and the attempt to base a positive denial of supersensuous realities — as materialism for example does — on the supposed validity of our sense experience is thus put out of court. "I cannot share the opinion so frequently expressed by excellent and thoughtful men who, being fully conscious of the weakness of the proofs hitherto advanced, indulge in a hope that the future would supply us with evident demonstrations of the two cardinal propositions of pure reason, namely, that there is a God, and that there is a future life. I am certain on the contrary that this will never be the case. But there is the same apodictic certainty that no man will ever arise to assert the *contrary* with the smallest plausibility, much less dogmatically. For as he could prove it by means of pure reason only, he would have to prove that a Supreme Being, and that a thinking subject within us as pure intelligence, is *impossible*. But whence will he take the knowledge that would justify him in thus judging synthetically on things far beyond all possible experience? We may, therefore, rest so completely assured that no one will ever really prove the opposite that there is no need to invent any scholastic arguments." [1]

While accordingly we cannot by the use of the abstract logical reason attain any insight into the world of supersensible realities, the possibility remains that a noumenal reality *may* exist; and conceivably there may yet remain some other avenue of approach which will enable us, if not to know, at least to postulate it as a legitimate object of faith. Kant believes there is such an avenue; and in the *Critique of Practical Reason*, the second of the trilogy of works on which his chief fame rests, he goes on to modify to a certain extent the agnosticism of his first *Critique*.

The advantages of our determination of the possibilities of knowl-

[1] *Ibid.*, p. 741.

edge show themselves not least in connection with the problem of freedom. If the categories of our thought life really applied to the noumenal world, there would be no escape from determinism. The law of causality demands that everything whatsoever to which it properly applies shall be regarded as strictly necessitated. In so far as our acts enter into the course of the world, they become *ipso facto* members of the causal series; and if this world were the only world freedom would be excluded. But if above phenomenal existence, where natural causation rules, there exists the possibility, at least, of another and a noumenal realm, we have a means of extricating ourselves from the deterministic conclusion. From one side — the empirical — an event will be strictly determined. But this very causal relationship might have its source in a higher causality — a causality which belongs to the intelligible world outside the temporal series, and which itself determines phenomena instead of being determined by them.

"Among the causes in the phenomenal world, there certainly can be nothing that absolutely and from itself could cause a series to begin to be. Every act that produces an event is, as a phenomenon, itself an event or result which presupposes another state to serve as cause. Everything that comes to be is, therefore, merely a continuation of the series, and nothing that begins of itself can enter into the series. Hence all the modes in which natural causes act in the succession of time are themselves effects, for which there must again be causes in the series of time. It is vain to seek in the causal connection of phenomena for an *original* act by which something may come to be that before was not."

"But granting that the cause of a phenomenal effect is itself a phenomenon, is it necessary that the causality of its cause should be entirely empirical? May it not be that, while every phenomenal effect must be connected with its cause in accordance with laws of empirical causality, this empirical causality, without the least rupture of its connection with natural causes, is itself an effect of a causality that is not empirical, but intelligible? May the empirical causality not be due to the activity of a cause which in its relation to phenomena is original, and which, therefore, in so far as this faculty is concerned, is not phenomenal, but intelligible; although as a link in the chain of nature it must be regarded as also belonging entirely to the world of sense?"[1]

It is conceivable, then, that as a phenomenon an act may be strictly necessary, while yet in its reality, as it enters into the noumenal world, it is self-determined and free. The possibility of freedom is thus not excluded. But have we any reason for believing in its actuality? Briefly the answer is: Yes; it is necessary to postulate freedom and an intelligible world in order to satisfy the demands of the moral law.

In order to get the point of this it will be necessary to turn briefly to Kant's moral theory. The essence of the moral life consists in obedience to a law — the categorical imperative — which pretends to be absolute and universal — an obedience freed from every intermixture of personal interest and self-gratification, and going back simply to reverence for the law as such. In an ethical system remarkable for its stern rigor Kant endeavors to establish in all strictness such a separation between moral action, and action based on empirical motives and desires. This last — the field of "natural" good — has no claim to be called moral, since it leaves us with no court of appeal when wants conflict, as they continually are doing. What morality tells us is that there is something good always and for everyone, whether or not a taste for it actually exists; there are things no rational creature *ought* to want no matter how strong the desire may be. But a universal law cannot possibly come from empirical sources; and we must rule out therefore from the content of moral good all natural impulses and particular emotions.

But how then, it is natural to ask, are we to bring this highly abstract conception of our duty to bear on actual conduct? To this Kant has left himself only one answer; if duty is to be determined *a priori* by a rational law freed from any contingent matter, it can be derived from nothing but the formal aspect of law *qua* law. Put more simply, the law of duty has to be tested purely by its abstract self-consistency; since reason professes to be uni-

[1] *Critique of Pure Reason*, p. 543, Watson's translation.

versal, if anything is to be our rational duty it must be of such a character that it can be acted on by all rational beings under all circumstances without resulting in inner contradiction. Suppose I ask whether I am ever justified in breaking a promise. I should never be able by considering empirical consequences to assure myself that it might not on occasion be to my advantage to violate what I recognize as on the whole a useful rule. But if I were to put this question : Could I extend such a special dispensation so as to allow every man to break a promise whenever it seemed to be to his advantage? could I be content that such a maxim should hold good as a universal law? I at once see that my position would be logically a suicidal one. If there were no guarantees that promises would be kept, they would cease to be made, and the rule itself would lapse. Or take again the case of a man contemplating suicide as an escape from trouble; it is at once apparent that a system of nature of which it should be a law to destroy life through the very feeling of self-love whose special nature it is to impel to the improvement of life, would contradict itself, and so would not exist as a system of nature.

The first and fundamental principle of moral conduct is, accordingly : So act that you can also will that your action should become a universal law. This is the sole content of morality, and from it springs the only truly moral motive — an obedience to moral law that has no other source than a respect for the autonomy of the law itself. "Nothing in the whole world, or even outside of the world, can possibly be regarded as good without limitation except a *good will.*" "Even if it should happen that, owing to special disfavor of fortune or the niggardly provision of a stepmotherly nature, this will should wholly lack power to accomplish its purpose, then like a jewel it would still shine by its own light, as a thing which has its whole value in itself. Its usefulness, or fruitfulness, can neither add nor take away anything from its value." [1]

And so conceived, the moral law by its very nature demands the actuality of freedom. It calls on me to will and to act unconditionally, without regard to any consideration save the moral

[1] *Metaphysic of Ethics*, Abbott's translation, pp. 9, 10.

"ought"; and it has no meaning unless what I ought to do, I *can* do. Freedom is thus the absolute precondition of the validity of the moral life. And since now as a part of the phenomenal world my act is not free, there must in consequence be another and a noumenal realm within which it has that freedom which the moral life demands. The escape from determinism does not lie in denying to my particular empirical acts a causal explanation, but in denying the ultimate reality of that whole world in which causality rules, in favor of an intelligible world which indeed we cannot know, but whose existence we are nevertheless compelled to postulate. "The explanation of the possibility of categorical imperatives, then, is that the idea of freedom makes me a member of the intelligible world. Were I a member of no other world, all my actions *would* as a matter of fact always conform to the autonomy of the will. But as I perceive myself to be also a member of the world of sense, I can say only that my actions *ought* to conform to the autonomy of the will." [1]

The guarantee of the intelligible world is thus not knowledge, but the immediate realization of the claims of the moral law. It is practical rather than theoretical; the abstract reason which the Enlightenment had deified is definitely subordinated to a moral faith. "Morality requires us only to be able to think freedom without self-contradiction, not to understand it; it is enough that our conception of the act as free puts no obstacle in the way of the conception of it as mechanically necessary, for the act stands in quite a different relation to freedom from that in which it stands to the mechanism of nature. From the critical point of view, therefore, the doctrine of morality, and the doctrine of nature, may each be true in its own sphere; which could never have been shown had not criticism previously established our unavoidable ignorance of things-in-themselves, and limited all that we can *know* to mere phenomena. I have, therefore, found it necessary to deny *knowledge* of *God*, *freedom* and *immortality*, in order to find a place for *faith*." [2]

[1] *Metaphysic of Morality*, Watson's translation, p. 255.
[2] *Critique of Pure Reason*, Preface, Watson's translation, p. 6.

And with the intelligible world postulated to justify freedom and morality, we may note briefly the way in which Kant uses these results, somewhat inconsequentially it might seem, to make possible a practical assurance of God and immortality as well. Although the desire for happiness is entirely distinct from the content of the moral will, yet, since man belongs to the phenomenal as well as to the intelligible world, happiness must have a place for him in the idea of the highest good. This last may be defined as the union of happiness and virtue; and since it is not, and cannot ever be, attained in the present world, an endless life must be postulated for its achievement if reality is not to appear to us fundamentally irrational. As a final step, this moral order of the world has to be safeguarded and the end assured; and for such an assurance we need to assume the existence of a God. God is, it is true, a purely intelligible concept free from all intermixture of sense content and so incapable of being "known"; but for the same reason he comes into no competition with natural — phenomenal — laws, and so is placed forever beyond the reach of attacks from scientific materialism or scepticism.

At the start mention was made of two points of special significance in Kant's philosophy; and it is the second of these points at which we have now arrived. For Kant, the truths of the intellect are subordinate to the truths of the practical will, or of the moral insight; the spiritual demands of life have, equally with scientific reason, the right to induce belief, and in the end it is even true that their claim is the more fundamental one. This is an attitude which has come to be rather popular since Kant's day. For our human understanding science and its laws may represent the final word. But we are more than thinking beings; and if we once recognize that the processes of thought do not sum up in any final way the inner nature of reality, then there is left the possibility of a realm in which these other sides of our nature may take refuge undisturbed by fear of contradiction from the reason.

Such a gap between the results of reason and the postulates of the spiritual life has however certain obvious drawbacks. Kant himself felt this more or less distinctly, and in a third work, the *Critique of Judgment*, he tried to make the gap a little less absolute. There are two facts in particular which seem to suggest that the world in space and time, and the world of purpose or of meaning, are after all not so divorced from one another as the previous consequences go to show. In the aesthetic experience the natural world, alike in the beautiful object and in the workings of artistic genius, shows itself in unconscious harmony with the ideal requirements of the mind; and for any adequate account of the biological organism we find ourselves constrained to use the concept of end or teleology. But with Kant these facts, though they are suggestive, do not lead to any genuine reconstruction of his position; such judgments still fail to represent objective reality, and so cannot forthwith be imported into the absolutely real world.

LITERATURE

Kant, *Critique of Pure Reason; Prolegomena to any Future Metaphysic; Principles of the Metaphysics of Ethics; Critique of Practical Reason; Critique of Judgment; Religion within the Bounds of Pure Reason.* Translations: Meiklejohn (*Critique of Pure Reason*); Max Müller (*Critique of Pure Reason*); Watson (*Selections*); Abbott (*Critique of Practical Reason*); Bernard (*Critique of Judgment*); Mahaffy and Bernard (*Prolegomena*); Goerrvitz (*Dreams of a Spirit Seer*); Hastie (*Kant's Cosmogony*); Carus (*Prolegomena*); Semple (*Metaphysic of Ethics*).

Mahaffy and Bernard, *Paraphrase and Commentary.*

Stirling, *Text Book to Kant.*

Wenley, *An Outline Introductory to Kant's Critique of Pure Reason.*

Abbott, *Kant's Theory of Ethics.*

Caird, *Critical Philosophy of Kant.*

Adamson, *Philosophy of Kant.*

Wallace, *Kant.*

Fischer, *Kant.*

Schurman, *Kantian Ethics and the Ethics of Evolution.*

Watson, *Kant and his English Critics.*

Seth, *From Kant to Hegel.*

Seth, *Scottish Philosophy.*

Stuckenberg, *Life of Kant.*

Sidgwick, *Lectures on the Philosophy of Kant.*

Paulsen, *Immanuel Kant.*

Porter, *Kant's Ethics.*

Morris, *Kant's Critique of Pure Reason.*
Green, *Lectures.*
Prichard, *Kant's Theory of Knowledge.*
Wenley, *Kant and his Philosophical Revolution.*
Smith, *A Commentary on Kant's Critique of Pure Reason.*
Ward, *A Study of Kant.*

§ 36. *Fichte and Schelling*

1. *The Idealistic Development.* — In order to get the point of view of the further development of Idealism in Germany it may be well to start by distinguishing two different ways that the term "thought" or "reason" might be understood. On the one hand we may take it as the work of individual thinkers; thought then becomes a fact of psychology, distinct from the other factual realities that exist alongside it. It is only through an implicit reference to such human thinking that thought can be distinguished from reality, and so any meaning given to the Kantian thing-in-itself.

Meanwhile there is a broader way in which we might take the term — as the system of rational content, namely, which includes everything that is capable of being known; from this standpoint the individual thinker is only one among a vast number of objects of knowledge, a particular item in an intelligible universe which extends far beyond his private boundaries. It is with this that in his actual procedure Kant was mostly dealing. Kant's criticism of knowledge is not, or does not intend to be, a matter primarily of psychology. It is rather a logical inquiry into knowledge as a systematic structure abstracted from its connection with particular individuals; it attempts to criticise each factor in knowledge by reference to its place in a connected rational whole rather than by reference to the relation of any particular man's thought to an external prototype. And it is this second attitude to the exclusion of the other which is adopted explicitly by the later Idealists. The connection of thought with the psychological human self is almost entirely ignored; the Self, or Ego, means for the Idealists not the individual 'me,' but the unitary system of thought. One result is that things-in-themselves immediately tend to drop away. That there are difficulties in connection with the notion of a thing-in-itself is plain. If it is unknowable, what right have we to say anything at all about it? Kant himself had sometimes spoken of it as the cause of our sense experience; but causation applies only *within* experience, not to the connection between experience and a noumenal reality. Why not then simply reject it as a contradiction in terms which serve no useful end? Do we insist that it is necessary in order to supply the content of knowledge? But the attempt to account for knowledge from what is not knowledge is pure dogmatism, and no explanation at all; the true way is, as Kant had shown, to explain "things" as a thought construct through the application of the categories.

Reality, then, is the reality of experience, or thought; and the problem of philosophy has nothing to do with a noumenal world, but is only concerned with working out the systematic and logically interdependent character of thought itself. A starting point was found in connection with the gaps left in Kant's theory of knowledge. Kant's aim had been to trace back all experience to tne synthetic unity of the self; but he had failed to make the unity complete. There were, to begin with, the two factors in experience — thought and sensation — which Kant had assigned to different sources and so had made partly incompatible with one another. So likewise, in the moral world, he had left a break between the moral law and the life of sensuous impulse and desire. And on a larger scale there was the distinction between the noumenal and the phenomenal, the theoretical and the practical, the realm of freedom and the realm of necessity. The work of the Idealists who followed Kant had to do with an attempt to heal these divisions and to make experience one.

2. *Fichte.* — *Johann Gottlieb Fichte*, Kant's immediate successor, was born in Lusatia in 1762. An early writing which, on its first appearance, had mistakenly been hailed as the work of Kant himself and praised as such, gave him an immediate reputation, and he was soon recognized as the only man worthy to carry on Kant's task. He became professor at Jena, where his lectures aroused

widespread interest; but a naturally aggressive temper kept him continually in trouble, and occasioned at last the loss of his position. His work in awakening the German people to the need of united action in the wars with Napoleon has caused his name to be remembered, in his own country, as a patriot as well as a philosopher.

Fichte's philosophy starts from the attempt to take seriously Kant's conception of the unity of experience. If reason is in truth one in all its operations, it ought to be possible to deduce the various categories from a single source instead of leaving them, as Kant had done, in comparative isolation. Fichte finds this source in the pure *activity* of the Ego — an activity which reflection discovers to be involved in any fact of knowledge whatsoever, even the simplest and most formal. In this act the Ego first posits itself, asserts its own existence. It next proceeds to posit or set up a *not-self*, or object, which constitutes a check or limit to the self; no longer a pure unity, it now confronts an outer world, and difference as well as unity has entered into experience. Concrete knowledge thus implies the self and the world mutually limiting each other; at the same time the dualism is not absolute since both go back to the same source — the creative activity of the Ego. The fundamental fact in the universe is accordingly free Spirit, and the world is a creation of Spirit rather than, as the materialist would hold, its source.

Here an obvious question will arise. Why should the Ego thus create an external world? Why not be content with its original infinitude and indeterminateness? For an answer Fichte goes back to Kant's doctrine of the supremacy of the moral will, and in so doing undertakes to bridge the gulf between the two *Critiques*. It is because man is fundamentally a moral being that he finds it necessary to posit an outer world. For the moral life implies striving, action; and this would not be possible if the will were infinite and unlimited. It must, to become conscious of itself, set up a limit, in order that it then may overcome the limit. In its essence the external world is thus nothing but the stuff of moral action, the material which the will creates in order to give itself a field for its endeavor. "Not merely to know, but according to thy knowledge to do, is thy vocation." I have certain duties to be fulfilled by means of certain materials; and my world is the object and sphere of my duties, and absolutely nothing more.

But is it then I myself, Johann Gottlieb Fichte, who created the world I seem to find about me? It is a weakness in Fichte's system that his starting-point, and many of his arguments, seem to lead to this; but undoubtedly it is not what he intends. The Absolute Ego is very different from the individual self; it is not even a personal God. Rather we may regard it as the moral order of the universe — a power not ourselves that makes for righteous. ness, working in and through the individual selves we know. And as such it finds its ultimate interpretation in the theory of morals which is the most distinctive, and certainly the most interesting side of Fichte's philosophy.

This moral philosophy starts, like that of Kant, from the notion of freedom; but Fichte succeeds in giving this a meaning that comes considerably closer to man's common experience. More explicitly, he sets out to derive the content of the moral duties from two premises in particular, both of them also taken over from Kant — my obligation to respect my own dignity as a free being, and my obligation always so to act as not to violate the equal freedom of other men. Since, for example, I can act only through my body, I must preserve and cultivate the body as a tool for moral action. Rights of property, again, arise from the fact that property sup plies a necessary condition for the exercise of concrete freedom; and consequently we are under obligation not only to respect the property rights of others, but to own property ourselves, to exercise the prudential virtues such as thrift, and, in general, to live the life of a reputable citizen in society. In like manner of the sanctity, and even the duty, of marriage; purposely to remain unmarried is to incur guilt. Fichte indeed is able to show the absolute rationality not only of the marriage institution, but of the status of the German housewife, who, he argues ingeniously, enjoys the blessing of essential freedom in spite of, or rather because of, the fact that reason dictates she should devote herself solely to her husband, possess no independent rights of property or of citizenship, and make no foolish attempts at a career, for which her mind is not by nature suited. The same consideration of freedom applied to our social relations determines the duties of benevolence and justice; benevolence, for example, consists not in giving alms, but in promoting a life of active self-expression through helping men to secure the benefits of education, of safe and continued employment, and the like.

When accordingly Fichte urges duty for duty's sake as the one moral motive, this is to be interpreted in the light of such concrete freedom as a universal end. We are moral only when we act solely, not from personal desire, but with the lofty conception before our minds of a realm of freedom wherein the autonomy of every rational being shall become actualized. There is but one virtue — to forget one's personality; the one vice is to make self the object of our thoughts. The highest principle of ethics is the welfare of the moral community, where "moral" takes the form of loyalty to one grand motive — a sense of the unutterable dignity and authority of the ideal of a free humanity which has its being as the expression of a single all-embracing Moral Law.

It is this unfolding process which interprets the course of history as a great drama whose plot is the gradual realization of spiritual freedom. The human race starts as a natural phenomenon, engaged in satisfying natural wants. The first step toward morality takes place when the aggressive few, following their inner will to self-assertion, enslave the many, and thus bring to consciousness the demand for freedom through the sense of its suppression. The third age — Fichte's own — is marked by the revolt against these oppressive forces of society; it is the age of militant individualism, of rebellion against institutions and dogmas, in the interest of a freedom which, however, is as yet abstract and empty. But already there is dawning a new age of reconstruction wherein, through the agency of a scholar class under the lead of the metaphysician, the true significance of self and freedom and reason are being brought to consciousness. And the final epoch will realize man's goal in a form of society where this new knowledge is applied in detail to the affairs of life, and the benefits of freedom extended to the entire earth.

3. *Schelling.* — Apart from the question that might be raised about the satisfactoriness of a moral ideal which involves setting up a world simply for the sake of over-matching it, Fichte's philosophy is evidently too easy-going in its treatment of the realm of nature. In *Friedrich von Schelling* (1775–1854) this side of the philosophical problem again assumes an independent importance, though with no solid results. Schelling's account of nature was influenced by his connection with the romantic school of German poetry; it took the path of trying to point out, in a semi-poetical vein, the traces of intelligence, or of the Idea, in natural processes and forms. Meanwhile the combination of metaphysics with natural science gave rise to a dualism which threatened to pass into a contradiction. On the one hand nature is taken as a product of intelligence, the creation of the Ego; on the other intelligence, in man, itself appears as the highest product of the process already at work in nature. As a consequence Schelling found himself led to postulate a common root for nature and intelligence alike, in which the differences of the two lose themselves in an abstract identity — a position to a certain extent suggesting that of Spinoza. From this abstraction — the night, as Hegel says, in which all cows are black — it was of course impossible to get back to the concrete facts of experience again; and in his later philosophy accordingly, which took successively a number of forms, Schelling resorts more and more to mysticism.

LITERATURE

Fichte, *Science of Knowledge; Science of Rights; Science of Ethics.* Translations: Kroeger (*Science of Knowlegde, Science of Ethics, Science of Rights*); Smith (*Popular Works*).

Schelling, *Transcendental Idealism.*

Everett, *Fichte's Science of Knowledge.*

Adamson, *Fichte.*

Thompson, *The Unity of Fichte's Theory of Knowledge.*

Watson, *Schelling's Transcendental Idealism.*

Seth, *Hegelianism and Personality.*

Seth, *From Kant to Hegel.*

Leighton, *Typical Modern Conceptions of God.*

§ 37. *Hegel*

Georg Wilhelm Friedrich Hegel was born at Stuttgart in 1770. At Tübingen, where he entered in 1788, he came in contact with the group of young men of which Schelling was the acknowledged leader; and to him he attached himself as a disciple, though Schelling was five years his junior.   Among his associates he was regarded as a hard worker, but not as particularly brilliant.   With Schelling he founded a philosophical journal to which he contributed various articles in defence of the Schellingian philosophy.   He broke with Schelling by the publication, in 1807, of his first important work, the *Phenomenology of Spirit*, in which, not without a touch of sarcasm, Schelling's position was criticised.   From this time on he was occupied with the laborious working out in detail of his own philosophy.   His success was soon assured. and he passed from Nuremburg to Heidelberg, and from Heidelberg to Berlin, where he became the dictator of the German philosophical world.   He died in 1831.

It is a matter of great difficulty to convey any clear notion of Hegel's philosophy, by reason not only of the inherent obscurities which have given rise to various interpretations of its meaning, but also because of the extreme subtilty of its logic and the vast field which it covers.   What follows will of necessity have to be very general in its nature.

I. THE GENERAL NATURE OF HEGEL'S PHILOSOPHY

1. We perhaps may get a starting-point for understanding Hegel's thought by saying that it is, on one of its sides at least, the philosophical expression of the new sense for history.   The world of experience is a progressive embodiment of reason — such is his general thesis.   For the man of the Enlightenment reason, it has appeared, had been a rather abstract faculty by means of which the individual is able to decide for himself, affirmatively or negatively, such questions as may arise — the existence of God or of matter, the obligatoriness of moral law, the foundations of justice and society, or whatever it might be.   For reason so con-

ceived, a thing was either true or false, and that was all there was to say; moreover, most of the opinions of the past were false, so that reason's chief function was critical and destructive. The historical method has changed all this. Instead of encouraging us to judge everything by a particular standard that happens to be ours, it rather says: A thing is to be evaluated in terms of its surroundings, its natural history, the part it plays in a more inclusive setting; we should put ourselves at the point of view of the thing we wish to estimate, and not try to measure it by a yardstick of our own. Reason is objective in things, not subjective in ourselves; what we have to do is to watch experience itself unfold, and detect the laws involved in this unfolding. Reality exists, and reveals itself in the history of man; it is our part to accept it and to find its meaning, not to praise or blame. A thing is condemned only by the logic of events; and even this will only mean that it no longer is able to perform its function, not that it did not once have a function which was its sufficient justification. We cannot therefore understand reality by making abstract statements about it; we must take it in its concrete fulness of detail, and in the habitat where it belongs. Philosophers have argued, perhaps, that there is a God; but of what value is such a bald assertion? It has no meaning until we give it a content; and that content is nothing less than the concrete facts of life and history and religion. This is the way God manifests himself; the more we know about it the more we know what God is, and the less we know the less we are acquainted with his actual nature.

It is Hegel's contention that experience is such a system of reason with its own laws; and his whole philosophy is an endeavor to unfold its implications. This is what he means by his assertion that thought and reality are identical. The statement might be taken to imply, either that our individual thoughts are the sole reality, or that reality is a set of intellectual abstractions opposed to sense and feeling. The first of these interpretations is evidently absurd, and Hegel has not the least intention of affirming it; though the relation of human thought to the ultimate Thought does involve difficulties which he never succeeds in clearing up. Nor, again, does he mean that reality is a system of abstract thought concepts; concrete experience is its starting-point and end. But this experience is *rational* throughout. Every element of experience is connected with a rational whole in which it has a definite place and function, and which enables it to be thought understandingly. The reality of a thing is just its possession of significance for the great process of experience into which it enters; its existence and its intelligibility are one and the same thing. There is no opaque thing-in-itself beyond experience, no transcendent truth distinct from the reason that lies in things themselves. With the system of significant experience reality is absolutely coextensive; that which does not enter into experience is for us nothing at all. Such a rational system in its entirety is God; and God thus is the most certain thing in the world, since he is implicated in the existence of any reality whatsoever. The course of history is not the process simply by which man comes to a consciousness of God and of the world; it is the process as well by which God comes to a consciousness of himself.

The problem of philosophy is, accordingly, to show the meaning of each factor of experience that has ever revealed itself to man, by discovering its organic relationship to the rational whole to which it belongs. The instrument by which this is brought about is in general the concept of *development* — a logical development, that is, not primarily a process of historical development in time. This gives the schema of Hegel's dialectic method — a schema of three stages, in which thesis is followed by antithesis, and that again by the synthesis which includes them both. What in other words we are disposed at first to take as immediate and self-complete presently, by reason of the fact that it is not such a complete whole but only a portion of reality, shows its incompleteness by passing into its opposite; and then follows the process of reconciliation through which both sides get their rights. Every partial truth is thus preserved, and enters into the final synthesis of reason; but it enters only as a part, an aspect, and not as something that is self-sufficient and that has no broken edges.

What Hegel has in mind is abundantly illustrated in the history of the intellectual experience. Most men have had occasion to recognize the fact that any ordinary truth, if pushed too far, is apt to lead to contradictions; and these contrary considerations have to be kept in mind as limits or qualifications before we can feel ourselves on solid ground. Thus for example, in the practical realm, if I press what I call my abstract rights beyond a certain point it is almost certain to lead me into wrong, or injustice; concrete justice commonly means a balancing, a compromise. Or we may think of examples such as have presented themselves on a large scale in the history of thought. Thus the principle of authority and obedience in the Middle Ages passed in the Enlightenment, by a natural reaction, into the contradictory and equally one-sided principle of an arbitrary liberty; the solution does not lie in denying either principle, but in combining both in the conception of a concrete freedom — a freedom which is not the mere abstract possibility of doing anything we please, but which realizes itself by limiting itself, turning its undefined possibilities into definite channels, and submitting to the conditions and laws required for actual accomplishment. The mental temper which insists upon taking things in their isolation, which cannot see more than one side of a truth at a time, and which will always have it either that a thing is so or that it is not so without compromise or limitation, represents what Hegel calls the *understanding;* whereas *reason* in its true sense is that more comprehensive and adequate way of looking at things in their relationships and many-sidedness.

Hegel's central thought is, then, that only the whole is real; the partial fact is only an abstraction, which needs to be brought into connection with the whole in order to gain validity. "The bud disappears in the bursting forth of the blossom, and it may be said that the one is contradicted by the other; by the fruit, again, the blossom is declared to be a false existence in the plant, and the fruit is judged to be its truth in the place of the flower. These forms not only distinguish themselves from one another, but likewise displace one another as mutually incompatible. But their transient and changing condition also converts them into moments in an organic unity in which not alone do they not conflict, but in which one is as necessary as the other; and this very necessity first constitutes the life of the whole." We may sum this up in a combination of two main theses; reality is rational, and it is a system. The first thesis opposes itself to philosophies of naturalism or of psychological empiricism; the second opposes itself alike to the common rationalisms which stop with a number of particular intuitive truths, and to the pantheisms in which a bare unity has swallowed up all differences and distinctions. Difference *in* unity, the concrete universal, is our true tool for thinking the world. Whereas the lower rationalism of the Understanding splits the world up into *disjecta membra*, *either* this *or* that, and in consequence is always running up against contradictions, the method of Reason takes such an analysis only as a starting-point. The existence of contradictions should be a challenge to the philosopher to look farther, and to find some larger and more systematic concept within which each alike of the opposing claims may get its relative justification. Dialectic is the process whereby, starting from the abstracter categories, thought thus makes its way progressively toward the truth, not by subjective guesses, but by following the inner clue of Reason itself, until at the end we reach a comprehensive unity of thought in which all partial truths are summed up and find their ultimate significance.

2. Accordingly in his various writings Hegel attempts to explicate the reason that is in the world by applying his method to the entire content of experience. He starts with a Logic. Here, beginning with the abstractest concept possible — the concept of Being — he tries to show that the categories, or thought terms, which we use in thinking the world — terms such as quantity and quality, substance and causality, essence, existence, and the like — belong to a connected system; they pass one into another by a dialectical process until they culminate in the complete notion which includes them all. This last is essentially the notion of self-consciousness, which thus remains the supreme category for interpreting the world. After Logic we have the Philosophy of Nature, where this same Reason is examined in the form in which it becomes externalized in the objective world. The Reason which is present in nature advances from the purely mechanical realm until it attains its

highest form in the human body; and this serves as a transition to the Philosophy of Mind, or Spirit. Here again there are three stages: Subjective Mind as it is dealt with by Anthropology and Psychology; Objective Mind as it actualizes itself in objective social institutions; and Absolute Spirit, where Spirit finally attains to complete self-consciousness and to the unity of the subjective and the objective in Art, Religion and Philosophy.

We may stop for a moment to ask in what sense Hegel intends this development to be taken. Is it a true temporal development, a process which goes on in reality itself? There are difficult questions involved in an interpretation of Hegel here. Perhaps the simplest and clearest way would be to suppose that we have to do merely with a logical process in the human mind; if we as human thinkers take a certain concept as complete, then by reference to our fuller knowledge it shows its partial nature, and leads us on to its connection with the larger fact of which it has all the time been actually a part. This however hardly does justice to all of Hegel's claims; and it does not seem to account fully for that large portion of his work which is concerned with the actual experience of mankind, and in which he is dealing with what most certainly is a true development. In the philosophy of history, for example, or of religion, or in the history of philosophy, the reference to the temporal growth of human knowledge and experience is hardly a matter of option. It is doubtful whether Hegel can be made wholly consistent and intelligible. In the end he undoubtedly means to deny that actual development in time is the final truth of things; the goal must somehow be present in the earlier stages, must somehow be eternally complete and non-temporal. But how our concrete experience, which assuredly is in some real sense an actual growth, connects with this absolute reality, or how it stands related to the conceptual development of the Logic, Hegel does not very satisfactorily clear up.

2. THE STAGES IN THE DEVELOPMENT OF SPIRIT

1. *Logic.* — The *Logic* represents probably Hegel's greatest work; but its nature is such that no brief summary can do it justice.

It subjects to an acute analysis all the more important concepts which we are accustomed to use in thinking the world, and attempts to show their relative character, the limitations which attend their application, and their interpretation in the light of Mind as a self-conscious and organic whole. It begins with the simplest possible category — that of Being. That it *is*, represents the very least we can say of anything. But just because it is so very abstract there is nothing final about it. To say that a thing is, and stop there, is practically to say nothing at all; Being passes into its opposite — Not-Being, or Nothing. And then the one-sidedness of both terms leads to the third member of the triad — Becoming — which includes within itself the truth of each — is, and is not. This is an example of the general method by which Hegel seeks to unfold the entire content of the life of thought.

The *Logic* as a whole falls into three sections. The first, which is called the doctrine of Being, represents roughly the realm of immediate, unanalyzed knowledge, and includes, besides Being, such categories as Quality and Quantity, which come to us as immediate data of experience. The second section bears the name of Essence, and is perhaps the most important and enlightening of the three. It deals with the concepts used in ordinary scientific analysis and explanation, where the fact is no longer taken in its immediacy but is referred to something else as its ground; here are included the categories of identity and difference, ground and consequence, essence and phenomenon, substance and attributes, cause and effect, and the like. Hegel is very successful in pointing out the difficulties into which we fall when we take these terms independently of their relations — when for example we try to understand substance as a mere substratum, distinct from its qualities, rather than as something whose nature these qualities reveal. The third section — that of the Notion — has to do with the categories through which the first two groups enter into a higher synthesis in terms of their relation to the teleological unity of self-conscious thought, or Spirit.

2. *Philosophy of Nature and Subjective Mind.* — We pass next to the more concrete application of this logical framework to reality.

The Philosophy of Nature is of no great importance here. Nature is, indeed, a necessary factor in the growth of Spirit; it is the natural environment that furnishes the plastic material for Spirit's self-expression. But the relation of nature to the rest of Hegel's system is obscure, and the treatment he gives it confessedly the weakest part of his philosophy. The realm of Subjective Spirit is likewise of relatively subordinate interest. This is the field occupied by what are called the sciences of anthropology and psychology; man appears purely as a natural object which, though possessed of consciousness, is essentially one thing among others. It is in the treatment of Objective Spirit that the real significance of Hegel's philosophy begins to come to light. Here the inner life is first given concrete content in the form of institutions which, though at first they seem foreign to the individual and imposed on him externally, in reality find their real justification in their spiritual character as an expression of man's true self, apart from which his life would be meaningless and bare.

3. *Objective Mind.* (a) *Philosophy of Law, Ethics, Society.* — We may start then with the understanding that the true ground of any philosophy of the ethical and social life is to be found, not in institutions regarded as external, nor yet in purely individual motives such as constitute the morality of the private conscience, but in the concrete life of man in society as a progressive revelation and realization of his nature. In beginning with *abstract right*, accordingly, we are not to think, with the French Revolutionists, that the whole social problem can be solved in terms of certain inherent rights, dogmatically assumed, which belong to man as an individual apart from the social whole. The conception of the human will as existing by itself over against a world of relations into which as yet it has not entered is only a tool of analysis, and not a stage of history through which real men have passed. Keeping this in mind, however, for theoretical purposes we may start by supposing such a formal power of entering into relations that are still undetermined; and the possessor of such a formal freedom is in legal terms a *person*. It is here we find the abstract basis of abstract right, or law. But such law, by reason of its abstract

character, is necessarily only negative, made up of "Thou shalt nots," with no content or concrete existence; to become real, it must first enter into a relation to the objective world. The act by which the will gives itself an objective existence, gets a fulcrum in the real world, is *possession* or *property;* and it is with what this act involves accordingly that abstract law is concerned.

An object becomes property in so far as through seizure, use and alienation it has come into relation to a human will and been made an attribute of a "me"; it is objectified will. Property is thus a necessary requirement for concrete freedom, and is proportionately sacred. However — here lies the fault in the reasoning of the Revolutionists — its abstract equality does not mean a natural right to equality for everyone; abstract law says nothing as to what or how much property any individual should possess in any organic state where differences are implied. Meanwhile the property relation is not really established except as my right is recognized and allowed by my neighbor; it involves not simply my will, but the consenting will of another, and hence is the objectification of this common will. In this way the relation between things becomes the relation between wills. Persons are related to each other through their properties; they can hold property only as they also respect each other's property.

Such an objectification of the common will forms the basis of *contract* — contract, it is to be noticed, underlies not of all social relationships whatever, as earlier philosophers had thought, but only our relationships to particular external things which are not intrinsically connected with the will; institutions which, like marriage, are an expression of the essential nature of man are not contractual. As contracts are arbitrary and accidental, there is no guarantee against their passing into *injustice* or *wrong*. This may take the form either of unconscious wrong, or of fraud, or of crime, whereby through my property violence is used upon my will. But since freedom is the basis of all right, in attacking the freedom of another the criminal is attacking himself and his own right; his act is self-contradictory and self-destructive, and force may legitimately be used to defeat it. This is the foundation of the right of com pulsion. And as the crime exists not in the external world, but in the will of the criminal, compulsion thus appears as *punishment* — the reaction upon the will of the perpetrator of his criminal act so that its essential self-contradictoriness comes home to him. The punishment is the completion of his own deed, and is called for by justice to the criminal himself; in receiving punishment the offender is really being treated with the honor due to a presumptively rational being. But such a reaction should not in its turn be arbitrary and individual — that is but adding one wrong to another; it should proceed from a reflective interpretation of the principle involved. Here therefore the demand arises for a particular will that can at the same time will the universal; and thus we rise to the stage of subjective, reflective will, or *morality*.

In morality man becomes aware of the universal character of those acts which hitherto he has performed unreflectively and so with the possibility of discord; his acts are now brought home to the *conscience*. But conscience, so long as it remains at the stage of mere self-determination, is itself also only a stage in the attainment of true moral freedom. I may will the good, but who shall tell me what the good really is? "Duty for duty's sake," "Do right though the heavens fall," sound very well; but what *is* right and what *is* duty in any particular case? Through the absence of any grounded answer to this question, conscience in its popular sense often comes to mean simply what my particular desires or unintelligent prejudices impel me to do; its action reveals itself as the result of blind feeling, and may as well be bad as right. There is need not only for self-determination, but for self-determination by reference to an objective standard. I transform the realm of subjective morality into a true ethical life only as I give up the purely individual right of private judgment, whose logical issue is anarchy, and become a member of an objectively constituted society whose authority I acknowledge as my guide, and whose institutions and customs I accept as giving enlightenment, control and definiteness to my moral life. Here, in the ethical relations of the family, civil society, the state, and, finally, of humanity, the true life of the will is concretely realized. Abstract rights and abstract duties now become concrete and specific, and thereby the individual liberates and elevates himself to real and substantial freedom.   Only in society does man really exist, really attain to selfhood and individuality.

The individual first comes to himself in the *family*.   The family is thus not a mere device of nature to propagate the species, nor an external contract which leaves each of the contracting parties unchanged essentially; it is a new and concrete form of reality in which the individual merges his identity and finds thereby that, far from losing his liberty, he for the first time has discovered his true being as part of a larger whole.   The principle of the family is love, which includes all the members and unites them in a living bond. It involves (1) marriage, in which the physical union is transformed into a spiritual one and the two persons submit to limitations in order to gain fuller self-realization; (2) the family property, which gains now an ethical value by becoming common property; (3) the education of the children to maturity.

But the family is still not adequate to the full nature of man.   As the children leave the home and families separate, the need arises for another and higher unity to hold together this newly emerging independence; and this brings us to the second stage of the ethical world — *civil society*.   In its first phase, society assumes the aspect of an external power by which the conflicting interests of individuals are restrained and a field for their activity secured.   This is society on the side of government, and represents the conception of society which the Enlightenment brought to the front.   On such a showing men are separate existences possessing private interests, and bound to aggrandize themselves to the top of their power; and since if liberty were unrestrained these conflicting interests would clash, it is held desirable to give up a certain amount of liberty, in so far as it conflicts with the liberty of others, in order to gain the advantage of security.   Government is thus thought of as a police arrangement which prevents actual aggression, but adopts the policy of *laissez faire* in all other directions.   Under this head Hegel takes up the various organs and functions of civil society and shows how after all the real motive force revealing itself is not such an abstract conception of government, but rather the ideal which finds its expression in the truer reality of the *State* or *Nation*.

It is this latter reality as the organic unity of the feelings, customs and genius of a people immanent in their whole activity — a moral personality, a temple whose building is of living stones, the work of God in history realizing the moral order of the world — which represents the consummation of the moral life of humanity, and makes man for the first time truly human. The State is the true end of man, not merely a means. It is the reconciliation of the private interests of the individual with universal aims — the interest of the public. As such it does not repress personality, as did the ancient state; it builds upon it. But personality is not mere individuality. The true person is a social person, who has his rights and his duties only as a member of society. Consequently his rights and his duty are identical; duty is not imposed upon him by authority, but is the path by which his own satisfaction is secured. And duty exists only in terms of those expressions of the universal will which have been objectified in law and custom. The striving for a morality of one's own is futile; by its very nature it is impossible of attainment. In regard to morality the saying of the wisest man of antiquity is the only true one: to be moral is to live in accordance with the moral traditions of one's country. These traditions are but the progressive revelation of the universal will, the spirit of the national genius; to alter them, one must not set himself outside them as a judge relying on his private conscience, but must act rather from within as himself the organ of the immanent Spirit advancing to a more complete realization.

This idea of the state Hegel goes on to consider (1) in its immediate existence in the individual state; (2) in the relation of the single state to other states — external polity; and (3) as the universal Spirit of Humanity, superior to the individual state, and realizing itself in the process of history. As regards the internal constitution of the State, its essential principle is the organic relation of powers in a unity, not the notion of a mechanical aggregate of mutual "checks" to which the purely negative conception of government leads. These essential factors are (1) the power to define and determine the universal in the form of law — the Legislative power; (2) the power to apply this universal in particular spheres and to single cases — the governing or Executive power; and (3) the power of ultimate decision — the power of the Prince — in which the different powers are brought together into an *individual* unity. The highest form of the State, accordingly, Hegel finds in a Constitutional Monarchy.

(*b*) *Philosophy of History.* — As the human being is not a person except in relation to other persons, so the State is not an individual save in relation to other states; and the highest phase of this, when it becomes internalized, is found in that organic relation which constitutes the History of Humanity. In his *Philosophy of History*, which is one of Hegel's most interesting works, he tries to unfold the "grand argument of human existence," to trace the law of development which runs through the whole past life of the race, to discover the particular genius which each great world power has displayed, and to relate this to the all-comprehensive Idea which is immanent in the entire process.

What then is the plot of this great drama? Briefly, history is progress in the consciousness of rational freedom; it is the story of that discipline of the uncontrolled natural will which finally brings it into obedience to a universal principle. In its first form, in Asia, Spirit is still immersed in Nature. Law and morality are regarded as something fixed and external; they need not coincide with the desire of the individual, and the subjects of the state are consequently like children who obey their parents without will and insight of their own. In the law men recognize not their own will but a will foreign to them; justice is administered only on the basis of external morality, and government exists only as the power of compulsion. So too religion and the State are not distinguished, and the constitution generally is a theocracy. This is the childhood of history.

The Greek world may be compared with the period of adolescence, for here we have individualities forming. This is the second main principle in human history. In Greece the principle of universality is impressed upon the individual himself, and he finds himself in immediate harmony with its outer expression in nature and the State; he himself wills that which is laid on the Oriental as an external constraint. The "natural" is thus transformed into an expression of spiritual truth. But since the freedom of Spirit still is conditioned by some stimulus which nature supplies, spirituality is not yet absolutely free and self-produced. The Idea is not seen in its essence but is bound up with the real, as in a beautiful work of art. The Greek Spirit is the plastic artist, forming the stone into a work of art. The artist cannot get along without stone, colors, sensuous forms, to express his spiritual conception; and because the Idea was thus too closely bound up with a particular material form, was not yet recognized as purely spiritual, the Greek Spirit did not prove enduring.

In the next phase of history the Idea becomes separated, but only as an *abstract* universal. This is the *Roman* State, which represents the severe labors of the manhood of history. The State begins now to have an abstract existence and to develop itself for a definite object; and in doing this there is involved a recognition also of its members as abstract individuals — as persons with definite rights before the law. But while individuals have a share in the purpose of the State, it is not one that calls their whole being into play. Free individuals are sacrificed to the demands of national ends; the geniality and joy of soul that existed in the Athenian Polis have given place to harsh and vigorous toil. True and substantial freedom is attained only in the fourth phase of world history — the German. This would answer, in a comparison with the periods of human life, to its *old age*. But while the old age of nature is weakness, that of Spirit is its perfect maturity and strength.

4. *Absolute Mind.* (*a*) *Art.* — But the State still does not represent man's full experience, and political life is not his highest and truest activity; complete freedom he can find only in the life of Spirit as such. Above the State, accordingly, there exist the free realms of Art, Religion and Philosophy, where the opposition of outer and inner is still more completely overcome, and man sees himself at last for what he truly is — pure Spirit. In Art this triumph of the idea over matter is achieved only in part. The

material of the artist bodies forth his idea immediately, but the material which the idea employs is not perfectly plastic. In this greater or less rebelliousness of character we find the basis for the distinction between the various arts. In *architecture* — the elementary stage — idea and form are still distinct. The cathedral may symbolize religious aspiration, but it is still far removed from the idea for which it stands; it may by its vast proportions express solemnity and grandeur, but it cannot even suggest the finer shades of feeling. This dualism partly disappears in *sculpture*. Sculpture has this in common with architecture, that it employs as its material gross matter; but it is more capable of transforming and spiritualizing this. It is able to utilize every detail instead of leaving many that are unessential to the idea, as architecture does. But it cannot represent the soul itself as revealed in the eye; this belongs to *painting*. In painting too the material is somewhat less gross; it is the plane surface, in which depth is represented only by appearance. It is still objective art however — is still bound to matter; and so, like architecture and sculpture, it is incapable of expressing anything beyond a single moment of life. This limitation is overcome in *music*, the subjective, immaterial art, which can reproduce all the infinite variety of the inner life. But its subjectivity is likewise a limitation. Music is still symbolic, and so is capable of various interpretations. The complete union of the subjective and the objective is brought about in the art of arts — *poetry*. Poetry converts the vague and indefinite sound which is the material of music into articulate and definite sound — language — where the material is wholly subordinated to the idea. Poetry sums up in itself all the other arts: *epic poetry* corresponds to the material arts; *lyric poetry* to music; while the crown of all, reconciling the two, and constituting the supreme artistic expression of the highest civilization, is *dramatic poetry*.

On the historical side, Oriental art is symbolical; it delights in allegories and parables, and shows its inability to cope with its material by its lack of form and its fondness for exaggeration. In Greek art symbolism is superseded by direct expression, in which matter and idea perfectly coincide; but Greek art is defective through its very perfection. The idea is so completely identified with its matter that it becomes purely naturalistic; the spiritual character of the idea is sacrificed to physical beauty. This fault is corrected in Christian art. Here art is recalled from the physical world, and the ideal of physical beauty is subordinated to that of spiritual beauty — the worship of the Virgin supersedes the cultus of Venus. Just because, however, the moral ideal is so far beyond the power of matter to embody, Christian art, despairing of adequately expressing it, lapses into the contempt of form which characterizes Romanticism.

(*b*) *Religion and Philosophy.* — The identification of thought and the object, of the finite and the infinite, which receives a partial expression in art, is raised to a higher power in *religion*. Here again there is no question, for Hegel, of *proving* the reality of God and the truth of religion in the ordinary sense; he is interested rather in the religious experience itself. This experience exists as a fact given to philosophy to understand, not to create; and since God has his existence within experience, not outside of it, the more comprehensive the experience the more adequately is God revealed in it. Accordingly he has no patience with the temper of the Enlightenment, which would reject positive religions as false and man-made and confine belief to a few abstract dogmas of Deism. Religion exists just in the process of religious development; and the stages of this development are to be interpreted, not judged, except as they are judged by the further historical development that supersedes them.

The same failure to embody the Idea fully that was found in Art, in Religion gives rise to a new dualism — the dualism of the finite and the infinite; and the progress of religion is the healing of this separation. In Oriental religions the idea of the infinite is paramount. God is everything (Pantheism), and man is nothing; God is what the despot is in the political sphere — an all-potent being upon whose will men are wholly dependent, so that nothing is left for man but submission. The religion of the Greek, on the contrary, is a religion of naturalism and the finite. Man is the final object of his worship; his gods are essentially human attributes concretely embodied and raised by art to the position of types.

These two extremes are reconciled in Christianity, the absolute religion, for which the important thing is neither God by himself nor man by himself, but the concrete unity of the divine and human in Christ — the God-man. Christianity finds God, the infinite, implicated *in* the finite — in human consciousness and in the process of the world. Its dogmas are to be taken in this way as shadowing forth in terms of the imagination the eternal progress of the Idea, not as the statement of historical events that happened eighteen hundred years ago. But for this reason also — that religion is still in the realm of imaginative representation — there is still a higher stage. The truths which are but shadowed forth in religion get their fully adequate and rational statement, and so the Idea comes to full consciousness of itself, in that development of pure thought which constitutes the History of Philosophy, and which has its outcome in the philosophy of Hegel.

5. *Conclusion.* — Hegel's faith that at last the Absolute had attained to complete self-consciousness was not borne out by subsequent events. His influence, supreme at his death, was not destined to continue long unchecked. Within his own school there was presently a split over the interpretation of his attitude toward religious problems; while without opponents sprang up on every side, among whom *Herbart* is perhaps the most important. It may be well to note briefly the chief weaknesses in Hegel's system that were responsible for this.

And first, while his attempt to show the rationality of the universe constitutes Hegel's main claim to recognition, there can be little doubt that he exaggerated the extent to which this rationality is a necessary and transparent one for human thought. If we were to judge by some of the utterances of Hegel and his disciples, all mystery is at last dispelled in the clear light of reason, and the whole course of creation may be watched as it moves with logical necessity from one step to the next. As against this rather presumptuous gnosticism it is not surprising that a call went out for a "return to Kant," and his limitation of the human faculties to a knowledge of phenomena. In opposition to Hegel's logical idealism we find accordingly, now a resort to faith or intuition as a substitute for reason, now the assertion of an ultimate agnosticism, occasionally an insistence, even, on the positive *ir*rationality of the world, or again a widely prevalent disposition to displace metaphysics altogether by the sober methods of science.

It was perhaps the last motive that was most responsible for the discredit into which Hegel's philosophy for a time fell. For the human side of life he had done much. But he had had almost nothing of importance to say about the world of physical objects on which man's experience depends, and which appears for the most part so indifferent or antagonistic to his spiritual interests; Hegel's treatment of this had been weak and fanciful, and he had even set himself actively against what have proved to be fruitful scientific ideas. Before any final philosophical rendering could be attempted with any promise of success, much more needed to be learned about what has happened and is still happening in the world of nature. This was the task of the great scientific development which dominates the thought of the nineteenth century.

Finally, there were new social and political demands afloat which Hegel failed conspicuously to satisfy. For him it had been the task of philosophy simply to interpret the movement of universal Spirit as it had already embodied itself in social institutions; it was not the philosopher's business to construct ideals. Hegel's whole effort had been to show that truth is to be found in the actual, and that between thought and reality, the ideal and the real, there is no separation. Substantial freedom consists in accepting the duties of our station in society as we find it, not in setting our finite wills in rebellion against the world-spirit. To the new temper which was beginning to demand social justice, and a reconstruction of society such as should give something for the mass of men to hope for and should relieve the miseries of those with whom the Idea had not seen fit to concern itself, Hegel seemed to have nothing to say. Indeed to men of such a temper he appeared even a reactionary — one who had found the highest expression of human freedom, beyond which it was idle to attempt to look, in that latest development of History — the Prussian state.

In this later development of philosophy it is probably useless to try to find any single guiding clue, even so slender a clue as earlier periods have revealed; for one thing, it is too close to us, and it is the outcome of social conditions far more complex and tortuous than have ever before existed. It will be enough to take up in succession a few of the most representative names and movements.

LITERATURE

Hegel, *Phenomenology of Spirit; Logic; Encyclopedia of Philosophical Sciences; Philosophy of Right; Philosophy of Religion; Aesthetics; Philosophy of History; History of Philosophy.* Translations: Wallace (*Logic, Philosophy of Mind*); Sibree (*Philosophy of History*); Dyde (*Philosophy of Right*); Bosanquet (*Philosophy of Art*); Hastie (*Aesthetics*); Haldane (*History of Philosophy*).
Sterrett, *The Ethics of Hegel.*
Caird, *Hegel.*
Kedney, *Hegel's Aesthetics.*
Morris, *Hegel's Philosophy of the State and of History.*
Harris, *Hegel's Logic.*
Seth, *From Kant to Hegel.*
Seth, *Hegelianism and Personality.*
Wallace, *Prolegomena to the Study of Hegel.*
McTaggart, *Studies in Hegelian Dialectic.*
McTaggart, *Studies in Hegelian Cosmology.*
McTaggart, *Commentary on Hegel's Logic.*
Ritchie, *Darwin and Hegel.*
Baillie, *Origin and Significance of Hegel's Logic.*
Hibben, *Hegel's Logic.*
Mackintosh, *Hegel and Hegelianism.*
Croce, *What Is Living and What Is Dead in Hegel's System*
Stace, *The Philosophy of Hegel.*

MORE RECENT TENDENCIES IN PHILOSOPHY

§ 38. *Schopenhauer*

Arthur Schopenhauer was born in 1788. His father died when he was a youth, and between himself and his mother, who was a popular novelist of the day, so little sympathy existed that they found it advisable to live apart. Schopenhauer's system was conceived early in life, and his chief work — *The World as Will and as Idea* — was published in 1819. The cold reception which it received was a severe blow to Schopenhauer's vanity, which was considerable; and it increased his disgust with the reigning philosophy. He was convinced there was a conspiracy among the school philosophers against him, and he could find nothing too disparaging to say of them in turn, particularly of Hegel. He had come in contact with Hegel at Berlin, where he was appointed *Privatdocent* in 1820. He apparently had cherished hopes that he could triumph over the great philosopher, whose popularity was then at its height; and he deliberately set himself in rivalry by choosing the same hour for his lectures. When in consequence he found his own lectures unattended and Hegel's classroom thronged, he was greatly disappointed and embittered, and finally was led to give up all thought of an academic career. The rest of his life was spent in quiet at Frankfort-on-the-Main. Toward the close of his life the recognition he had failed of in his youth seemed on the point of coming to him. His book began to be talked about and to find converts, if not among the technical philosophers at least among the laity. This growing fame soothed his last days. He died in 1860.

1. *The World as Will.* — The two notable things about Schopenhauer's philosophy are (1) his doctrine of the Will as the thing-in-itself, and (2) the way in which he erects on this foundation the

first systematic philosophy of Pessimism. As a metaphysician Schopenhauer relates himself to Kant — to whom he professes to go back in opposition to the tendency which culminated in Hegel — and to Kant's contention that the world as we know it is a phenomenal construction of the self. " ' The world is my idea ' — this is a truth that holds good for everything that lives and knows, though man alone can bring it into reflective consciousness. If he really does this, he has attained to philosophical wisdom. It then becomes clear and certain to him that what he knows is not a sun and an earth, but only an eye that sees a sun, a hand that feels an earth; that the world that surrounds him is there only as idea, that is, only in relation to something else — the consciousness which is himself." [1]

But while the world is illusion, mere appearance, there exists behind it a reality which appears — the thing-in-itself of Kant, which Schopenhauer defends against the attacks of the Idealists. Is this thing-in-itself really unknowable however, as Kant had claimed? Here Schopenhauer strikes out for himself. He agrees that we cannot reach it by the pathway of the reason; it cannot be demonstrated in the strict sense of the word. Our insight into its nature is rather the outcome of a direct intuition of genius. Nevertheless we have every right to believe this intuition justified. For we are ourselves a part of the real universe, and in ourselves we come upon reality at first hand. We have only to get at our own true nature, therefore, to be able by analogy to extend this to other things as well; for it is natural to assume that reality is all of a piece.

Now the inner essence of man's nature is *will*. It is as will that the reality of his own body comes home to him immediately. The various parts of the body are the visible expression of desires; teeth, throat and bowels are objectified hunger, the brain is the will to know, the foot the will to go, the stomach the will to digest. It is only as a secondary outcome of this original activity that the thought life arises. We *think* in order to *do;* the active impulse precedes, and is the necessary basis for, any conscious motive.

[1] *The World as Will and Idea.* Translation by Haldane and Kemp. Vol. I, p. 1, Paul, Trench, Trübner & Co.

And this insight, once attained, throws a flood of light on the outer world. The eternally striving, energizing power which is working everywhere in the universe — in the instinct of the animal. the life process of the plant, the blind force of inorganic matter — what is this but the Will that underlies all existence? "If we observe the strong and unceasing impulse with which the waters hurry to the ocean, the persistency with which the magnet turns ever to the north pole, the readiness with which iron flies to the magnet, the eagerness with which the electric poles seek to be reunited and which, just like human desire, is increased by obstacles; if we see the crystal quickly take form with such wonderful regularity of construction, which is clearly only a perfectly definite and accurately determined impulse in different directions, seized and retained by crystallization; if we observe the choice with which bodies repel and attract each other; lastly, if we feel directly how a burden which hampers our body by its gravitation toward the earth increasingly presses and strains upon it in pursuit of its one tendency — if we observe all this, I say, it will require no great effort of the imagination to recognize, even at so great a distance, our own nature. That which in us pursues its ends by the light of knowledge, but here, in the weakest of its manifestations, only strives blindly and dumbly in a one-sided and unchangeable manner, must yet in both cases come under the name of Will, as it is everywhere one and the same; just as the first dim light of dawn must share the name of sunlight with the rays of the full mid-day."[1]

Reality, then, is Will; and Will is one and indivisible. All apparent multiplicity is due to those subjective forms of human thought which come between us and the truth — namely, space and time. "As the magic lantern shows many different pictures which are all made visible by one and the same light, so in all the multifarious phenomena which fill the world together, or throng after each other as events, only one Will manifests itself, of which everything is the visibility, the objectivity, and which remains unmoved in the midst of this change."[2] And if this is so, of course we must leave out of our conception of the universal Will that action

[1] I, p. 153.   [2] I, p. 199.

for intelligent ends which characterizes human willing. Intelligence is only a surface phenomenon — a form which existence assumes for the attainment of its hungry striving, but a form quite foreign to its real nature. In itself will is blind and irrational. In all its lower aspects it is without knowledge; the nests of birds and the webs of spiders are not the product of intelligence, but of unforeseeing instinct. It is only as its manifestations become more complex that it kindles for itself, in intellect, a light to aid it in the task of dealing with the disadvantages that arise from this complexity. The will is thus far deeper seated than the intellect; it is the blind man carrying on his shoulders the lame-man who can see.

2. *The Philosophy of Pessimism.* — And this supplies the metaphysical basis for Schopenhauer's pessimism; pessimism follows from the very nature of will. All willing arises from want, and so from deficiency, and so from suffering. "The satisfaction of a wish ends it, yet for one wish that is satisfied there remain at least ten that are denied. Further, the desire lasts long, and demands are infinite; the satisfaction is short and scantily measured out. It is like the alms thrown to a beggar, that keeps him alive to-day that his misery may be prolonged till the morrow. So long as we are given up to the throng of desires with their constant hopes and fears, so long as we are the subjects of willing, we can never have lasting happiness or peace. It is essentially all the same whether we pursue or flee, fear injury or seek enjoyment; the care for the constant demands of the will continually occupies and sways the consciousness." [1] The subject of willing thus is constantly stretched on the revolving wheel of Ixion, pours water into the sieve of the Danaides, is the ever-longing Tantalus. No possible satisfaction in the world could suffice to still the longings of the will, set a goal to its infinite craving and fill the bottomless abyss of its heart.

Life is therefore fundamentally an evil; as Calderon says: The greatest crime of man is that he was born. "There is no proportion between the cares and troubles of life, and the results or gain of it. In the simple and easily surveyed life of the brutes, the emptiness

[1] I, p. 253.

and vanity of the struggle is more easily grasped. The variety of the organizations, the ingenuity of the means whereby each is adapted to its element and its prey, contrasts here distinctly with the want of any lasting final aim; instead of which there presents itself only momentary comfort, fleeting pleasure conditioned by wants, much and long suffering, constant strife, *bellum omnium*, each one both a hunter and hunted, pressure, want, need and anxiety, shrieking and howling. And this goes on *in secula seculorum*, or till once again the crust of the planet breaks."

"Let us now add the consideration of the human race. Here also life presents itself by no means as a gift for enjoyment, but as a task, a drudgery to be performed; and in accordance with this we see, in great and small, universal need, ceaseless wars, cares, constant pressure, endless strife, compulsory activity with extreme exertion of all the powers of mind and body. Many millions, united into nations, strive for the common good, each individual on account of his own; but many thousands fall as a sacrifice for it. Now senseless delusions, now intriguing politics, excite them to wars with each other; then the sweat and the blood of the great multitude must flow to carry out the ideas of individuals or to expiate their faults. In peace, industry and trade are active, inventions work miracles, seas are navigated, delicacies are collected from all ends of the world, the waves engulf thousands. All strive, some planning, some acting; the tumult is indescribable. But the ultimate aim of it all — what is it? To sustain ephemeral and tormented individuals through a short span of life, in the most fortunate case with endurable want and comparative freedom from pain, which however is at once attended with ennui; then the reproduction of this race and its striving. In this evident disproportion between the trouble and the reward, the will to live appears to us from this point of view, if taken objectively, as a fool, or subjectively, as a delusion, seized by which everything living works with the utmost exertion of its strength for something that is of no value." [1]

"The enchantment of distance shows us paradises which vanish like optical illusions when we have allowed ourselves to be mocked

[1] III, pp. 112 ff.

by them. Happiness, accordingly, always lies in the future or else in the past, and the present may be compared to a small dark cloud which the wind drives over the sunny plain; before and behind it all is bright, only it itself always casts a shadow." Pleasure is merely negative, and only evil is real. We feel pain, but not painlessness; care, but not the absence of care; fear, but not security. Hence all poets are obliged to bring their heroes into anxious and painful situations so that they may be able to free them from these. The happiest moment of the happy man is the moment of his falling asleep. "The earthquake of Lisbon, the earthquake of Haiti, the destruction of Pompeii, are only small playful hints of what is possible. A small alteration of the atmosphere causes cholera, yellow fever, black death, which carry off millions of men; a somewhat greater alteration would extinguish all life. A very moderate increase of heat would dry up all the rivers and springs. The brutes have received just barely so much in the way of organs and powers as enables them to procure, with the greatest exertion, sustenance for their own lives and food for their offspring; therefore if a brute loses a limb, or even the full use of one, it must generally perish. Even of the human race, powerful as are the weapons it possesses in understanding and reason, nine-tenths live in constant conflict with want, balancing themselves with difficulty and effort upon the brink of destruction." [1] "Whence did Dante take the materials for his hell but from this our actual world? And yet he made a very proper hell of it. And when on the other hand he came to the task of describing Heaven and its delights he had an insurmountable difficulty before him, for our world affords no material at all for this."

It is wholly impossible, then, to find a purpose or meaning in life. Why the whole tragi-comedy exists cannot in the least be seen, since it has no spectators, and the actors themselves undergo infinite trouble with little and merely negative pleasure. "What then is a short postponement of death, a slight easing of misery or deferment of pain, a momentary stilling of desire, compared with such an abundant and certain victory over them all as death?

[1] III, p. 396.

What could such advantages accomplish taken as active moving causes of a human race, innumerable because constantly renewed, which unceasingly moves, strives, struggles, grieves, writhes, and performs the whole tragi-comedy of the history of the world, nay, what says more than all, *perseveres* in such a mock existence as long as each one possibly can. Clearly this is all inexplicable if we seek the moving causes outside the figures, and conceive the human will as striving in consequence of rational reflection after those good things held out to it, the attainment of which would be a sufficient reward for its ceaseless cares and troubles. The matter being taken thus, every one would rather have long ago said: '*Le jeu ne vaut pas la chandelle*,' and have gone out. But on the contrary every one guards and defends his life like a precious pledge intrusted to him under heavy responsibility. The wherefore and the why, the reward for this, certainly he does not see; but he has accepted the worth of that pledge without seeing it, upon trust and faith. The puppets are not pulled from without, but each bears in itself the clockwork from which its movements result. This is the *will to live*, manifesting itself as an untiring machine, an irrational tendency, which has not its sufficient reason in the external world." [1] It is this blind pressure, without goal or motive, which drives us on, and not anything that we can rationally justify. "We pursue our life with great interest and much solicitude as long as possible; so we blow out a soap bubble as long and as large as possible, although we know perfectly well that it will burst." Accordingly we often see a miserable figure, deformed and shrunk with age, want and disease, implore our help from the bottom of his heart for the prolongation of an existence the end of which would necessarily appear altogether desirable if it were an objective judgment that determined here. Surely if one knocked on the graves and asked the dead whether they wished to rise again, they would shake their heads.

3. *The Way of Salvation.* — Such are the facts of life; is there no deliverance? Can we never for a moment be set free from the miserable striving of the will, keep the sabbath of the penal servitude

[1] III, p. 115.

of willing while the wheel of Ixion stands still? Yes, in a more or less complete way man may free himself from this all-devouring will to live. The first and partial road to deliverance is through art. Art has to do, not with the particular things of the phenomenal world which can serve as a satisfaction to our desires, but rather with the eternal types which are represented in the objectification of the World Will — the stages which it has assumed. Art is concerned with ideas. It repeats or reproduces the essential and abiding in all the phenomena of the world, the eternal ideas grasped through pure contemplation. In relation to these, the details of the natural world and the multitudinous events of history are just as foreign and unessential and indifferent as the figures which they assume are to the clouds, the form of its eddies and foam flakes to the brook, or its trees and flowers to the ice. Astonishment at the complete sameness of all its million phenomena and the infallibility of their occurrence is really like that of a child or a savage who looks for the first time through a glass with many facets at a flower, and marvels at the complete similarity of the innumerable flowers which he sees. The one source of art is the knowledge of the ideas; its one aim the communication of this knowledge. "While science, following the unresting and inconstant stream of the fourfold forms of reason and consequent, with each end attained sees farther, and can never reach a final goal any more than by running we can reach the place where the clouds touch the horizon, art, on the contrary, is everywhere at its goal. For it plucks the object of its contemplation out of the stream of the world's course, and has it isolated before it. And this particular thing which, in that stream, was a small perishing part, becomes to art the representative of the whole, an equivalent of the endless multitude in space and time. It therefore pauses at this particular thing; the course of time stops; the relations vanish for it; only the essential, the idea, is its object." [1]

In the pure contemplation of these Platonic ideas the soul finds thus a momentary release from striving, and by the disinterestedness of contemplation it denies for a time the remorseless will to live.

[1] I, p. 239.

Knowledge breaks free from the service of the will, and loses itself in the object; man forgets his individuality, his will, and only continues to exist as the pure subject, the clear mirror of the object — the pure, will-less, painless, timeless subject of knowledge. The faculty of continuing in this state of pure perception, and of enlisting in this service the knowledge which originally existed only for the service of the will, is what we call *genius.* Genius is the power of renouncing entirely one's own personality for a time, so as to remain pure knowing subject, clear vision of the world. The common mortal, the manufacture of nature which she produces by the thousand every day, is not capable thus of observation that in every sense is wholly disinterested; he can turn his attention to things only so far as they have some relation to his will.

But such moments as art can give are too fleeting for complete deliverance; that can come about only by the complete suppression of the will to live. This cannot be attained by suicide. The destruction of its phenomenal manifestation, the body, leaves quite unchanged that underlying will which is the true cause of our misery. The real source of the conditions we are trying to escape remains untouched by death. "If a man fears death as his annihilation, it is just as if he were to think that the sun cries out at evening : Woe is me! for I go down into eternal night." The suicide, therefore, goes to work the wrong way. Instead of denying the will, he gives up living just because he cannot give up willing. True deliverance comes by rejecting, not life, but the desire for life; not by shunning sorrows, but by shunning joys. To the attainment of this happy consummation *morality* is a step. Morality is in essence the crushing out of the egoistic self-assertion which is ready to annihilate the world in order to maintain its own self — that drop in the ocean — a little longer. It does this through a recognition of the fact that, after all, it is only phenomenally that I differ from my neighbor. In reality, each man must say to himself with reference to other things: *This art Thou.* Down beneath the appearance of difference which the space and time forms give, it is the same unitary will which constitutes your life and mine; and so our interests are not different, but identical. The true root of all morality, therefore, is *sympathy;* for sympathy is nothing but the obscure perception of this identity between myself and my neighbor.

But while morality is a partial abandonment of the striving will in so far as it sinks the law of self-preservation in a sense of human brotherhood, it is only the starting-point. He who through morality renounces every accidental advantage, and desires for himself no other lot than that of humanity in general, cannot desire even this for long. True salvation only comes when striving ceases altogether, when we mortify the deeds of the body by voluntarily crushing out all desire and all activity. "Every gratification of our wishes won from the world is like the alms which the beggar receives from life to-day that he may hunger again to-morrow; resignation, on the contrary, is like an inherited estate, it frees the owner forever from all care." [1]

The highest ideal is thus that ascetic starvation of the impulses which results in the attainment of Nirvana, the heaven of the extinction of consciousness. "Then nothing can trouble a man more, nothing can move him, for he has cut all the thousand cords of will which hold us bound to the world and, as desire, fear, envy, anger, drag us hither and thither in constant pain. He now looks back smiling and at rest on the delusions of this world which once were able to move and agonize his spirit also, but which now stand before him as utterly indifferent to him as the chessmen when the game is ended, or as in the morning the cast-off masquerading dress which worried and disquieted us in the night in carnival. Life and its forms now pass before him as a fleeting illusion, as a light morning dream before half-waking eyes, the real world already shining through it so that it can no longer deceive; and like this morning dream they finally vanish altogether without any violent transition." Is it said that this is an ideal of nothingness? — it is not denied. "Rather do we freely acknowledge that what remains after the entire abolition of the will is, for all those who are still full of will, certainly nothing; but conversely, to those in whom the

[1] I, p. 504.

will has turned and has denied itself this our world which is so real, with all its suns and milky ways — is nothing." [1]

LITERATURE

Schopenhauer, *Fourfold Root of the Principle of Sufficient Reason; World as Will and as Idea.* Translations: Haldane and Kemp (*World as Will and as Idea*); Hillebrand (*Fourfold Root*); Bax (*Essays*); Saunders (*Essays*).
Wallace, *Schopenhauer.*
Sully, *Pessimism.*
Caldwell, *Schopenhauer's System in Its Philosophical Significance.*
Wenley, *Aspects of Pessimism.*
Whittaker, *Schopenhauer.*

§ 39. *Comte and Positivism*

1. Among the streams of tendency that go to make up the intellectual history of the nineteenth century, a new type of social philosophy plays not the least important rôle. In general this is marked, on the one hand, by an attempt to enlist the prestige of science, and on the other by a strong reaction against the authority of the past, in the interest of a more satisfying social state than the undirected course of history had left behind. The tendency took two directions which interacted, but in which the emphasis was differently placed. In England the direction was toward individualism and a curtailing of the power of the state; on the continent the main trend was rather toward authority, located however in a new form of social structure that should extend the benefits of civilization to those classes which had hitherto had little share in them. On the practical side this found expression in the rise of various brands of socialism; in a more speculative form it takes shape in Positivism and the philosophy of Comte.

In Positivism philosophy again returns to a recognition of the claims of the Baconian conception of science as a servant of human life. *Auguste Comte*, born in 1798, was influenced in early life by the socialist St. Simon, and from him he got the germ at least

[1] I, pp. 504, 532.

of the idea that was to lead him to subordinate his scientific interests to the conception of man and society. His *Cours de philosophie positive*, published in 1839–1842, gave him a position among the most important thinkers of his day. Positivism quickly attracted enthusiastic disciples; in England not only did it influence such men as J. S. Mill and Herbert Spencer, but it presently took on a sectarian form, and a Positivistic church was established in London to which a number of very able men attached themselves. Comte's death occurred in 1857.

Positivism means the definite abandonment of all search for ultimate causes, and the turning of human attention rather to the *laws of phenomena* as the only kind of knowledge that is both attainable and useful. Knowledge is of value to us because it helps us modify conditions in the physical and the social world; to do this we need to know how things act, and that is all we need to know. This necessary limitation of all knowledge to phenomena Comte hardly attempts to demonstrate. He assumes it to be self-evident to all minds that are abreast of their age; it is the great lesson which the history of human thought has to teach. This is the outcome of Comte's "Law of the Three Stages." Man starts in by explaining the phenomena of nature *theologically;* he attributes the activities of things, that is, to an arbitrary will such as he finds in himself. In its earliest and most thorough-going form this is *fetichism*, which obviously leaves but little room for the recognition of positive law. Later on the notion of a separate will in each material thing becomes generalized, and we have the *polytheistic* stage. Polytheism is more general and abstract in character than fetichism; the gods act through things, but the things themselves are no longer thought of as being alive. And by reason of this greater abstractness the secondary details of phenomena are accordingly set free for scientific observation.

The final stage of theological thought is *monotheism*. Here we have everything brought back to a single abstract will; and consequently a still wider extension of scientific observation is made possible in connection with the details of nature. Just because it is so abstract, however, monotheism cannot yield any permanent satisfaction, and must give place to a strictly scientific explanation. But it cannot do this immediately — a transition stage must intervene; and this is the stage of *metaphysics*. Metaphysics drops, to be sure, the idea of a personal will; but it substitutes therefor, not positive law, but metaphysical essences and powers, which are mere abstract repetitions of the earlier gods, the dry bones of the living creatures of poetry. They furnish in consequence no real explanation, but are only the phenomena over again with an abstract name substituted for the concrete facts. To the metaphysical stage succeeds the final goal of human thought, the *positive* stage, which occupies itself solely with the facts of experience and the laws which they reveal, without making the impossible attempt to penetrate behind phenomena to the unknown real.

The first part of Comte's task is to sum up and organize the laws of the various sciences. This organization he tries to carry out in a definite hierarchy of the sciences, beginning with the most abstract — mathematics — and passing, in the order of greater and greater complexity, through astronomy, physics, chemistry, to biology, each science basing itself on, and making use of, the results of the science beneath it. Meanwhile there remains one great class of facts which has not been touched — the facts of the social life; and here we come to the center of Comte's doctrine, and that which gives him his historical importance. He proposes to crown the whole system of the sciences by founding a new science — the positive science of society, or *sociology*. Not only will he thus bring within the scope of positive or scientific method the entire round of experienced facts, but he will also give to what has preceded its unity and rational justification. For as each group of sciences enters into the next higher group, so the whole science of physical nature gets its reason and end in the service of humanity. Here we have not, to be sure, an objective and absolute principle of unity based on the inner essence of reality, which we have seen to be unknowable. But at least we have a subjective and practical basis. That basis is humanity, whose life we can modify because we know its laws; and it is for the service of humanity that science exists. Humanity is our highest concept. Whatever the foundation of things may be in itself, however indifferent or hostile to human progress, at least things may up to a point be compelled to enter the service of man. And only in so far as knowledge can turn the laws of things into an instrument of service need we pay them any attention.

2. The object of Comte in his Sociology is in a way the same as that of Hegel — to discover definite laws in the development of social experience. With Comte there is the added purpose, however, of showing how these laws point to a more adequate social state in the future. He is trying, that is, to get a satisfactory social *ideal*, not as an arbitrary construction, but as the carrying-out of those tendencies and forces that are already at work in society. The general form of the result which he reaches is already involved in the principle of the three stages; he has now to elaborate this in connection with the actual facts of the social life.

Briefly the connection is as follows: The theological stage represents the socialization of the human race. For any real social union a certain community of belief is required, and this common doctrine is furnished by theology, least adequately in its earlier and fetichistic stage, more completely in its latest or monotheistic. In this grade of social attainment there are however certain defects involved. To begin with, the close union of the temporal with the spiritual power, universal in the earlier stages of society, is detrimental to the best interests of the latter. The great function of the priesthood is to supply those moral and social sanctions which keep society together; but this necessitates intellectual gifts that are not identical with the gifts called for by the immediate work of social administration. Unless the two offices, therefore, are kept distinct, the more insistent and practical needs will prevail; and this will involve the supremacy of a lower order of intelligence inadequate to its spiritual functions.

It was the great merit of the Middle Ages — the one period of history to which Comte looks back with admiration — that they brought about the separation of these two functions, giving to the priesthood a supremacy in the way of guidance and advice, while secular affairs, matters of action, were handed over to a secular power. In this way the conflict between men of action and men of thought was reconciled. Moral and intellectual eminence could now win position, as it could not expect to do in the practical field. At the same time morals by being released from service to this or that particular state — where they were bound always to be dominated by the military spirit necessary for self-preservation — were given a general and universal character; and this in turn reacted upon politics and helped to moralize it.

But while this separation of the spiritual and secular powers in the Middle Ages represents on the formal side a true ideal, the work of supplying adequate material out of which the spiritual power should construct those common beliefs on which social unity must rest was not one for which monotheism was prepared. It could only be accomplished on the basis of facts so compelling as to insure their general acceptance; which means that only Positivism is equal to the task. Before however this desirable result could come about there had to be a preliminary clearing of the ground; and this is the work of the metaphysical stage, which corresponds to the period of the Enlightenment. It is by reference to such a negative task that all the characteristic dogmas of the Enlightenment have to be judged; they represent a denial of this or that aspect of the old social order based on theology. Here belong the doctrines of the right of private judgment, of universal equality, of government as a police power and nothing more. It is only because the Enlightenment is in antagonism with the ancient order that it is led to represent *all* government as being the enemy of society. So its emphasis on liberty of conscience is merely the abstract expression of that temporary state in which the human mind was left by the decay of the theological philosophy; it has no further validity after a more adequate social philosophy appears to supply a new positive content of belief.

The result of the negative or metaphysical stage is that a division arises between the heart and the intellect; and this must continue until the intellect shows itself capable of producing a new system that can sustain the social order more securely than the fictions of theology had done, and more completely satisfy the affections and spiritual aspirations of man. The reconciliation is found in Positivism. In opposition to the individualistic dogmas of the Enlightenment, Positivism goes back for its ideal to the Middle Ages. Like the Middle Ages it insists upon the need for an independent spiritual power to formulate the doctrines on which society is to be founded and morality based. But these doctrines are no longer theological; they are the outcome of science. To regenerate social doctrine there has to be raised up out of the midst of anarchy a new spiritual authority which, after having disciplined the human intellect and reconstructed morals, will without violence become the basis of a final system of human society.

With knowledge placed thus upon a positive basis, "freedom of conscience" can no longer have any justification. When social questions are given scientific treatment liberty of conscience is as much out of place as it is, for example, in astronomy or physics. There are few people who consider themselves fitted to sit in judgment on an astronomical problem; can it be supposed that the most important and most delicate of questions, with which in the nature of things only a small number of highly trained intellects are capable of dealing, are to be abandoned to the arbitrary and variable decisions of the least competent minds? A dissolution of the social state would follow if this were allowed. Social order must ever be incompatible with a perpetual discussion of the foundations of society. The convergence of minds requires a renunciation by the greater number of their rights of individual inquiry on subjects about which they are not qualified to judge, and which require more than any others a real and permanent agreement. The spiritual power in the new society is consequently to be in the hands of a priestly guild made up of the highest order of intellects, and prosecuting the work of science not on its own account — specialism in science is forbidden — but in the interests of humanity. Such a priesthood is preserved from all temptation to prostitute its position by being entirely removed from civil power, and held strictly to its function of moral influence and good advice.

What next is to be the constitution on the civil side? Here another principle comes into play, which likewise is involved in the survey of social development. This development has been a progress from a *military* to an *industrial* basis. The military organization necessarily comes first in time; the growth of industry presupposes the existence of a considerable social attainment such as could not have taken place till isolated families had been connected by the pursuits of war. War too has laid the foundation for the virtues of regularity and discipline; while slavery, the consequence of war, gives rise directly to habits of industry. But with its work accomplished, a military civilization must give way to an industrial.

In this new society, when it is placed consciously and completely on an industrial basis, the "equality" of the Revolution will find no place. Since society is an organism, different members have different parts to play; and thus necessarily they have different degrees of value, and cannot claim equal rewards for their services. And as in the sciences, the principle of subordination can only be that of the degree of generality. The more particular the industrial function, the greater the subordination; the more general it is, and the more it involves a coördination of activities, the higher the rank which the wielder assumes. The logical consequence is a capitalistic régime headed by "captains of industry" and culminating in the banker, who, as exercising the most general function of all, is the leader of society on the side of its active work. In this general organization all workers will find their place, and so all distinction between public and private functions will be dropped

The dangers of this capitalism are to be avoided by the growing moralization of society, by the moral influence which a disinterested priesthood will exert, and by the power on the part of labor to refuse coöperation — peaceful strikes. The positive foundation given to the laws of conduct will exercise a compulsion unknown before; moral rules will have acquired a new energy and tenacity when they rest on a clear understanding of the influence which the actions and the tendencies of each individual must exercise on human life. The mere fact that each man is consciously working for the general welfare of society will arouse a new enthusiasm. Other men would feel, if their labor were but systematized, what the private soldier feels in the discharge of his humblest duty — the dignity of public service and the honor of a share in the general economy. The priests and the workers will be natural allies, and their union will be enough to counteract the selfish tendencies of the civil power and keep it true to the service of humanity.

3. So much for the earlier form of Comte's philosophy. In later years he lost much of the sanity of his earlier views, and attempted to convert his philosophy into a religion of humanity. Unable to satisfy the longings of the heart by truth, Comte was led to substitute for this poetry. The *Grand Être* — Humanity — is worshiped as the mediator between the outer world and man and the real author of the benefits for which thanks were formerly given to God — a worship to which was added that of the earth as the Great Fetich, and of space as the Great Medium. An elaborate and fanciful ritual was introduced to give impressiveness to this worship. Nor was this a matter of option merely; the paternalism always implicit in Comte's thought comes more and more to the front in a rigid subordination of the members of the new society to every whim of the High Priest of Humanity. On this side Comte's thought has had but little influence.

LITERATURE

Comte, *Positive Philosophy*. Translation by Harriet Martineau.

Mill, *Comte and Positivism*.

Caird, *The Social Philosophy and Religion of Comte*.

Watson, *Outline of Philosophy*.

Fiske, *Darwinism and other Essays*.

Mackintosh, *From Comte to Benjamin Kidd*.

Martineau, *Essays*.

Martineau, *Types of Ethical Theory*.

Morley, *Auguste Comte* (in *Critical Miscellanies*).

Levy-Bruhl, *Philosophy of Auguste Comte*.

§ 40. *Utilitarianism. Bentham, the Mills*

1. *Bentham.* — In England the early part of the nineteenth century is marked by the growing ascendency of that type of thought to which Hegel had been most violently opposed. Its theoretical basis is the psychological individualism of the previous age. This individualism continually is moving toward the "social," but it does this without any thoroughgoing reconstruction of its premises; the justification of the social character of man is found in empirical considerations brought to light in the first instance by psychological analysis, and later on by consequences implicit in the new scientific theory of evolution.

The former tendency is that which goes by the name of Utilitarianism. Utilitarianism was primarily an ethics, but an ethics in which the good of particular men is distinctly subordinated to a political and social interest. As a distinct school of thought it takes its start from *Jeremy Bentham* (1748–1832). Bentham was himself not primarily a philosopher, or even an ethicist in the narrow sense; his interest lay in the matter of legal and legislative reform. He sets out, to be sure, from the nominalistic thesis that all abstract or general terms are purely fictitious and verbal entities, and that the only thing that actually is real is the particular instance. But in saying this he is not really concerned with the problem of universals as a philosophical speculation; what he wants is to remove a very real obstacle to the work of the reformer — the readiness of the human mind, that is, to be impressed by glittering generalities and eulogistic terms — the fig leaves for covering the unseemly parts of the mind — while losing sight of the concrete facts out of which such terms were originally derived.

It is in this light that we are to interpret accordingly the fundamental principle of the utilitarian ethics — that pleasure, or the avoidance of pain, is the sole end of man's action and the sole content of human good. Talk about liberty, justice, honor, patriotism, and you may mean anything or nothing; it is only when you get down to particular consequences in the way of actual and individual satisfactions that you are in sight of a real standard

by which to determine the value of laws and social institutions.
The "greatest happiness of the greatest number" is thus the social
test of what is morally defensible in conduct, and the true method
is a "felicific calculus" which takes account not only of the intensity and duration of pleasures, but of their certainty, propinquity,
purity, fecundity and extent; the ablest moralist will be he who
best calculates the maximum of happiness, and the most virtuous
man he who most successfully applies right calculation to conduct.
On this showing duty, or obligation, naturally takes a second place;
if the word "ought" be admissable at all, Bentham remarks, it
"ought" to be banished from the vocabulary of morals. The only
meaning duty properly carries is in terms of penalties or sanctions;
that is my duty to do which I am liable to be punished according to
law for not doing.

To the test which settles the goodness or badness of an act by its
concrete results for human happiness — utility meaning of course
usefulness for bringing these pleasant results about — there are, so
Bentham thinks, only two alternatives. An ethical theory which
does not accept utility must either say that *un*happiness is good —
which is the principle of asceticism — or else that the good is anything for which I, or anybody else, happens to feel a sentiment of liking or approval. It is this last "principle of caprice," in the form
either of a despotic forcing of my special preference on other men or
of an anarchical acceptance of all sorts of contradictory preferences,
under which most of the historical theories of ethics fall; and it is
sufficiently condemned by the mere statement of its nature.

A further conclusion drawn from the utility criterion is that the
goodness of an act depends entirely on its intention, and not upon
its motive. By "intention" Bentham means the entire group of
objective consequences aimed at; by a "motive" he means to
distinguish the *cause* of the intention as a desire for this or that
particular sort of pleasure moving the will to action. The value of
a motive is itself entirely dependent on the consequences of the act.
Thus benevolence is not virtuous when it gratifies a benevolent motive — by giving alms to beggars for example — in a way that really
harms the recipient or society at large; and on the same showing

we cannot morally condemn malevolence in the cases, somewhat rare indeed, where it performs a public service, as when personal animosity prompts a man to bring to justice an enemy who has committed a crime.   That the object of approval or condemnation is not the motive is further shown by the fact that the same motive may be the source of various acts differing in moral quality; thus the abolition of the slave trade and the tortures of the Inquisition might both be said to spring from the motive of benevolence.   In fact we might even say that, *as such*, every motive is a good motive, since it never aims at anything but pleasure, and since in so far as a thing is pleasant it is good.

Bentham's primary interest lay, as has been said, in the work of reforming English law along more rational lines.   Meanwhile experience made it clear to him that before this had much chance of being accomplished a preliminary task would have to be undertaken.   This was the task of reforming that stronghold of the "sinister interests" which could be counted on to stand out against reform — government, namely.   The problem as he saw it was in substance this: how are we to get rid of private and class interests in men in authority — interests hostile to the general welfare?   On Bentham's own showing men are fundamentally selfish; and as every one loves power and wealth he will, if given power over others, naturally and necessarily exploit them for his selfish ends.   The only radical remedy is to remove the distinction between rulers and ruled by investing sovereignty in the people themselves.   A pure democracy is indeed in modern times impossible; but by letting people choose their representatives, and then by binding these representatives so closely as to give them no opportunity to betray their masters, an approximate identity of interest can be secured. The political ideal of the Utilitarians therefore lay, first in the direction of extending the ballot, and then in originating devices that should subject representatives as strictly as possible to popular control.

2. *James Mill.* — In terms of Bentham's special problem, for which morality has to do not with a man's private life but with the action of society in order to protect its interests, the method of a

calculus of specific consequences in the way of pleasure can make out a very good case for itself. But as a complete theory of morals it has several vulnerable points. Bentham for instance never very seriously attempted to explain how, if psychologically a man is concerned only with getting the utmost pleasure for himself, we are entitled to set up the greatest happiness of the greatest number as a moral standard. It was left to some of his successors to try to fill up the logical gaps which his opponents were quick to seize upon, and to render his hedonism somewhat more acceptable to the natural temper of the moralist.

Bentham's most important immediate disciple was *James Mill.* Mill's chief work in the field of theory was to give to Bentham's doctrine a more adequate psychological foundation by endeavoring to show in detail how every item of man's mental furniture — and this of course includes his ethical approvals — can be reduced to a complex of Locke's simple ideas associated in various ways. The principle in particular of which he makes use is that of an "inseparable association" that may grow up between things that are not connected by nature; the stock illustration is that of the miser for whom money, which originally is important only for what it will buy, takes on the form of an end interesting and valuable in itself. The practical importance which this has for Mill is of course its service in getting rid of obstinate moral prejudices which are immune to rational interpretation and reconstruction; if a man has only to appeal to an immediate intuition that such and such a thing is right or wrong, the possibilities of social argument, and so of social reform, are blocked at the start. "The notion" says J. S. Mill, "that truths external to the mind may be known by intuition or consciousness independently of observation or experience is, I am persuaded, in these times the great intellectual support of false doctrines and bad institutions. By the aid of this theory every inveterate belief and every intense feeling is enabled to dispense with the obligation of justifyng itself by reason, and is erected into its own self-sufficient voucher and justification. There never was such an instrument devised for consecrating all deep-seated prejudices." To show that such beliefs are capable of being reduced to particular connections of ideas, and have in them therefore nothing sacred or compelling, is the first service that the associationist psychology conceived itself to be performing.

But beside this negative value, the doctrine has another and more positive side. If early association can produce the intense conviction which we now observe in undesirable beliefs, then, if rightly controlled, it might be equally effective in leading to a more salutary issue. It has very generally been objected to schemes of social regeneration that they may be ideally desirable, but that they are impracticable so long as human nature remains what it is. Very well, the Utilitarian in effect replies; but what is human nature? A complex of particular associations of ideas. But these you can easily conceive changed. Accordingly the association theory points to one ultimate panacea for human ills — Education. Education properly conducted is capable of almost anything; and society has therefore in its own hands the power of creating the social material to make possible its ideals of social justice.

3. *J. S. Mill.* — Mill's actual treatment of ethics is decidedly dogmatic. He is so sure that the way has at last been found for freeing ethics from authority that he is not disposed to enter sympathetically into possible objections; most of these did not appeal strongly to his own severely unsentimental type of mind. His son however, *John Stuart Mill*, was less oblivious to the deficiencies in Bentham's standpoint, and his contribution to ethics takes the form of an attempt to obviate some of these, while still remaining true to the fundamental principles which Bentham and his father had laid down.

John Mill is on the whole the most influential English philosopher belonging to the middle period of the nineteenth century. Subjected by his father to a very strenuous course of education on associationist principles, he was able while still a young man to take his place among the recognized intellectual leaders of the day. His most permanent contribution to philosophy is probably his *System of Logic* — the first thoroughgoing attempt to do for the inductive logic of scientific inquiry what Aristotle had accomplished for logic on its formal side.

In ethics his work had to do, generally speaking, with the attempt to find a place within the framework of Utilitarian doctrine for those feelings and sentiments which make man more than a creature aiming at the utmost pleasure for himself, in this way rendering it more acceptable to that idealistic strain with which Mill had decidedly more natural sympathy than his predecessors, and which had by no means been eradicated by his father's rigorous training. Owing largely to a nervous breakdown in early life during which his customary interests had gone stale, he had come to feel the insufficiency of the associationist machinery for building up pleasure associations strong enough to be depended on in crises. Any connection of ideas that can be made can also be broken; and this insecurity is, to say the least, not lessened by the habit of psychological analysis. Mill thought he had found an antidote in the "natural" feelings elicited by poetry and by human social relationships; and thereafter he showed a constant disposition to mellow the Utilitarian creed by trying to take some account of them as well. Thus into ethics he introduces, along with the quantitative differences which alone Bentham had recognized, the notion of a differing "quality" in pleasures also; some pleasures, though they may be less intense, are "higher," and these the intelligent man who is in a position to know what both are like will prefer as suited to a certain sense of dignity or elevation in human nature which he does not want to violate.

Mill's change of emphasis shows most clearly in a new spirit which appears in his attitude toward the social ends which always remain his ultimate concern. A considerable part of the practical effectiveness of the Utilitarian movement was due to its alliance with the new political economy which Adam Smith in his *Wealth of Nations* had started, and which had been carried forward by Malthus and David Ricardo. This in its inception was a protest against the interference of government in industrial affairs; and its general outcome had been to exalt the principle of free competition leading to the survival of the industrially most fit. As a consequence the economists and their Utilitarian allies were to be found arrayed not only on the side of free trade against protection and in opposition to bureaucracy in general, but also against the growing tendency to correct by legislative action abuses due to the exploitation of labor, as well as against the disposition on the part of the working classes to improve their conditions by forming unions.

To the general principle of individualism Mill himself remained true; indeed his *Essay on Liberty* is still its classical expression. But he rests his case not on industrial benefits, but on the value of freedom to man's dignity as a human being, and to society through the need for free experiment in living in order to counteract the cramping effects of custom and authority. And this more human emphasis led him to an increasing sympathy with the new demands for social justice, and to a large modification of the *laissez faire* attitude toward "socialistic" measures such as the more orthodox Utilitarians were engaged in combating.

LITERATURE

Bentham, *A Fragment on Government, Introduction to the Principles of Morals and Legislation.*

Mill, James, *Essay on Government, Analysis of the Human Mind.*

Mill, J. S., *System of Logic, On Liberty, Utilitarianism, Auguste Comte and Positivism.*

Stephen, *The English Utilitarians.*

Albee, *History of English Utilitarianism.*

Courtney, *The Metaphysics of J. S. Mill.*

Douglas, *J. S. Mill.*

Green, *Works.*

Seth, *The Philosophical Radicals.*

Watson, *Outline of Philosophy.*

Watson, *Hedonistic Theories.*

Sorley, *Ethics of Naturalism.*

Courtney, *Life of J. S. Mill.*

§ 41. *Evolution. Darwin, Spencer*

1. *Darwin.* — The scientific doctrine whose philosophical results in the last century have been most far-reaching sprang from English soil. It is not the purpose here to describe in detail the

theory of evolution; in its general outlines it is now familiar to every one. The old conception of God which places him outside a world which he influences only arbitrarily and miraculously, and to which therefore he has a direct relation only in so far as we get beyond the sphere of natural law, had made a stand on the existence of organisms. It had claimed that here, at least, an outside interference has obviously taken place. For the different organs — the eye for example, or the hand — are clearly designed to perform their various functions; and design implies an outside designer, an intelligent cause. Each separate species, then, must be regarded as created outright by an act of God.

To *Charles Darwin* belongs the merit of having brought the world of organic life, as previous science had brought the inorganic world, under the reign of natural law, by pointing out a *vera causa* which goes a long way at any rate toward accounting for the origin of species without reference to such a miraculous agency. It is a fact that no organism is an exact reproduction of a preceding organism; there are always minute variations in one direction or another from the parent forms. It is also a fact that some of these variations are likely to be more helpful to the animal than others; some will be in a direction to prove of advantage to it in dealing with its environment, while others will be useless or positively detrimental. Now if the world were an easy place to get along in, if there were food in plenty for all and no rivalry, this would not be a matter of much consequence; but such is not the case. Vastly greater numbers of all kinds of animal life come into the world than can be supported in it. There is as a result a continual struggle for existence, and in the natural course of things it is the weaker individuals — the ones, that is, less adapted to their environment — that go to the wall.

But here we have all the data for an explanation of the existing adaptation of organisms without the need of having recourse to an external designer. Grant that variations are constantly taking place, some of which are fitted to give the possessor a slight advantage in the struggle for existence; then this more favored individual is likely to survive at the expense of his brothers and sisters. And if, as our knowledge of heredity would suggest, these inborn variations are transmitted to the animal's descendants, the basis is laid for a progressive development which, given time enough, might result in the highly specialized forms of the present day. It is no longer necessary to say, for example, that animals in the north have fur *in order to* protect them from the cold; they are protected from the cold *because* they have fur. In this way the whole aspect of the organic world has changed. Instead of having a number of distinct and permanent species which, if they are looked at simply by themselves, seem too complex and teleological to be accounted for as a purely natural product, we have a continuous stream of process in which each step is connected with the rest by a series of slight changes, and where each organ therefore is to be explained genetically by reference to the whole development which here reaches a temporary climax. And to this universal law of development man is of course no exception.

The theory of evolution was left by Darwin still incomplete. The importance of natural selection as an agency is now indeed generally admitted, but also it is widely believed that it does not explain all the facts. For one thing, it is plain that selection does not *cause* advance in the first place. Selection can only take place on the basis of an advance already made; and so we have to ask the further question: What is the cause and nature of the original variations that are afterwards selected out, as well as of the factor of heredity which Darwin also took for granted. Evolution is therefore not necessarily identical with Darwinism. That Darwin was right however in maintaining that there has been a gradual development of organic forms may now be taken as established; and the recognition has changed the whole direction of human thought. Not only in the biological sciences, but also in the realm of human experience, the principle has been applied with results that have put a new face on all our knowledge.

2. *Spencer.* — It was inevitable that the new emphasis should be given a more general philosophical expression. An attempt in this direction was made in Germany by the biologist *Ernst Haeckel*, whose *Riddle of the Universe* attained wide popularity. Such a

motive had its most comprehensive and influential expression however in the English thinker, *Herbert Spencer*. Spencer was born in 1820. His academic training was slight; his education did not proceed along the conventional lines but followed the direction of his natural preferences, which were scientific and sociological rather than literary or historical. In his earlier years he engaged actively in the profession of engineering. But intellectual interests became more and more compelling; and finally, as the underlying principle which had been present in his thinking from the start gradually became clearer to his mind, he determined deliberately to devote his life to expounding it. The outline of a Synthetic Philosophy was drawn up, to whose working out Spencer was to devote over forty years of his life. The work was carried on under many discouragements. At times he was at the point of being compelled to abandon it through lack of money; and throughout he was handicapped by a chronic semi-invalidism brought on by overwork. But the task was finally completed, substantially on the lines laid down at the beginning. Spencer died in 1903.

There are two characteristics of Spencer's intellectual temperament on which the special character of his philosophy largely depends. One is the tendency, alike natural to him and developed by his father's early training, to look for causes — natural causes — of everything he came across. The second characteristic was his remarkable powers of generalization; he had an unusual gift for penetrating to the common features of apparently disconnected facts. For exercising these capacities, he had as a young man come into contact with a relatively new idea — the idea of development. Of course the idea was as such not really new; even in biology, the starting-point and center of modern evolutionary doctrine, it had been formulated in a well-known hypothesis — that of Lamarck. But by scientists as a whole it was not yet taken very seriously. Spencer came in contact with this biological theory in a book intended to controvert it; but his sympathy remained rather with the view he found criticised. Not that he had any special competency to solve the biological problem; it was simply a leaning due to his natural bias. Organisms *must* have developed, he argued, because the only other alternative is a supernatural creation which is the denial of scientific intelligibility. Even before Darwin's theory had convinced scientists that, as a scientific explanation, evolution furnishes the most satisfactory account of the origin of species, Spencer had accordingly accepted the idea in its broader form as, in an almost self-evident way, true of things generally, and had used it to throw light on a variety of problems.

Meanwhile there was growing up in his mind the recognition that, if development rules the world, there must be laws which hold concerning it that are of universal application. This evolution of the Law of Evolution was a gradual and somewhat laborious affair, which finally took shape in the famous Spencerian formula: Evolution is a continuous change from indefinite, incoherent homogeneity, to definite, coherent heterogeneity of structure and function, through successive differentiations and integrations.

The meaning of this is not as formidable as might appear on the surface. Eliminating secondary matters, the main point is simply this: that development involves on the one hand a growing specialization and division of labor, while, on the other, these specialized organs and functions are bound more and more intimately together to form an organic unity or system. This is the sum and substance of the evolutionary philosophy. Spencer tries to show, also, not only that this is true as an empirical generalization, but that it is necessarily true. After reaching it inductively he turns around, following his favorite method, and attempts to prove that as a deduction from a certain — to him — self-evident truth — the law of the persistence of force — this is the course that events *had* to take. Without stopping to consider the cogency of this deduction we may simply ask wherein the value of the formula consists.

And it seems evident it cannot lay claim to settling all the problems of philosophy; to suppose that the universe has been accounted for when you have said that things are all the time becoming more complex and more unified is to have a very limited notion of the philosopher's task. It is a large and useful generalization; but a generalization never explains anything. It is not even a true cause of certain particular phenomena, as Darwin's law is. Where its real and positive significance lies is mainly in the shift of emphasis which it effected. It brings to the front an immensely important idea that had been neglected. While development does not settle the problems of philosophy — on the contrary it creates new ones — it does change their face; and no question can be settled finally without reference to it. Spencer was very largely influential in making this idea a power in modern thought, and thereby giving a new impulse to every sphere of intellectual activity. He was fortunate in becoming possessed of an illuminating conception just at the moment when forces were preparing for its favorable reception; and by conceiving the new principle in a universal way he came, even more than Darwin, to be regarded as its high priest. This impression which he was able to make on his contemporaries was immensely strengthened by the remarkable fertility with which he was able to apply the principle to the facts of experience in detail. Probably no man in his generation started a greater number of fruitful scientific theories in the most varied fields than Spencer. Many, indeed most, of these theories are now recognized as at best only partial; but they had the merit of starting inquiry along lines that have led to permanent results.

Spencer's scientific work was in four main fields — Biology, Psychology, Sociology and Ethics. Omitting the first, we may turn briefly to his *Psychology*. The thing of chief importance is, once more, the new point of view for regarding the psychological life. This is primarily a *growth;* and so it can be best understood genetically, in the light of its history. Taken thus, the apparently so diverse aspects of the developed consciousness can be traced back to simple undifferentiated forms of functioning. This genetic point of view, and the corresponding emphasis upon the relationship of mind to the developing biological organism, has had far-reaching effects upon modern psychology. Of Spencer's psychological doctrines in particular, perhaps the one with the most direct bearing on philosophy is that which has to do with the much discussed problem of innate ideas. Hitherto the empiricists, in denying the existence of metaphysically valid innate ideas, had tended to ignore the fact that actually human beings do not enter the world without any bias whatever, a mere sheet of blank paper on which experience writes its lessons. We have ways of reacting, even in the mental life, which are too general and necessary to be easily explained through the accidents and uncertainties of each man's personal experience. The theory of evolution enabled Spencer, as he thought, to effect a compromise between the warring schools. He agreed with the intuitionalists that each individual man does find himself possessed of ways of apprehending the world which go back of any experience in his own lifetime. But on the other hand this does not mean that such ideas are to be accepted as a divine and indubitable revelation independent of all experience. To experience they go back, and in terms of experience they can be explained, as the empiricists maintained; but it is the experience of our ancestors, not ourselves. Innate in us, acquired in the race — this Spencer thought would combine the relative truth of both sides.

The biological conception Spencer applies likewise to sociology. Social institutions also are not made; they grow. The organic conception of society is now a commonplace, and Spencer did much to bring this about. Here again one aspect only of his social doctrine need be mentioned. There are two opposing tendencies in modern social movements. One is the tendency to look to the State for interference in behalf of desirable social ends. The other is inclined to restrict such activity on the part of the State, assigning to it police functions while leaving all further initiative to private citizens. Of this individualism Spencer is the chief modern representative. Primarily it is with him a matter of temperament. His natural independence and assertiveness of character make the thought of State interference intensely disagreeable, as an interference with his rights. The most fundamental moral right of a man is the right to do as he pleases, unrestricted by anything save the equal rights of others to the same freedom. If man were a perfectly moral being, he would voluntarily restrict himself to such limits. But a part of his inheritance from a primitive state, where egoistic self-assertion was necessary, is that tendency to disregard others' rights which constitutes an imperfection in his adjustment to present conditions; and so long as the existing maladjustment lasts, there is need of an organ to bring about the mutual forbearance that society demands. This organ is found in what we call government.

But here Spencer is able to get into connection with his formula, and lend to his natural bias the weight of a concordance with his philosophy. In two ways he justifies his individualism. First and chiefly, according to the law of Evolution functions become more and more specialized in definite organs. Now government is such a special organ. Its one definite and fundamental work is to prevent mutual aggression. For that it is necessary; other social needs can be met by private initiative and association. By the general law of things it ought to confine itself, therefore, to its special work. If it gets beyond these bounds, and tries to do the work for which there is other machinery, it will not only do this poorly, but it will lose that much energy for the proper performance of its own special task.

There is another way in which the thing appeals to Spencer — a way that brings to light one of the presuppositions which, without his trying adequately to prove them, form the background of his whole system. This is the assumption that things work out in the evolving universe by purely natural laws with which it is quite impossible for man successfully to interfere. Natural laws represent for Spencer not merely facts to be recognized, but to some extent, also, ideals that have a claim upon us. As one of his friends once said, "The laws of nature are to him what revealed religion is to us." To attempt to interfere with them is not only foolish and meddling; it is almost impious as well. By reason of this attitude, which it may be noticed is by no means a necessary consequence of evolution, he was led still further to discount the value of human efforts for remedying social conditions. Things will improve only when, in their own good time, the impersonal laws of nature work themselves out; our interference only helps to keep alive those who are socially unfit, and whose elimination in favor of a higher type is nature's method of advance. Evils can only rectify themselves by a self-adjusting process, which we cannot hasten, though apparently we may hinder it.

In the *Ethics* the idea of development is still further applied, this time to the facts of the moral experience. Here may be mentioned three points in particular : the use once more of the distinction between the individual and the race experience to settle the quarrel over the so-called moral sense, or moral intuitions; the explanation of conscience as having its origin in social commands and restrictions; and the attempt to arbitrate between egoism and altruism by making the moral life a composite of the two. A more general point is the application of evolution in the criticism of Utilitarianism. Spencer agreed with the Utilitarians that pleasure and avoidance of pain represent in a way the end of life. But he held Utilitarianism faulty for its inability to lay down any rules for the attainment of this end save those of pure empiricism — finding out by trial. To be a science, ethics must be able to deduce its results; and for this there is needed a more objective statement of the end than the mere feeling of pleasure supplies. Spencer found this in the evolutionary conception of adjustment to environment. Such an adjustment involves natural laws; by discovering these laws we can determine beforehand therefore what course of conduct will secure happiness, since happiness is to be found only in a perfectly adjusted functioning. As such a perfection of adjustment does not now exist, it follows that the principles of a scientific ethics apply, strictly and without modification, not to our present conduct, but to a future society where the process of evolution shall have reached an equilibrium. When such a state shall have been attained our troubles will be over, the idea of duty will disappear as no longer needed, and we shall all do the right thing by instinctive preference.

In conclusion we may turn back to a point to which reference already has been made. Any final estimate of Spencer's philosophy as a reasoned system must be considerably affected by the fact that its main outcome is an empirical generalization, which ignores in so far most of the fundamental problems that philosophy has been accustomed to consider. The recognition of development is compatible, that is, with a variety of opposing philosophies. Spencer has it is true an answer to give to these further problems, or to many of them; but his answer for the most part rests rather too strongly on a temperamental attitude which is seldom fairly brought to the light and scrutinized on its merits. This attitude is that to which the name of Naturalism has been given. Naturalism means that the natural laws of science are taken as everywhere the final word of explanation; in particular, man and man's ideals are purely natural products in the sense that they can be fully accounted for in terms which involve nothing not already found in those physical processes out of which they spring. More generally, the complex can always be reduced without remainder to the simple, the higher to the lower. This may very well be true; but it needs a more adequate proof than it ever occurred to Spencer to give.

Only at one point does he really face ultimate questions; and his Agnosticism is not his strongest claim to philosophical attention. It is possible, so he thinks, to show that by the nature of our minds we are necessarily shut out from a knowledge of ultimate reality; we are as incompetent to think it as a deaf man to understand sounds. The proof of our incapacity is briefly this: we can think only by relating one thing to another; but Absolute reality, by definition, is not relative, but absolute, and is in consequence beyond our grasp. On the other hand an Absolute is implied in all our relative knowledge even, since there would be no sense in calling this relative were there not something absolute to which it is contrasted. Although we cannot then think the Absolute, we have a sort of vague, indefinite assurance that it really exists in some unknown form. That which comes closest to a description of this unknown reality Spencer finds in the term Force.

The Unknowable supplies what for Spencer is the only possible religion for the modern man of science. Historical religions are of course subject to a naturalistic explanation, and are discredited by their origin. But hidden away in all positive religions there is an irreducible minimum which science does not touch. This is the feeling of awe in the presence of the mysteries of the universe. If anything, science tends to emphasize the ultimate mystery of existence. A feeling of awe, then, in the face of the unknowable force from which all things spring, is the final form that religion is destined to take.

LITERATURE

Spencer, *Synthetic Philosophy.*
Darwin, *Origin of Species. Descent of Man.*
Huxley, *Works.*
Wallace, *Darwin.*
Romanes, *Darwin and after Darwin.*
Schurman, *Ethical Import of Darwinism.*
Fiske, *Darwinism and other Essays.*
Watson, *Outline of Philosophy.*
Ritchie, *Darwin and Hegel.*
Bowne, *Philosophy of Herbert Spencer.*
Collins, *Epitome of the Synthetic Philosophy.*
Hudson, *The Philosophy of Herbert Spencer.*
Royce, *Herbert Spencer.*
McPherson, *Spencer and Spencerism.*
Thomson, *Herbert Spencer.*

§ 42. *Idealism*

1. *Lotze and Fechner.* — After the death of Hegel, the idealism which he represented began almost at once to split up into a number of opposing tendencies. Among the more hard-headed Hegelians of the so-called Left there began a movement toward a naturalism that was distinctly unsympathetic toward religion; here we may note for example the application of a rationalistic criticism to the beginnings of Christianity by *Friedrich David Strauss* in his famous *Life of Jesus*, and the doctrine of economic determinism into which the progress of the Idea was translated by *Karl Marx*. On the other side there was a considerable group of thinkers with a direct interest in religion — sometimes supplemented by a recognition of the new scientific tendencies — who broke with absolutism, and experimented with a freer and less logically rigorous idealism which should take more account of human personality; reality is still regarded as spiritual in its nature. but insight appealing to a

reasonable analogy is what reveals this to us rather than a necessary logic. Representing this last tendency the most widely influential name is that of *Rudolf Hermann Lotze*. Lotze was among the first to reëmphasize the rights of naturalistic and mechanical explanation in the field of science; but he subordinated these to an ultimate idealism. Perhaps his most significant doctrine is in connection with causality. The conceivability of causal interaction such as is involved in scientific explanation he tried to show would be excluded were the elements really separate, as mere mechanism seems to leave them; the possibility that one thing should influence another is only intelligible in case they are in reality parts of a single whole, states of a unitary being. Thus science itself points to an ultimate monism in the world of nature, which Lotze interprets after the analogy of selfhood. Several influential American thinkers have been followers of Lotze.

In this connection one other name also deserves attention as the representative of a tendency which has reappeared in a great variety of forms in recent philosophy. The formulation of the law of the conservation of energy, one of the outstanding achievements of modern science, had given a new emphasis to the indisposition on the part both of scientists and philosophers to resort to consciousness for explaining bodily actions. If the law is not to be violated, the physical universe forms a closed system in which there is no apparent place for a new influence, such as consciousness would be, that comes in from the outside to modify the result. As a consequence there has been a tendency to accept the doctrine of the automatism of the physical body, and to regard psychical processes as running alongside physical movements without exerting any influence upon them. This is called the doctrine of *psycho-physical parallelism* — a doctrine which has been further strengthened by the tendency of psychology as an empirical science to find a physiological correlate to every aspect of the conscious life.

This parallelism needed however some further explanation; and such an explanation was found by going back to Spinoza and Leibniz. According to both of these philosophies, mind and body are ways of looking at a single ultimate reality; either this reality is unlike them both, or else one series alone is real and the other only an appearance. This last alternative proved the more popular, and it gets an interesting formulation in the German philosopher *Gustav Fechner*. The reality of what we call our body is the conscious life which we immediately experience; it is only the outside observer looking at this who sees it as a material fact. But then we must interpret every physical object in the same way, and find the true being not alone of animals, but of plants and inanimate things, in a conscious life like our own, only less complex. All these minor consciousnesses have their unity in the one great life of God, as the things which are their phenomenal appearances are brought together in the all-embracing unity of scientific law. One of the many recent advocates of this doctrine is *Friedrich Paulsen*.

2. *Green.* — Meanwhile in England idealism in a form much closer to its Hegelian meaning was revived by an important group of thinkers, who used it to combat the hedonism of the Utilitarians and the whole naturalistic tendency which this represented. The most important name here is that of *Thomas Hill Green*. Green sets out to call philosophy back from the empiricism and subjectivism out of which, as Hume supposedly had shown, nothing but scepticism can result. The human mind indubitably possesses knowledge in a variety of fields; it is the business of philosophy to accept this, and to ask what its implications are. Green, following Kant, finds that the possibility of knowledge depends on the presence in our experience of a principle of unity, not identical with the succession of events, through which the flow of feeling is constituted a real "object," and ultimately a universe. This is the very meaning of reality; nothing is real for us that does not enter into the organized unity of such a knowledge system. This disposes of empiricism; knowledge cannot have its origin in an association of sensations, because there is no such thing as a *mere* sensation. A feeling *is* at all only as it is this or that feeling in particular; and it cannot be something in particular except as it is part of a definite relational context involving distinction from, and connection with, other particulars. What we call sensations are

not the original of knowledge, but a relatively late product of analysis by mind.

Green himself is chiefly interested in the consequences this has for ethics and religion. Here again the great enemy is that "naturalism" which takes man primarily as an animal, a secondary product of unintelligent forces; and the answer is in principle the same. Mind cannot be explained by nature, because there would be no natural world were the spiritual principle of the unity of self-consciousness not already presupposed. The world is "real" only for knowledge; and what is necessary to constitute a world cannot therefore be a passive product of this world. We can know a temporal series of events *as* a series only as the facts are held together by something present alike to each of them, and itself, consequently, out of time; and such a timeless principle can never be a result of the process of change. The unity of self-consciousness is not of course the human self, which is only one item in the natural world; it is a universal Consciousness, or God — a consciousness involved in the very possibility of thinking the world of science as a connected whole. With this eternally existing Self our own "true" self is identical, otherwise we should have no explanation of our human capacity for knowing; in knowledge man participates in the actual life of God. The particular human self is thus a compound of the finite and the infinite; it is an animal organism used as the vehicle of an eternally complete consciousness.

This granted, we have left behind hedonism and utilitarianism with its reduction of the moral life to the satisfaction of particular desires. Desires as such are no more real than sensations as such. Before an animal want can represent a conscious desire and motive it must become the presentation of a wanted "object"; and an object already presupposes a connected world, and so involves the presence of that universal spiritual principle which is not an aspect of the natural life at all. Not feeling, but *self-realization*, is the true end of man — the realization of a self whose satisfaction can never be found in any number of events in time, but only in a permanent well-being which does not pass away with this or that transient pleasure. For the same reason man finds his good not in isolation, but only in so far as he is a member of a spiritual community where the self-realization of his fellows is bound up with his own. Moral growth consists in the progressive discovery that the things which, in nature and our fellow-men, and in the institutions of society, at first seem a hindrance to the individual's freedom, are in reality themselves a means to his development — a process which in the end leads beyond man to religion, and to the sense of our identity with the universal Self implicit in the fact of knowledge. It is true we do not know precisely in what this perfect life consists. But the certainty that such a vast and eternal good is somewhere actual is nevertheless an effective agent of progress; it renders us dissatisfied with any existing attainment, and fills us with a divine discontent that keeps us pressing forward.

3. *Bradley.* — For several decades the type of idealism which Green represents exercised a dominant influence on British and American philosophy. In England it was given a peculiar twist by *F. H. Bradley*, whose subtle dialectic made him for a time the most provocative thinker of his day. According to Bradley, the only notion we can form of reality is in terms of "experience" — the sort of thing that comes home to us in immediate feeling; and in the end this experience must be thought of as a *single* experience, the reality which transcends our present state of feeling joining on continuously to its edges and forming with it an immediate feeling whole. So far we have a fairly common type of theory to which various names — panpsychism, pantheism and the like — might be given. The peculiarity of Bradley's position is that in extending explicitly the notion of reality to include feeling as well as thought, he abandons the Hegelian faith in the power of thought, as one special aspect of experience, to grasp reality in its ultimate nature. Thought sets the ideal of a completely rational whole free from self-contradiction — an ideal we must accept and trust if we elect to play the game of thinking at all; and it tells us how in outline its demands are to be met. But also it makes plain to us, through the inevitable self-contradictions into which it falls, that we can reach the goal only by leaving thought as such behind; the truly and completely rational is to be attained only as thought gives up its

self-identity, and is resurrected in a new form as an aspect of a higher unity in which "relations" — thought's special tool — are reabsorbed into the immediacy of feeling.

4. *Royce.* — The influence of Bradley's agnosticism proved relatively transient; the main direction of the idealistic movement still continued along more orthodox lines. Bradley's most influential follower, *Bernard Bosanquet*, returned to an essentially Hegelian faith in the universe as an individual whole of spiritual meaning which is capable, ideally at least, of being given a logical explication. The American philosopher *Josiah Royce* took Bradley's notion of "experience" as opposed to thought more seriously, but without his agnosticism. Reality is knowable as an ultimate and all-inclusive consciousness, or self, into which human selves enter to supply a content. A good share of Royce's thinking centers about the attempt to explain this relationship, and to show how the focussing of reality in human selves is to be understood so as not to give up either their genuine individuality, or their ultimate identity with the more truly individual whole. He started by asking what one means when he says that an idea "intends" or "refers to" an object other than itself; and he finds an answer in the empirical situation where an anticipation is met by some later experience that fulfils it. This implies that thought can know an object, can be sure what really it is pointing at, only in so far as idea and object have come within a single unity of consciousness where they can be compared. Accordingly in order to explain how valid knowledge can be possible we are led to an absolute experience in which all possible objects of thought are concretely realized. Even the possibility of error or mistaken judgment implies such an all-inclusive consciousness; unless thought and its object are actual parts of a larger thought I cannot in any intelligible sense so much as doubt.

To explain how this universal consciousness can be individuated into human selves Royce has recourse to the notion of *will* as aiming at the satisfaction of an unique interest or purpose. A human self is such a plan or interest demanding a specific form of fulfilment; and as a consequence it is not swallowed up and abolished in the divine life, but is essential to the reality and perfection of the whole. In this way the "object of knowledge" gets reinterpreted as a specific end already present implicitly and potentially in my idea, which has its explicit fulfilment in that wider consciousness of the Absolute where both the purpose and its realization coexist.

5. *Croce.* — On the continent the most widely influential reinterpretation of idealism is that of the Italian philosopher *Benedetto Croce.* Croce starts from the assumption, common to the idealistic movement, that reality has no assignable meaning except in terms of what is real for Mind or Spirit — more simply, except as it stands in some significant relation to the life of man. What is new in his philosophy comes largely from a shift of emphasis from logic — the conceptual activity of thought — to certain "cultural" values, more particularly art and history. Croce attempts to show that Mind gets expression at four — and only four — stages or levels of activity. The lowest or basic stage is that of aesthetic intuition — the production of concrete and individual imagery. This is presupposed and given further content in the second or logical stage — the activity of conceptual thinking, of reflection and criticism, whose function it is to bring to light the universal characters implicit in the concrete intuition. The two together constitute the theoretical life. But man also is a being who acts as well as knows; he not only understands reality, but he makes it. This practical activity also has two stages — the economic and the ethical. As knowing presupposes intuiting, so action presupposes knowledge; will independent of knowing is unthinkable. The four stages are the expression of four values — beauty, truth, utility, goodness; and with these values reality is identified. Each of them is a distinctive and concrete expression of Mind, and one is lower than another only in the sense of being a necessary condition of its existence; it is not annulled in a higher stage, as in Hegel's dialectic. Thus, in the life of conduct, goodness does not supplant utility. Utility wills individual ends, while goodness wills universal ones that transcend my individual self-interest; but the goal of ethics is not to leave individual ends behind. We cannot conceive of universal good except in terms of individual good; it is only as

a universal good becomes *my* good that it constitutes an end at all. There is no good action which does not depend on some utility, and no useful action in which goodness is not implicit as a universal meaning.

Croce's influence has been in considerable measure due to the theory of aesthetics implicit in this general construction. The aesthetic value is identical with that image-forming activity of Mind which underlies the possibility of all the rest. In this immediacy of intuition, this absorption in the pure joy of creation which knows as yet no distinction of reality and unreality but which accepts the image just for what it is, beauty as a value consists. "Objects" are not beautiful in themselves; they are extrinsic to the aesthetic quality as such. The work of art is the translation of the artist's inner vision into physical phenomena — color, shape or sounds — and so belongs to the stage of action; beauty itself resides in the artistic intuition, which must be there before it is embodied. The one who enjoys a work of art is thus in his own right an artist. It is his own intuition which he is expressing; in living through the aesthetic experience he is himself creating, by virtue of a fundamental activity of mind in which all share alike. That some men are called artists in a special sense is due only to their ability to enable those of us with lesser gifts to rise to higher reaches of intuition than we could otherwise have done.

The other most distinctive feature of Croce's doctrine is his identification of philosophy with history — history conceived not as a mere record of past events, but as a concrete manifestation of the full reality of experience in a present which retains the meaning of the past and is moving toward the future. The aim of philosophy is to realize and interpret at each stage of history this indwelling life which expresses itself in action. For this reason there is no final or absolute philosophy; Mind is not static, but is an eternal activity of new creation. A problem of philosophy is not therefore something to be answered once for all; it is part of an unending process, with the future constantly posing new questions and calling for new interpretations.

LITERATURE

Lotze, *Microcosmus.*

Green, *Introduction to Hume, Prolegomena to Ethics.*

Caird, J., *Introduction to the Philosophy of Religion.*

Nettleship, *Memoir of T. H. Green.*

Bradley, *Ethical Studies, Principles of Logic, Appearance and Reality.*

Royce, *Religious Aspect of Philosophy, Spirit of Modern Philosophy, World and the Individual.*

Croce, *Aesthetic, History, Logic, Philosophy of the Practical, Conduct of Life.*

Carr, *Philosophy of B. Croce.*

Piccoli, *B. Croce.*

§ 43. *Nietzsche. Bergson. Pragmatism*

1. *Introduction.* — The normal tendency in science and philosophy alike has always been to take the human mind as an instrument which can in general be relied on, when critically employed, to put us in touch with something like the actual truth about the world; otherwise there would not be much point in embarking on the search for truth. Every now and then scepticism had intruded to cast doubt on this assumption; but scepticism is relatively not a natural human state, and it had not exercised very much permanent influence on the course of thought. The rise of the theory of evolution might perhaps have been expected to modify this confidence; if mind is a by-product of a process that has as such no relation to intelligence, its haphazard origin and subordinate status might appear to reflect on its authority. But we should not know the truth about evolution itself if we could not trust the mental tools we have at our disposal. In philosophies of evolution, consequently, mind still holds its own as a trustworthy means of getting at the real facts — the empirical facts at any rate — about the world; the ideas which it uses are sufficiently accurate copies of real causes.

But evolution will at least suggest that mind represents no final goal of nature. Like everything else organic, it has originated for some purpose other than itself; it is an instrument rather than an end. Such a view of intellect has appeared already in Schopenhauer; here thought is a secondary product of the will to live, and must be reinterpreted in the light of its subordinate function. In more recent thinking such a view of thought as instrumental has been rather widely prevalent. Something of this appears even among scientists themselves; the notion of a scientific law has tended to lose its rigidity as a definite mould in which nature's processes are cast — not an unnatural result in view of the rapidity with which "laws" have been discarded and replaced in modern times. A law is rather an hypothesis, a convenient shorthand for ordering the facts and keeping them in mind; it is determined less by the principle of objective truth than by that of an economy of thought, and is to be abandoned therefore as soon as a more useful formula is hit upon. This way of viewing scientific laws appears in various quarters — in the German scientist *Ernst Mach*, the French mathematician *Henri Poincaré*, the Englishman *Karl Pearson*. The interest here still lies in the intellectual field — the field of scientific method. But by interpreting particular laws in terms not of their absolute truth but of their utility, the way is opened to a more radical revaluation of the whole nature of mind or intellect.

2. *Nietzsche.* — Here is perhaps the most convenient place to say a few words about a thinker whose influence — in the field of general culture for the most part rather than among technical philosophers — has been very considerable. *Friedrich Nietzsche's* general philosophical background is the Will of Schopenhauer, intensified and heightened; the essence of reality is Force, expressing itself in what Nietzsche calls, not the Will to Live, but the Will to Power. In this last phrase, interpreted as a certain specific ideal of human character and living, Nietzsche's fundamental interest lies. On its positive side this is the aristocratic ideal of a superabundance of vitality taking form in the creation of artistic beauty — an ideal which he identifies with the early Hellenic ideal of Olympian beauty and power before the Greeks had been corrupted by morals. On the whole its more distinctive character however — the special source of its influence at any rate — lies less in its positive nature than in the things it sets out to discredit and to overthrow.

These are, in brief, everything that approves itself to the average man — morality, religion, progress, truth. Thus Nietzsche rejects utterly all the humanitarian and equalitarian tendencies of the modern state; the only form of state that justifies itself is the despotic rule of the strong — those courageous souls who aim at power and full living for themselves, and who use without scruple their authority to further this. Democracy and socialism, with their talk of liberty and equality and justice, are merely devices whereby the weak, through the unheroic qualities of prudence, cunning and hypocrisy, keep in check their natural masters. Such a state aims to tame men and to turn them into cattle; it encourages mediocrity, an insipid ideal of peace, contentment and security; it is the enemy of all that is exceptional, powerful, all that makes men great. War, not peace, is the soil of the heroic virtues; "you say, A good cause sanctifies even war; but I say, A good war sanctifies every cause." "Life is a well of delight; but when the rabble also drink then all fountains are poisoned."

No more is science and the search for truth worthy of respect; the scientist is an anemic individual who shuts his eyes to everything outside the narrow field of his specialized interest, demanding only peace and quiet for his work — a smug optimist who thinks science justified by its extension of creature comforts to the multitude. In reality there is no such thing as truth; "truth is that kind of error without which a certain sort of living being cannot exist." Every one of our ideas — space, time, causality — is a practical tool which, like everything else, has survived only because it has proved useful in the preservation of the species under particular conditions; it has no more "necessity" than has the species which uses it, and if the conditions change we may look to see ideas changing also.

Most emphatically is this the case with those moral truths or standards which claim authority on the conscience. The new race of men for which Nietzsche aims to prepare the way has indeed what might be called a morality of its own; but it is one that reverses all accepted values. It is a master-morality, whose virtues are exuberance of life, ruthless egoism, arrogance, revenge against equals, hate and anger: it is brave, strong, daring, unscrupulous. It aims to master the passions, but not to destroy or weaken them; the great man is great on account of the freedom with which he gives vent to his passions, and through the still greater power which he manifests in keeping these wild animals in check and placing them at his service. "Not contentment, but more power; not peace at any price, but war; not virtue, but efficiency (virtue in the Renaissance sense, *virtu*, free from all moralic acid)."

What men ordinarily call virtue is just the opposite of this; it is a slave-morality, the morality of weaklings, the product of degeneracy, exhausted vitality, fear. Here everything that elevates the individual above the herd and is a source of fear to his neighbor is henceforth called evil, and a mediocrity of desires attains to moral distinction and honor; to be good, in a word, is to be stupid. Virtues such as modesty, industry, benevolence, chastity are exalted — all of them just so many obstacles in the way of an heroic purpose and a noble existence for oneself; everything well-constituted, proud, high-spirited and beautiful is offensive to the "moral" man. In religion the weakling has created the greatest of his instruments for bringing into subjection those nobler natures which, since he cannot emulate them, he envies and hates. For Christianity in particular Nietzsche entertains the deepest aversion. Impotence that is too feeble to do anything is changed by Christianity into "goodness," ignoble cowardice into humility, submission to those one hates becomes obedience. The God of the Christian is the God of the poor and humble, of love and forgiveness and sympathy, the God of a subject rather than a conquering race.

In truth pity and sympathy are worse than any vice; they are opposed to all the tonic passions that enhance the energy of the feeling of life. Sympathy increases suffering without adding to beauty; it drags down the one who yields to it to the level of the sufferer while leaving his sufferings unassuaged. That those who are sick and degenerate should not communicate their illness and degeneracy to those that are healthy, that the weak and botched should perish and should even be helped to perish in the interest of a higher race — this ought surely to be the first condition on earth. The strong man must escape the stifling air of compassion; instead he must exalt cruelty, hardness, contempt for the right of the weak. He will even aim to increase suffering and pain rather than to abolish them; for suffering is essential to the creation of beauty, to the great art in which life alone finds its justification. It is conflict and exploitation that constitute the fearful delight of tragedy — the highest art. Suffering intensifies the love of life in those who are strong enough to surmount it and take pleasure in its contemplation; only as one is able to inflict and witness suffering can he taste the joys of artistic creation. To create, then, an aristocratic and heroic race of Over-men in whom the Will to Power is incarnate, who are beyond all good and evil, a hothouse for the cultivation of rare and strange plants, who create beauty, live dangerously, play dice for death, and who use the weaker race of men as a foundation and scaffolding on which to elevate themselves to a higher existence — this is the only worthy goal of human effort.

3. *Bergson.* — The instrumental character of thought and its consequent inadequacy for speculation hold a more central place in the French philosopher *Henri Bergson*. The fundamental truth of existence Bergson finds in the conception of a "vital impulse," a spontaneous living force, akin to consciousness, out of whose urge to action and creation the world process springs. What Bergson wants chiefly to emphasize as against nearly all historical philosophies, we may see by turning to life as man knows or experiences it in himself. "Knows" is not the best word here. When we stand off and look at life through the eyes of the intellect our unavoidable tendency is to break it up into separate bits of conscious fact; the fleeting shades which in experience itself merge into one another we turn into distinct and, so to speak, solid colors set side by side like the beads of a necklace. But this is not the reality we immediately feel. Actually nothing stays for a single moment fixed. We change without ceasing; to exist is to change, to change is to mature, and to mature is to go on creating oneself endlessly. Time, felt duration, is the very stuff of which the psychical life is made; and duration means invention, the creation of forms, the continual

elaboration of the absolutely new. So looked at, creation is no mystery; we experience it in ourselves whenever we act freely. Life is a continuous and irreversible process in which every moment of action is the confluence of our entire past issuing in a new creative act. It is true we "think" only with a small portion of our past; our conscious memory picks out only a few odd recollections for which it has some immediate use. But it is with our whole past — with the "character" that has been shaped by everything that has gone before — that we desire, will and act. And because life is thus a continual process of growth in which the same concrete reality never recurs, each new pulse of life is something unique and unpredictable.

Turning this now into a metaphysics, we may conceive reality itself in the same fashion as an original process of creation. But to account for "nature" we need to add here a further aspect. Just as in ourselves, the life force acts not steadily but in spurts; it arises only to fall back again as its efforts are expended. As in the flux of Heracleitus, there are two opposing streams; and it is this second aspect that we call matter, or materiality. Physics is psychics inverted, a relaxation of the intensive into the extensive, of liberty into necessity. Matter thus approximates in its nature to passivity, whose limit is pure space; though to this it never attains completely, since that would be to step out of duration altogether. In this sense matter to be sure is not to be identified with particular material objects; the division of matter into separate bodies is the work of our senses. It is a general principle which conditions everywhere the pure activity of consciousness, and out of which arise the concrete possibilities of experience as we know it.

In its more sober interpretation, we perhaps may think of this in terms of conscious activity relapsing into unconscious or semi-conscious "habits," such a habit in turn providing a starting-point for new creative action. Bergson figures it as a series of jets gushing out from the immense reservoir of life, each of which falling back is a world; or again we may describe it as a center from which worlds shoot out like rockets in a fire-works display — provided we do not present this center as a "thing," but only as a continuity of shooting out. To the rocket whose extinguished fragments fall back as matter, as well as to the persisting energy which passes through the fragments and lights them up, we may give the name of consciousness or supra-consciousness, though in the strict sense consciousness, while it is a *need of creation*, is made manifest to itself only when actual creation is possible. Because life is confronted thus with matter it cannot create absolutely, and is forced to find expression in many different guises; and in overcoming the obstacle it individuates itself, and so cuts out of the movement of reversion the living beings which it leaves all along its track.

Such a view of the nature of organic life has, Bergson recognizes, to meet the opposition of our natural tendencies of thought, and of their extension in a higher degree of refinement and exactness in the form of science. Science sets the ideal before itself of explaining everything, life included, in terms that have no place for novelty and creation, and that account for each new step by what has gone before. To obviate such an objection we need to examine more closely what thinking really is and does.

Bergson's second fundamental thesis is that thought is not an instrument for knowing reality; it is a tool which the vital impulse has created purely to serve practical needs. The intellect is a flame which lights up the coming and going of living beings in the narrow passage open to their action; and this lantern glimmering in a tunnel we have no right to convert into a sun which can illuminate the world. An object of physics is no more than a plan of our eventual action. As an action like every pulsation of life is discontinuous, so too is knowledge; individual things are due to acts of attention governed by a practical interest which ignores such aspects of reality as do not cast light on the present situation and its needs. We may liken knowledge to a cinematograph film; it is a series of snapshots of a reality that in itself is continuous. Having in this way split up reality into discontinuous parts, it of course is at a loss when it attempts to recreate the original flow of life. It has to represent becoming as a series of distinct and separate states, to try to build up continuity and movement out of immobilities put together.   Naturally it fails in this; and consequently it is irresistibly driven toward the denial of real duration and real creation, and to an insistence that the present contains no more than the past, the effect no more than its cause.   For its own purpose this is justified; it is not interested in recreating the real process, but in replacing it with a practical equivalent.   To modify an action we have to arrest its flow and to picture it as durable and discontinuous; for practical control we must turn our attention not to what is unique in the situation, but to what is like something already known — to the aspect of repetition, withdrawn from the action of real time.   Accordingly the ideal of scientific explanation consists in resolving the new and unforeseeable into old and familiar elements arranged in a different order; and so we are led to the notion of a system of stable mechanical relationships which postulates the totality of the real as complete in eternity, the apparent duration of things expressing merely the infirmity of a mind that cannot know everything at once.

But whatever the value of this as a method, it nevertheless involves a falsification of the real.   For certain purposes it may be useful to conceive of childhood and manhood as two termini between which we insert as many arbitrary sub-divisions as we find convenient.   But meanwhile the *transition* from childhood to manhood has slipped between our fingers; and it is this actual transition, which one lives through as a continuity, that reveals to us the ultimate nature of life itself.   Science needs therefore to be supplemented and corrected by a deeper insight.   We do not think real time, but we live it; and life transcends intellect.   As life ripens into acts, the intellect may then be able to look back and to resolve it indefinitely into intelligible elements; but life itself always escapes its grasp.

What science is unable to reveal, however, *intuition* may sympathetically divine.   Consciousness, turning round suddenly against the push of life which it feels behind, may have a vision, even though it be a fleeting vision, of life complete; it may plunge back into the pure duration in which the past, always moving on, is swelling into a present that is absolutely new, and in which our whole being and personality concentrates itself into a point, or rather a sharp edge pressed against the future and cutting into it increasingly. Perhaps the best illustration of the difference between the two points of view will be found in the experience of artistic creation. A work of art, once in existence, can be analyzed, and its various elements singled out and put in juxtaposition. But a scientific criticism of art never can be made to explain the artist's genius. Through the words, lines and verses which supply the material of the poet's self-expression runs the inspiration which *is* the poem in its wholeness, and this is unpredictable; not even the artist could have foreseen exactly what the outcome was to be, for to predict it would have been to produce it before it was produced.

Reality, then, is a never-ceasing flow which assumes a vast variety of experimental forms as the primal urge takes this or that way of creative activity. Some of them lead into blind alleys — the vegetative life for instance, or the animal life of instinct. Instinct is in a sense closer to the vital impulse than thought; but it is so tied to particular objects and situations that it is soon brought to a standstill. It is in man, with his power to detach himself from particulars and to set before his mind alternatives of action, that life reaches its fullest possibility. In this strictly guarded sense man is the end of creation. This does not mean the substitution of teleology and final causes for a mechanistic philosophy; finality in this form is only an inverted mechanism. It equally presupposes a preëxistence, in the form of idea, of the future in the present; it merely holds in front of us the light with which it claims to guide us instead of putting it behind. Life has no "end" in the ordinary sense. But of the various highways along which the creative impulse has proceeded, only the one that leads through the vertebrates up to man has been wide enough to allow free passage to the full breadth of life. The aim of life has been to create, by means of matter which is pure necessity, an instrument of freedom; to make a machine that should triumph over mechanism; to use the mechanism of nature to pass through the meshes of the net which nature itself has spread — meshes in which everywhere, except in man, consciousness has let itself be caught. In his rise man has abandoned, along with much cumbersome baggage, some valuable possessions also. While intuition still remains, it is as a lamp almost extinguished. But it still glimmers whenever a vital interest is at stake. On our personality, our liberty, the place we occupy in the whole of nature, and perhaps also on our destiny, it throws a light which is feeble and vacillating indeed, but which none the less pierces the darkness of the night in which intellect leaves us.

4. *Pragmatism.* — That thought primarily is the tool for action is likewise, in a less spectacular form, the thesis of a widespread tendency which originated in America, and to which the name of Pragmatism has most commonly been applied. The tendency first came to general notice through the writings of *William James*, in whose case however it represents a large interest or point of view rather than a well-thought-out system of philosophy. James was a psychologist to begin with, and his *Principles of Psychology* had a good deal to do with the displacement of the older sensationalism by the more modern biological emphasis. James starts not with "states of consciousness," but with the "stream" of consciousness, out of which particular elements are selected by the teleological needs of the organic life. As a natural consequence, thought too will have to be regarded not primarily as an independent organ engaged in envisaging a realm of "truth"; its whole procedure and the tools with which it works arise in connection with the needs of animal conduct, and continue to serve these needs. In large measure James' pragmatism is a corollary of this general standpoint.

It was natural that some critics should be inclined to interpret this as a bread and butter philosophy, a concession to the "materialistic" character of American life. But in James' case, at any rate, this was far from his intention; indeed he was blamed by others for letting down the bars to beliefs that leave the natural world too far behind. Perhaps nothing James ever wrote was more widely read and discussed than a little essay called the *Will to Believe*. Among scientists the current tendency had been strongly against granting the human mind the right to entertain beliefs beyond a very limited range. *Thomas Huxley* had recently coined the term

Agnosticism to stand for this attitude. Agnosticism in Huxley's sense is not, as with Spencer, an attempt to demonstrate that reality is unknowable; it is a confession of ignorance, and rests wholly on the impotence of human thinking to get anywhere when it abandons the field in which empirical verification is possible. An insistence on the moral duty therefore of confining belief to science and its laws, and on the wickedness of allowing it to roam beyond these limits, had among naturalistic thinkers come very generally to be an article of faith that was held almost with religious fervor; he who would deserve well of his fellows, writes for example *W. K. Clifford*, one of the most brilliant of the younger scientists of his time, "will guard the purity of his belief with a very fanaticism of jealous care, lest at any time it should rest upon an unworthy object and catch a stain which can never be wiped out."

James' "will to believe" is a repudiation of agnosticism in this sense. Not only do scientific laws themselves represent a faith that goes far beyond the empirical evidence, but science tends to ignore the existence in man of other needs and instincts that have a claim to satisfaction. This does not give us the right to believe anything we like. But when belief attaches to momentous issues where decisive evidence is lacking, there is nothing to hinder us if we keep in mind its tentative character from extending belief to matters in which scientific proof no longer is attainable, especially when the issue is "forced," so that to withhold a decision is equally to lose the advantage that would follow from accepting it if the belief were a true one. There will be risks in such an attitude. *Cardinal Newman* had already used something the same principle to justify an acceptance in full of the dogmas of the Catholic Church; and by *A. J. Balfour* it had still more explicitly been utilized to subordinate the claims of science to the interests of an ethical and religious faith. But it is no part of a human ideal that it should be too safe and sane; an element of adventure and a readiness to take chances belongs no less to the intellectual than to the physical life. In James' case the general outcome, not very systematically worked out, was in the direction of a pan-psychist conception of the world

— a conception to which in his later years he added certain features of the "neo-realism" to be mentioned presently.

Pragmatism assumed a less equivocal and more systematic form at the hands of *John Dewey*, thereby qualifying as a distinct "school" which has had a large influence not on philosophy alone, but also, and especially, on the social and political tendencies of the day. Here James' principle that thought is not an otiose reproduction of reality but that it always "makes a difference," is given a more precise meaning. In this to be sure there is implied the "truth" of a certain specific account of thought and of reality; but the account once accepted, it absolves us from the need of bothering further with most of the traditional problems of metaphysics, and leaves thought free to pursue its proper business as an aid to the practical affairs of conduct.

Dewey begins by identifying thought with "thinking" and reality with "experience" — experience, that is, not as *my* experience, or indeed as the experience of anyone, but as just Experience, within which both selves and things make their appearance under specifiable conditions. "Life" and "activity" are other names we might apply to this reality. From such a starting-point Dewey sets out to show that we always think not for the sake of thinking, but as a stage in the business of living. Reason is not something handed down from above to render experience rational, as the idealists had held; it is something that *happens* to experience under definable conditions. So long as life moves smoothly we do not think — we act. It is only when the impulses that normally lead to action conflict with one another, and the issue becomes confused and doubtful, that we have to call a halt to the immediate business of living, and turn our attention instead to the means of reconstructing our interrupted activity. This last is what constitutes the special phase of experience which we call thinking. In such a process a diremption of experience takes place. On the one hand there emerges the "fact," the object, the datum — those elements of the situation namely, the outcome of past experience crystallized in habit, which while they are not final — else no trouble would have started — are yet sufficiently stable for us to count upon them for the moment and look to them to furnish the material out of which the new and desired method of control can be constructed. On the other hand there is the concept or idea which, on the basis of the given, attempts in the form of an hypothesis or plan of action to effect the desired change. And the validity or truth of the idea is reducible wholly to its success or failure in this task; "that which guides us truly is true." The true object of a judgment is thus in the end a practical issue, relating to what we are called upon to do; knowing has reference only to the future, and is neither a contemplative survey of existence, nor the working out of a timeless logical process.

And this suggests the underlying motive of Dewey's philosophy; it is an attempt to furnish a sound logical basis for progress. Pragmatism is the experimental use of intelligence to liberate and liberalize action. Thinking is not the reduplication of a reality already complete; it is the method of social advance — a method that is to free us alike from the unchanging ideals of the conservative, and from a spasmodic demand for novelty or freedom working under no principle of control from the past. The moral experience is not a movement toward some settled goal which reason can anticipate, and to reach which we have authoritative guide-posts in the shape of universal maxims and established virtues; it neither attains nor aims at an ultimate good, but goes on endlessly to gather up fresh resources of insight and of satisfaction.

For me as an individual this means that the emphasis has shifted from a conscientious performance of accepted duties to the task of moral education. My obligation is not to be loyal to some model of perfection, but to learn how my conception of the good may keep pace with expanding opportunities and knowledge; instead of its being a merit never to let moral convictions waver, we shall have to be always on our guard against their hardening into forms that put a stop to growth. The difference is still more conspicuous when we turn to the field of social action. In opposition to stereotyped ideals Dewey proposes the method of experimental science. The pragmatist does not pretend to know just what the future will bring forth; but meanwhile we have some acquaintance with our immediate surroundings, and with the particular occasions for readjustment brought home to us by the failure of the satisfaction that belongs to unimpeded action. A man for example does not need to have settled views about the destiny of capitalism to be convinced that monopolistic tendencies are having empirical results not altogether to his liking; and it is the business of political reason to discover how these difficulties in particular can be remedied in view of man's actually existing opportunities and limitations. On the one hand then it calls for a realistic recognition of natural facts and conditions unadulterated by idealistic prejudices; on the other it emphasizes the need for conscious social planning in order that progress may no longer be haphazard but may utilize intelligence and foresight. Such planning it is true will not be planning for an end clearly perceived and delimited in advance. The end emerges as we go along; the future type of society where man will be better adjusted to his surroundings than at present we shall in course of time find ourselves living in rather than consciously anticipate and create. But meanwhile the process is assisted by the habit of intelligent experiment on the small scale within our reach — a habit which it is the business of philosophy to substitute alike for utopianism and for an acquiescence in things as they are.

LITERATURE

Nietzsche, *Works.*

Bergson, *Matter and Memory, Time and Free Will, Creative Evolution.*

James, *Psychology, Will to Believe, Varieties of Religious Experience, Pragmatism, Pluralistic Universe, Meaning of Truth, Essays in Radical Empiricism.*

Dewey, *Influence of Darwin on Philosophy, Reconstruction in Philosophy, Human Nature and Conduct, Experience and Nature, Individualism Old and New, Quest for Certainty, Philosophy and Civilization.*

Chatterton-Hill, *Philosophy of Nietzsche.*

Salter, *Nietzsche the Thinker.*

Wright, *What Nietzsche Taught.*

Carr, *Henri Bergson.*

Cunningham, *Studies in the Philosophy of Bergson.*

Lindsay, *Philosophy of Bergson.*

Stewart, *Critical Exposition of Bergson's Philosophy.*
Boutroux, *William James.*
Kallen, *William James and Henri Bergson.*
Knox, *Philosophy of William James.*
Moore, *Pragmatism and its Critics.*
Schiller, *Humanism.*
Schiller, *Studies in Humanism.*
Pratt, *What is Pragmatism.*
Perry, *Present Philosophical Tendencies.*

§ 44. *Conclusion*

In the academic philosophy of the British and American universities there had been a period during which idealism of the German type appeared to be having things pretty much its own way. Pragmatism was the first to make a serious breach in this citadel; and pragmatism was soon followed by other movements that have left the older idealism rather on the defensive. There will be no attempt here to give an account of the profusion of new tendencies that enter into the present situation. Some of these are popular and more or less extemporaneous philosophies — Freudianism, for example, which turns a special therapeutic method into a drastic revaluation of man's traditional ideals, or Behaviorism with its generalization of a scientific method in psychology into a materialistic metaphysics. Other tendencies represent a variety of motives of a more technical sort, for the most part in a form that interests the professional philosopher more than it does the general public. It perhaps will be enough to mention three of these as sufficiently representative; in each case they take their name from a coöperative volume of essays by which the movement was inaugurated.[1]

Of these movements Personal Idealism was the first and least distinctive. In general, as the name implies, it sets itself against the logical proclivities of German idealism by an emphasis on the human self, alike as a genuine existent and as a clue to philosophic understanding. This is much the same general tendency that Lotze had earlier represented, and it is a German thinker, *Rudolf*

[1] *Personal Idealism*, 1902; *The New Realism*, 1912; *Critical Realism*, 1920.

Eucken, who has been its most prolific and most popularly effective advocate. Eucken conceives the task of philosophy primarily as one of spiritual redemption. Its interest lies for him not so much in systems of philosophy as in those larger tendencies that consti- tute "culture systems," or general ways of looking at life and its meaning; and he undertakes to defend the life of "spiritual" values — a term not very explicitly defined — against its main com- petitors — naturalism, subjectivism, pantheism. The only new note here is an emphasis on action rather than meditation as a cure for modern doubt and instability; the problems of life are to be solved by a spiritual heroism, which reveals to us our transcendence of the natural world through a coöperation, with other men and with God, in the task of transfiguring the universe into a realm of spiritual ideals.

Neo-Realism is in the first instance a renewed attack on the problem of knowledge. Its general outcome is to vindicate the immediate presence in consciousness — this is a repudiation of any dualism between knowledge and the things it knows such as throws doubt on its validity — of independently real existents standing in relations that, some of them, are more or less external to the things themselves; as such it stands opposed to idealisms that identify reality either with a single whole of thought or with Berkeleyan states of consciousness. Critical Realism likewise at- tempts to vindicate the knowledge of real existents without having to regard perception as an intellectual inference starting from an original recognition of subjective feelings or sensations, but also without giving up the common-sense belief that such existents are separate from the conscious fact which mediates our knowledge of them.

If there is any single tendency peculiarly characteristic of the more recent period — and this is doubtful — it might perhaps most plausibly be looked for in a return to the Platonic notion of a realm of eternal Forms or essences. This has been influenced in par- ticular by the new developments in pure mathematics brought to popular attention by the revolutionary views of *Albert Einstein*. Such a tendency is visible in a variety of quarters which otherwise are separated by sharp differences. It is one of the leading motives in Neo-Realism, where such "subsisting" characters and relationships stand among the most important of the reals that may be present to awareness, and where a strong disposition sometimes shows itself, as in the case of *Bertrand Russell*, to create a practical ideal of life out of the intellectual contemplation of eternal logical forms — belonging not to this world simply but to all possible worlds — as alone capable of satisfying the spirit of the free man who refuses to abase himself before the God of things as they are. Again in the critical realist *George Santayana*, such a realm of pure essences — the infinite array of all possible intelligible "characters," removed from the limited field of existence, and capable on occasion of being intuited by "spirit" — is combined with the acceptance of a naturalistic realm of substance or existence which constitutes the "natural" world. This latter world is revealed not by immediate intuition but by "animal faith" — by assumptions arising spontaneously when the animal organism finds itself confronted by independently real conditions which call for some form of action, and through whose agency spirit is led to pick out from the infinite host of immaterial patterns this or that essence in particular to serve as a cue or sign for anticipating nature's behavior. And, in conclusion, we may note other philosophies in the making which are strongly influenced by mathematics, and which are moving toward a new metaphysics whose issue still is more or less obscure.

INDEX

Italics indicate the important place in which the subject is treated.